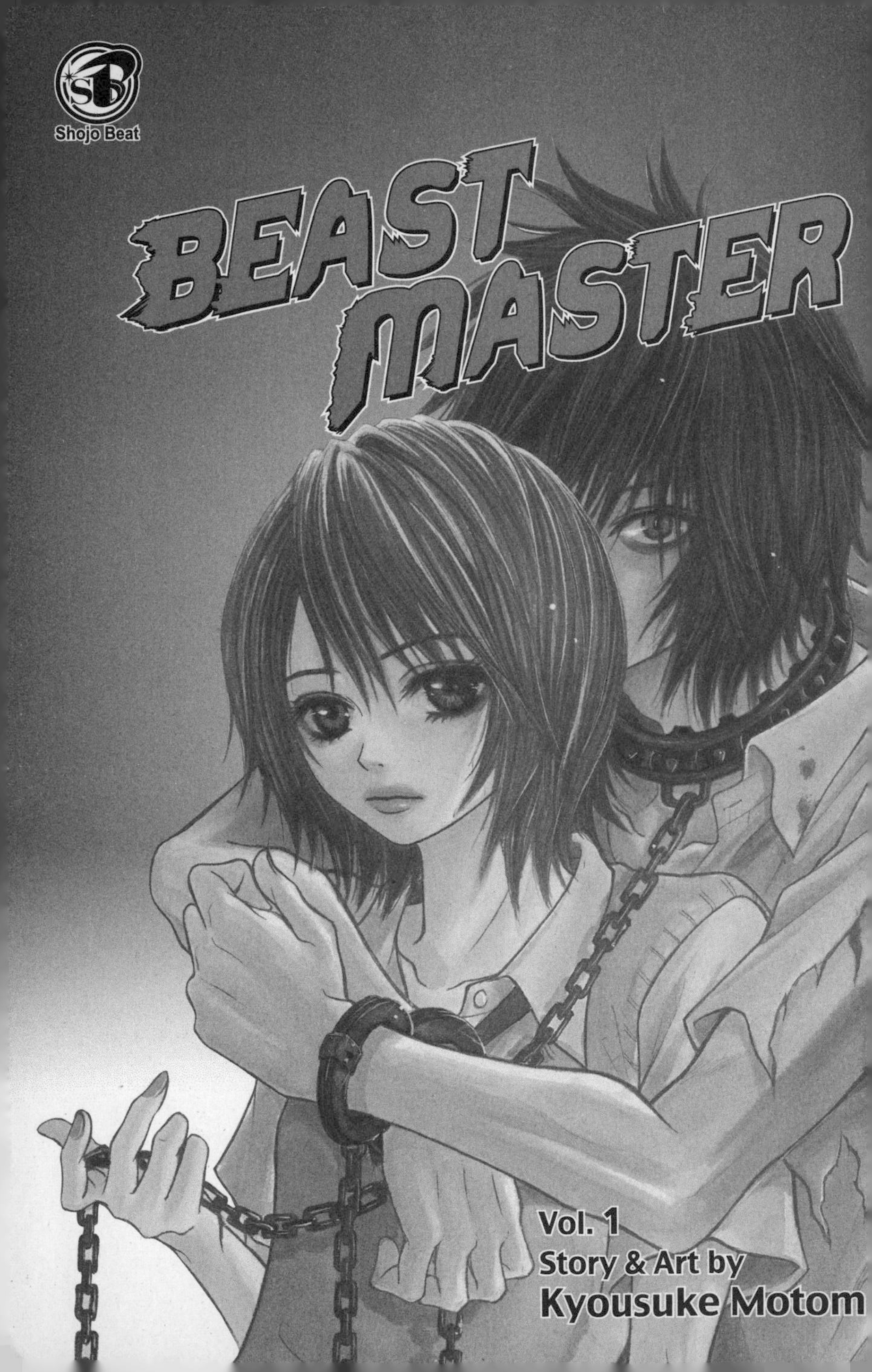
Shojo Beat
BEAST MASTER
Vol. 1
Story & Art by
Kyousuke Motom

Volume 1
CONTENTS

Chapter 1 🐾 5

Chapter 2 🐾 52

Chapter 3 🐾 89

Chapter 4 🐾 125

Fly 🐾 159

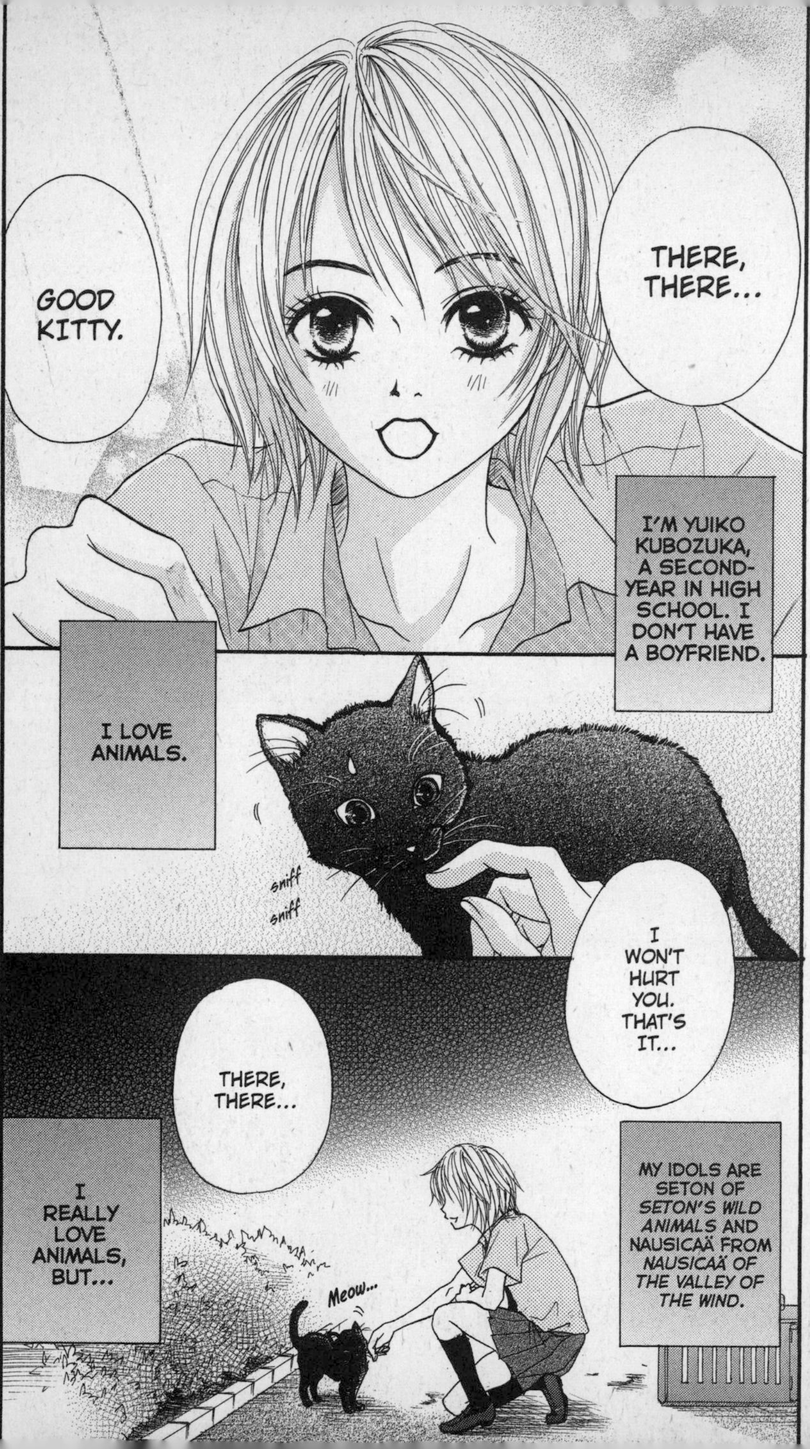
THERE, THERE...
GOOD KITTY.
I'M YUIKO KUBOZUKA, A SECOND-YEAR IN HIGH SCHOOL. I DON'T HAVE A BOYFRIEND.
I LOVE ANIMALS.
sniff sniff
I WON'T HURT YOU. THAT'S IT...
THERE, THERE...
MY IDOLS ARE SETON OF *SETON'S WILD ANIMALS* AND NAUSICAÄ FROM *NAUSICAÄ OF THE VALLEY OF THE WIND*.
Meow...
I REALLY LOVE ANIMALS, BUT...

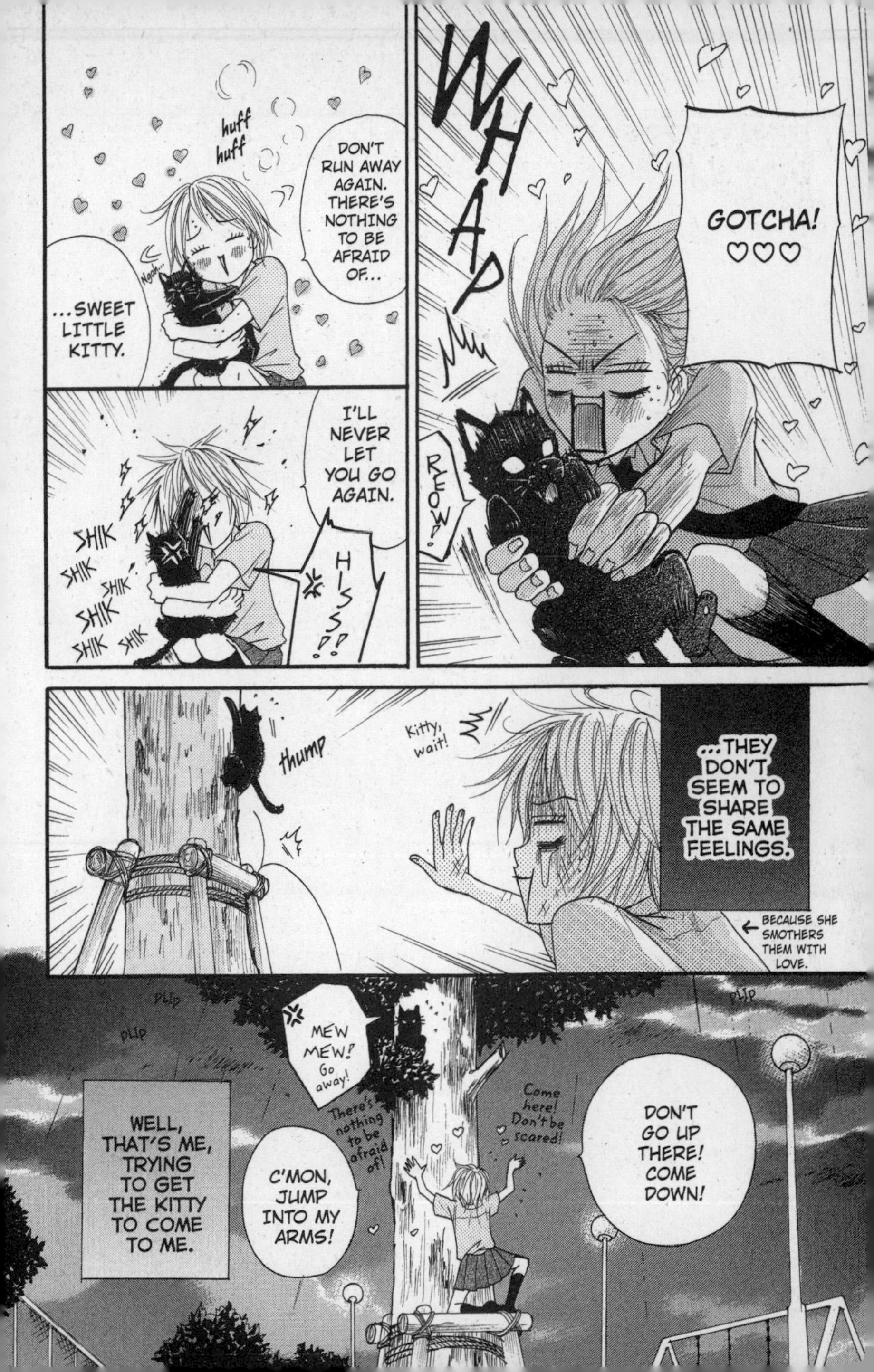
GOTCHA! ♡♡♡
WHAP
REOW!
huff huff
DON'T RUN AWAY AGAIN. THERE'S NOTHING TO BE AFRAID OF...
Ngah...
...SWEET LITTLE KITTY.
I'LL NEVER LET YOU GO AGAIN.
HISS!!
SHIK SHIK SHIK SHIK SHIK SHIK
...THEY DON'T SEEM TO SHARE THE SAME FEELINGS.
← BECAUSE SHE SMOTHERS THEM WITH LOVE.
Kitty, wait!
thump
plip
plip
plip
DON'T GO UP THERE! COME DOWN!
Come here! Don't be scared!
MEW MEW!? Go away!
There's nothing to be afraid of!
C'MON, JUMP INTO MY ARMS!
WELL, THAT'S ME, TRYING TO GET THE KITTY TO COME TO ME.

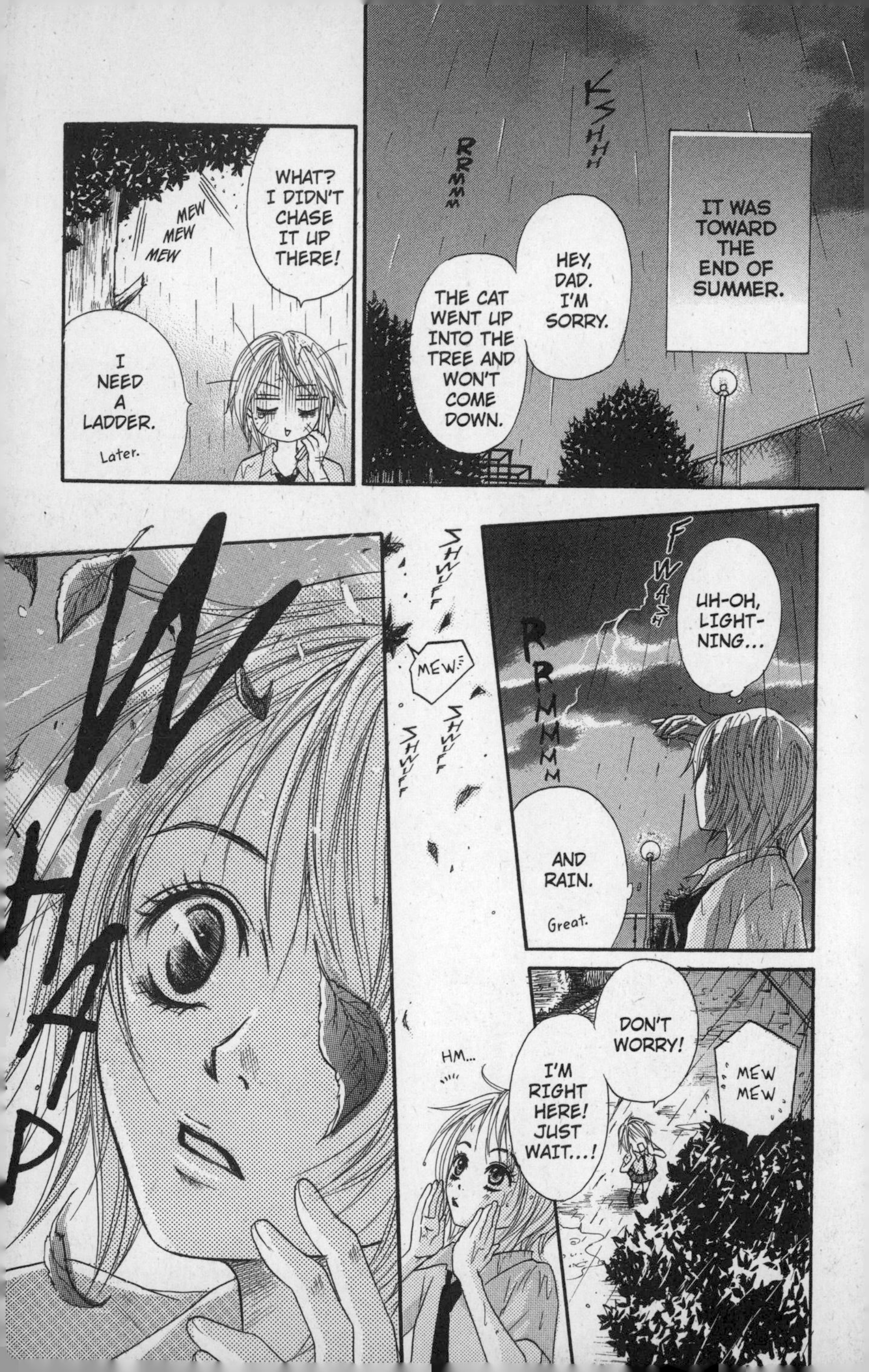
IT WAS TOWARD THE END OF SUMMER.
KSHHH
RRMMM
HEY, DAD. I'M SORRY.
THE CAT WENT UP INTO THE TREE AND WON'T COME DOWN.
WHAT? I DIDN'T CHASE IT UP THERE!
MEW MEW MEW
I NEED A LADDER.
Later.
FWASH
UH-OH, LIGHTNING...
RRMMMM
AND RAIN.
Great.
MEW MEW
DON'T WORRY!
I'M RIGHT HERE! JUST WAIT...!
HM...
SHWUFF
MEW
SHWUFF
SHWUFF
WHAP

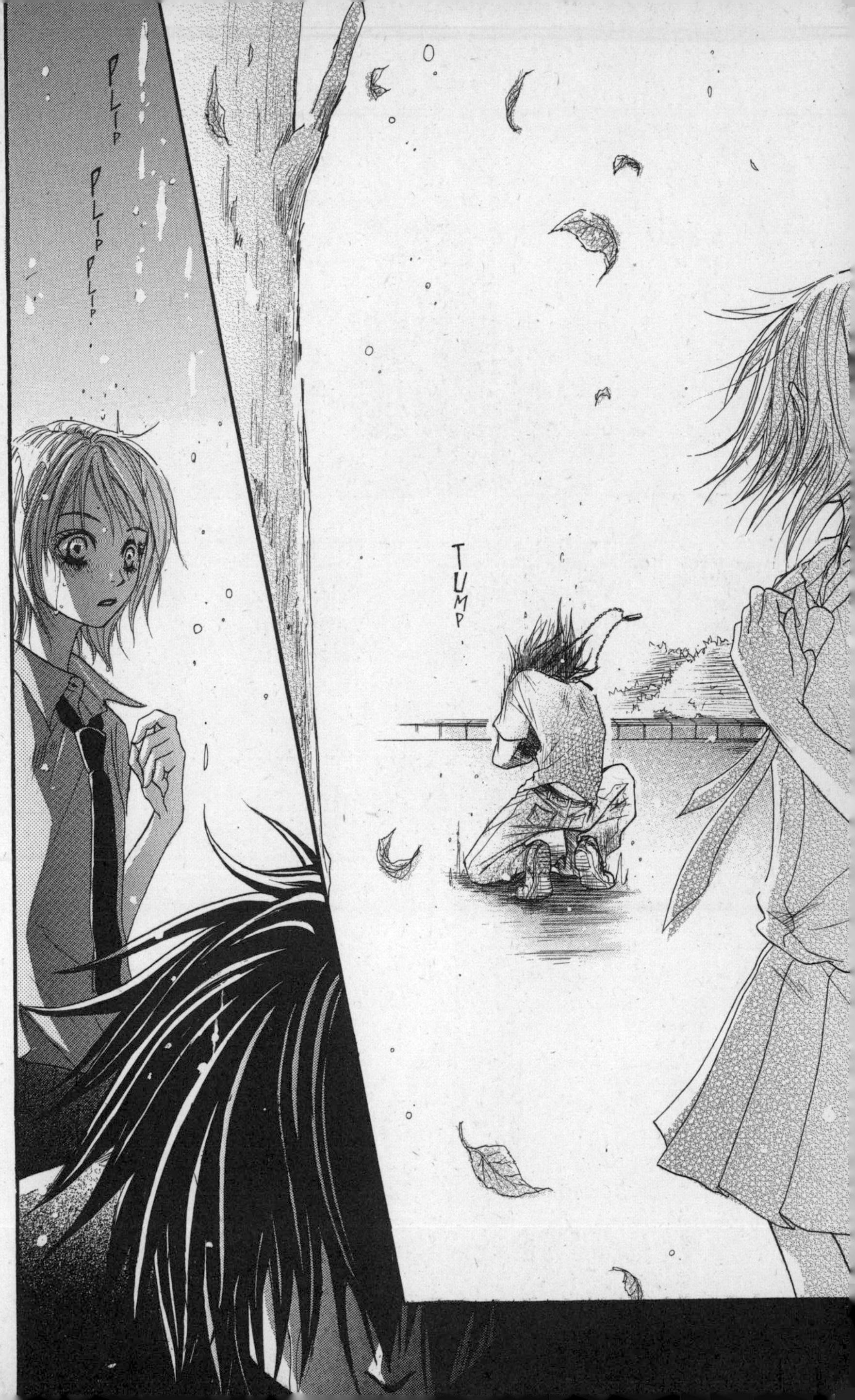
TUMP
PLIP PLIP PLIP PLIP

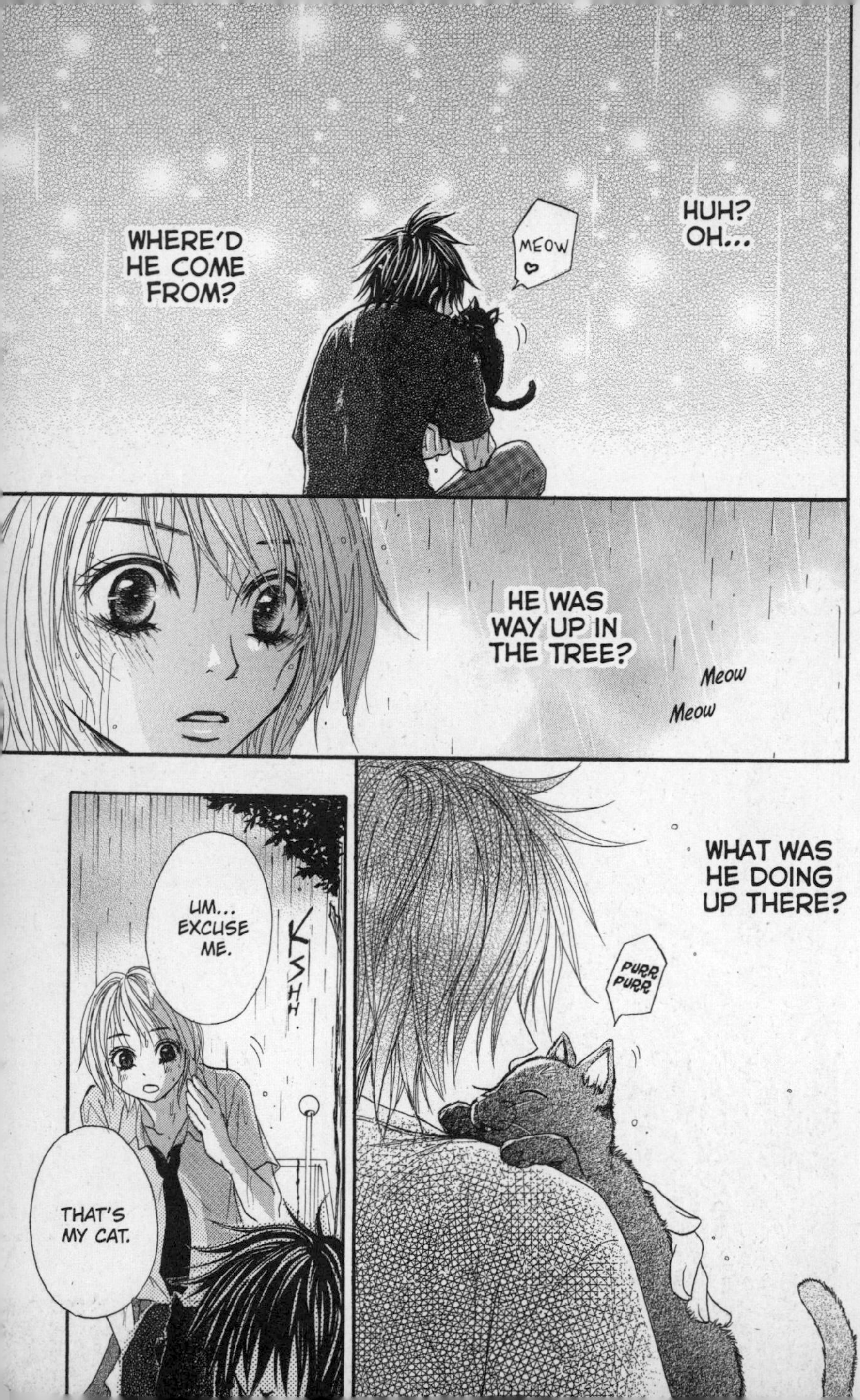
HUH? OH...
MEOW ♡
WHERE'D HE COME FROM?
HE WAS WAY UP IN THE TREE?
Meow
Meow
WHAT WAS HE DOING UP THERE?
PURR PURR
UM... EXCUSE ME.
SHH
THAT'S MY CAT.

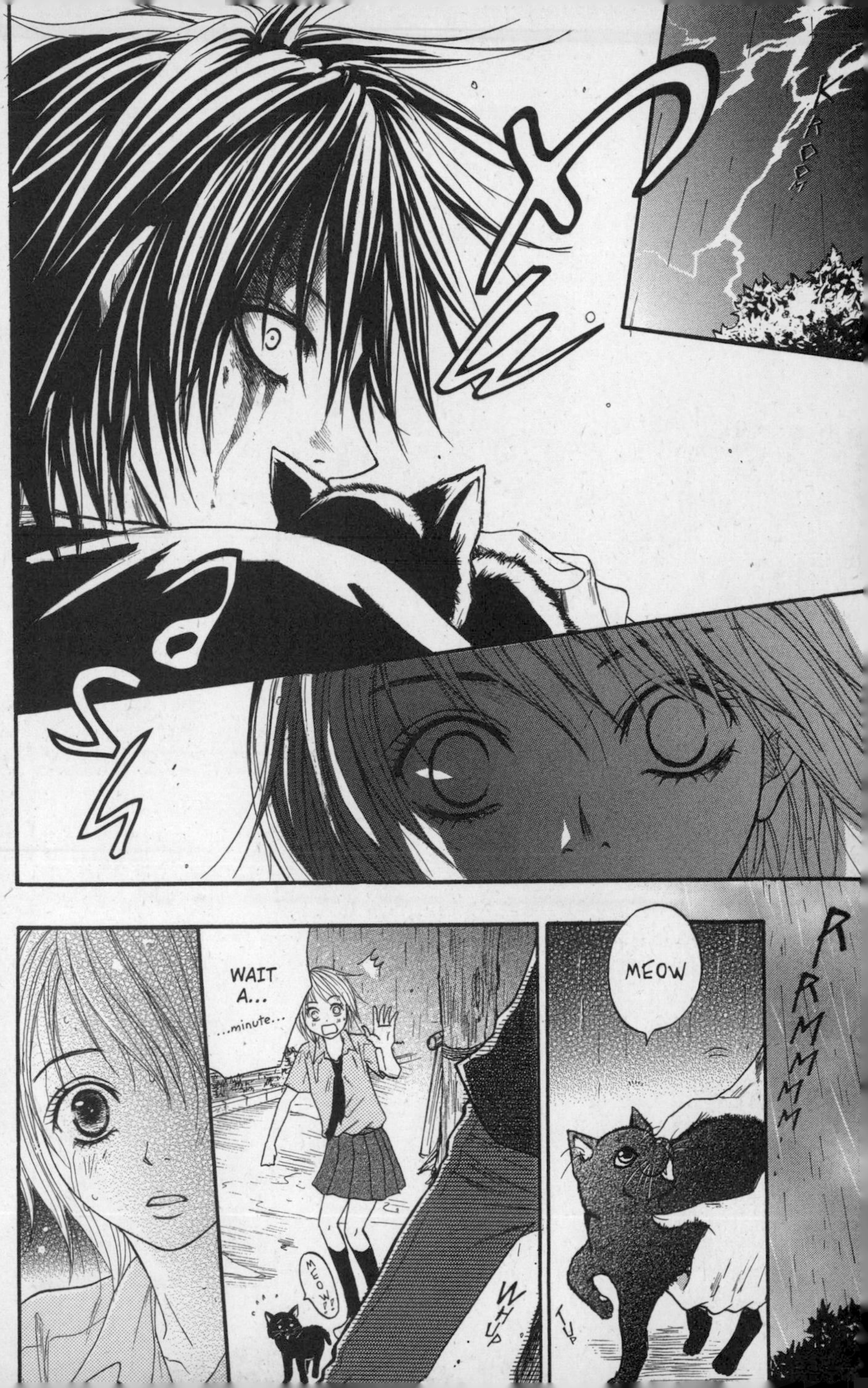
KROOM
RRRMMMM
MEOW
TUP
WHUP
WAIT A...
...minute...
MEOW?!

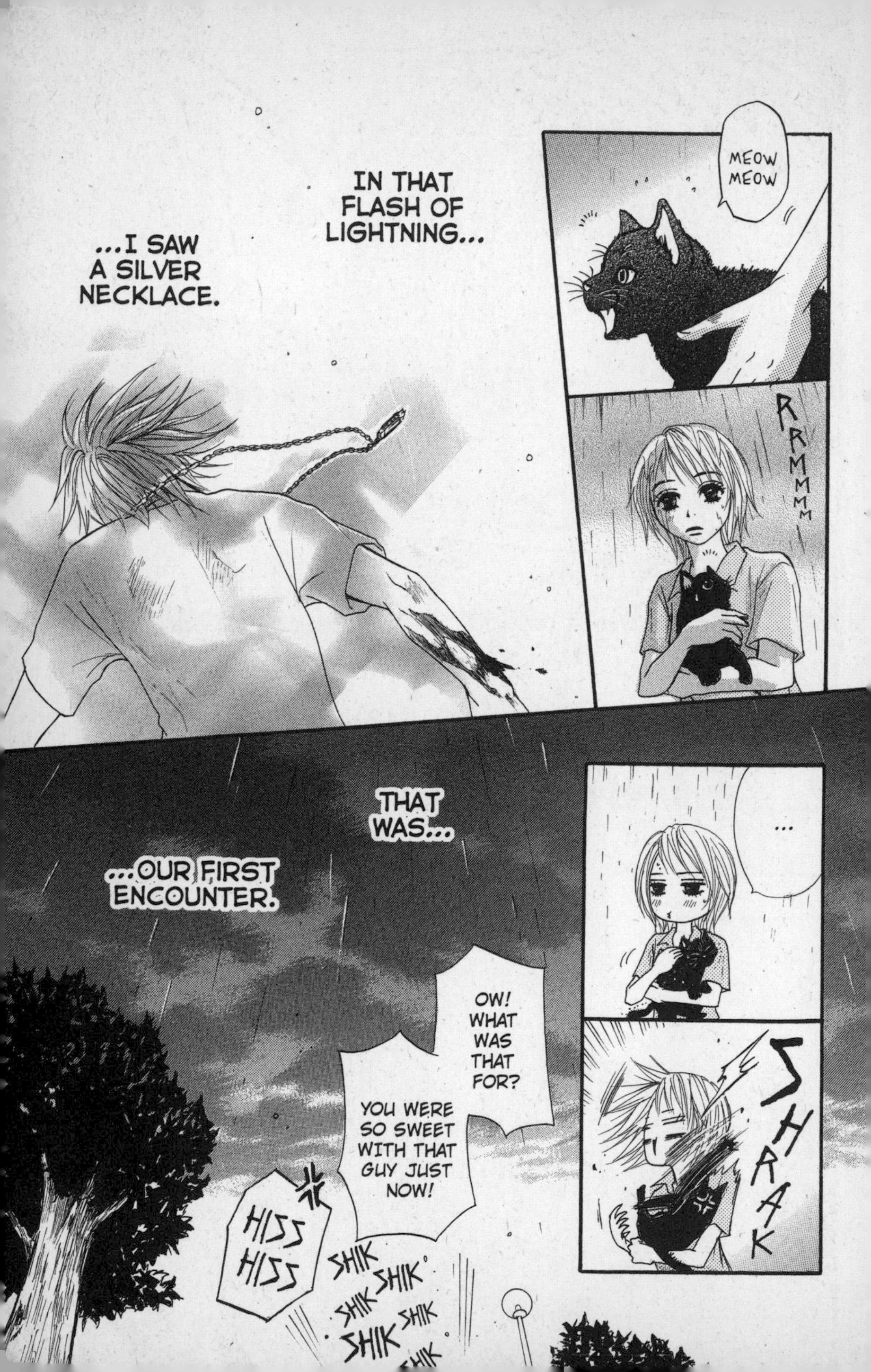
MEOW MEOW
RRMMMM
IN THAT FLASH OF LIGHTNING...
...I SAW A SILVER NECKLACE.
...
SHRAK
THAT WAS...
...OUR FIRST ENCOUNTER.
OW! WHAT WAS THAT FOR?
YOU WERE SO SWEET WITH THAT GUY JUST NOW!
HISS HISS
SHIK SHIK SHIK SHIK SHIK SHIK

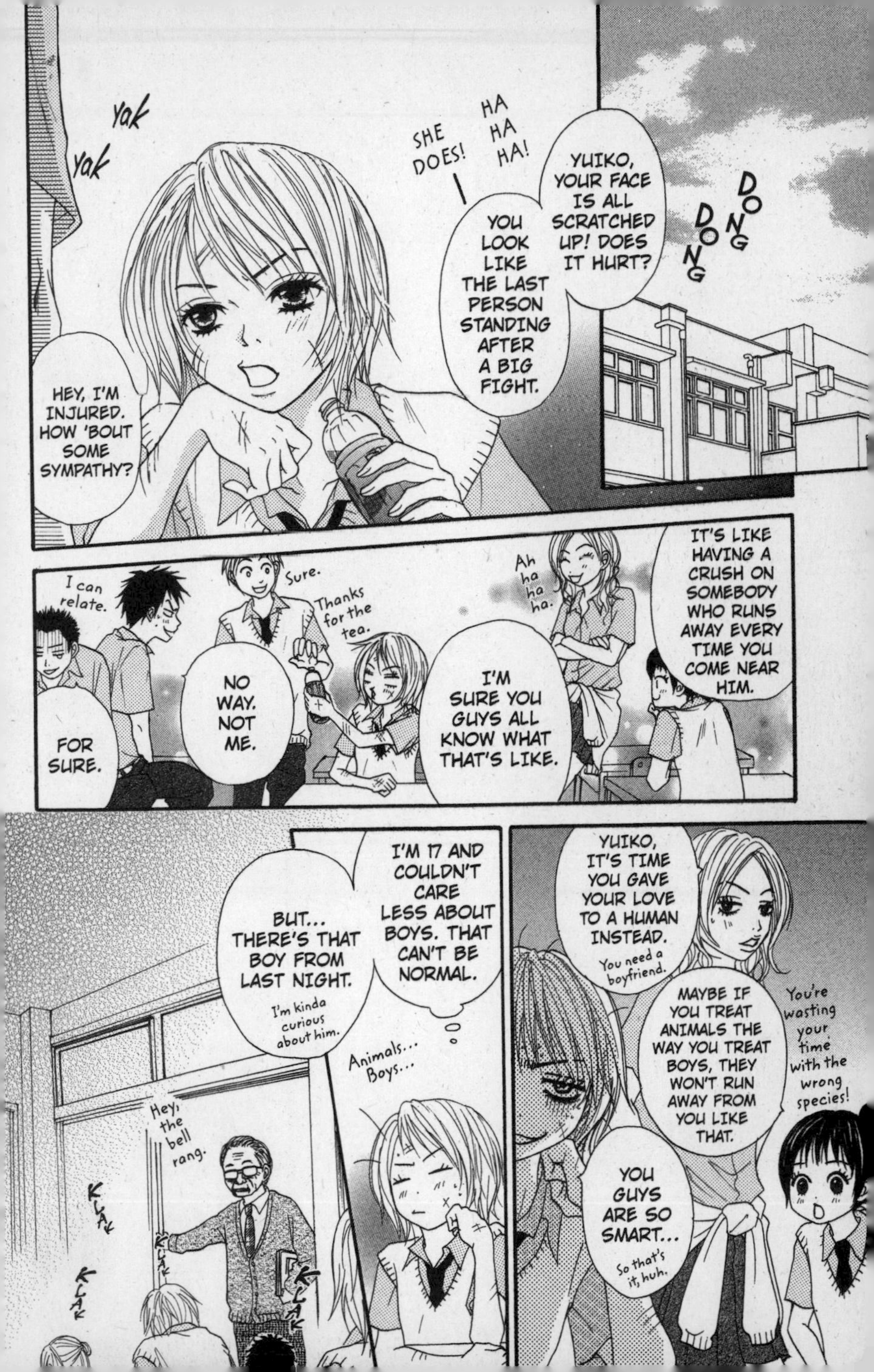
DONG DONG
YUIKO, YOUR FACE IS ALL SCRATCHED UP! DOES IT HURT?
YOU LOOK LIKE THE LAST PERSON STANDING AFTER A BIG FIGHT.
HA HA HA!
SHE DOES!
yak
yak
HEY, I'M INJURED. HOW 'BOUT SOME SYMPATHY?
IT'S LIKE HAVING A CRUSH ON SOMEBODY WHO RUNS AWAY EVERY TIME YOU COME NEAR HIM.
Ah ha ha ha.
I'M SURE YOU GUYS ALL KNOW WHAT THAT'S LIKE.
Thanks for the tea.
Sure.
NO WAY. NOT ME.
I can relate.
FOR SURE.
YUIKO, IT'S TIME YOU GAVE YOUR LOVE TO A HUMAN INSTEAD.
You need a boyfriend.
You're wasting your time with the wrong species!
MAYBE IF YOU TREAT ANIMALS THE WAY YOU TREAT BOYS, THEY WON'T RUN AWAY FROM YOU LIKE THAT.
YOU GUYS ARE SO SMART...
So that's it, huh.
I'M 17 AND COULDN'T CARE LESS ABOUT BOYS. THAT CAN'T BE NORMAL.
BUT... THERE'S THAT BOY FROM LAST NIGHT.
I'm kinda curious about him.
Animals... Boys...
Hey, the bell rang.
KLAK KLAK KLAK KLAK

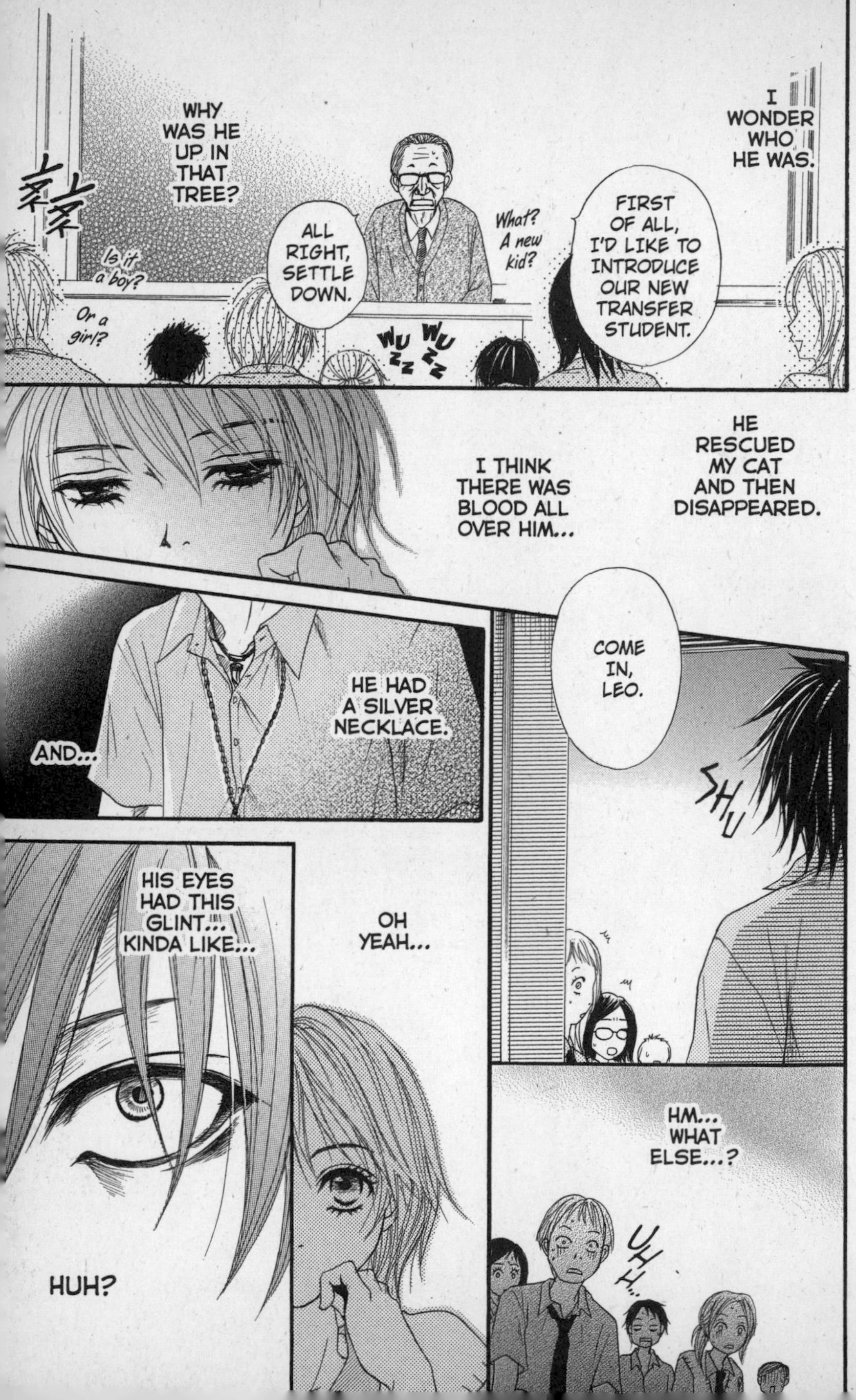
I WONDER WHO HE WAS.
FIRST OF ALL, I'D LIKE TO INTRODUCE OUR NEW TRANSFER STUDENT.
What? A new kid?
ALL RIGHT, SETTLE DOWN.
WHY WAS HE UP IN THAT TREE?
Is it a boy?
Or a girl?
WU ZZ WU ZZ
HE RESCUED MY CAT AND THEN DISAPPEARED.
I THINK THERE WAS BLOOD ALL OVER HIM...
COME IN, LEO.
SHU
HE HAD A SILVER NECKLACE.
AND...
HM... WHAT ELSE...?
UHH...
OH YEAH...
HIS EYES HAD THIS GLINT... KINDA LIKE...
HUH?

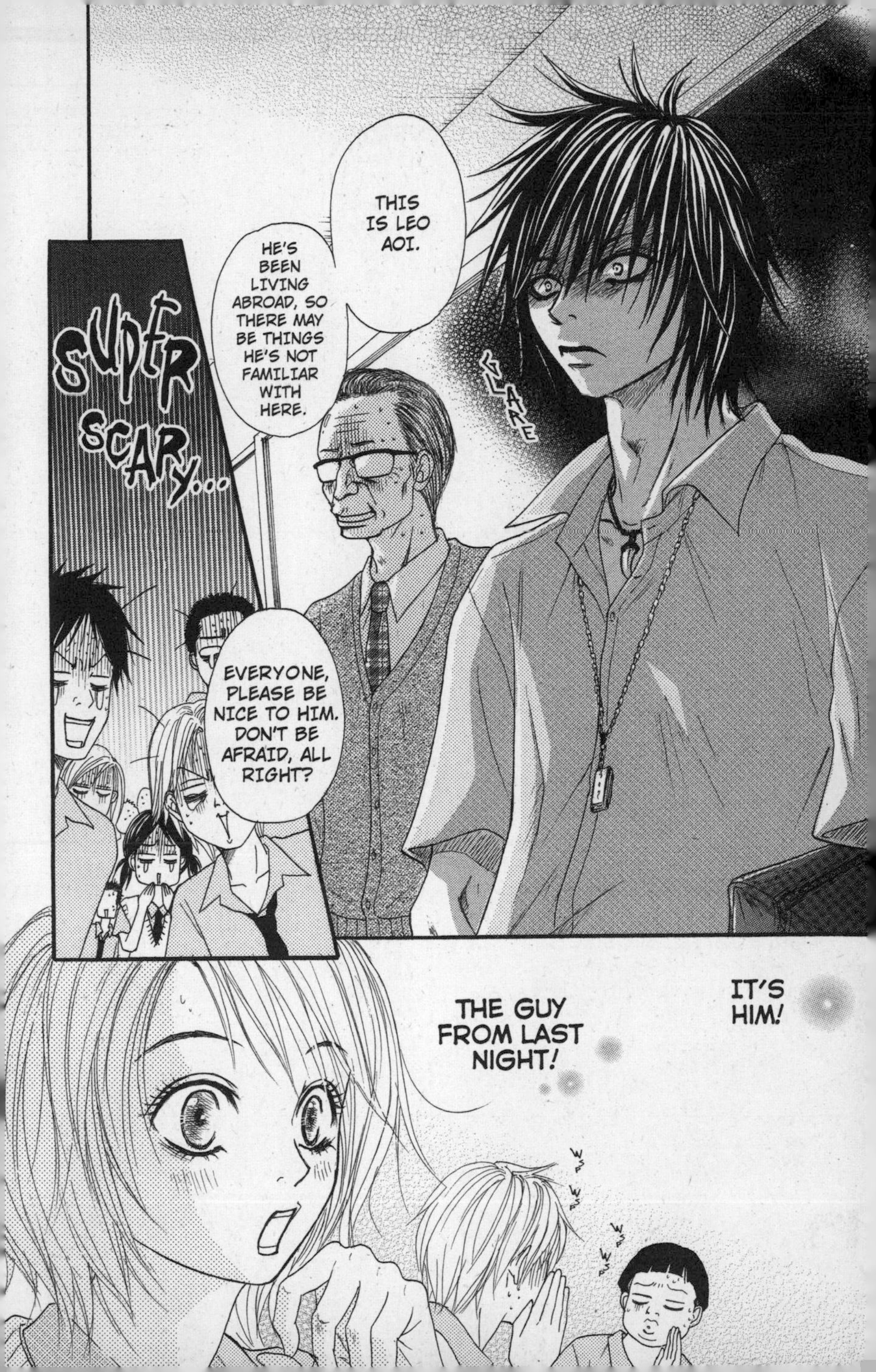
THIS IS LEO AOI.
GLARE
HE'S BEEN LIVING ABROAD, SO THERE MAY BE THINGS HE'S NOT FAMILIAR WITH HERE.
EVERYONE, PLEASE BE NICE TO HIM. DON'T BE AFRAID, ALL RIGHT?
SUPER SCARY...
IT'S HIM!
THE GUY FROM LAST NIGHT!

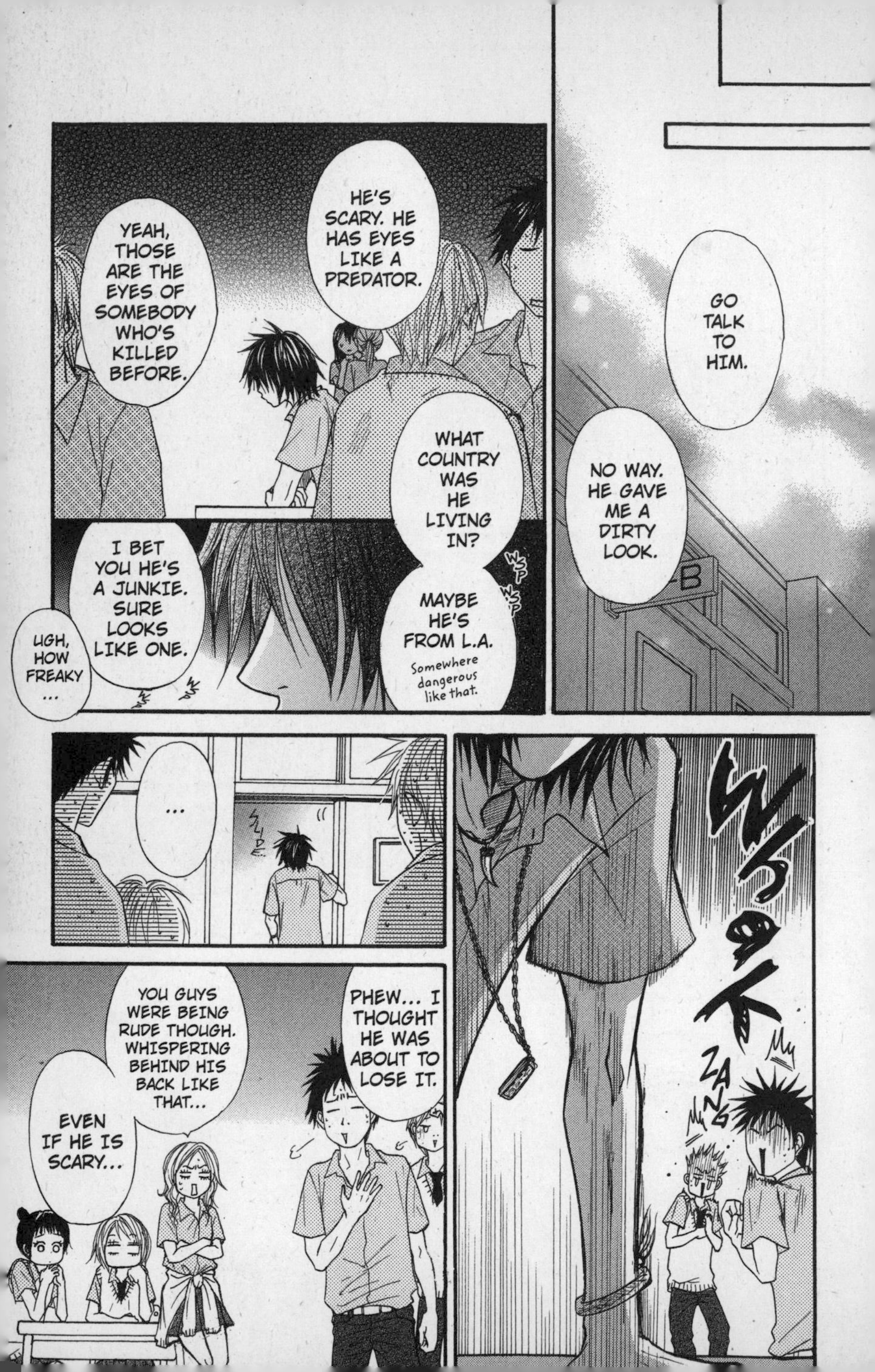
GO TALK TO HIM.
NO WAY. HE GAVE ME A DIRTY LOOK.
HE'S SCARY. HE HAS EYES LIKE A PREDATOR.
YEAH, THOSE ARE THE EYES OF SOMEBODY WHO'S KILLED BEFORE.
WHAT COUNTRY WAS HE LIVING IN?
MAYBE HE'S FROM L.A.
Somewhere dangerous like that.
WSP WSP
I BET YOU HE'S A JUNKIE. SURE LOOKS LIKE ONE.
WSP WSP
UGH, HOW FREAKY...
ZANG
...
SLIDE
PHEW... I THOUGHT HE WAS ABOUT TO LOSE IT.
YOU GUYS WERE BEING RUDE THOUGH. WHISPERING BEHIND HIS BACK LIKE THAT...
EVEN IF HE IS SCARY...

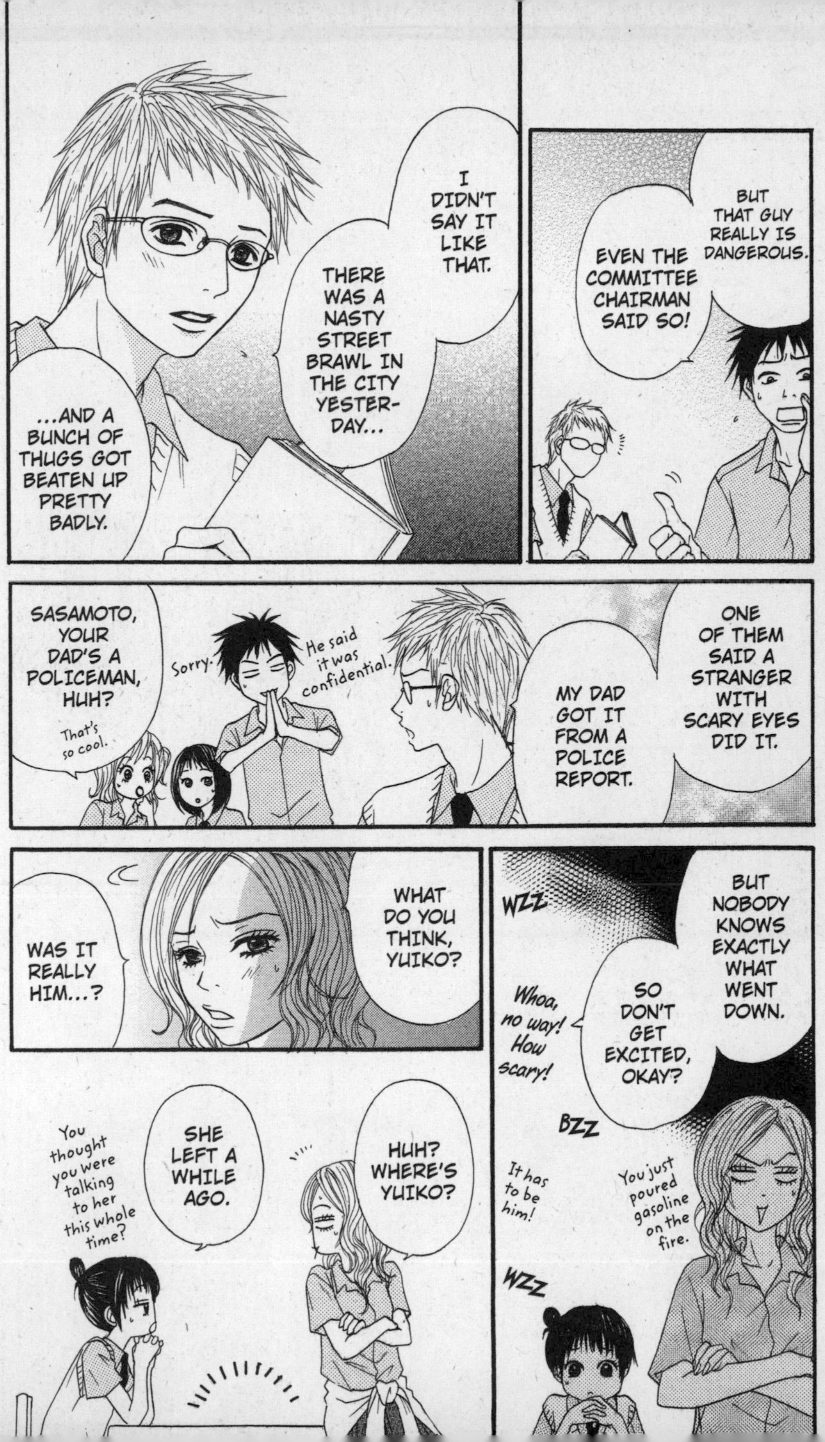
BUT THAT GUY REALLY IS DANGEROUS.
EVEN THE COMMITTEE CHAIRMAN SAID SO!
I DIDN'T SAY IT LIKE THAT.
THERE WAS A NASTY STREET BRAWL IN THE CITY YESTER-DAY...
...AND A BUNCH OF THUGS GOT BEATEN UP PRETTY BADLY.
ONE OF THEM SAID A STRANGER WITH SCARY EYES DID IT.
MY DAD GOT IT FROM A POLICE REPORT.
He said it was confidential.
Sorry.
SASAMOTO, YOUR DAD'S A POLICEMAN, HUH?
That's so cool.
WZZ
BUT NOBODY KNOWS EXACTLY WHAT WENT DOWN.
SO DON'T GET EXCITED, OKAY?
Whoa, no way! How scary!
BZZ
It has to be him!
You just poured gasoline on the fire.
WZZ
WHAT DO YOU THINK, YUIKO?
WAS IT REALLY HIM...?
HUH? WHERE'S YUIKO?
SHE LEFT A WHILE AGO.
You thought you were talking to her this whole time?

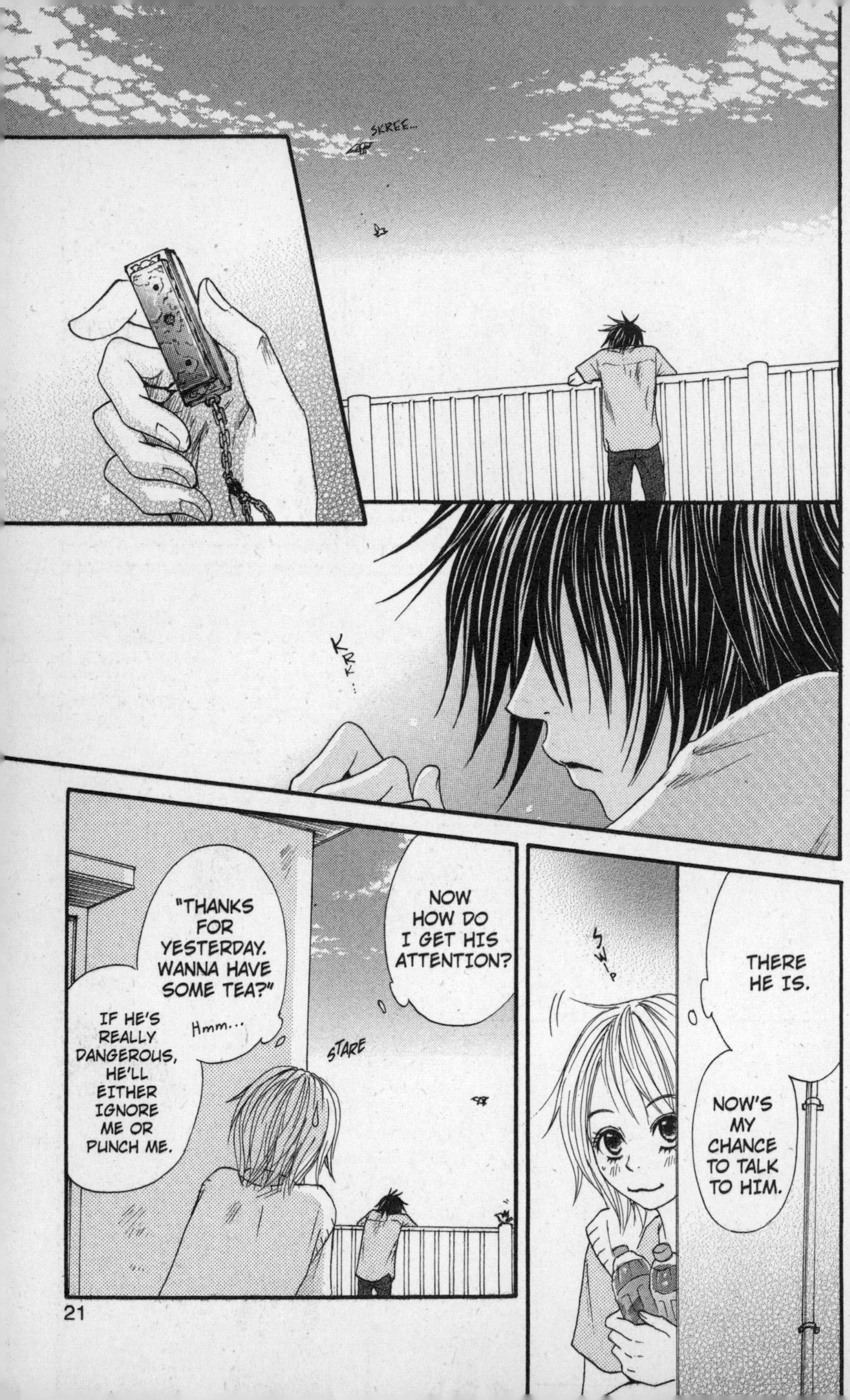
SKREE...
KRK...
SWIP
THERE HE IS.
NOW'S MY CHANCE TO TALK TO HIM.
NOW HOW DO I GET HIS ATTENTION?
STARE
"THANKS FOR YESTERDAY. WANNA HAVE SOME TEA?"
Hmm...
IF HE'S REALLY DANGEROUS, HE'LL EITHER IGNORE ME OR PUNCH ME.

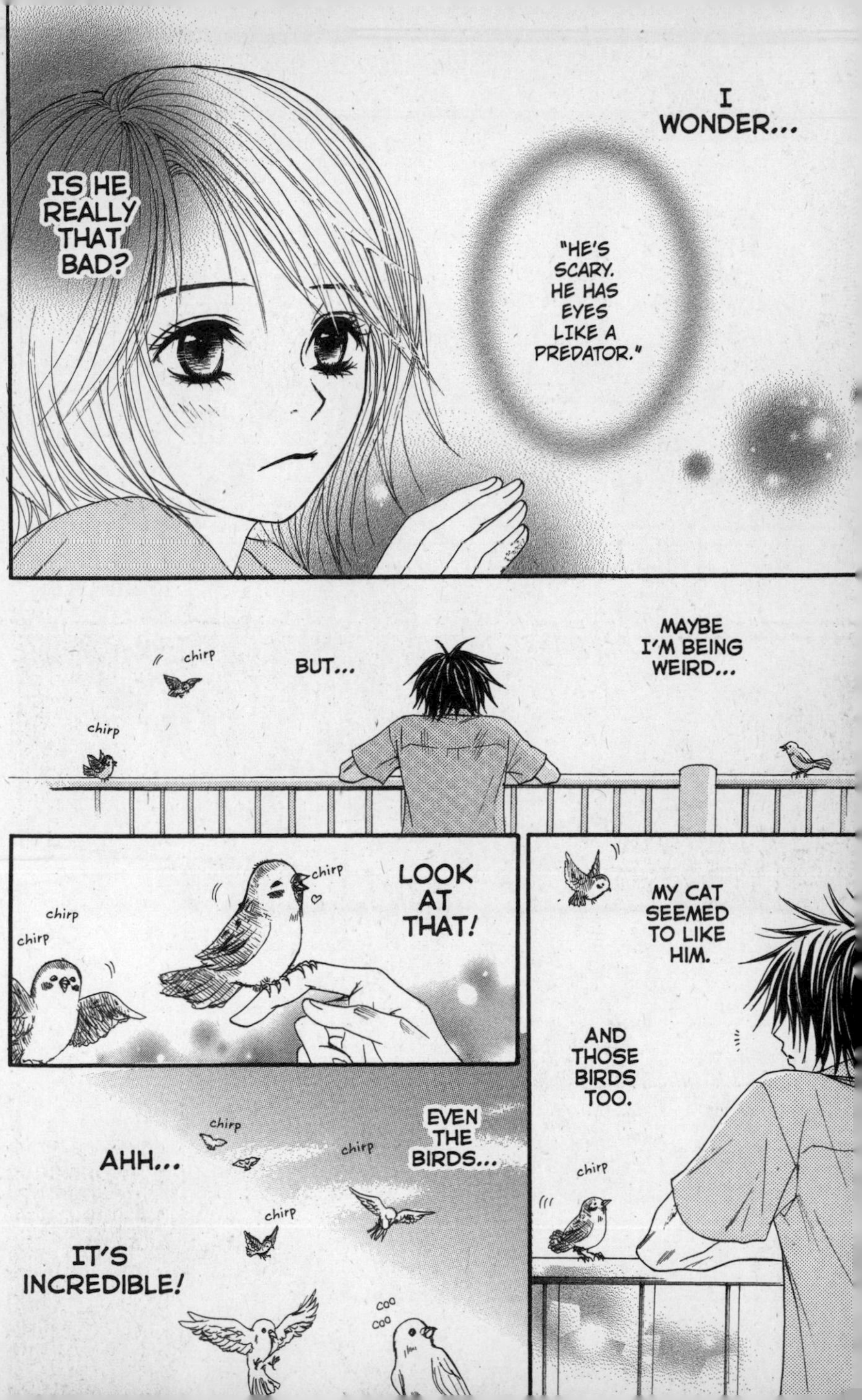
I WONDER...
"HE'S SCARY. HE HAS EYES LIKE A PREDATOR."
IS HE REALLY THAT BAD?
MAYBE I'M BEING WEIRD...
BUT...
chirp
chirp
MY CAT SEEMED TO LIKE HIM.
AND THOSE BIRDS TOO.
chirp
LOOK AT THAT!
chirp
chirp
chirp
EVEN THE BIRDS...
chirp
chirp
AHH...
chirp
IT'S INCREDIBLE!
coo coo

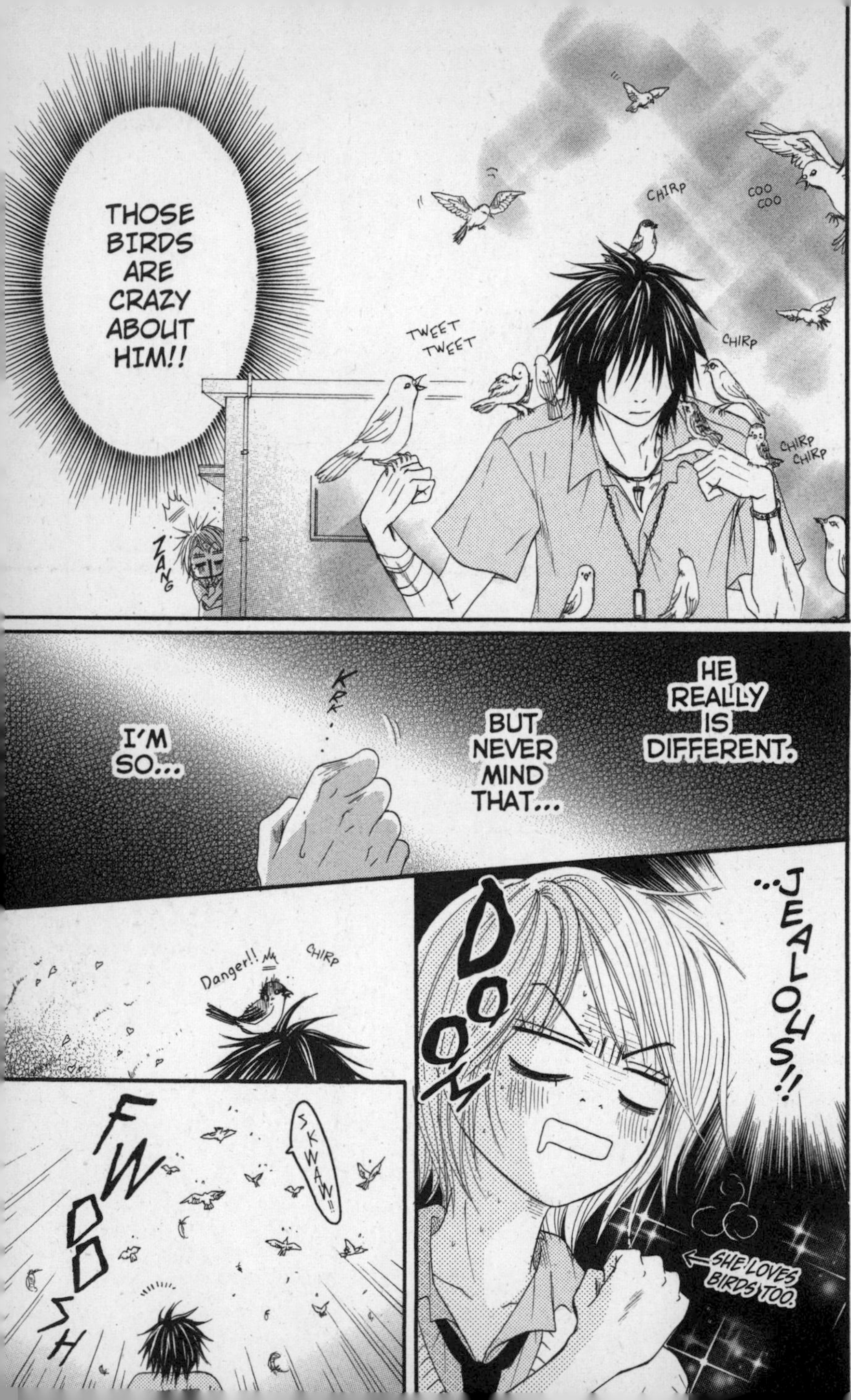
CHIRP
COO COO
CHIRP
CHIRP CHIRP
TWEET TWEET
THOSE BIRDS ARE CRAZY ABOUT HIM!!
ZANG
HE REALLY IS DIFFERENT.
BUT NEVER MIND THAT...
I'M SO...
...JEALOUS!!
DOOM
SHE LOVES BIRDS TOO.
CHIRP
Danger!!
SKWAW!!
FWOOSH

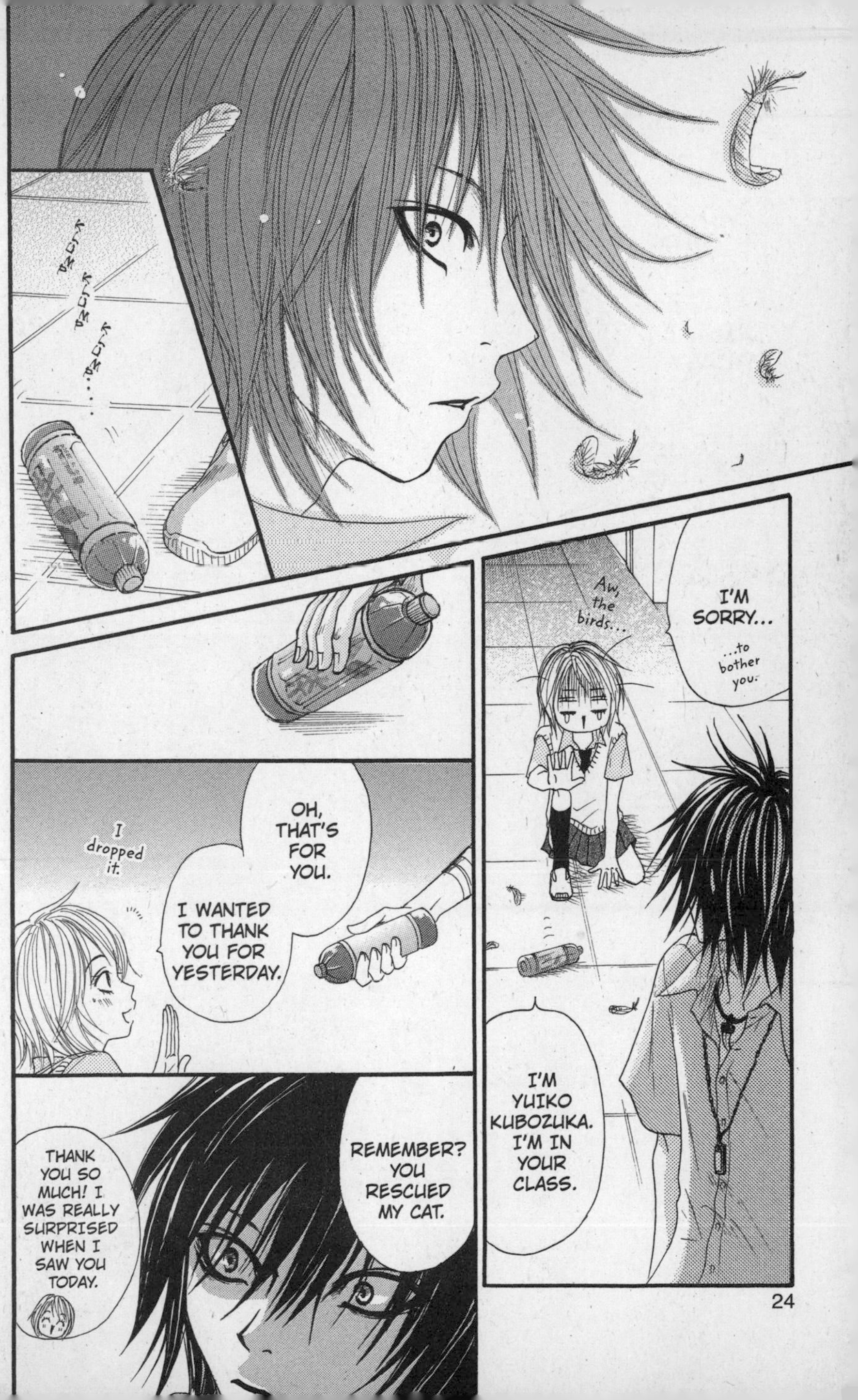
KLUMP KLUMP KLUMP...
I'M SORRY...
...to bother you.
Aw, the birds...
I'M YUIKO KUBOZUKA. I'M IN YOUR CLASS.
OH, THAT'S FOR YOU.
I WANTED TO THANK YOU FOR YESTERDAY.
I dropped it.
REMEMBER? YOU RESCUED MY CAT.
THANK YOU SO MUCH! I WAS REALLY SURPRISED WHEN I SAW YOU TODAY.

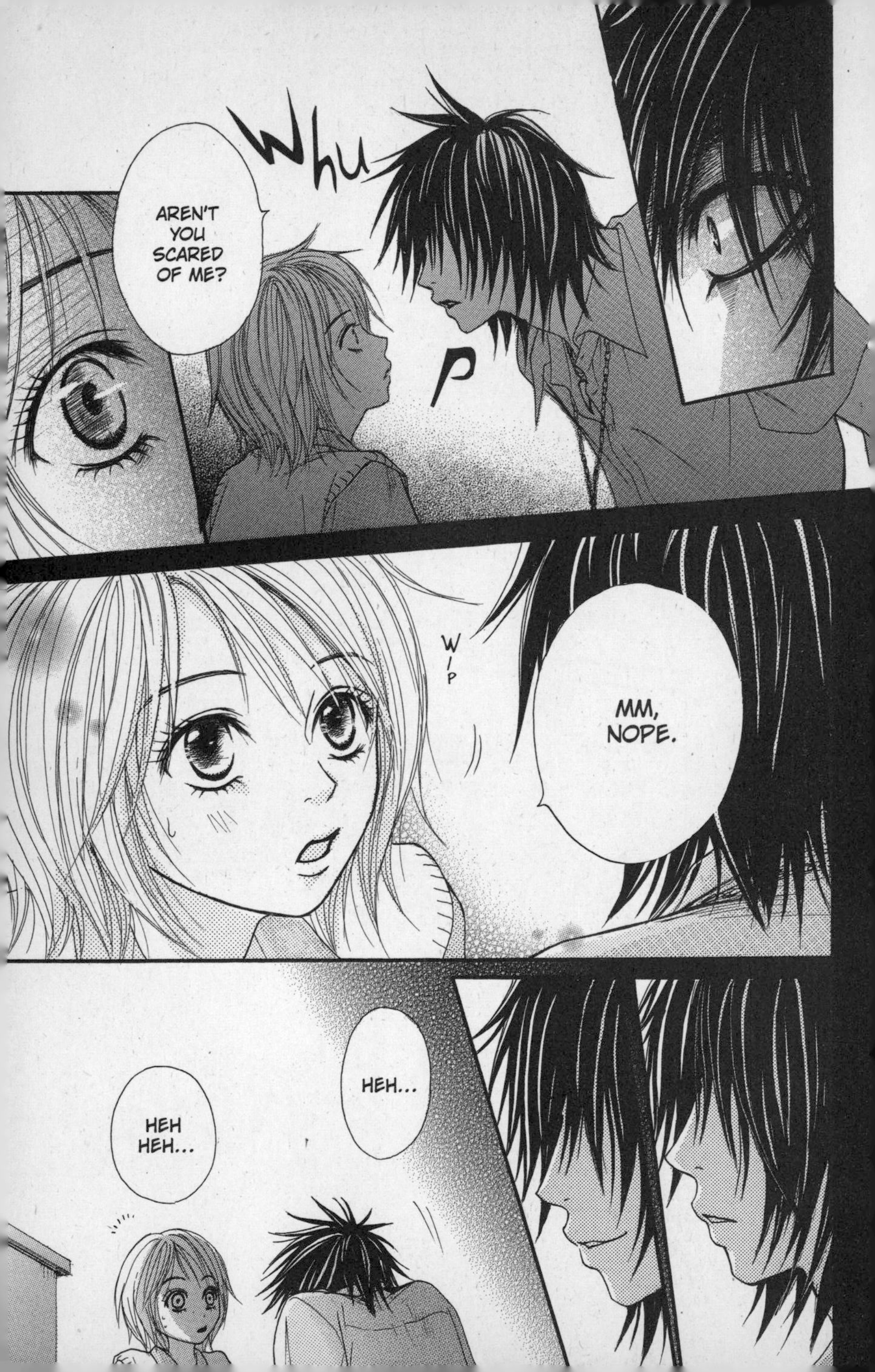
Whup
AREN'T YOU SCARED OF ME?
MM, NOPE.
WIP
HEH...
HEH HEH...

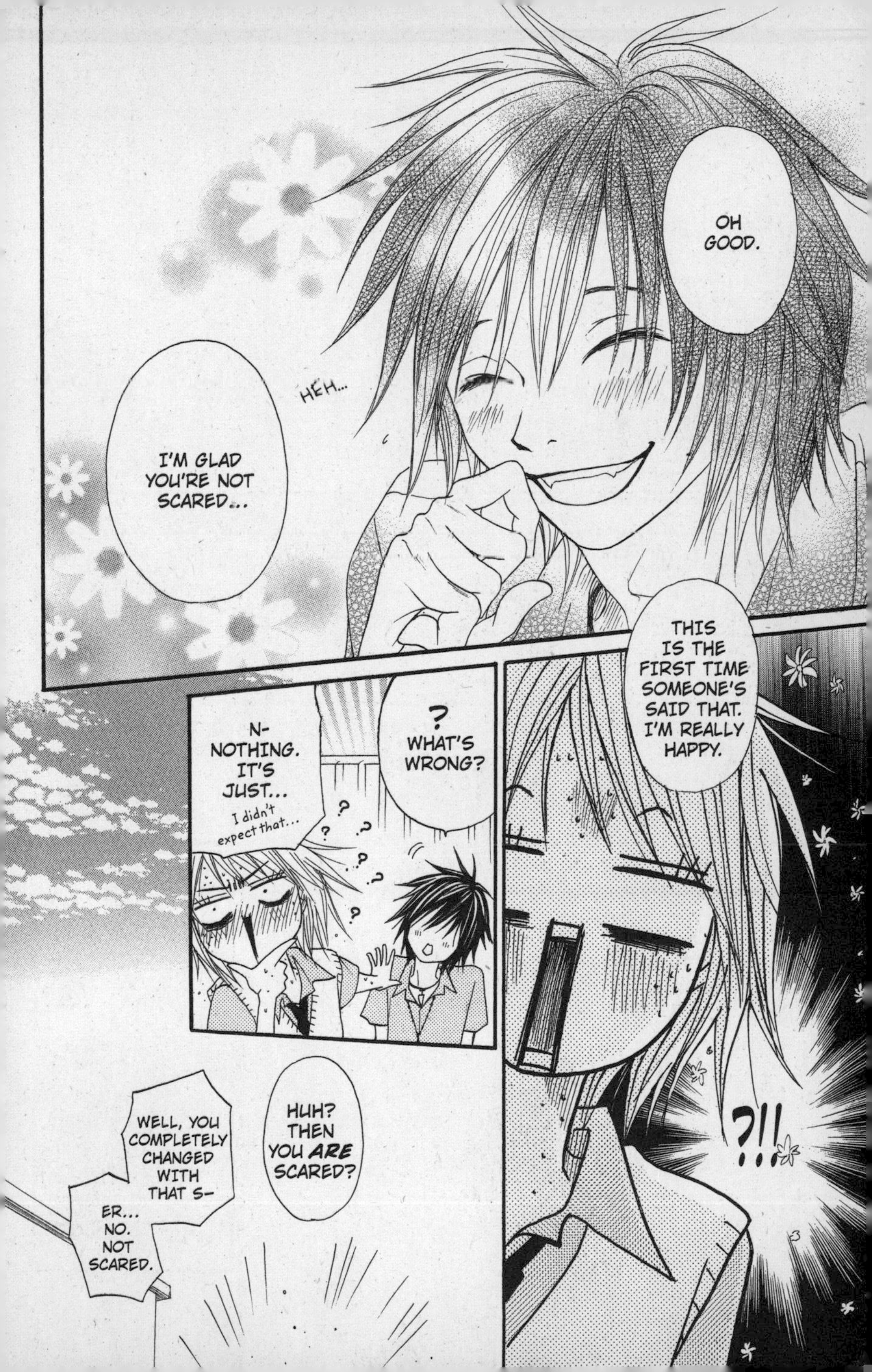
OH GOOD.
HEH...
I'M GLAD YOU'RE NOT SCARED...
THIS IS THE FIRST TIME SOMEONE'S SAID THAT. I'M REALLY HAPPY.
?!!
? WHAT'S WRONG?
N-NOTHING. IT'S JUST...
I didn't expect that...
HUH? THEN YOU ***ARE*** SCARED?
WELL, YOU COMPLETELY CHANGED WITH THAT S-
ER... NO. NOT SCARED.

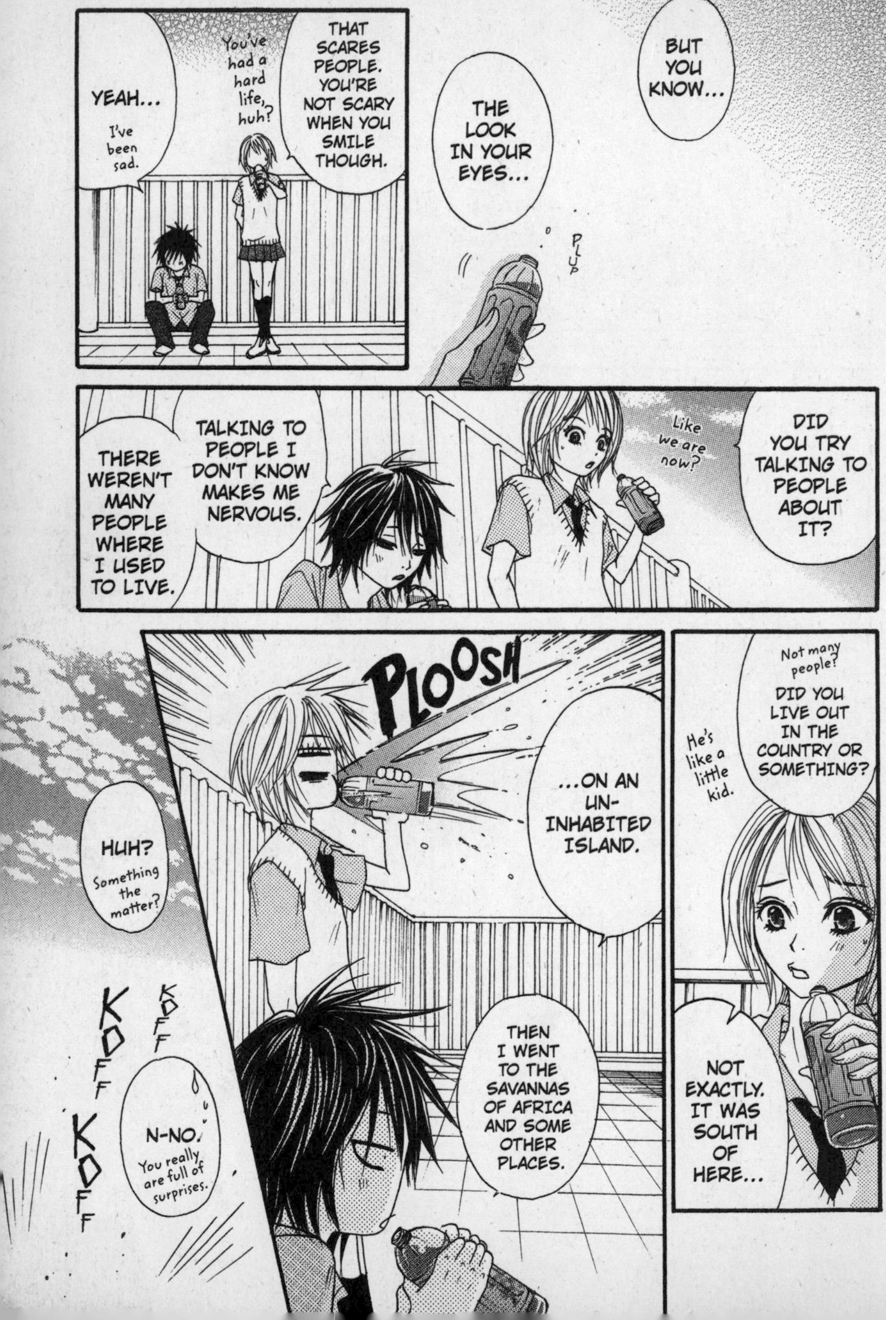
BUT YOU KNOW...
THE LOOK IN YOUR EYES...
PLUP
THAT SCARES PEOPLE. YOU'RE NOT SCARY WHEN YOU SMILE THOUGH.
You've had a hard life, huh?
YEAH...
I've been sad.
DID YOU TRY TALKING TO PEOPLE ABOUT IT?
Like we are now?
TALKING TO PEOPLE I DON'T KNOW MAKES ME NERVOUS.
THERE WEREN'T MANY PEOPLE WHERE I USED TO LIVE.
Not many people?
DID YOU LIVE OUT IN THE COUNTRY OR SOMETHING?
He's like a little kid.
NOT EXACTLY. IT WAS SOUTH OF HERE...
PLOOSH
...ON AN UN-INHABITED ISLAND.
THEN I WENT TO THE SAVANNAS OF AFRICA AND SOME OTHER PLACES.
HUH?
Something the matter?
KOFF
KOFF
KOFF
KOFF
N-NO.
You really are full of surprises.

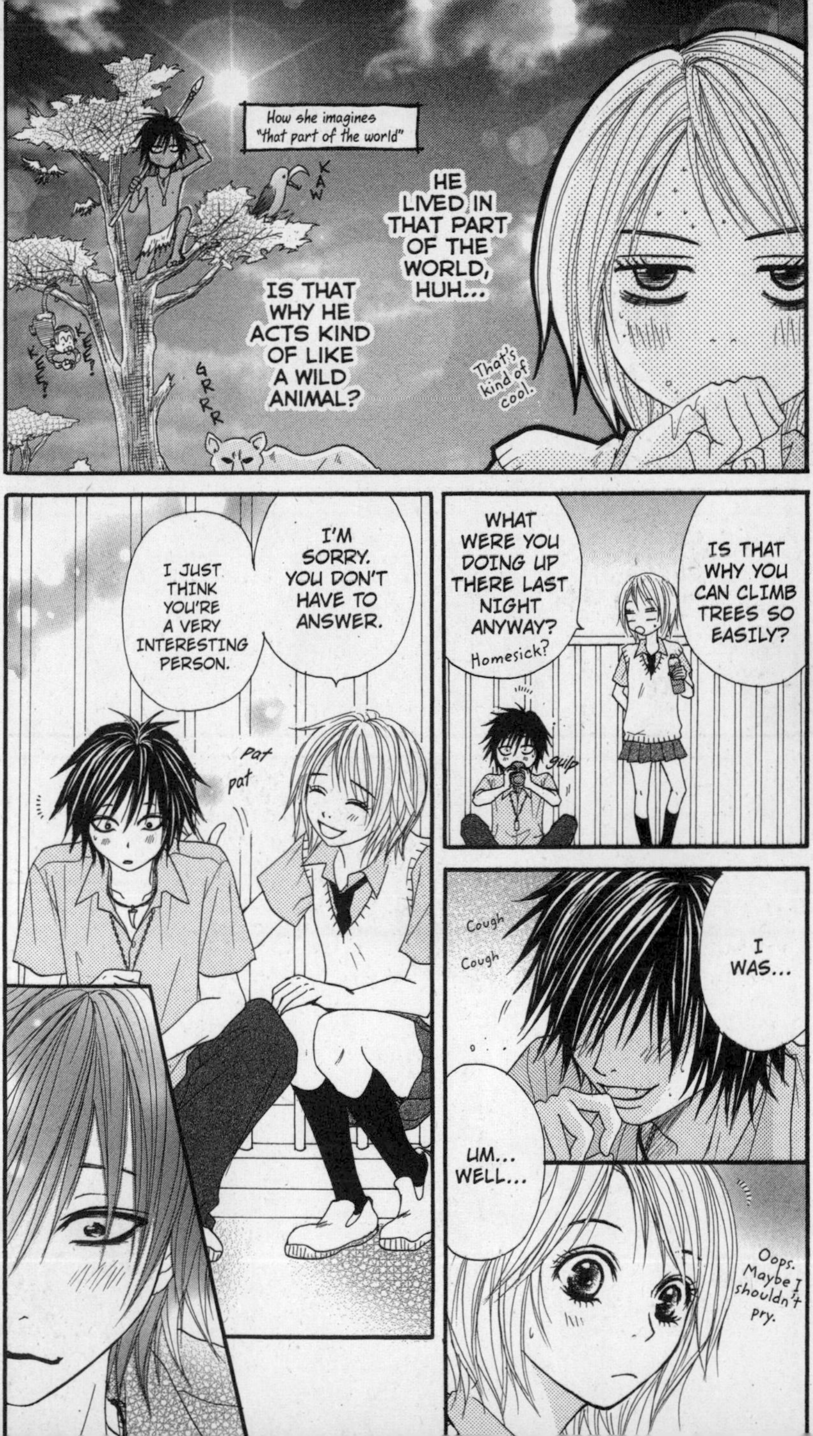
How she imagines "that part of the world"
KAW
KEE? KEE?
GRRR
HE LIVED IN THAT PART OF THE WORLD, HUH...
IS THAT WHY HE ACTS KIND OF LIKE A WILD ANIMAL?
That's kind of cool.
IS THAT WHY YOU CAN CLIMB TREES SO EASILY?
WHAT WERE YOU DOING UP THERE LAST NIGHT ANYWAY?
Homesick?
gulp
Cough
Cough
I WAS...
UM... WELL...
Oops. Maybe I shouldn't pry.
I'M SORRY. YOU DON'T HAVE TO ANSWER.
I JUST THINK YOU'RE A VERY INTERESTING PERSON.
pat pat

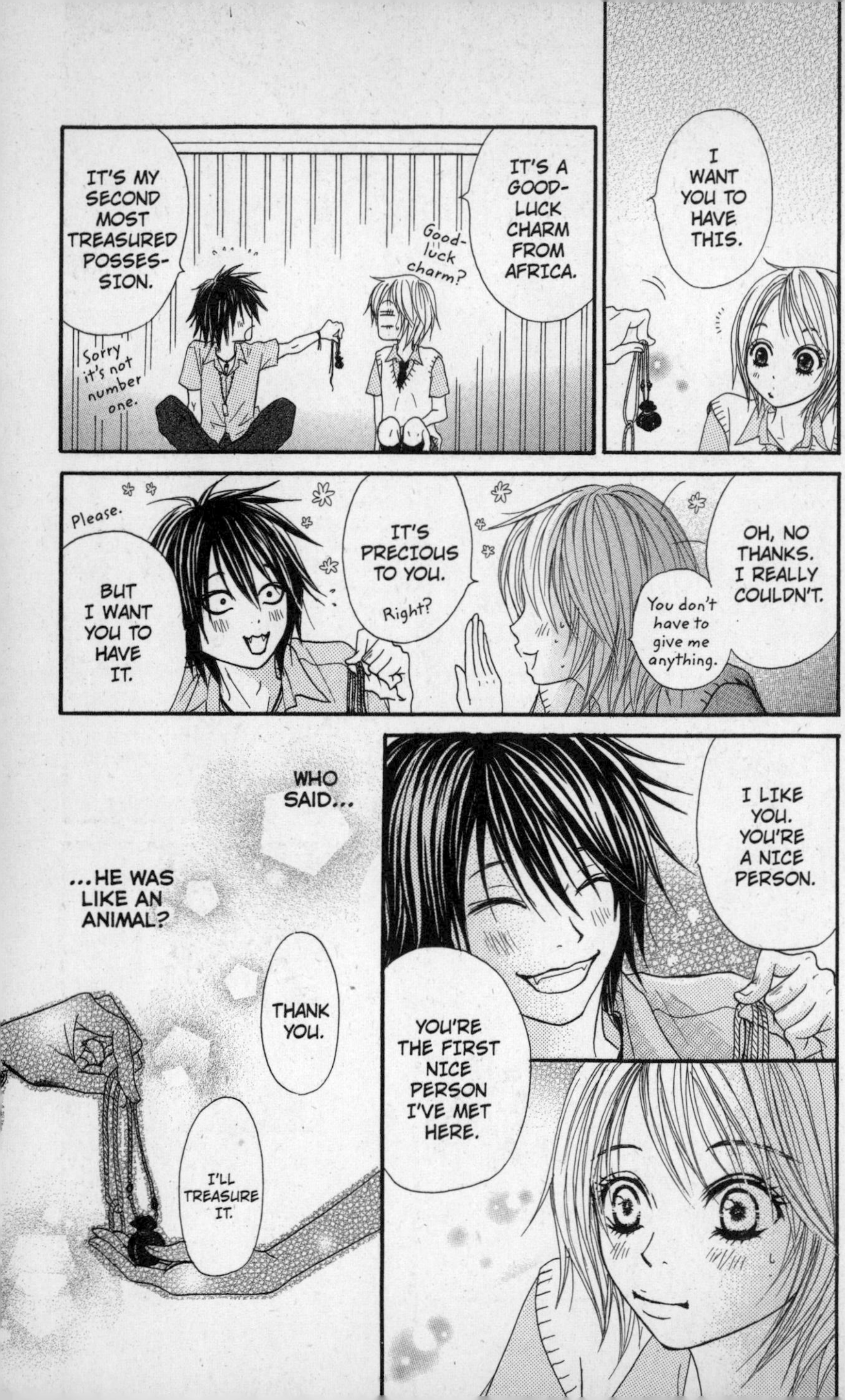
I WANT YOU TO HAVE THIS.
IT'S A GOOD-LUCK CHARM FROM AFRICA.
Good-luck charm?
IT'S MY SECOND MOST TREASURED POSSES-SION.
Sorry it's not number one.
OH, NO THANKS. I REALLY COULDN'T.
You don't have to give me anything.
IT'S PRECIOUS TO YOU.
Right?
Please.
BUT I WANT YOU TO HAVE IT.
I LIKE YOU. YOU'RE A NICE PERSON.
YOU'RE THE FIRST NICE PERSON I'VE MET HERE.
WHO SAID...
...HE WAS LIKE AN ANIMAL?
THANK YOU.
I'LL TREASURE IT.

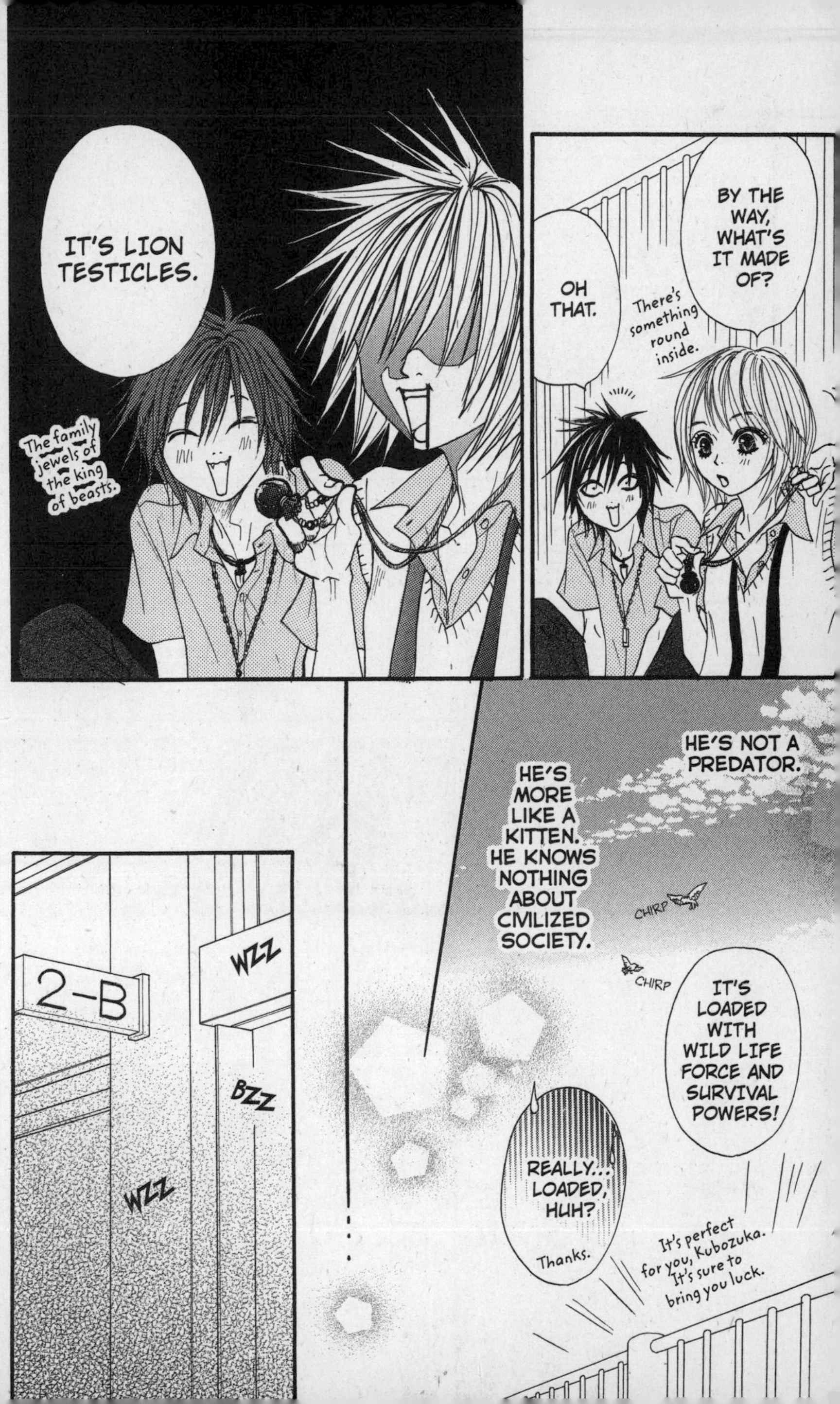
BY THE WAY, WHAT'S IT MADE OF?
There's something round inside.
OH THAT.
IT'S LION TESTICLES.
The family jewels of the king of beasts.
HE'S NOT A PREDATOR.
HE'S MORE LIKE A KITTEN. HE KNOWS NOTHING ABOUT CIVILIZED SOCIETY.
CHIRP
CHIRP
IT'S LOADED WITH WILD LIFE FORCE AND SURVIVAL POWERS!
It's perfect for you, Kubozuka. It's sure to bring you luck.
REALLY... LOADED, HUH?
Thanks.
2-B
WZZ
BZZ
WZZ

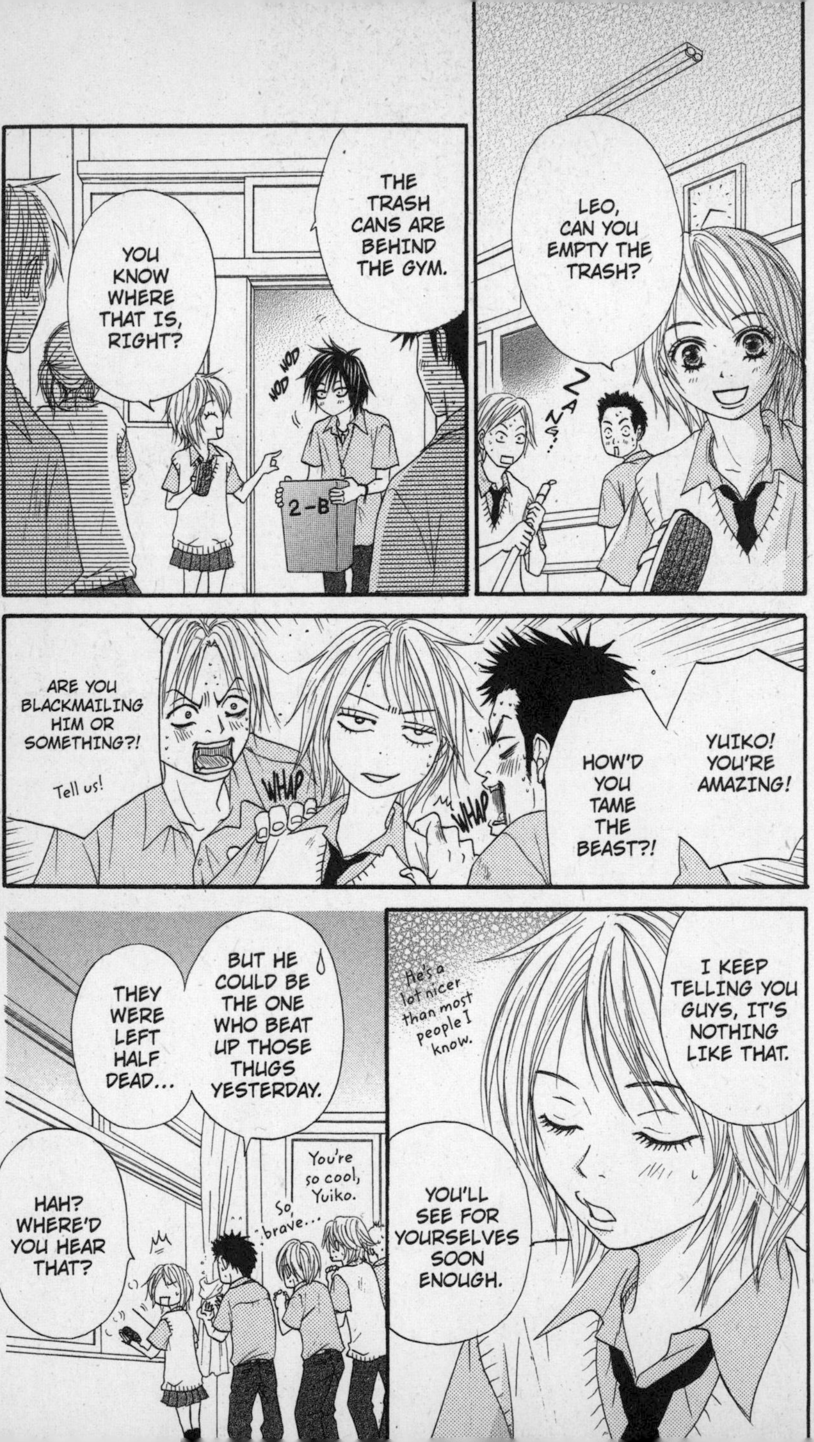
LEO, CAN YOU EMPTY THE TRASH?
ZANG...
THE TRASH CANS ARE BEHIND THE GYM.
YOU KNOW WHERE THAT IS, RIGHT?
NOD NOD
2-B
YUIKO! YOU'RE AMAZING!
HOW'D YOU TAME THE BEAST?!
WHAP
WHAP
ARE YOU BLACKMAILING HIM OR SOMETHING?!
Tell us!
I KEEP TELLING YOU GUYS, IT'S NOTHING LIKE THAT.
He's a lot nicer than most people I know.
YOU'LL SEE FOR YOURSELVES SOON ENOUGH.
BUT HE COULD BE THE ONE WHO BEAT UP THOSE THUGS YESTERDAY.
THEY WERE LEFT HALF DEAD...
You're so cool, Yuiko.
So, brave...
HAH? WHERE'D YOU HEAR THAT?

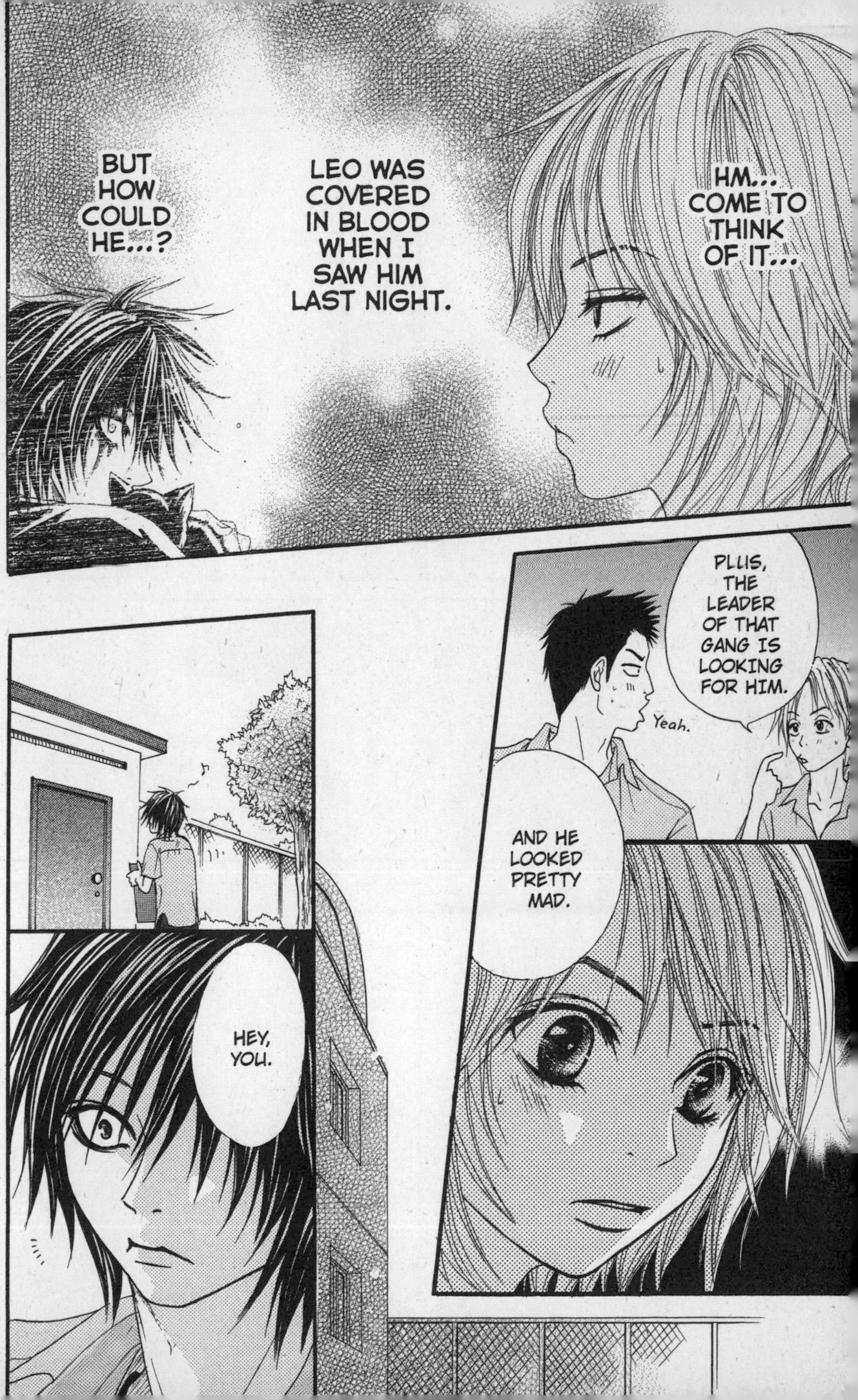
HM... COME TO THINK OF IT...
LEO WAS COVERED IN BLOOD WHEN I SAW HIM LAST NIGHT.
BUT HOW COULD HE...?
PLUS, THE LEADER OF THAT GANG IS LOOKING FOR HIM.
Yeah.
AND HE LOOKED PRETTY MAD.
HEY, YOU.

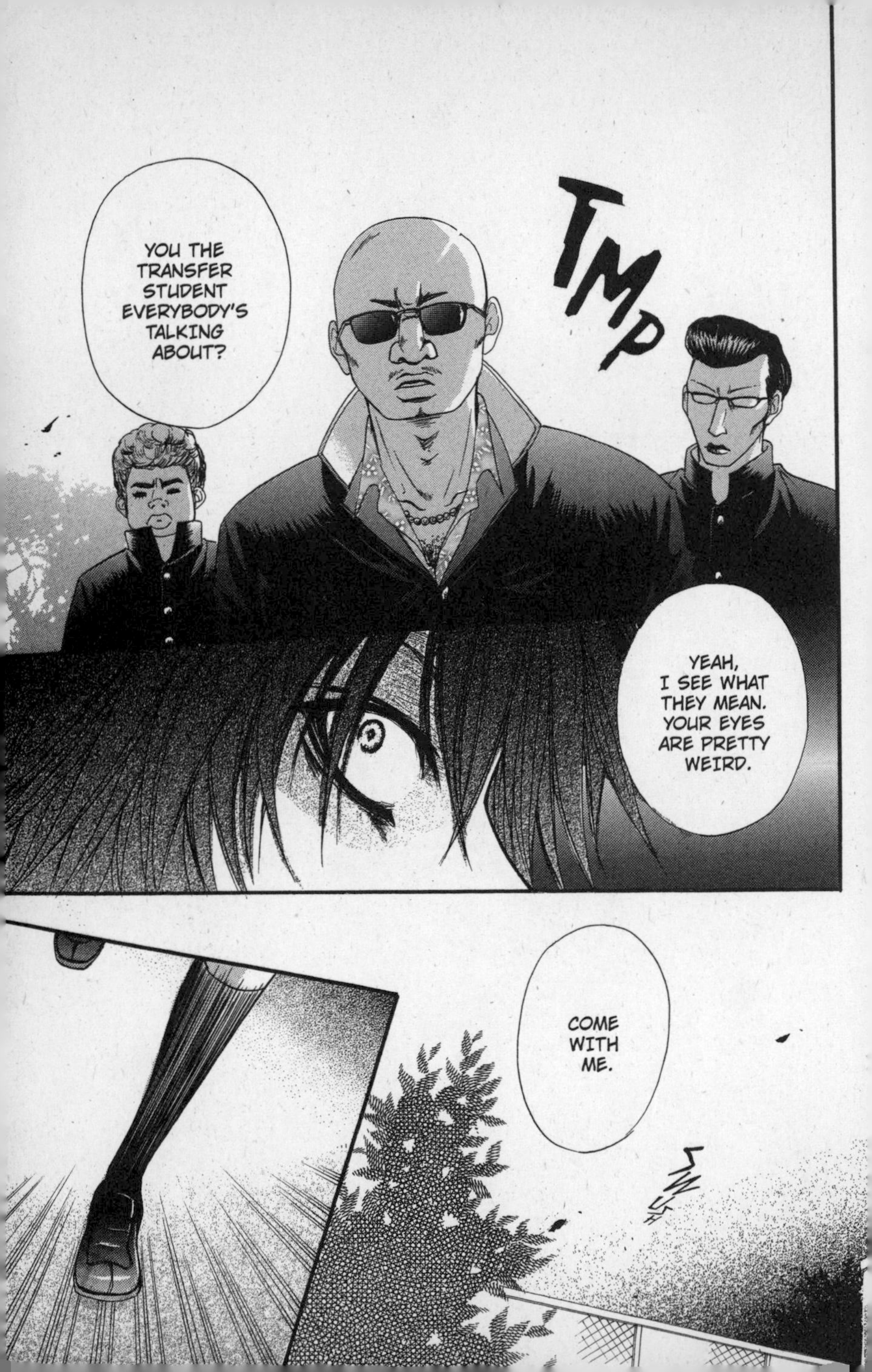
TMP
YOU THE TRANSFER STUDENT EVERYBODY'S TALKING ABOUT?
YEAH, I SEE WHAT THEY MEAN. YOUR EYES ARE PRETTY WEIRD.
COME WITH ME.
SWUSH

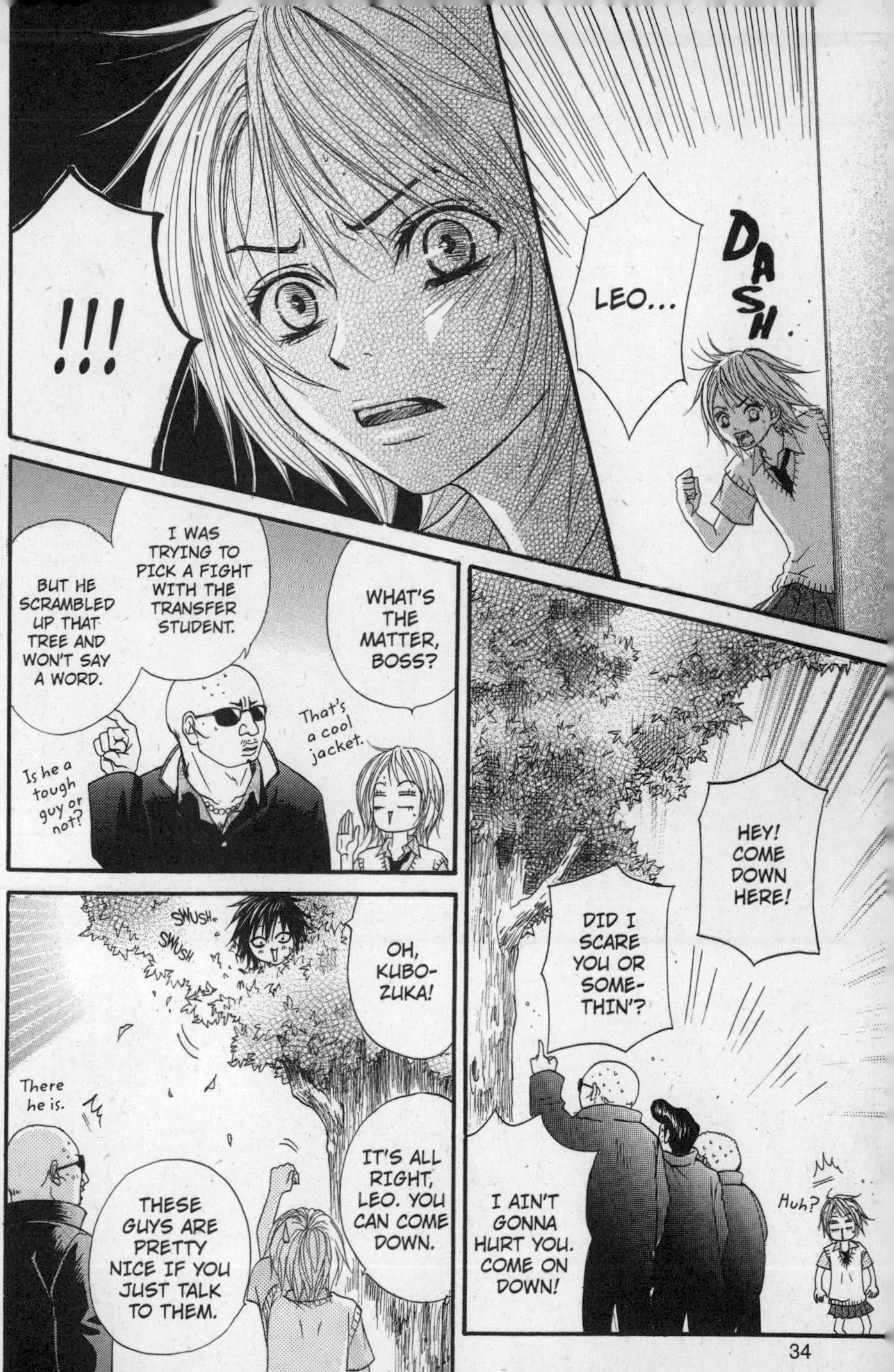
LEO...
DASH
!!!
HEY! COME DOWN HERE!
DID I SCARE YOU OR SOME-THIN'?
I AIN'T GONNA HURT YOU. COME ON DOWN!
Huh?
WHAT'S THE MATTER, BOSS?
I WAS TRYING TO PICK A FIGHT WITH THE TRANSFER STUDENT.
BUT HE SCRAMBLED UP THAT TREE AND WON'T SAY A WORD.
That's a cool jacket.
Is he a tough guy or not?
OH, KUBO-ZUKA!
SWUSH
SWUSH
IT'S ALL RIGHT, LEO. YOU CAN COME DOWN.
There he is.
THESE GUYS ARE PRETTY NICE IF YOU JUST TALK TO THEM.

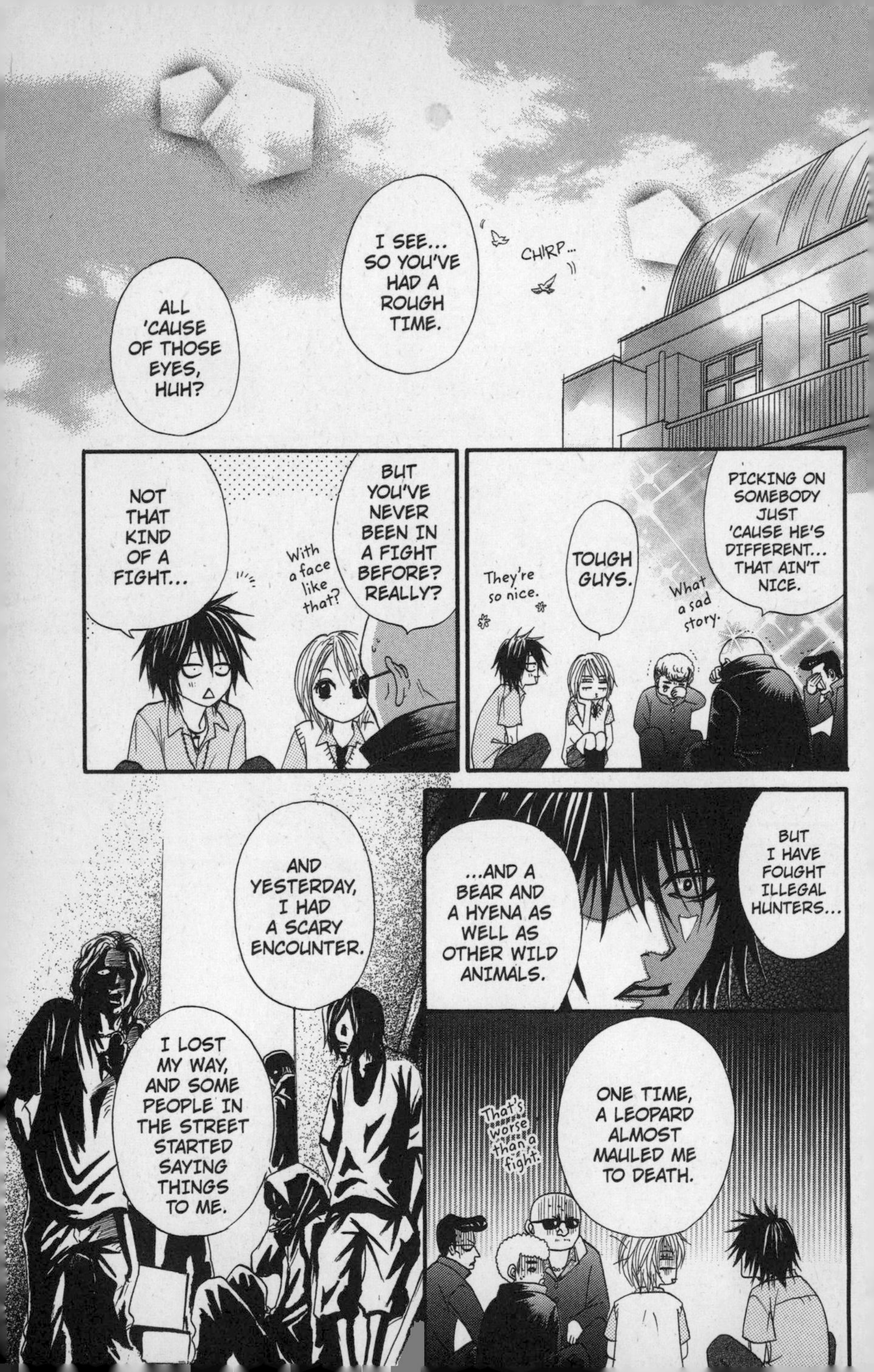
CHIRP...
I SEE... SO YOU'VE HAD A ROUGH TIME.
ALL 'CAUSE OF THOSE EYES, HUH?
PICKING ON SOMEBODY JUST 'CAUSE HE'S DIFFERENT... THAT AIN'T NICE.
What a sad story.
TOUGH GUYS.
They're so nice.
BUT YOU'VE NEVER BEEN IN A FIGHT BEFORE? REALLY?
With a face like that?
NOT THAT KIND OF A FIGHT...
BUT I HAVE FOUGHT ILLEGAL HUNTERS...
...AND A BEAR AND A HYENA AS WELL AS OTHER WILD ANIMALS.
ONE TIME, A LEOPARD ALMOST MAULED ME TO DEATH.
That's worse than a fight.
AND YESTERDAY, I HAD A SCARY ENCOUNTER.
I LOST MY WAY, AND SOME PEOPLE IN THE STREET STARTED SAYING THINGS TO ME.

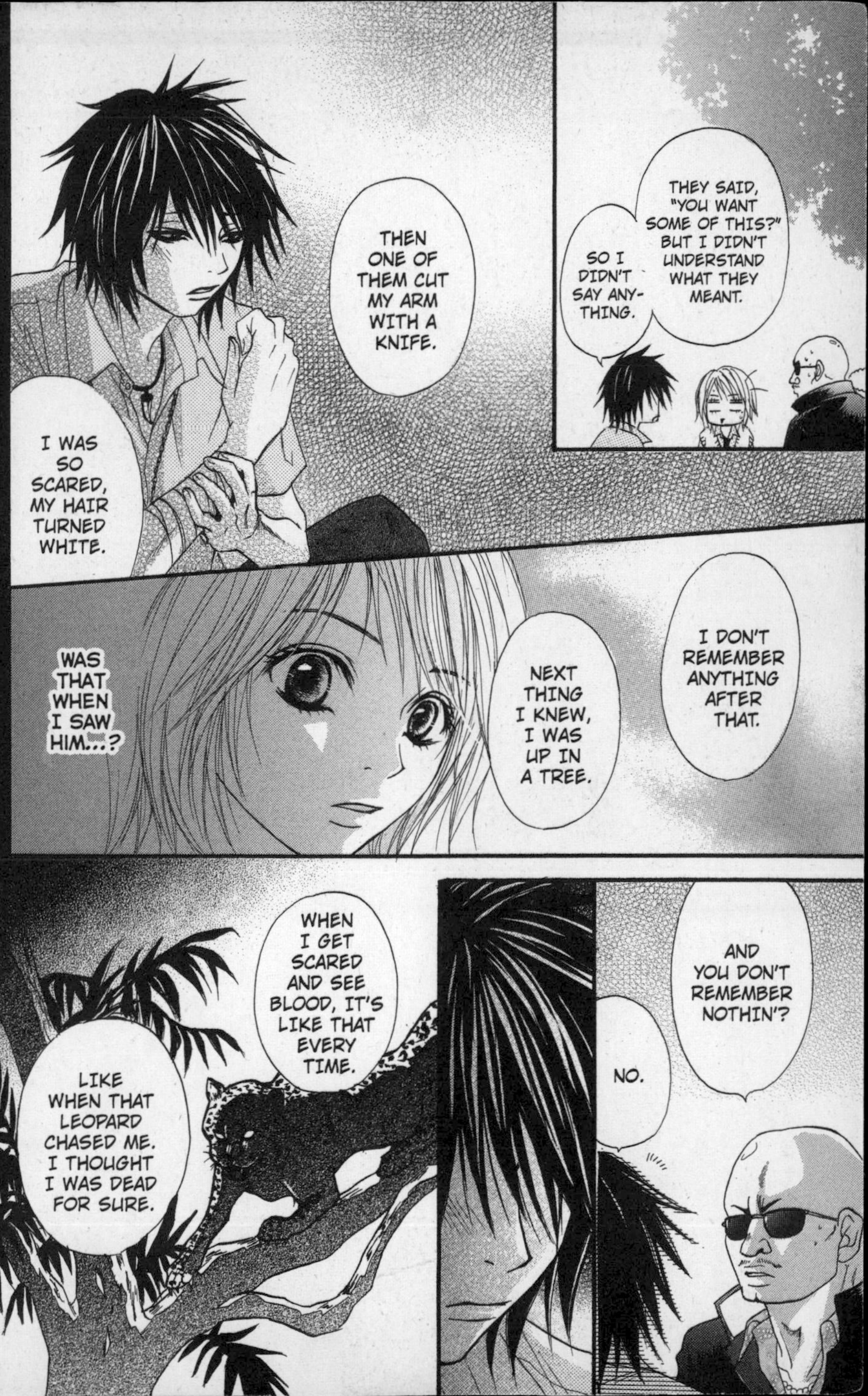
THEY SAID, "YOU WANT SOME OF THIS?" BUT I DIDN'T UNDERSTAND WHAT THEY MEANT.
SO I DIDN'T SAY ANY-THING.
THEN ONE OF THEM CUT MY ARM WITH A KNIFE.
I WAS SO SCARED, MY HAIR TURNED WHITE.
I DON'T REMEMBER ANYTHING AFTER THAT.
NEXT THING I KNEW, I WAS UP IN A TREE.
WAS THAT WHEN I SAW HIM...?
AND YOU DON'T REMEMBER NOTHIN'?
NO.
WHEN I GET SCARED AND SEE BLOOD, IT'S LIKE THAT EVERY TIME.
LIKE WHEN THAT LEOPARD CHASED ME. I THOUGHT I WAS DEAD FOR SURE.

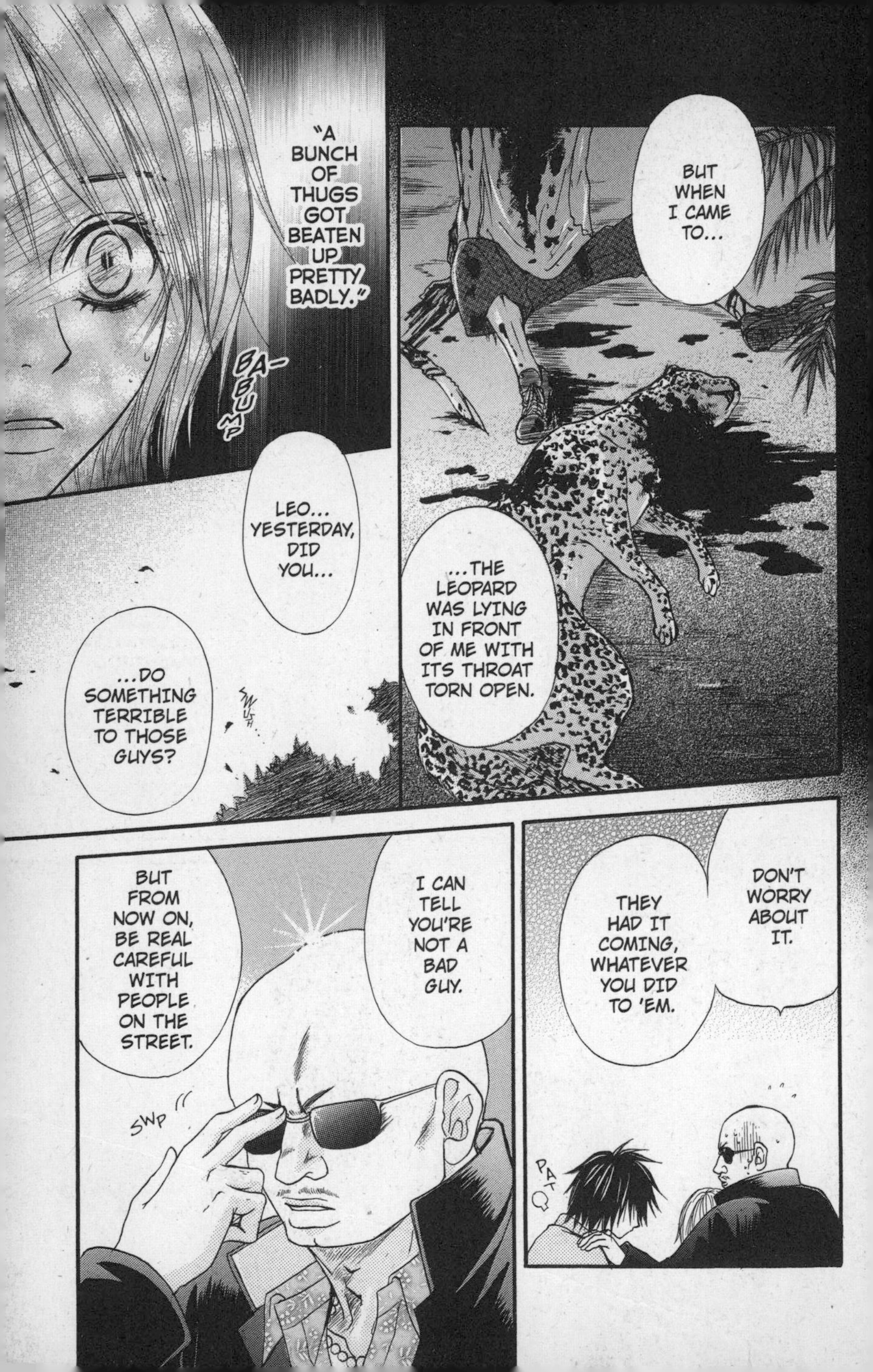
BUT WHEN I CAME TO...
...THE LEOPARD WAS LYING IN FRONT OF ME WITH ITS THROAT TORN OPEN.
"A BUNCH OF THUGS GOT BEATEN UP PRETTY BADLY."
BA-BUMP
LEO... YESTERDAY, DID YOU...
...DO SOMETHING TERRIBLE TO THOSE GUYS?
SWUSH...
DON'T WORRY ABOUT IT.
THEY HAD IT COMING, WHATEVER YOU DID TO 'EM.
PAT
I CAN TELL YOU'RE NOT A BAD GUY.
BUT FROM NOW ON, BE REAL CAREFUL WITH PEOPLE ON THE STREET.
SWP

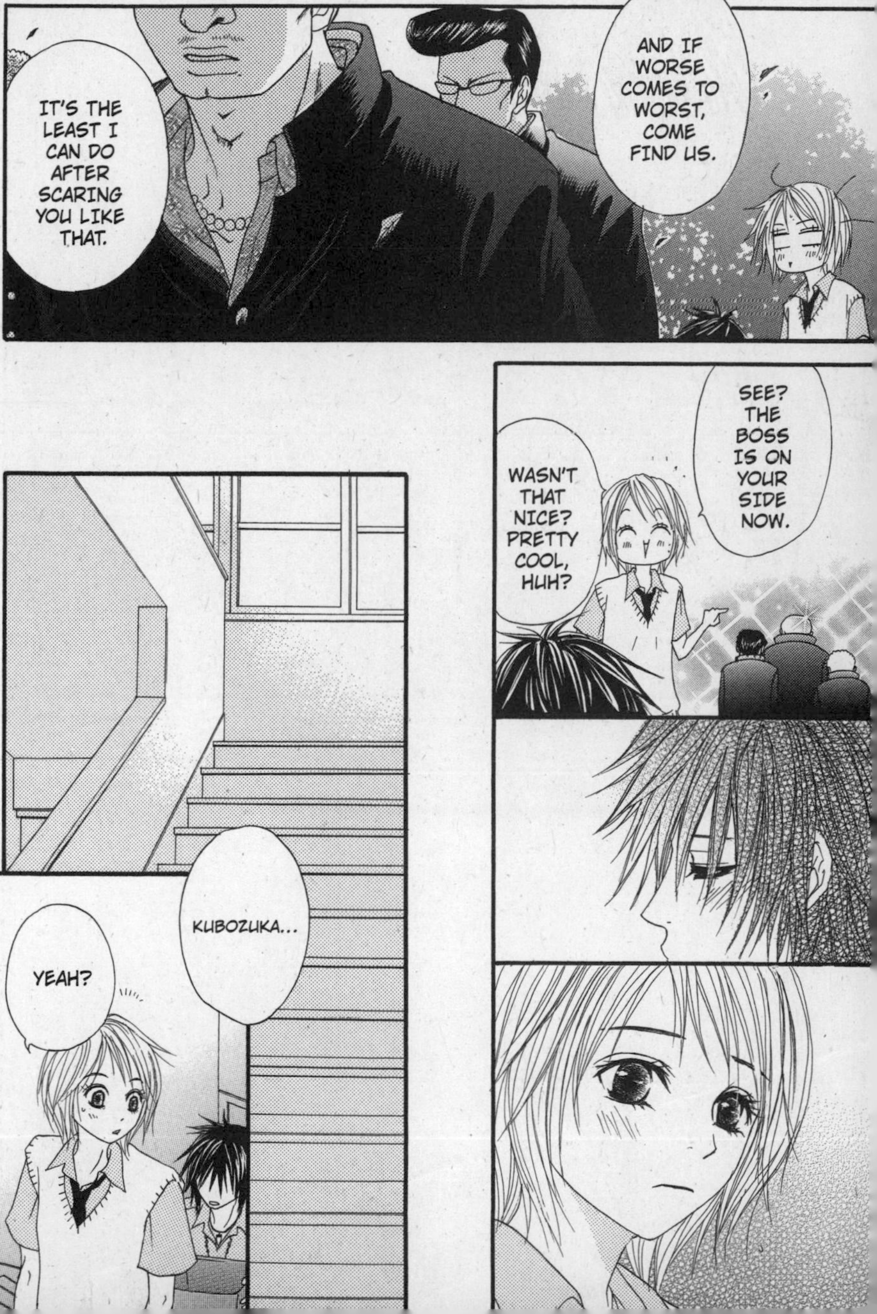
AND IF WORSE COMES TO WORST, COME FIND US.
IT'S THE LEAST I CAN DO AFTER SCARING YOU LIKE THAT.
SEE? THE BOSS IS ON YOUR SIDE NOW.
WASN'T THAT NICE? PRETTY COOL, HUH?
KUBOZUKA...
YEAH?

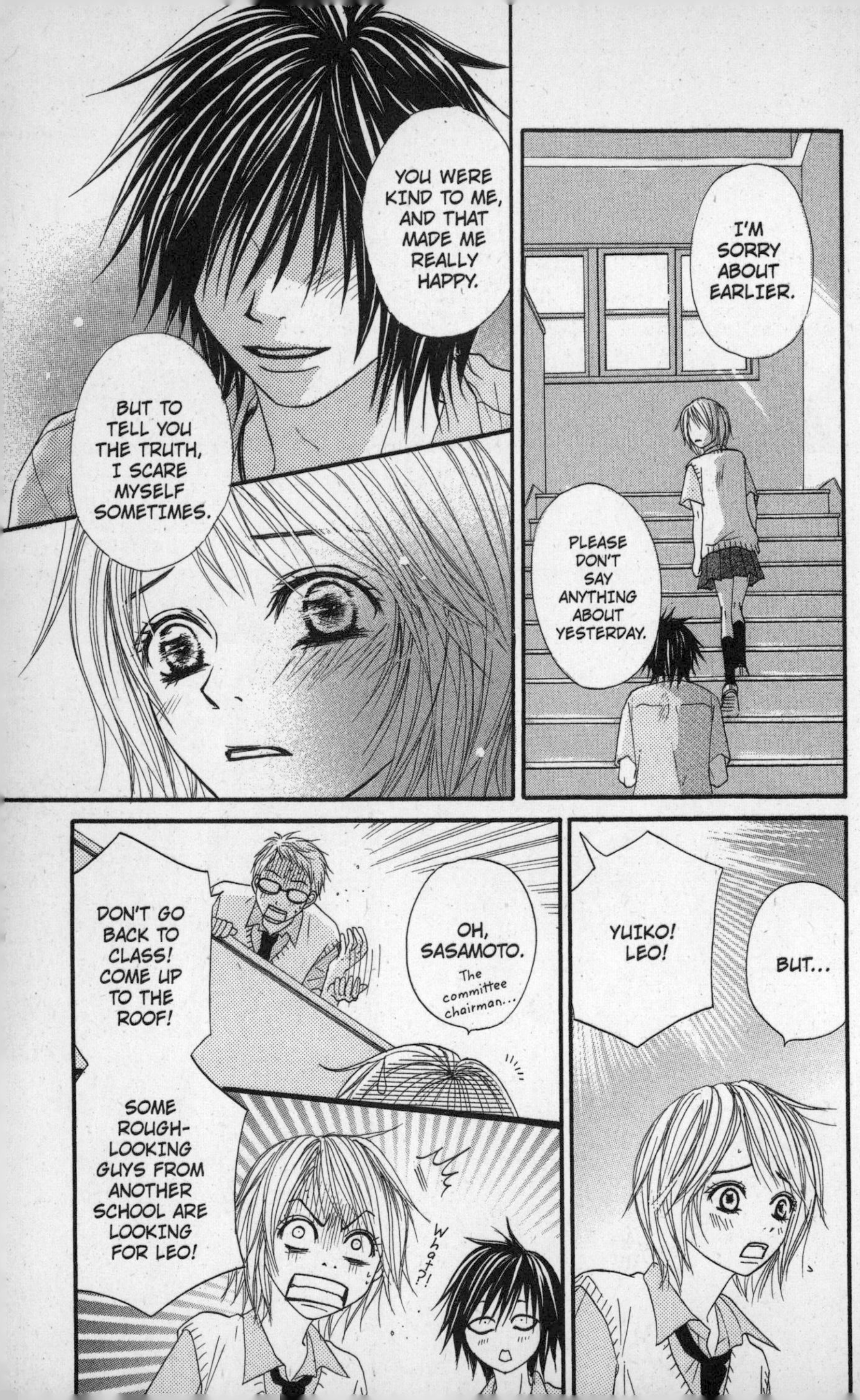
I'M SORRY ABOUT EARLIER.
PLEASE DON'T SAY ANYTHING ABOUT YESTERDAY.
YOU WERE KIND TO ME, AND THAT MADE ME REALLY HAPPY.
BUT TO TELL YOU THE TRUTH, I SCARE MYSELF SOMETIMES.
BUT...
YUIKO! LEO!
OH, SASAMOTO.
The committee chairman...
DON'T GO BACK TO CLASS! COME UP TO THE ROOF!
SOME ROUGH-LOOKING GUYS FROM ANOTHER SCHOOL ARE LOOKING FOR LEO!
What?!

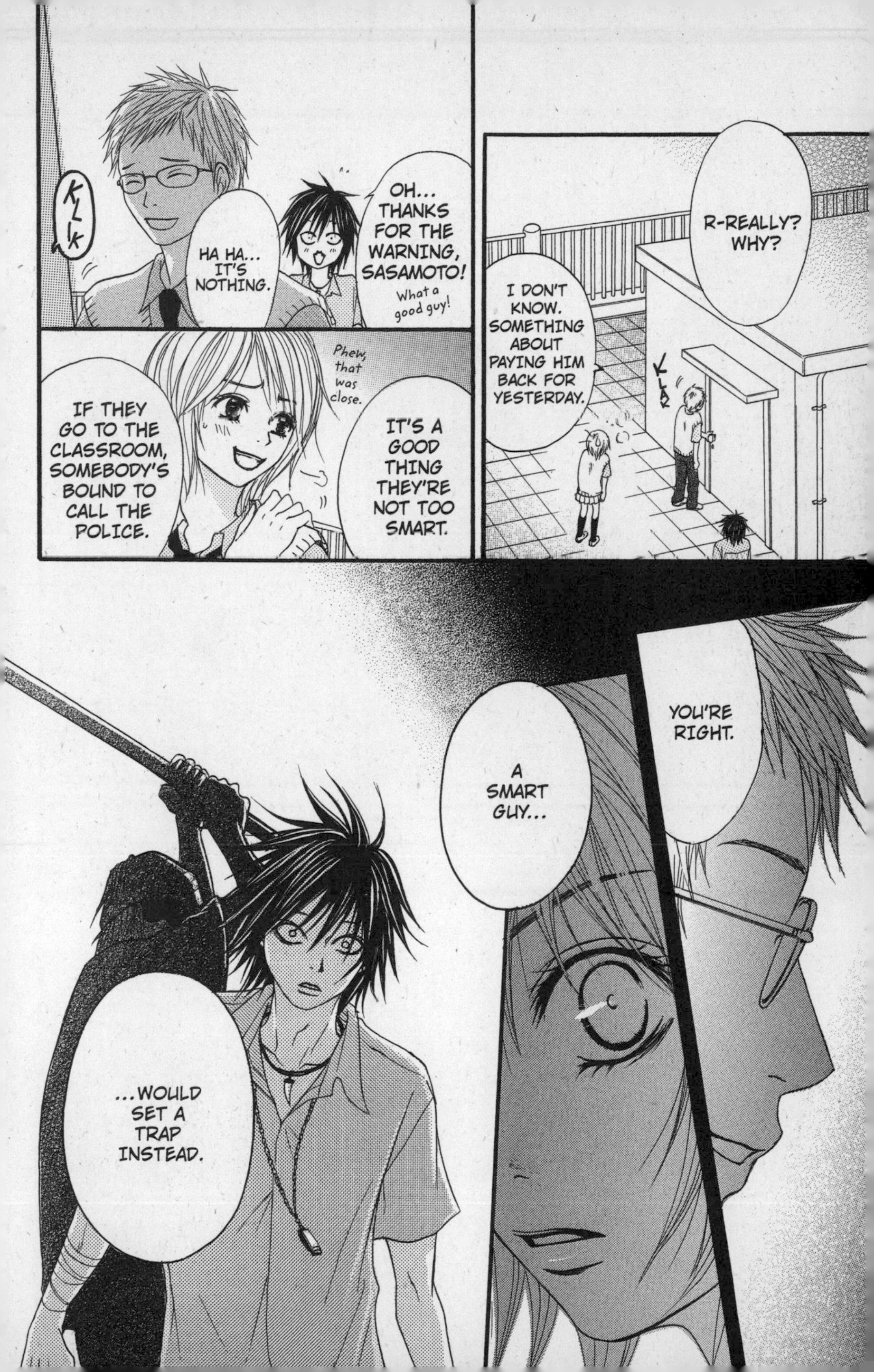
R-REALLY? WHY?
I DON'T KNOW. SOMETHING ABOUT PAYING HIM BACK FOR YESTERDAY.
KLAK
OH... THANKS FOR THE WARNING, SASAMOTO!
What a good guy!
HA HA... IT'S NOTHING.
KLIK
Phew, that was close.
IF THEY GO TO THE CLASSROOM, SOMEBODY'S BOUND TO CALL THE POLICE.
IT'S A GOOD THING THEY'RE NOT TOO SMART.
YOU'RE RIGHT.
A SMART GUY...
...WOULD SET A TRAP INSTEAD.

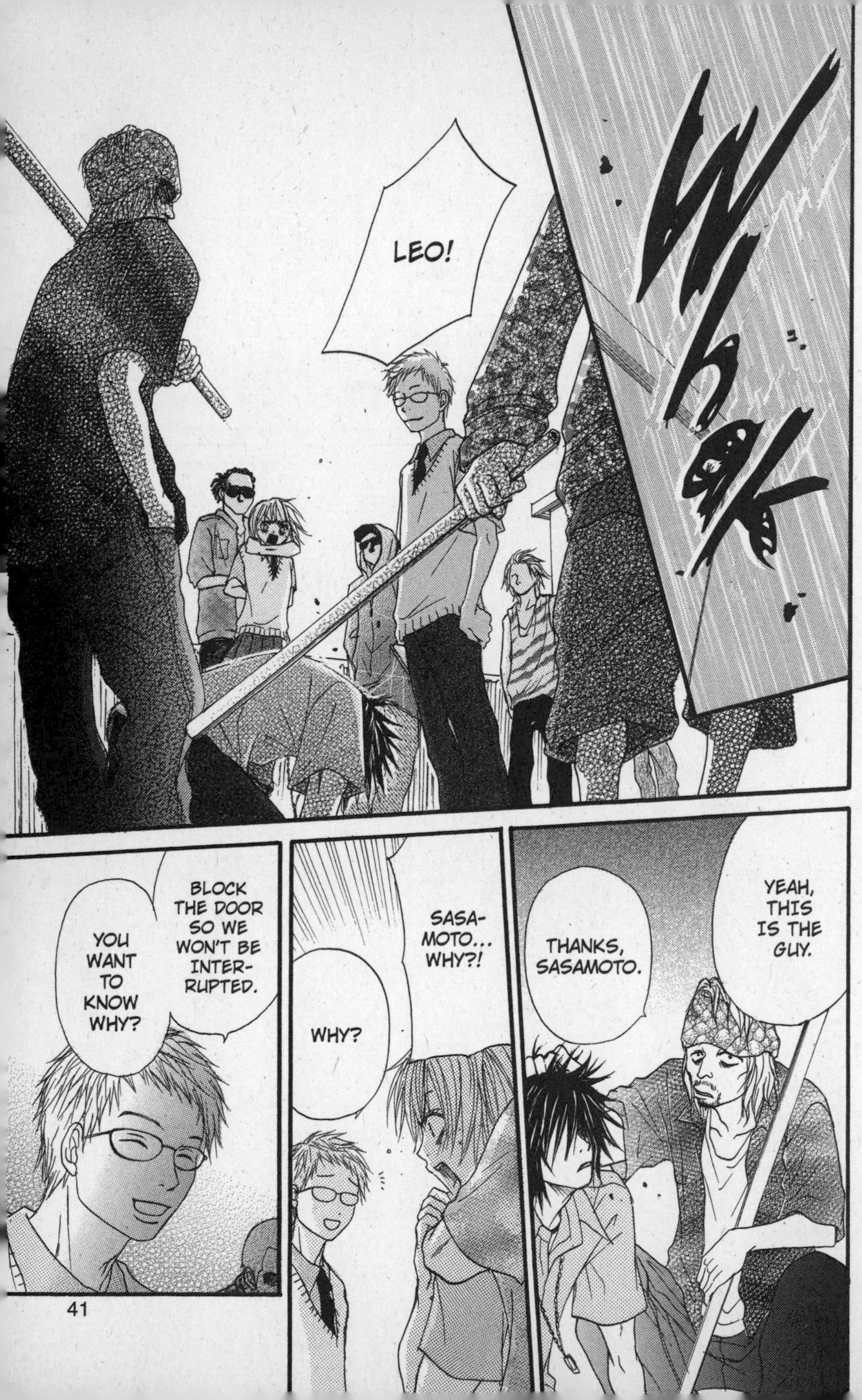
WHACK
LEO!
YEAH, THIS IS THE GUY.
THANKS, SASAMOTO.
SASAMOTO... WHY?!
WHY?
BLOCK THE DOOR SO WE WON'T BE INTERRUPTED.
YOU WANT TO KNOW WHY?

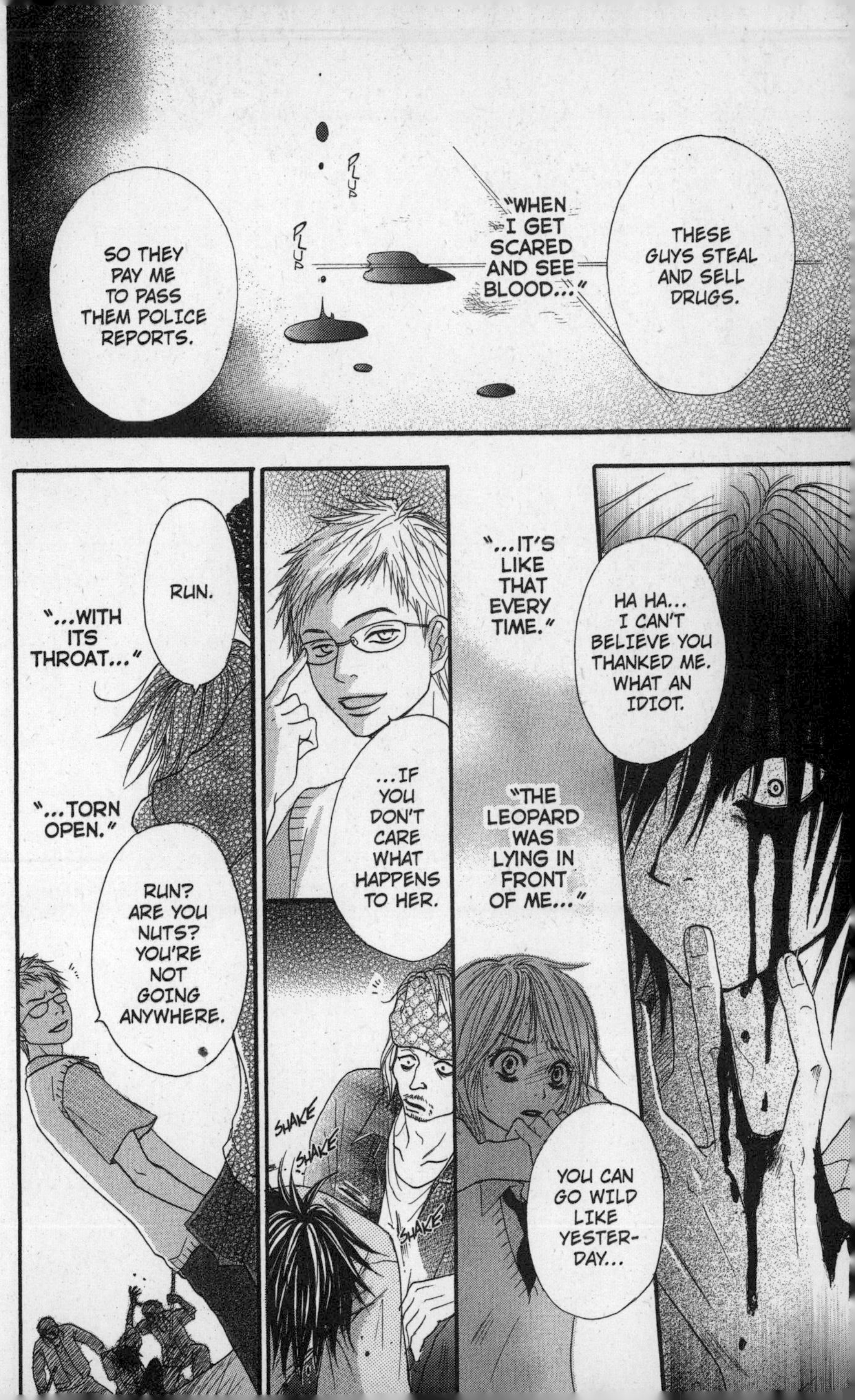
THESE GUYS STEAL AND SELL DRUGS.
"WHEN I GET SCARED AND SEE BLOOD..."
PLUP
PLUP
SO THEY PAY ME TO PASS THEM POLICE REPORTS.
HA HA... I CAN'T BELIEVE YOU THANKED ME. WHAT AN IDIOT.
"...IT'S LIKE THAT EVERY TIME."
"THE LEOPARD WAS LYING IN FRONT OF ME..."
YOU CAN GO WILD LIKE YESTER-DAY...
...IF YOU DON'T CARE WHAT HAPPENS TO HER.
SHAKE
SHAKE
SHAKE
RUN.
"...WITH ITS THROAT..."
"...TORN OPEN."
RUN? ARE YOU NUTS? YOU'RE NOT GOING ANYWHERE.

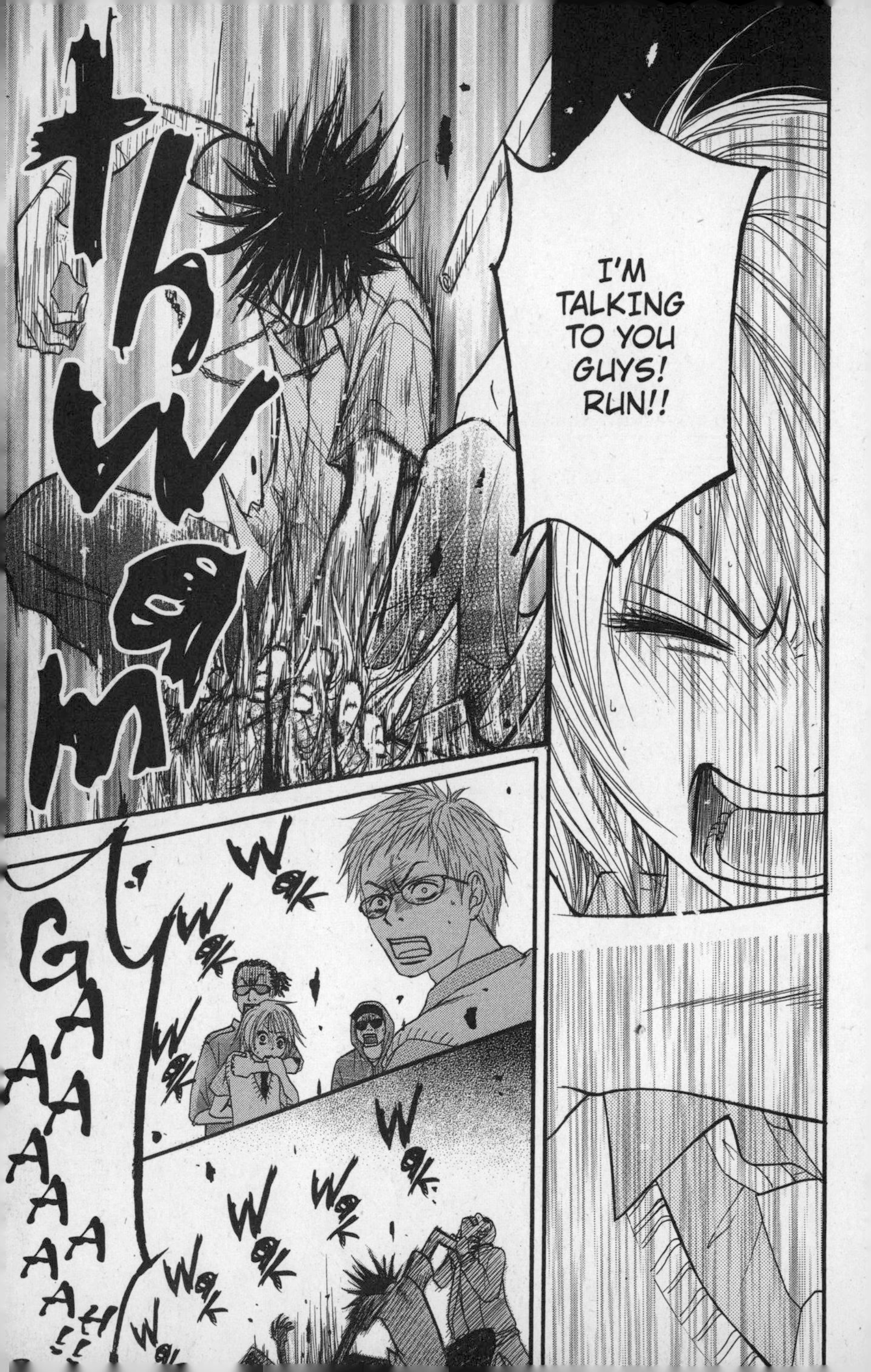
I'M TALKING TO YOU GUYS! RUN!!
thwam
GYAAAAAAAAAAH!!
Wak Wak Wak Wak Wak Wak Wak Wak

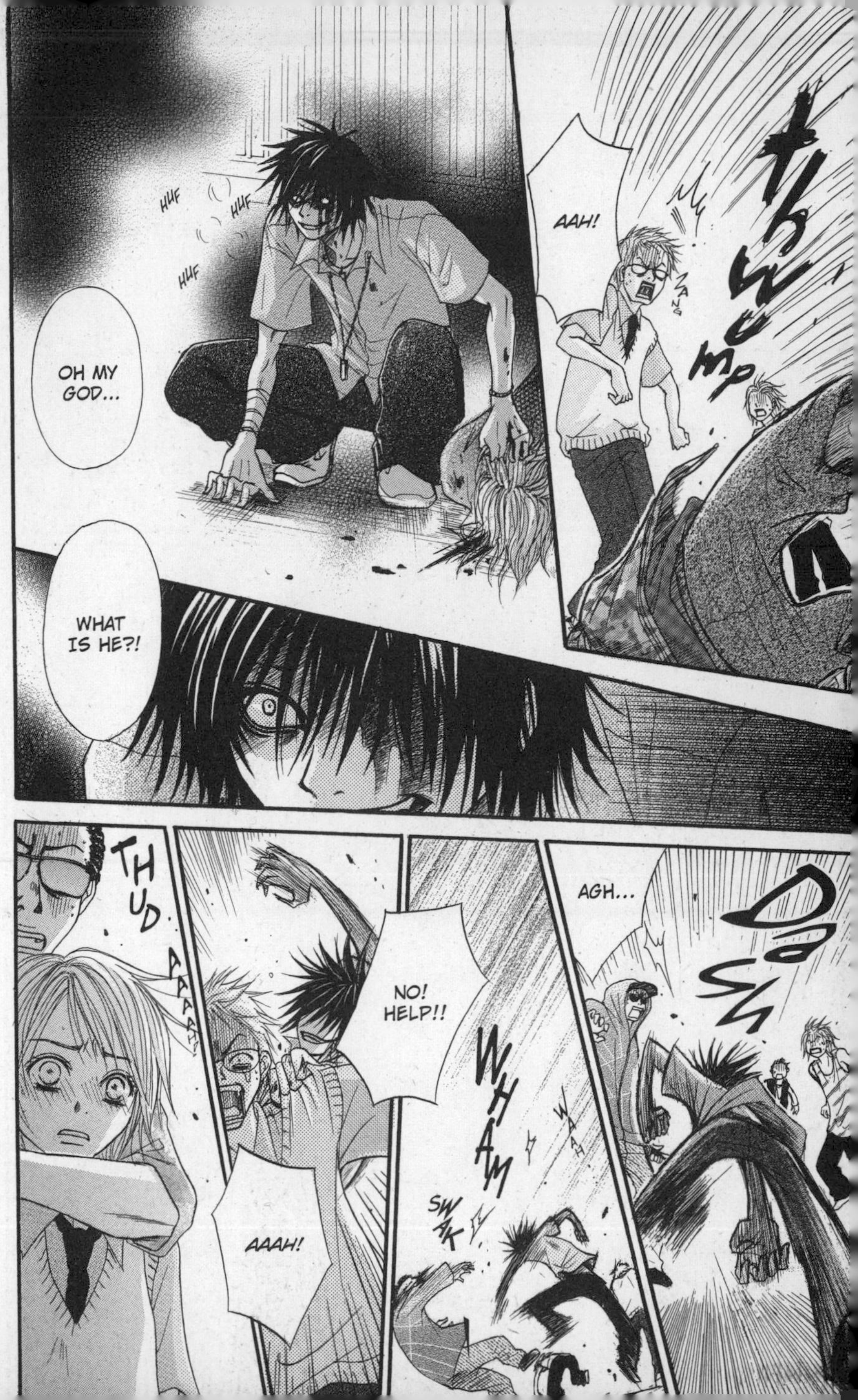
THWUMP
AAH!
ZANG
HUF
HUF
HUF
OH MY GOD...
WHAT IS HE?!
DASH
AGH...
WHAM
WAAH
SWAK
NO! HELP!!
AAAH!
THUD

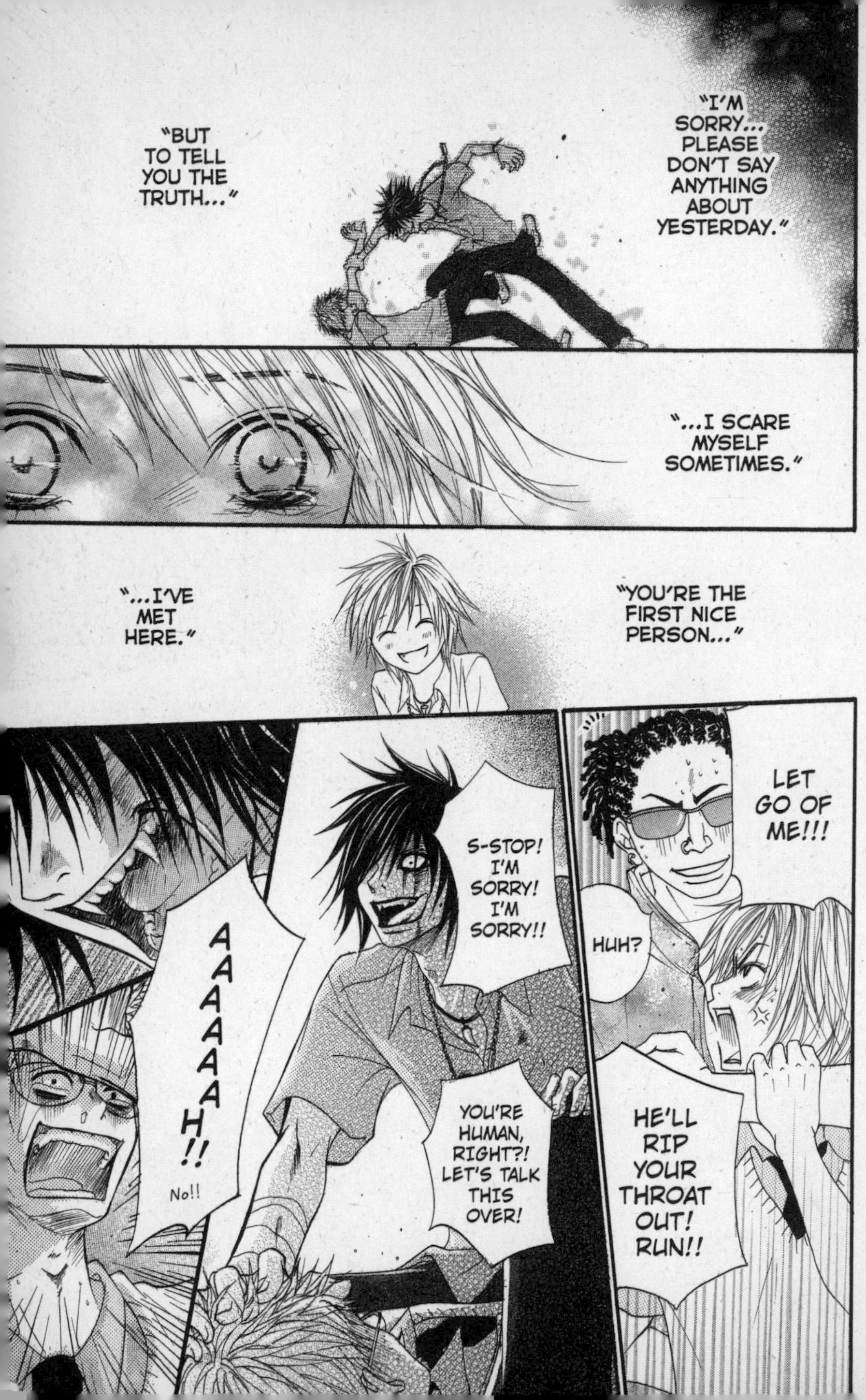
"I'M SORRY... PLEASE DON'T SAY ANYTHING ABOUT YESTERDAY."
"BUT TO TELL YOU THE TRUTH..."
"...I SCARE MYSELF SOMETIMES."
"YOU'RE THE FIRST NICE PERSON..."
"...I'VE MET HERE."
LET GO OF ME!!!
HUH?
HE'LL RIP YOUR THROAT OUT! RUN!!
S-STOP! I'M SORRY! I'M SORRY!!
YOU'RE HUMAN, RIGHT?! LET'S TALK THIS OVER!
AAAAAAAH!!
No!!

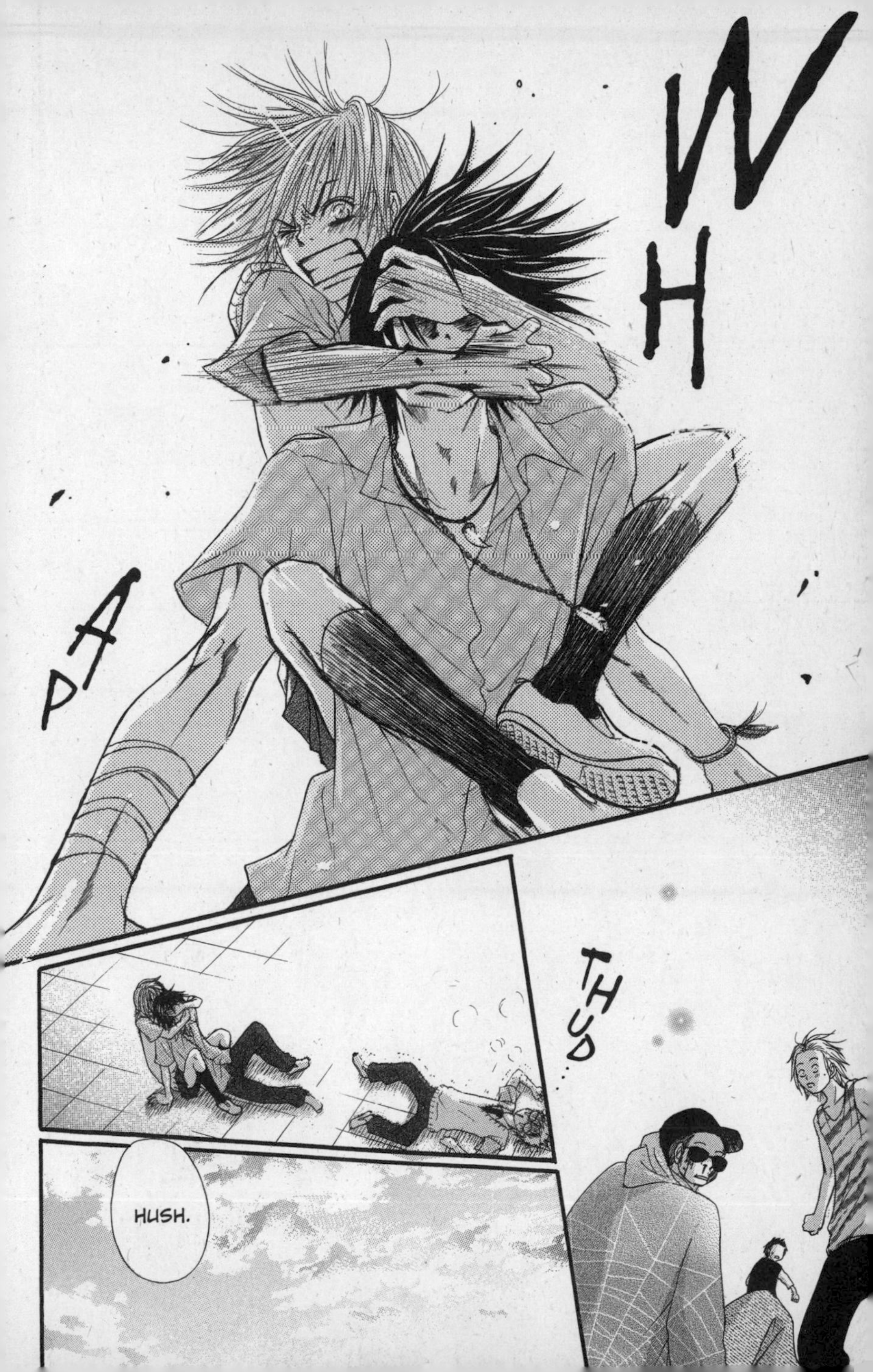
WHAP
THUD...
HUSH.

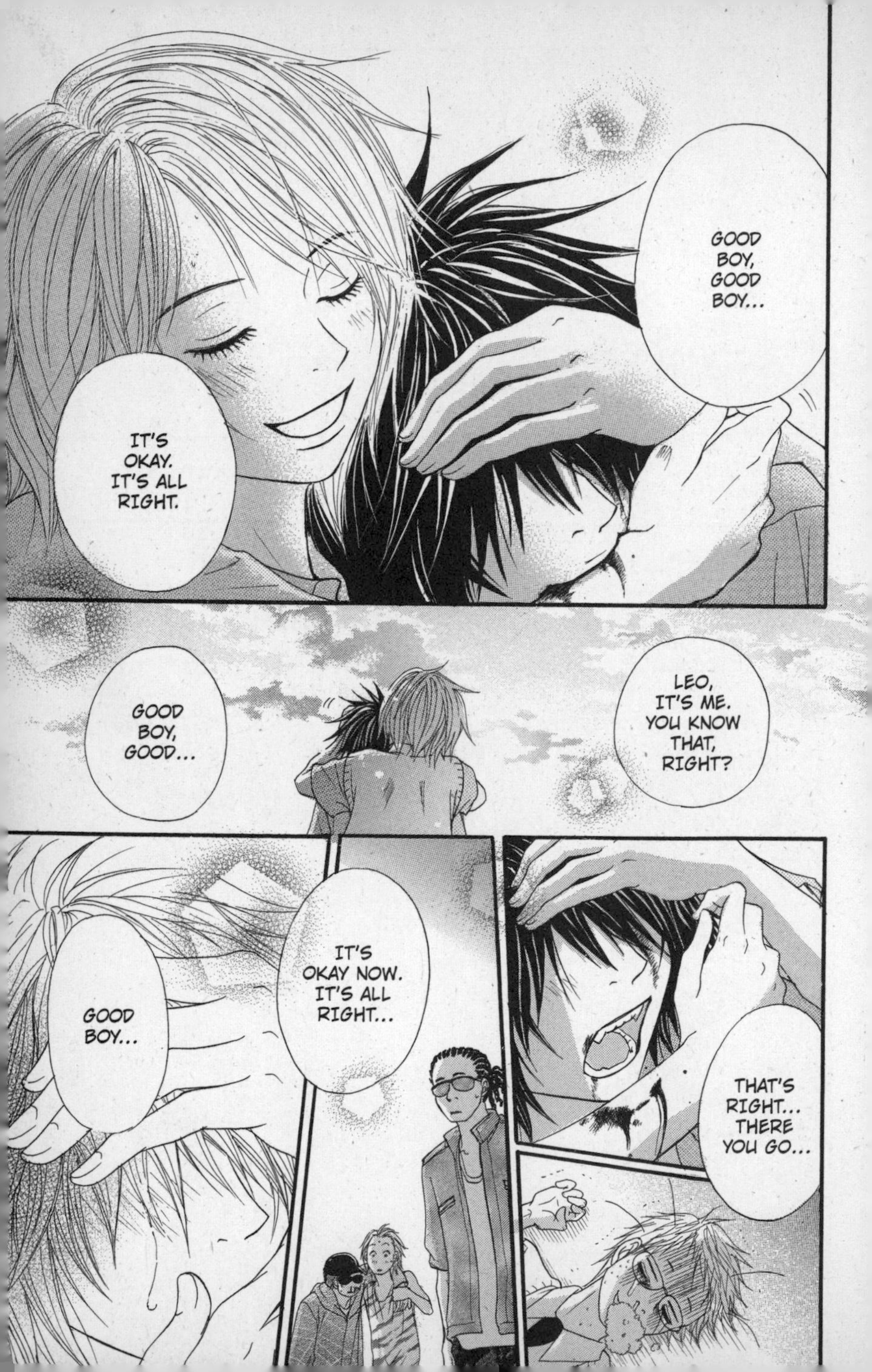
GOOD BOY, GOOD BOY...
IT'S OKAY. IT'S ALL RIGHT.
LEO, IT'S ME. YOU KNOW THAT, RIGHT?
GOOD BOY, GOOD...
THAT'S RIGHT... THERE YOU GO...
IT'S OKAY NOW. IT'S ALL RIGHT...
GOOD BOY...

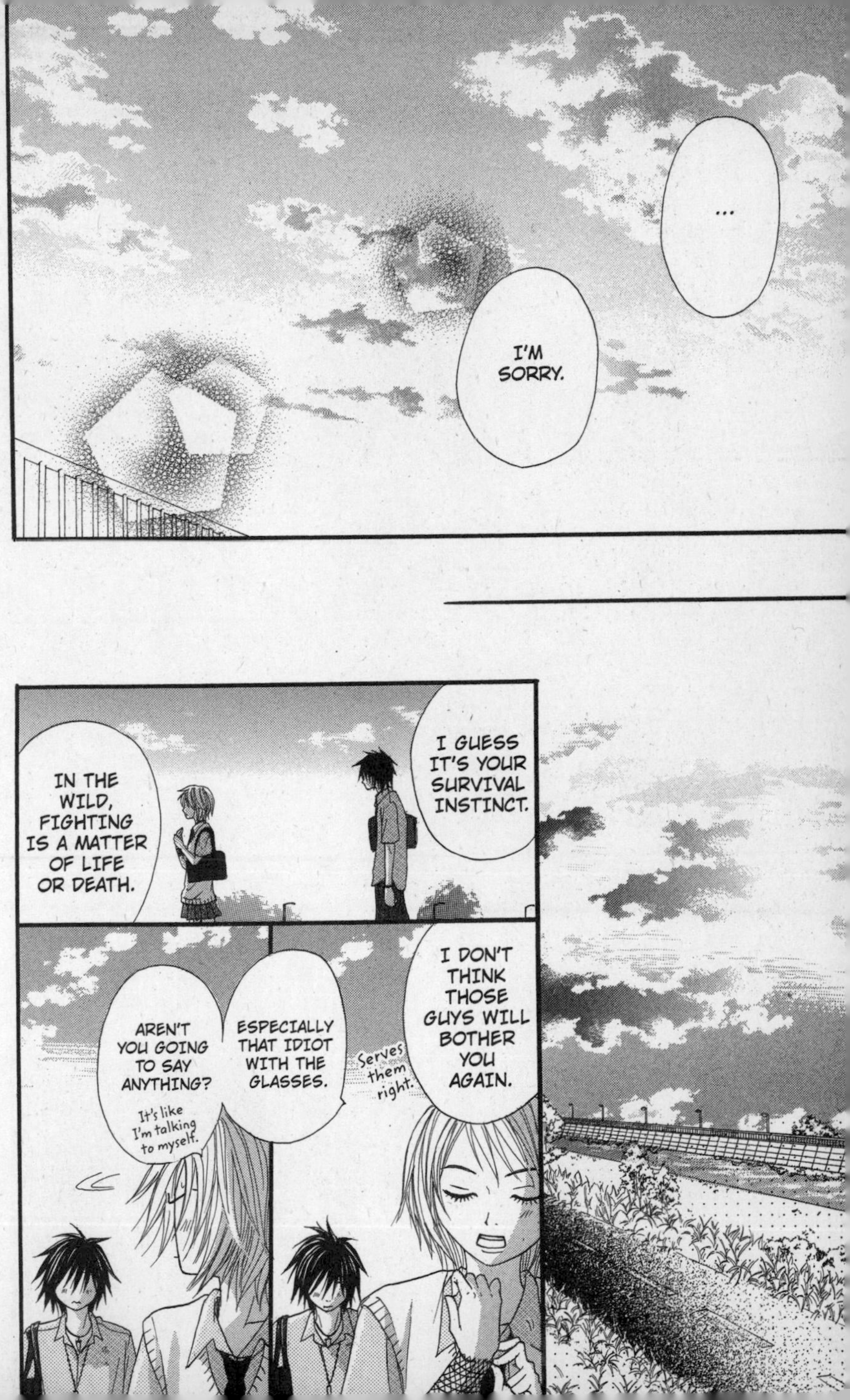
...
I'M SORRY.
I GUESS IT'S YOUR SURVIVAL INSTINCT.
IN THE WILD, FIGHTING IS A MATTER OF LIFE OR DEATH.
I DON'T THINK THOSE GUYS WILL BOTHER YOU AGAIN.
Serves them right.
ESPECIALLY THAT IDIOT WITH THE GLASSES.
AREN'T YOU GOING TO SAY ANYTHING?
It's like I'm talking to myself.

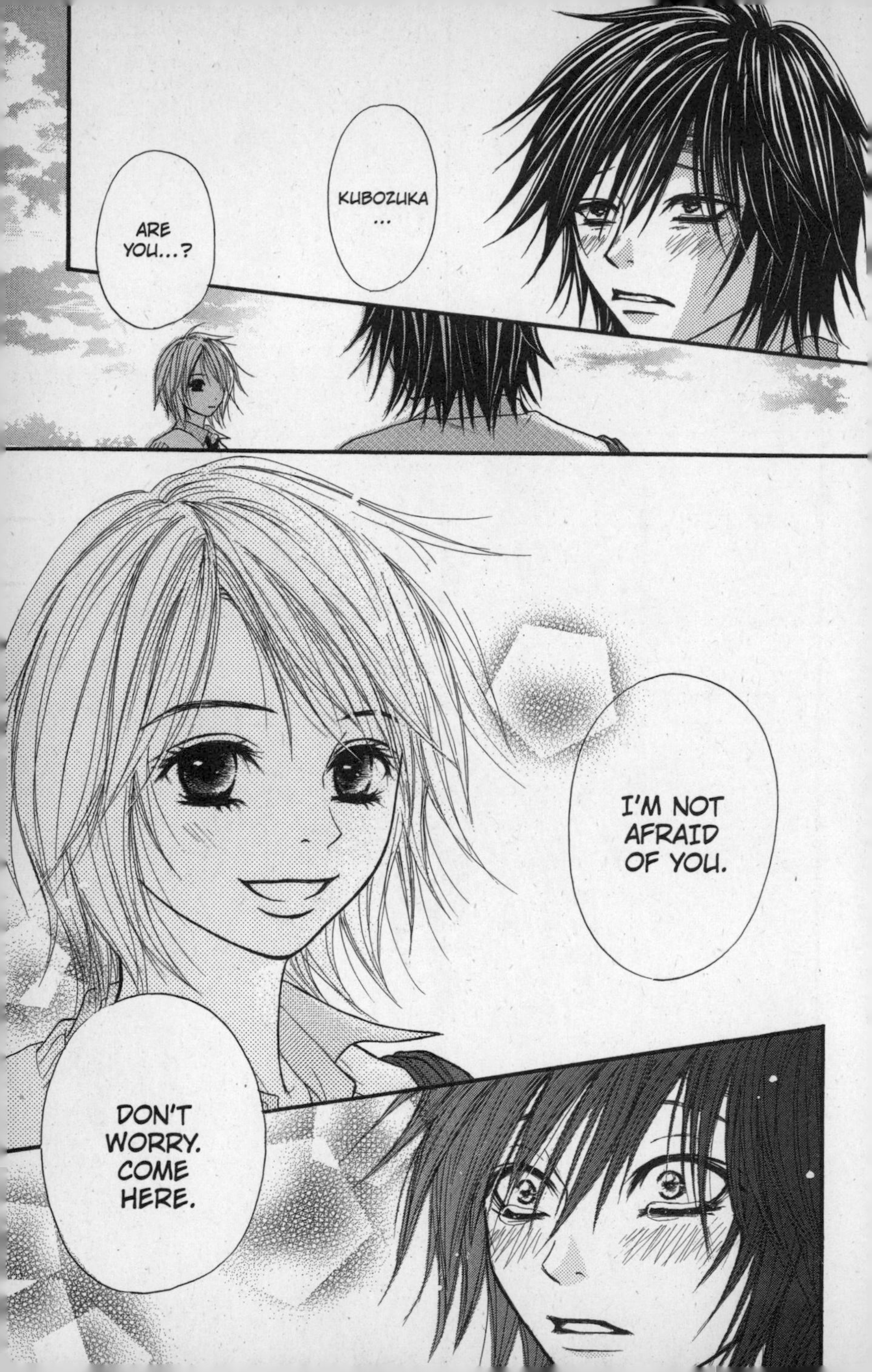
KUBOZUKA ...
ARE YOU...?
I'M NOT AFRAID OF YOU.
DON'T WORRY. COME HERE.

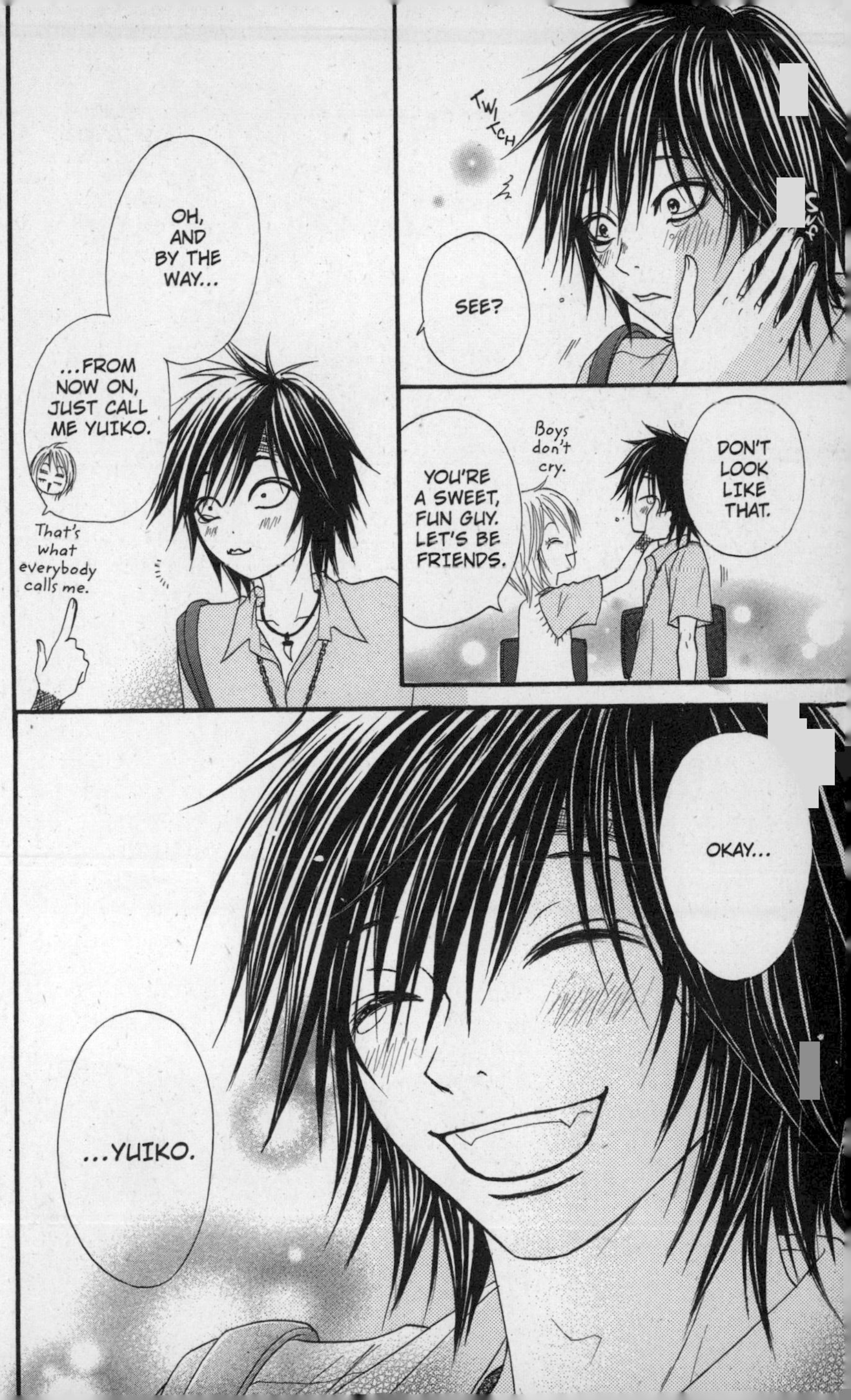
TWITCH
SEE?
DON'T LOOK LIKE THAT.
Boys don't cry.
YOU'RE A SWEET, FUN GUY. LET'S BE FRIENDS.
OH, AND BY THE WAY...
...FROM NOW ON, JUST CALL ME YUIKO.
That's what everybody calls me.
OKAY...
...YUIKO.

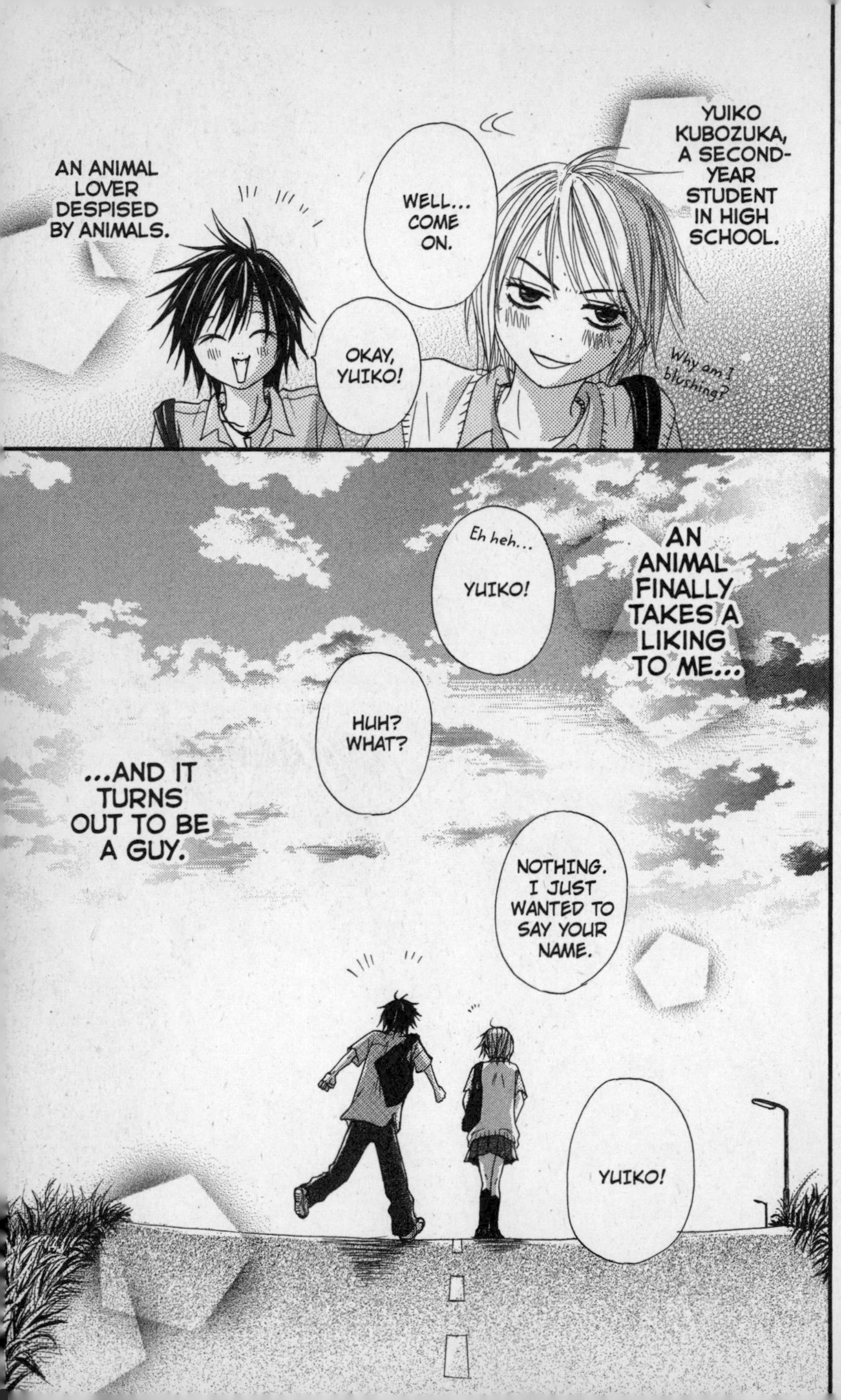
YUIKO KUBOZUKA, A SECOND-YEAR STUDENT IN HIGH SCHOOL.
Why am I blushing?
WELL... COME ON.
OKAY, YUIKO!
AN ANIMAL LOVER DESPISED BY ANIMALS.
AN ANIMAL FINALLY TAKES A LIKING TO ME...
Eh heh... YUIKO!
HUH? WHAT?
NOTHING. I JUST WANTED TO SAY YOUR NAME.
...AND IT TURNS OUT TO BE A GUY.
YUIKO!

BEAST MASTER

Chapter 2

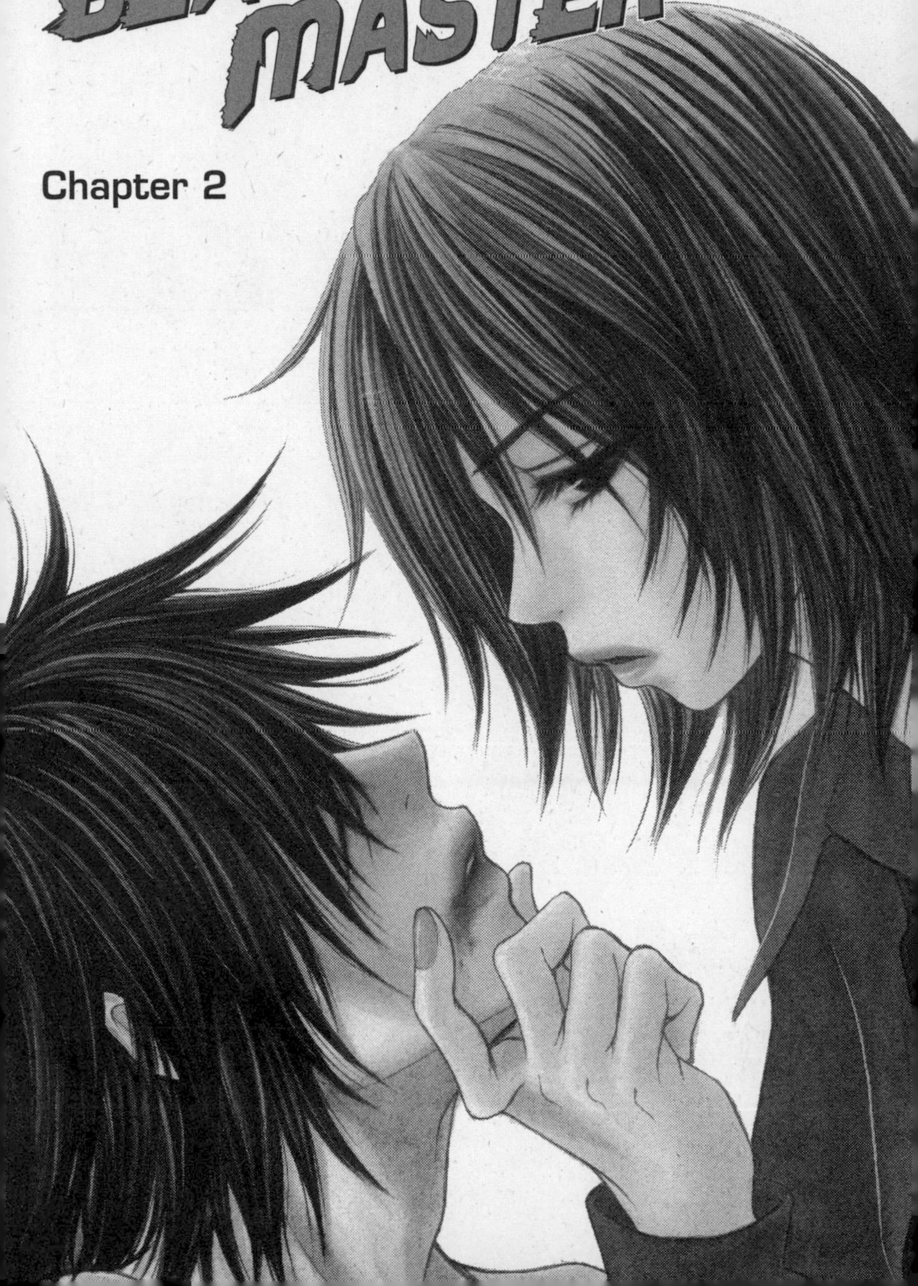

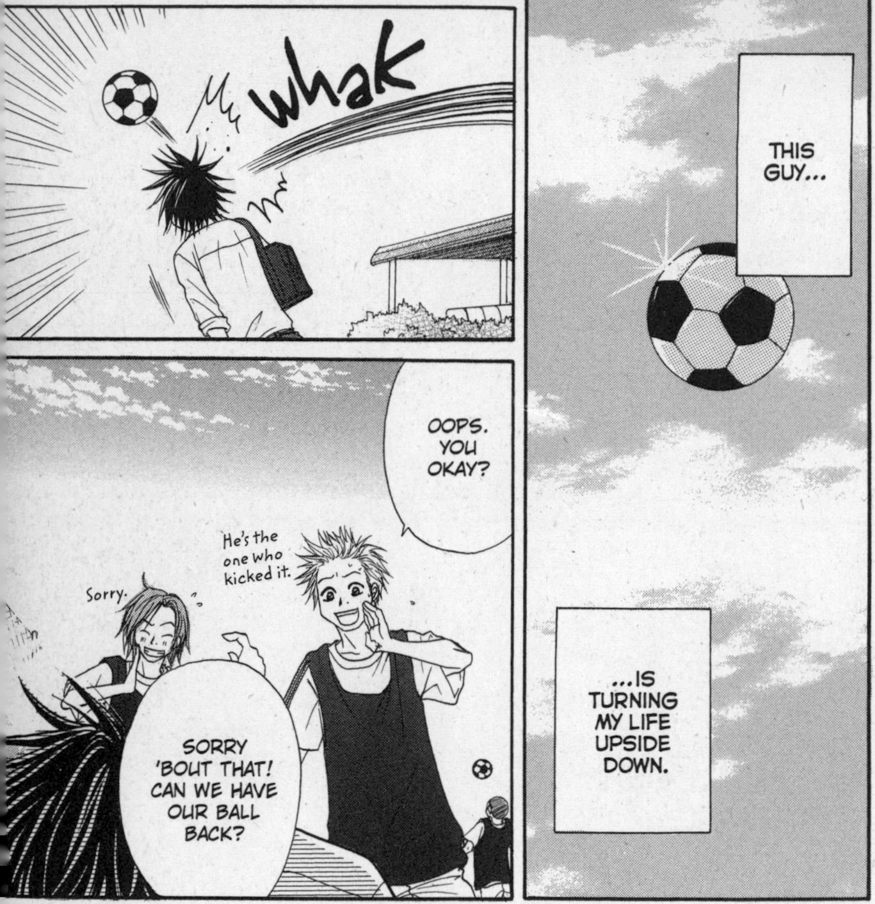
THIS GUY...
...IS TURNING MY LIFE UPSIDE DOWN.
whak
OOPS. YOU OKAY?
He's the one who kicked it.
Sorry.
SORRY 'BOUT THAT! CAN WE HAVE OUR BALL BACK?

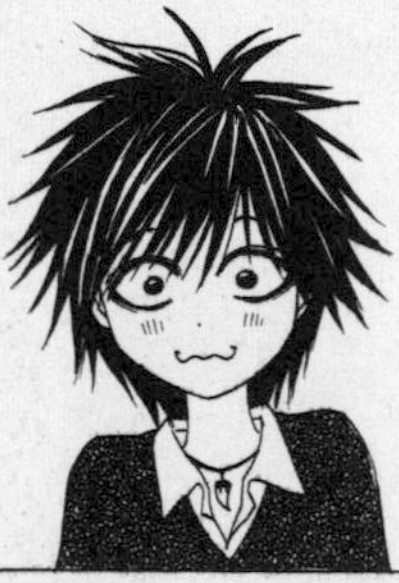

Leo

I'd never drawn a character with a face or personality like Leo's before, so he was quite a challenge. But he allowed me to discover how effective black eyes are in shojo manga. The more I care about a character, the more I agonize over him. Leo's appearance and name are lionlike, but when I first drew him, he reminded me of a black leopard. Lions seem older and more dignified, don't you think?

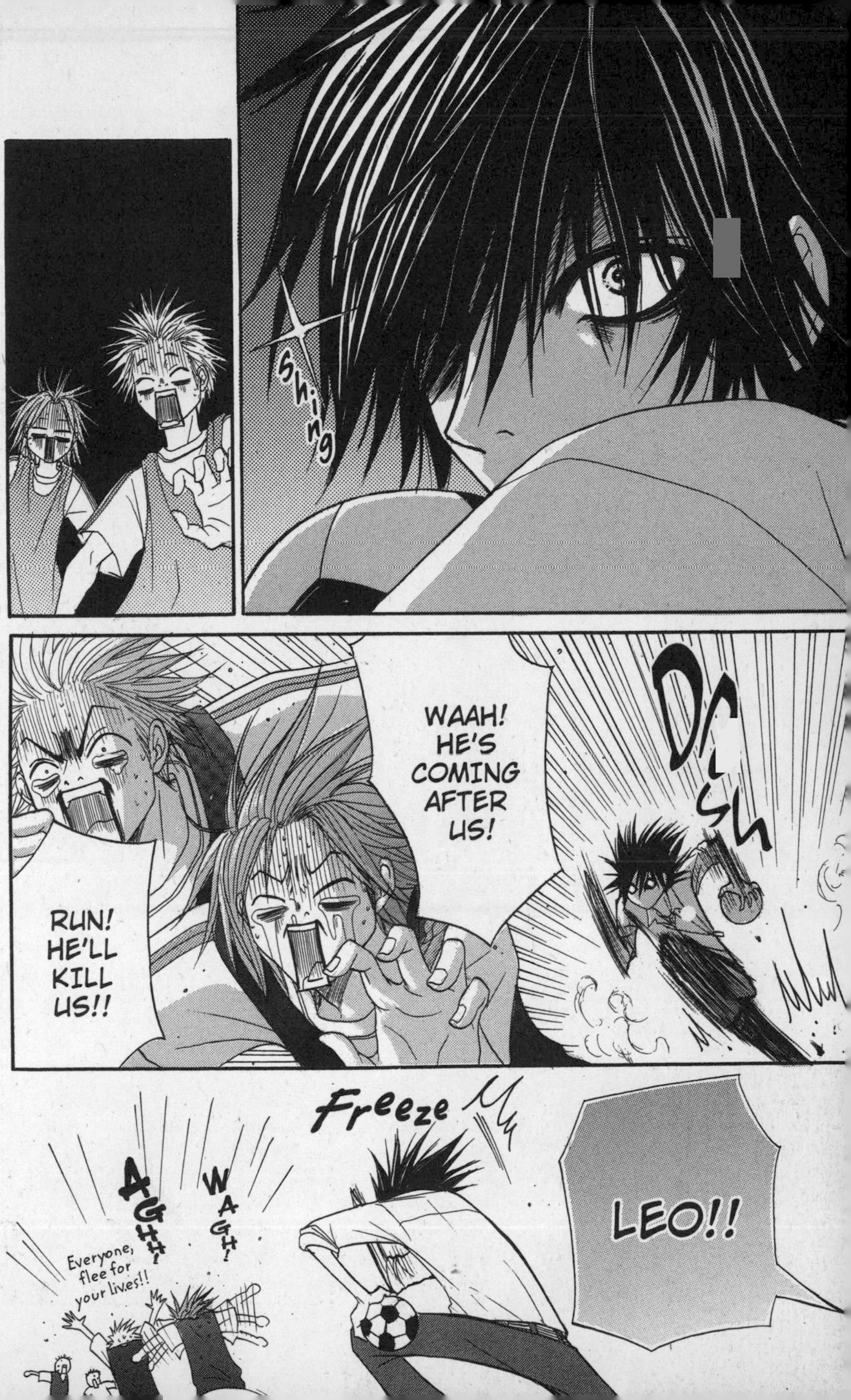
Shing
WAAH! HE'S COMING AFTER US!
RUN! HE'LL KILL US!!
LEO!!
Freeze
WAGH!
AGHH!
Everyone, flee for your lives!!

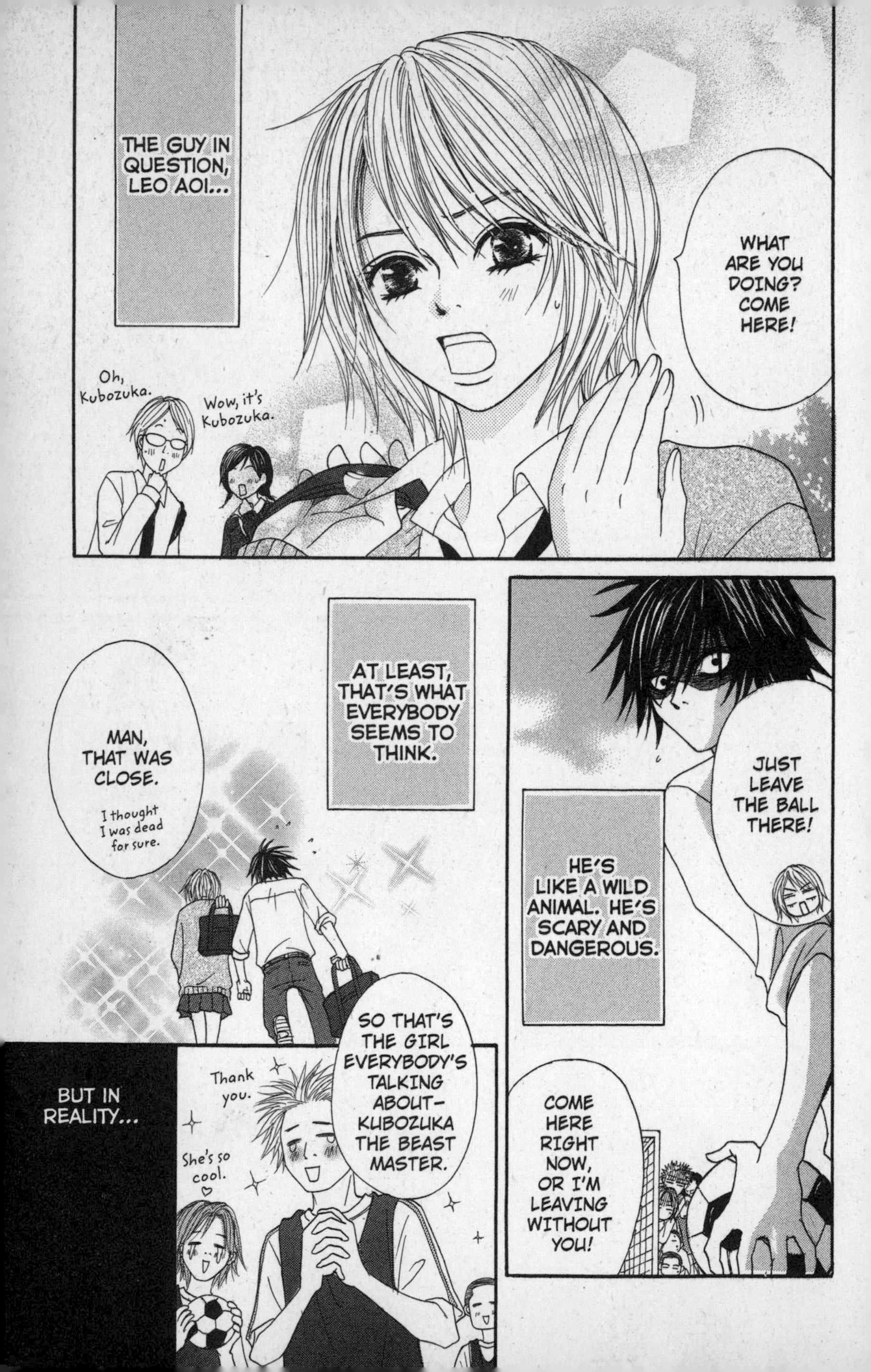
THE GUY IN QUESTION, LEO AOI...
WHAT ARE YOU DOING? COME HERE!
Wow, it's Kubozuka.
Oh, Kubozuka.
JUST LEAVE THE BALL THERE!
HE'S LIKE A WILD ANIMAL. HE'S SCARY AND DANGEROUS.
COME HERE RIGHT NOW, OR I'M LEAVING WITHOUT YOU!
AT LEAST, THAT'S WHAT EVERYBODY SEEMS TO THINK.
MAN, THAT WAS CLOSE.
I thought I was dead for sure.
SO THAT'S THE GIRL EVERYBODY'S TALKING ABOUT-KUBOZUKA THE BEAST MASTER.
Thank you.
She's so cool.
BUT IN REALITY...

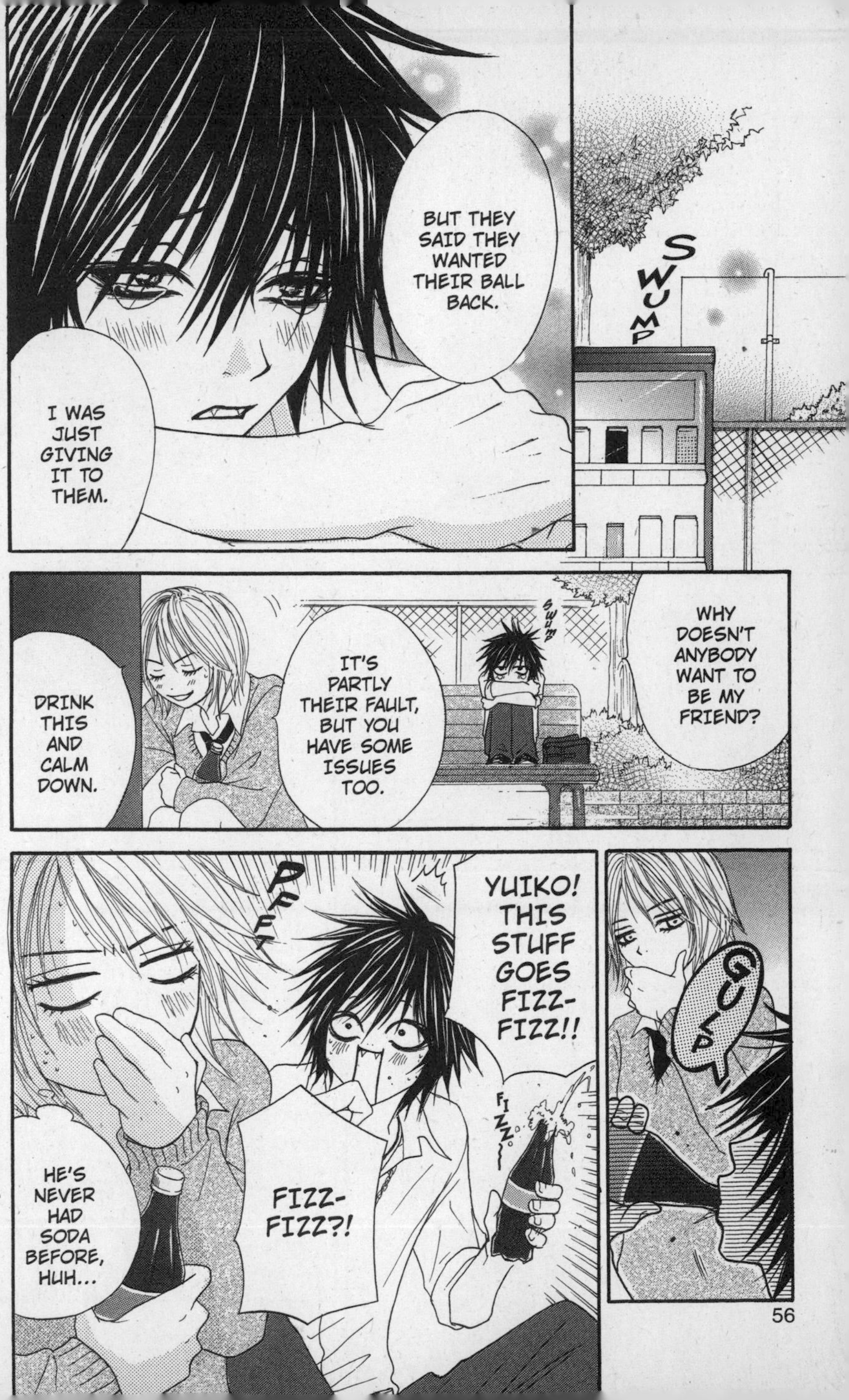
SWUMP
BUT THEY SAID THEY WANTED THEIR BALL BACK.
I WAS JUST GIVING IT TO THEM.
WHY DOESN'T ANYBODY WANT TO BE MY FRIEND?
SWUMP
IT'S PARTLY THEIR FAULT, BUT YOU HAVE SOME ISSUES TOO.
DRINK THIS AND CALM DOWN.
GULP
YUIKO! THIS STUFF GOES FIZZ-FIZZ!!
PFFT
FIZZ
FIZZ-FIZZ?!
HE'S NEVER HAD SODA BEFORE, HUH...

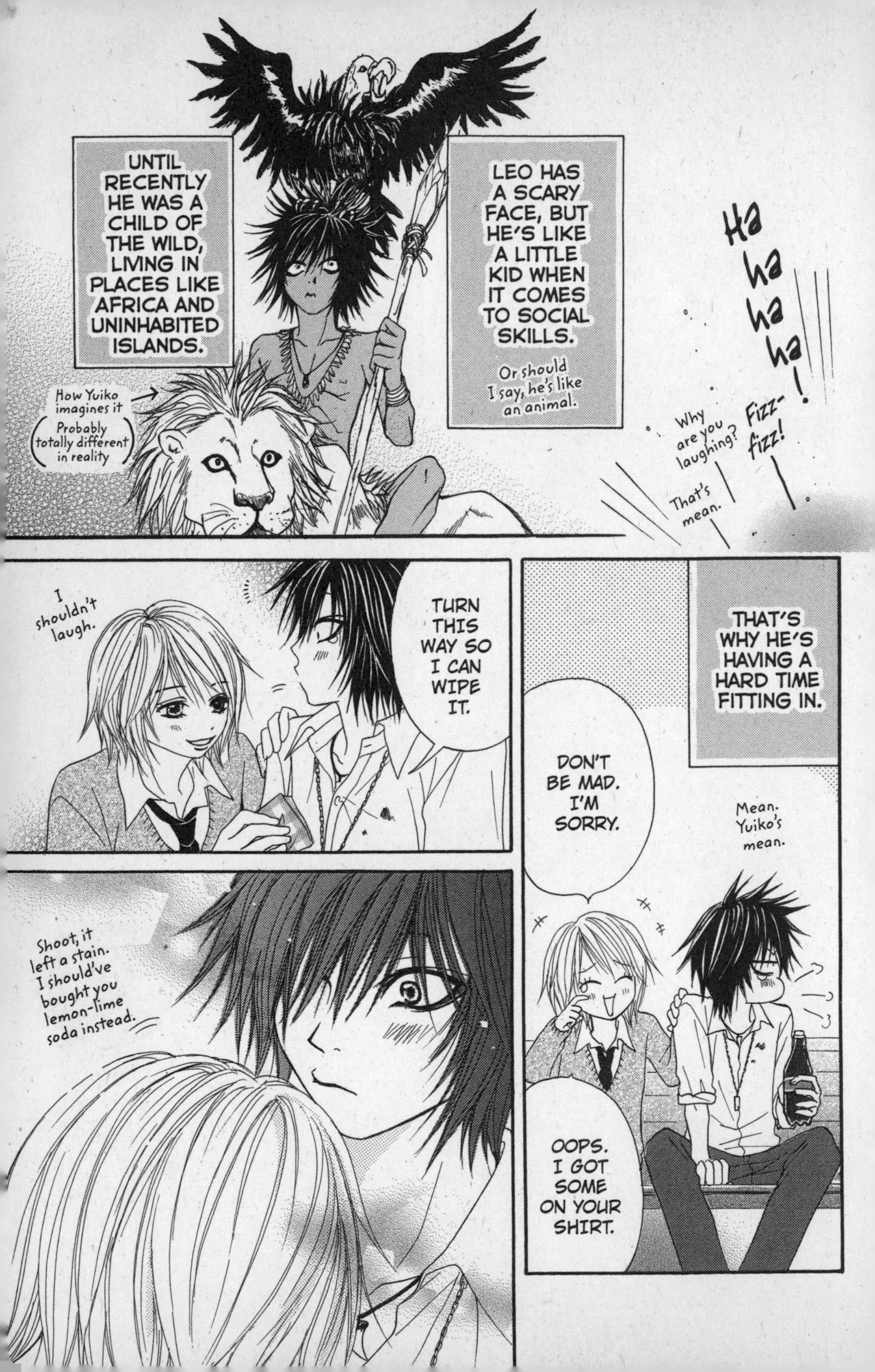
Ha ha ha ha!
Fizz-fizz!
Why are you laughing?
That's mean.
LEO HAS A SCARY FACE, BUT HE'S LIKE A LITTLE KID WHEN IT COMES TO SOCIAL SKILLS.
Or should I say, he's like an animal.
UNTIL RECENTLY HE WAS A CHILD OF THE WILD, LIVING IN PLACES LIKE AFRICA AND UNINHABITED ISLANDS.
How Yuiko imagines it
(Probably totally different in reality)
THAT'S WHY HE'S HAVING A HARD TIME FITTING IN.
DON'T BE MAD. I'M SORRY.
Mean. Yuiko's mean.
OOPS. I GOT SOME ON YOUR SHIRT.
TURN THIS WAY SO I CAN WIPE IT.
I shouldn't laugh.
Shoot, it left a stain. I should've bought you lemon-lime soda instead.

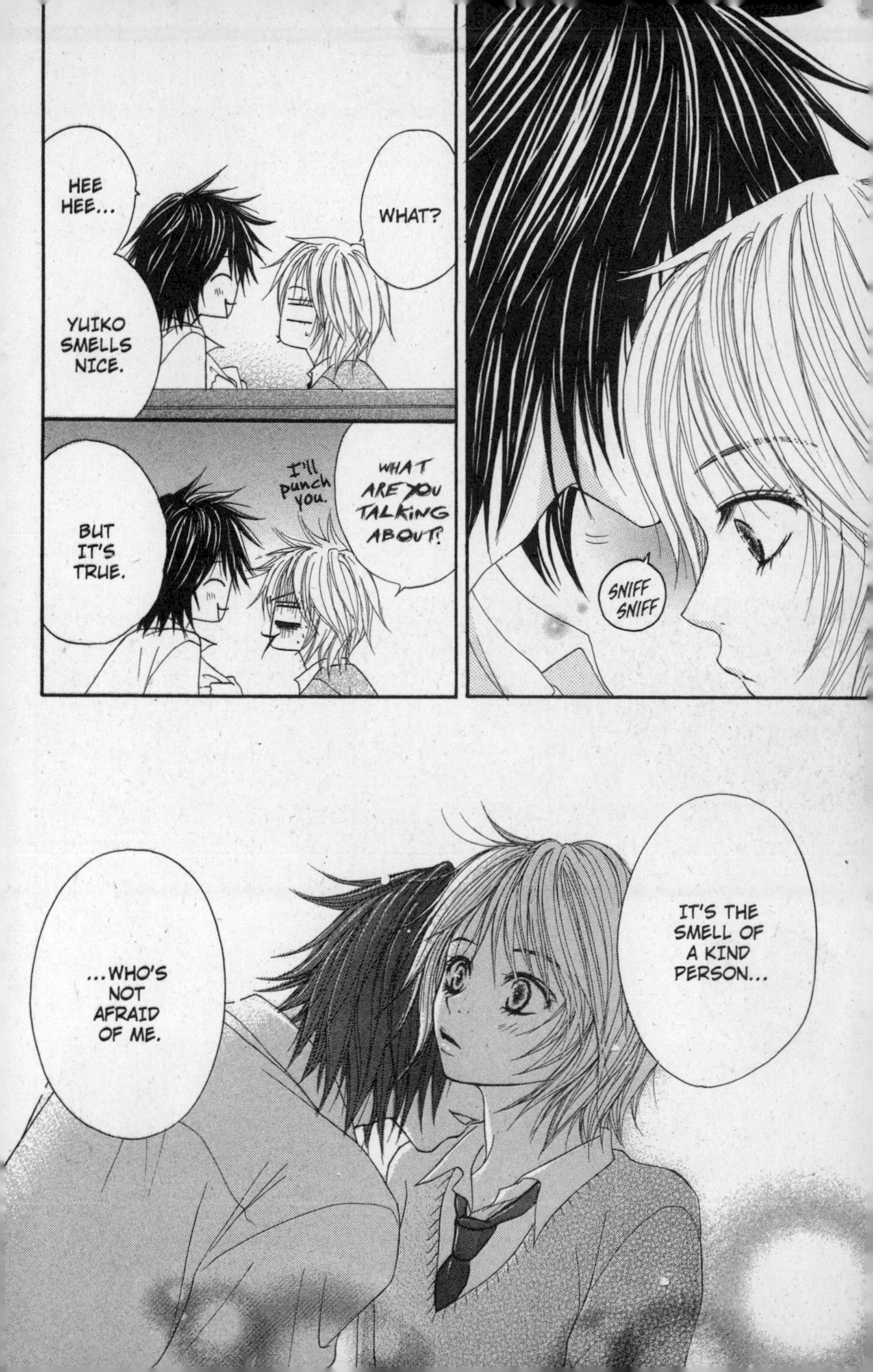
SNIFF SNIFF
HEE HEE...
YUIKO SMELLS NICE.
WHAT?
WHAT ARE YOU TALKING ABOUT?
I'll punch you.
BUT IT'S TRUE.
IT'S THE SMELL OF A KIND PERSON...
...WHO'S NOT AFRAID OF ME.

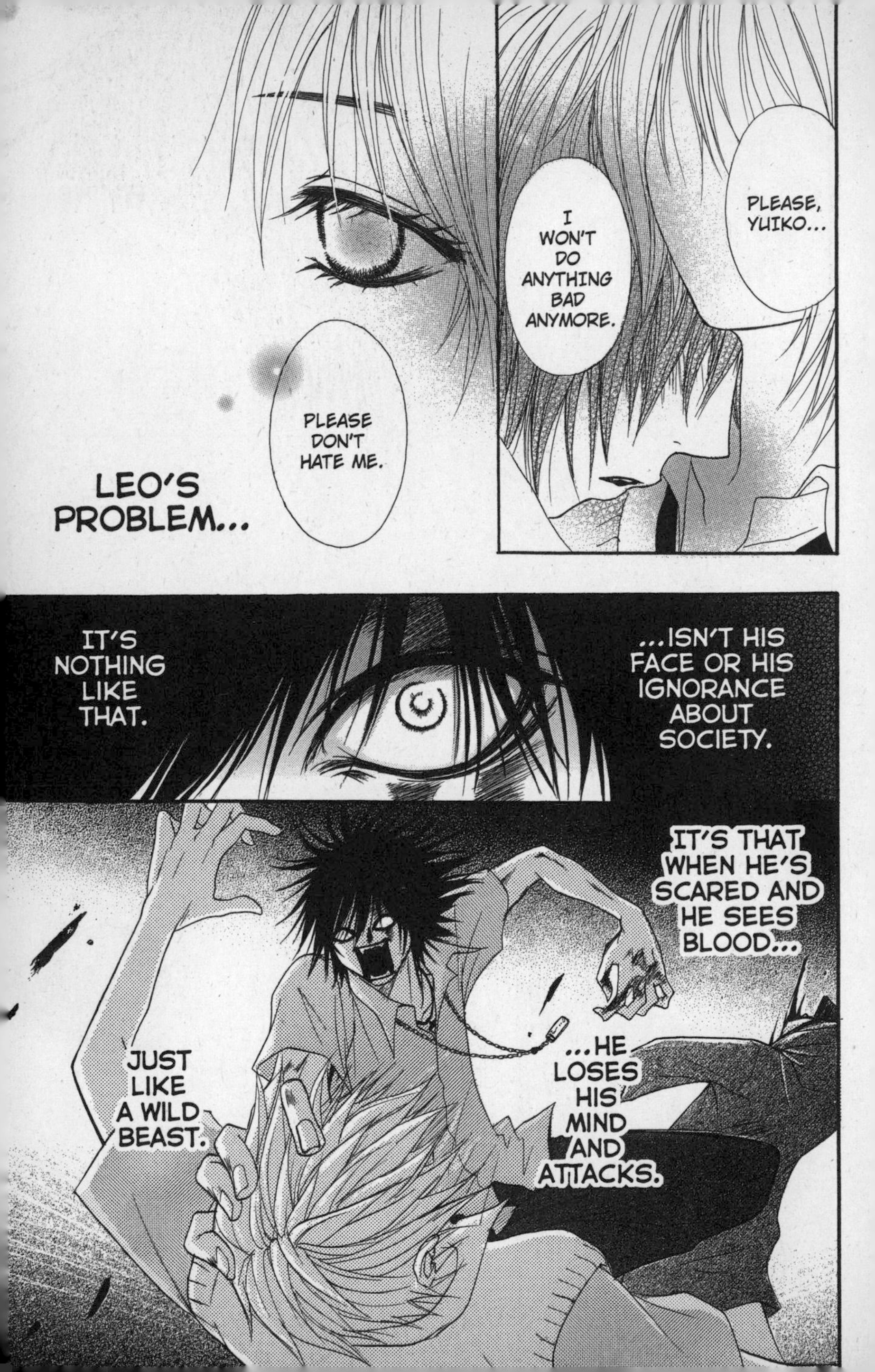

PLEASE, YUIKO...
I WON'T DO ANYTHING BAD ANYMORE.
PLEASE DON'T HATE ME.
LEO'S PROBLEM...
...ISN'T HIS FACE OR HIS IGNORANCE ABOUT SOCIETY.
IT'S NOTHING LIKE THAT.
IT'S THAT WHEN HE'S SCARED AND HE SEES BLOOD...
...HE LOSES HIS MIND AND ATTACKS.
JUST LIKE A WILD BEAST.

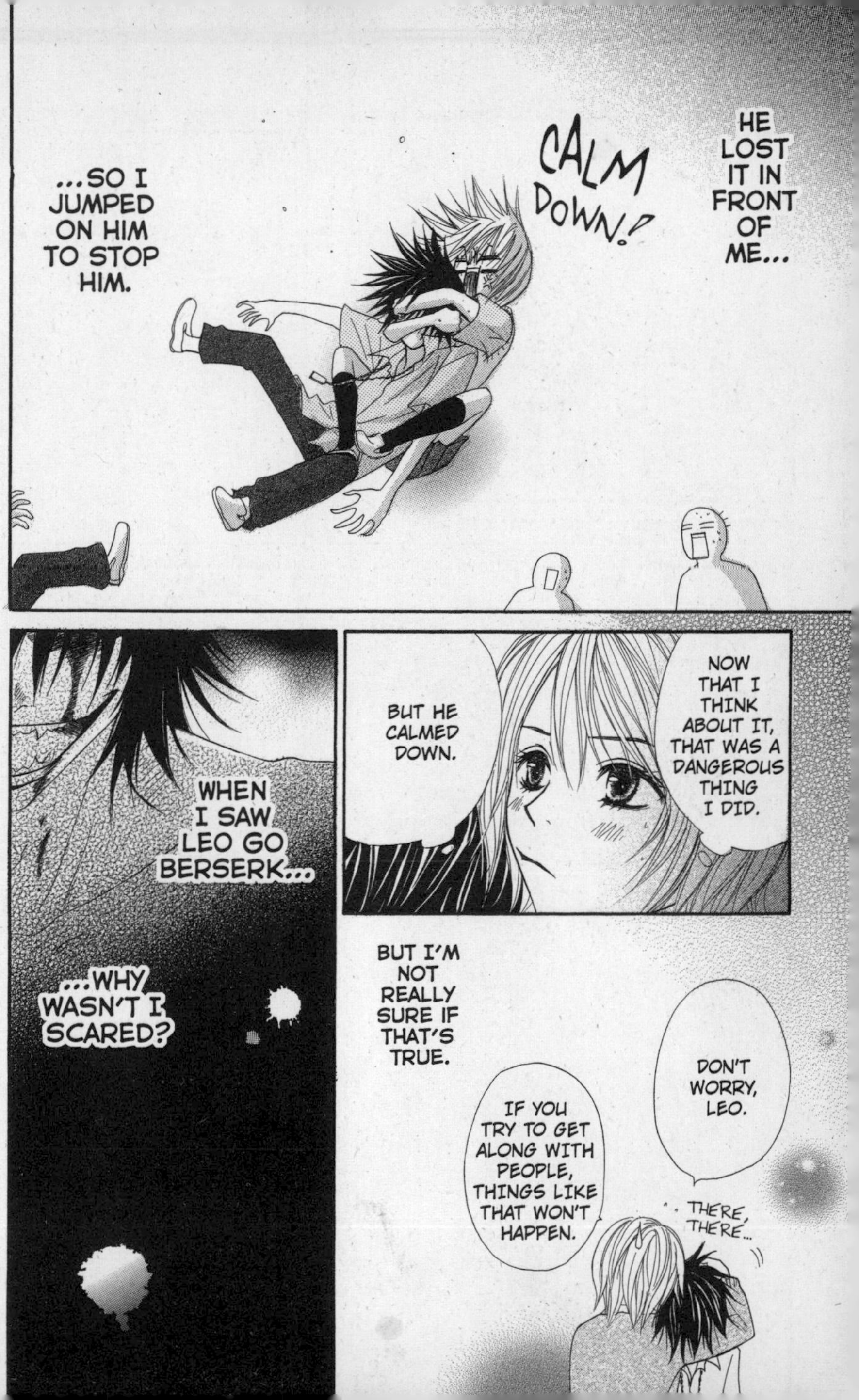
HE LOST IT IN FRONT OF ME...
CALM DOWN!!
...SO I JUMPED ON HIM TO STOP HIM.
NOW THAT I THINK ABOUT IT, THAT WAS A DANGEROUS THING I DID.
BUT HE CALMED DOWN.
DON'T WORRY, LEO.
IF YOU TRY TO GET ALONG WITH PEOPLE, THINGS LIKE THAT WON'T HAPPEN.
THERE, THERE...
BUT I'M NOT REALLY SURE IF THAT'S TRUE.
WHEN I SAW LEO GO BERSERK...
...WHY WASN'T I SCARED?

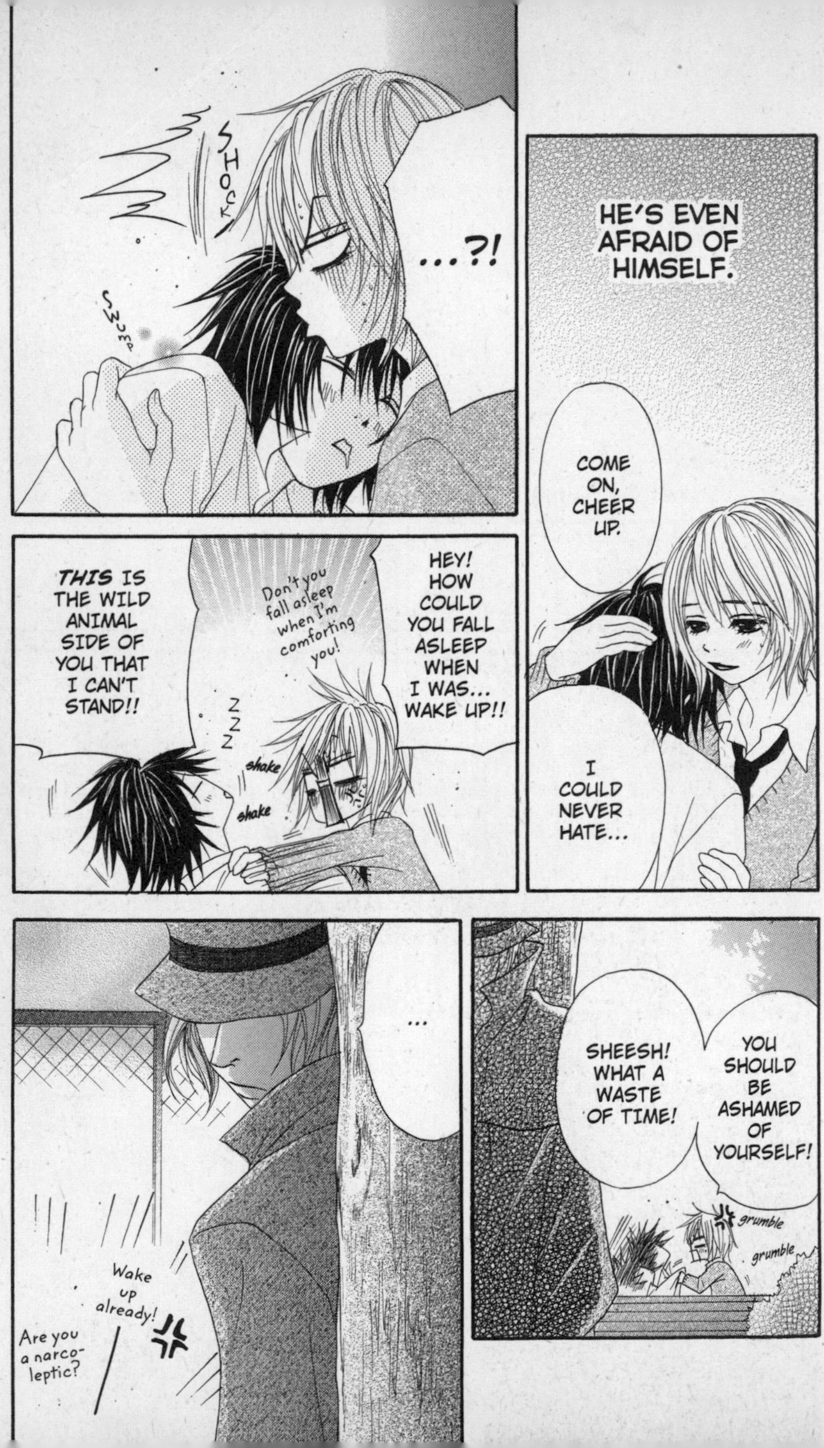
HE'S EVEN AFRAID OF HIMSELF.
COME ON, CHEER UP.
I COULD NEVER HATE...
SHOCK
SWUMP
...?!
HEY! HOW COULD YOU FALL ASLEEP WHEN I WAS... WAKE UP!!
Don't you fall asleep when I'm comforting you!
THIS IS THE WILD ANIMAL SIDE OF YOU THAT I CAN'T STAND!!
ZZZ
shake
shake
YOU SHOULD BE ASHAMED OF YOURSELF!
SHEESH! WHAT A WASTE OF TIME!
grumble
grumble
...
Wake up already!
Are you a narco-leptic?

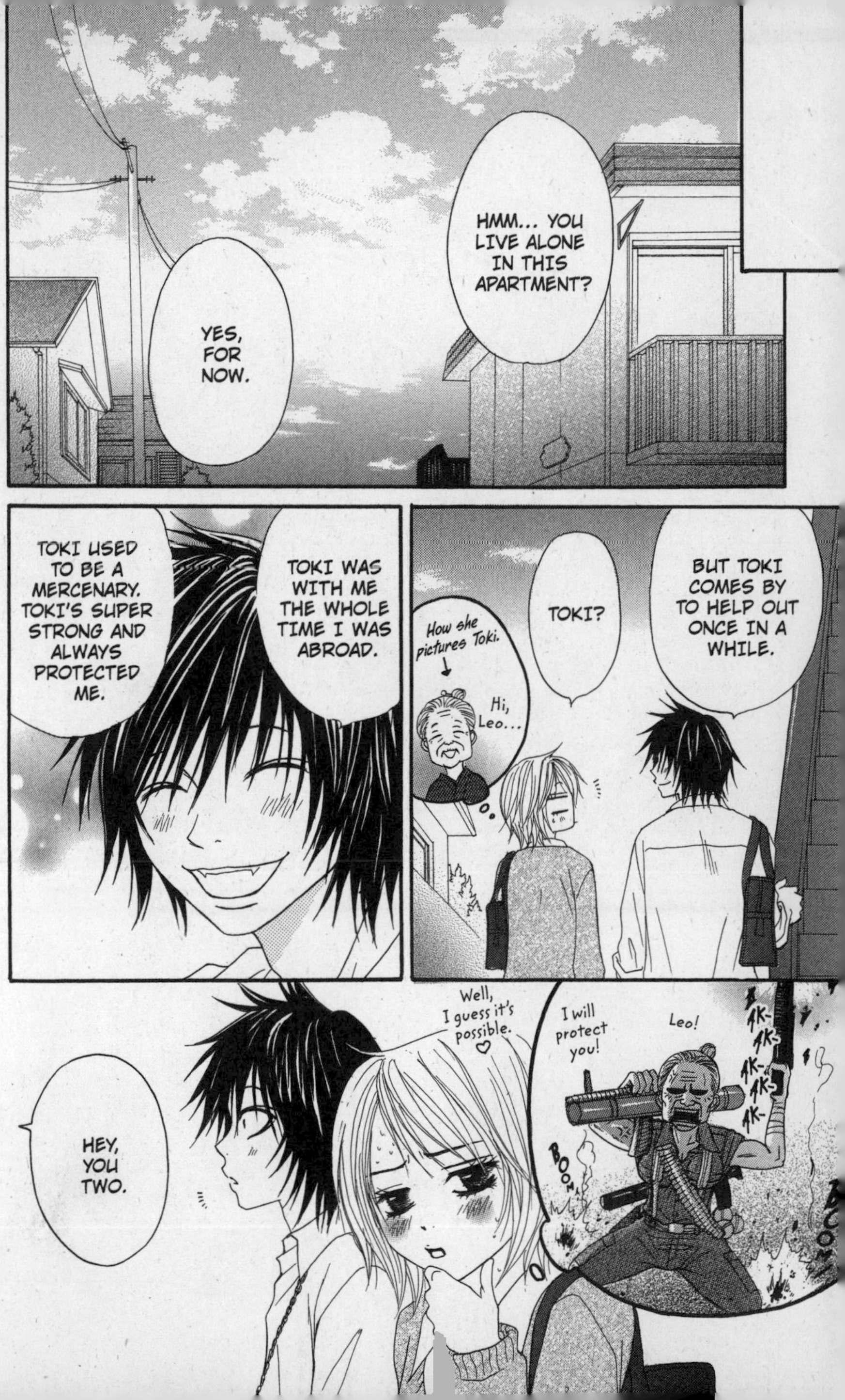
HMM... YOU LIVE ALONE IN THIS APARTMENT?
YES, FOR NOW.
BUT TOKI COMES BY TO HELP OUT ONCE IN A WHILE.
TOKI?
How she pictures Toki.
Hi, Leo...
TOKI WAS WITH ME THE WHOLE TIME I WAS ABROAD.
TOKI USED TO BE A MERCENARY. TOKI'S SUPER STRONG AND ALWAYS PROTECTED ME.
AK-AK-AK-AK-AK-
BOOM
Leo!
I will protect you!
BOOM
Well, I guess it's possible.
HEY, YOU TWO.

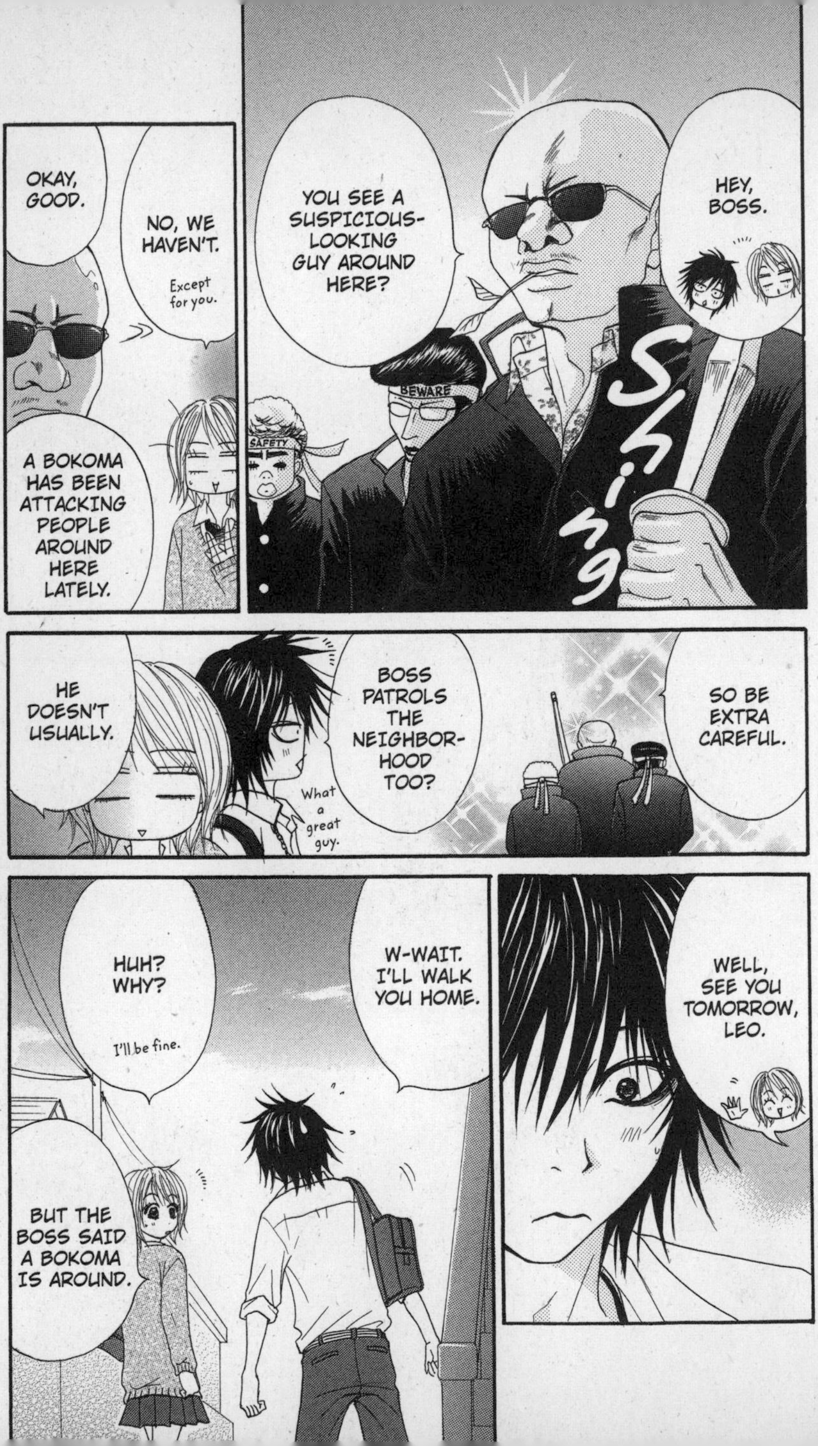
HEY, BOSS.
YOU SEE A SUSPICIOUS-LOOKING GUY AROUND HERE?
BEWARE
SAFETY
Shing
NO, WE HAVEN'T.
Except for you.
OKAY, GOOD.
A BOKOMA HAS BEEN ATTACKING PEOPLE AROUND HERE LATELY.
SO BE EXTRA CAREFUL.
BOSS PATROLS THE NEIGHBORHOOD TOO?
What a great guy.
HE DOESN'T USUALLY.
WELL, SEE YOU TOMORROW, LEO.
W-WAIT. I'LL WALK YOU HOME.
HUH? WHY?
I'll be fine.
BUT THE BOSS SAID A BOKOMA IS AROUND.

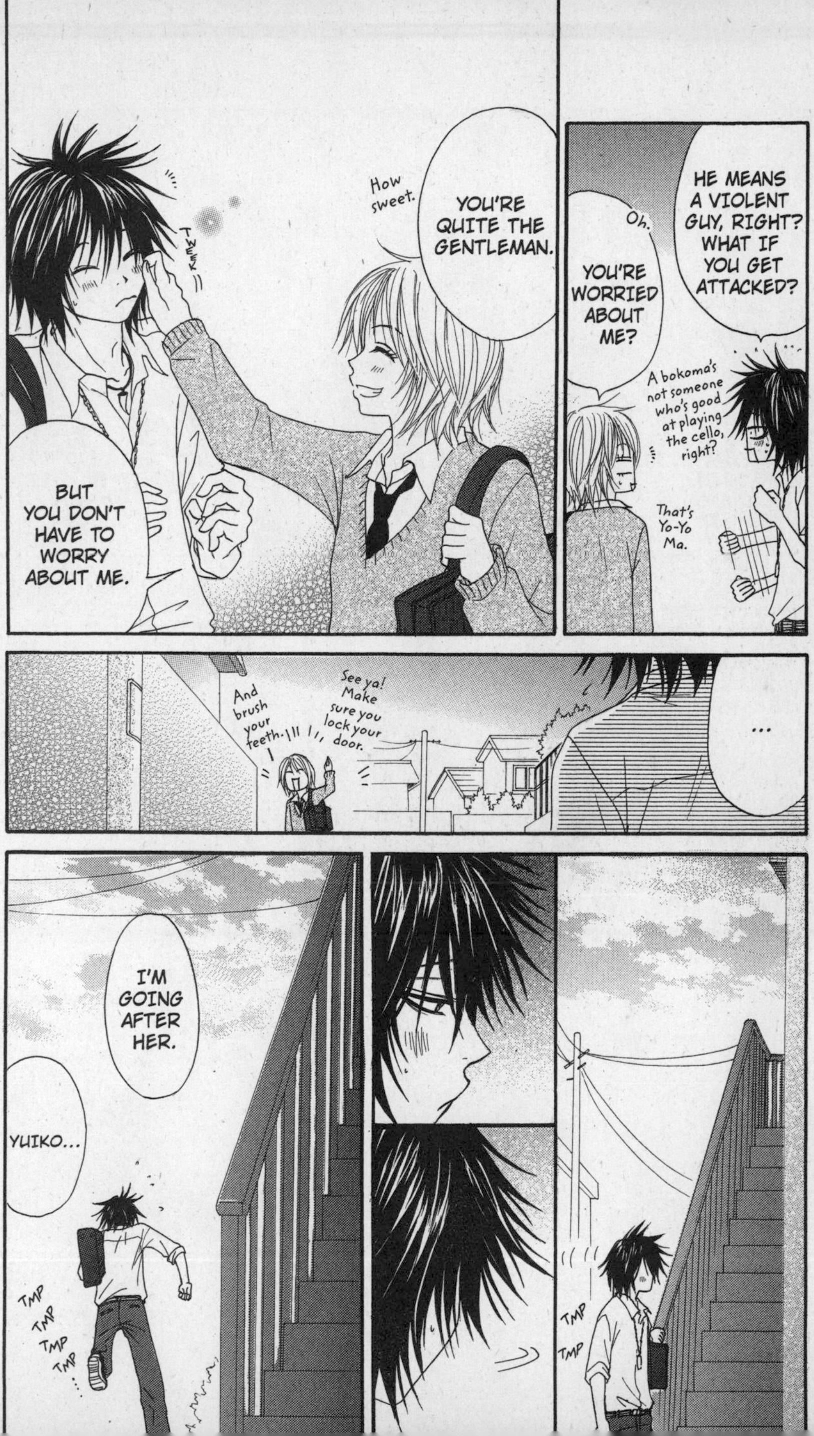
HE MEANS A VIOLENT GUY, RIGHT? WHAT IF YOU GET ATTACKED?
Oh.
YOU'RE WORRIED ABOUT ME?
A bokoma's not someone who's good at playing the cello, right?
That's Yo-Yo Ma.
YOU'RE QUITE THE GENTLEMAN.
How sweet.
TWEEK
BUT YOU DON'T HAVE TO WORRY ABOUT ME.
...
See ya! Make sure you lock your door.
And brush your teeth.
TMP
TMP
I'M GOING AFTER HER.
YUIKO...
TMP
TMP
TMP
TMP...

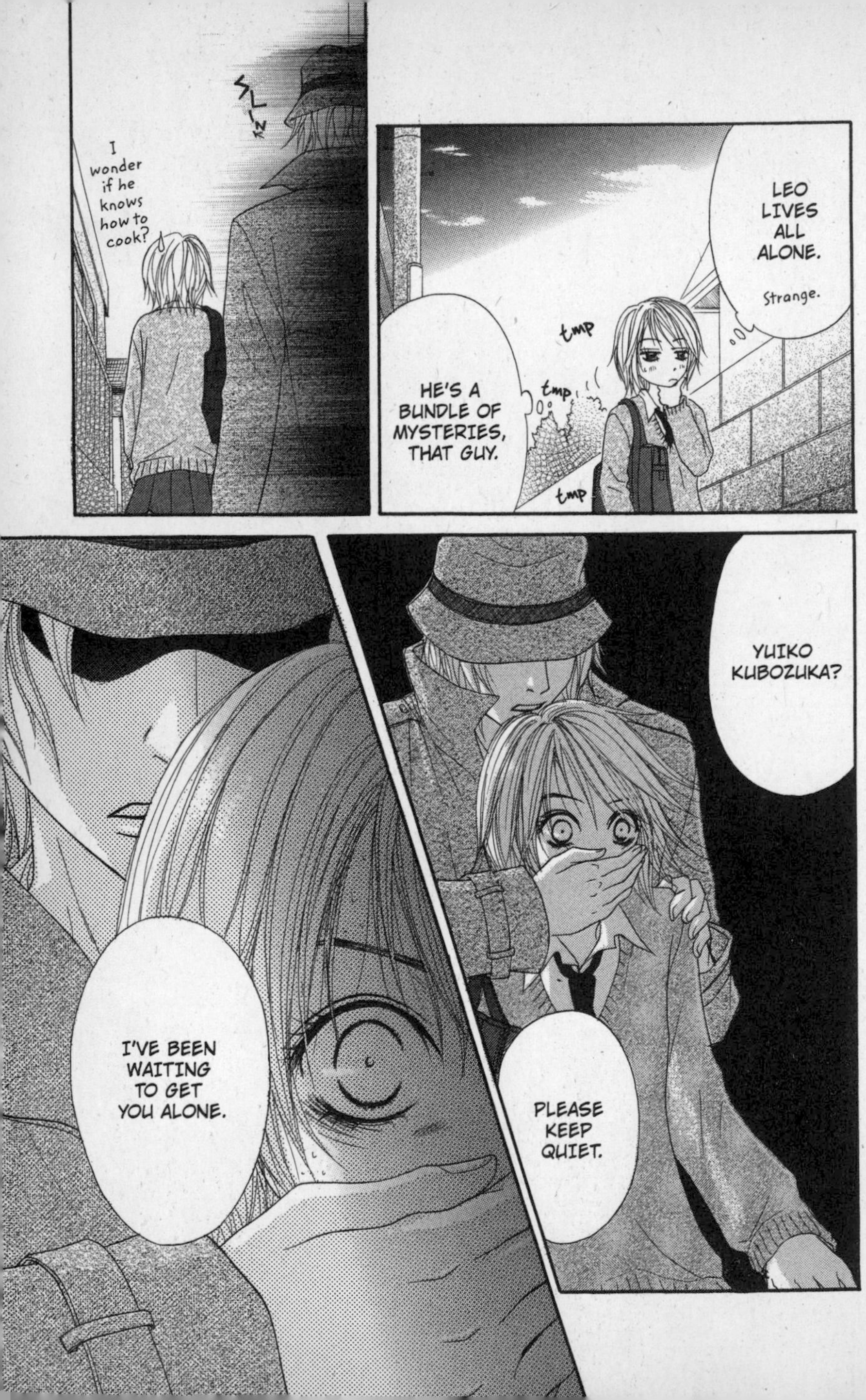
LEO LIVES ALL ALONE.
Strange.
HE'S A BUNDLE OF MYSTERIES, THAT GUY.
tmp
tmp
tmp
SLINK
I wonder if he knows how to cook?
YUIKO KUBOZUKA?
PLEASE KEEP QUIET.
I'VE BEEN WAITING TO GET YOU ALONE.

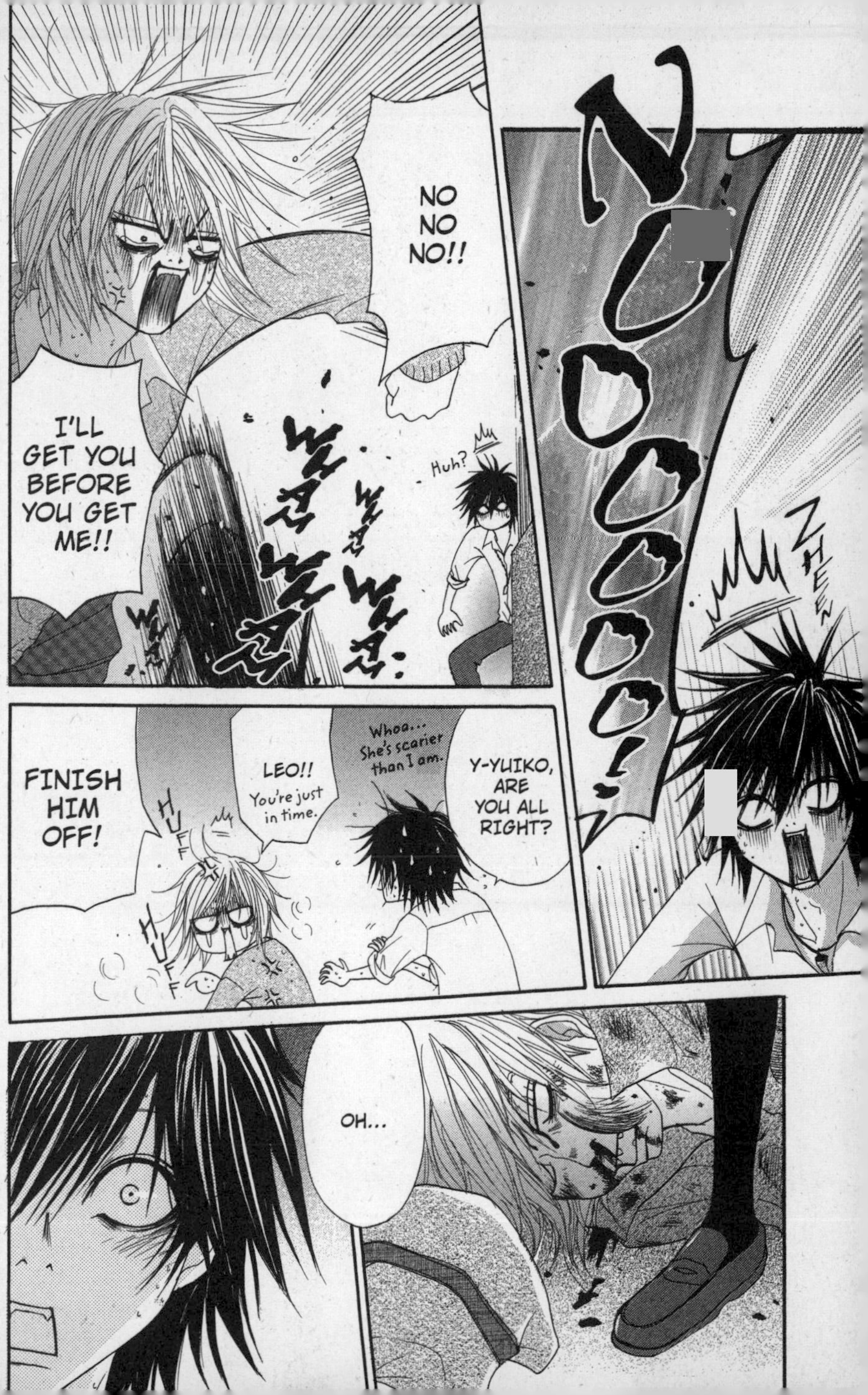
NOOOOOOO!!
ZHEEN
NO NO NO!!
I'LL GET YOU BEFORE YOU GET ME!!
WHAM WHAM WHAM WHAM
Huh?
Y-YUIKO, ARE YOU ALL RIGHT?
Whoa... She's scarier than I am.
LEO!! You're just in time.
FINISH HIM OFF!
HUFF HUFF
OH...

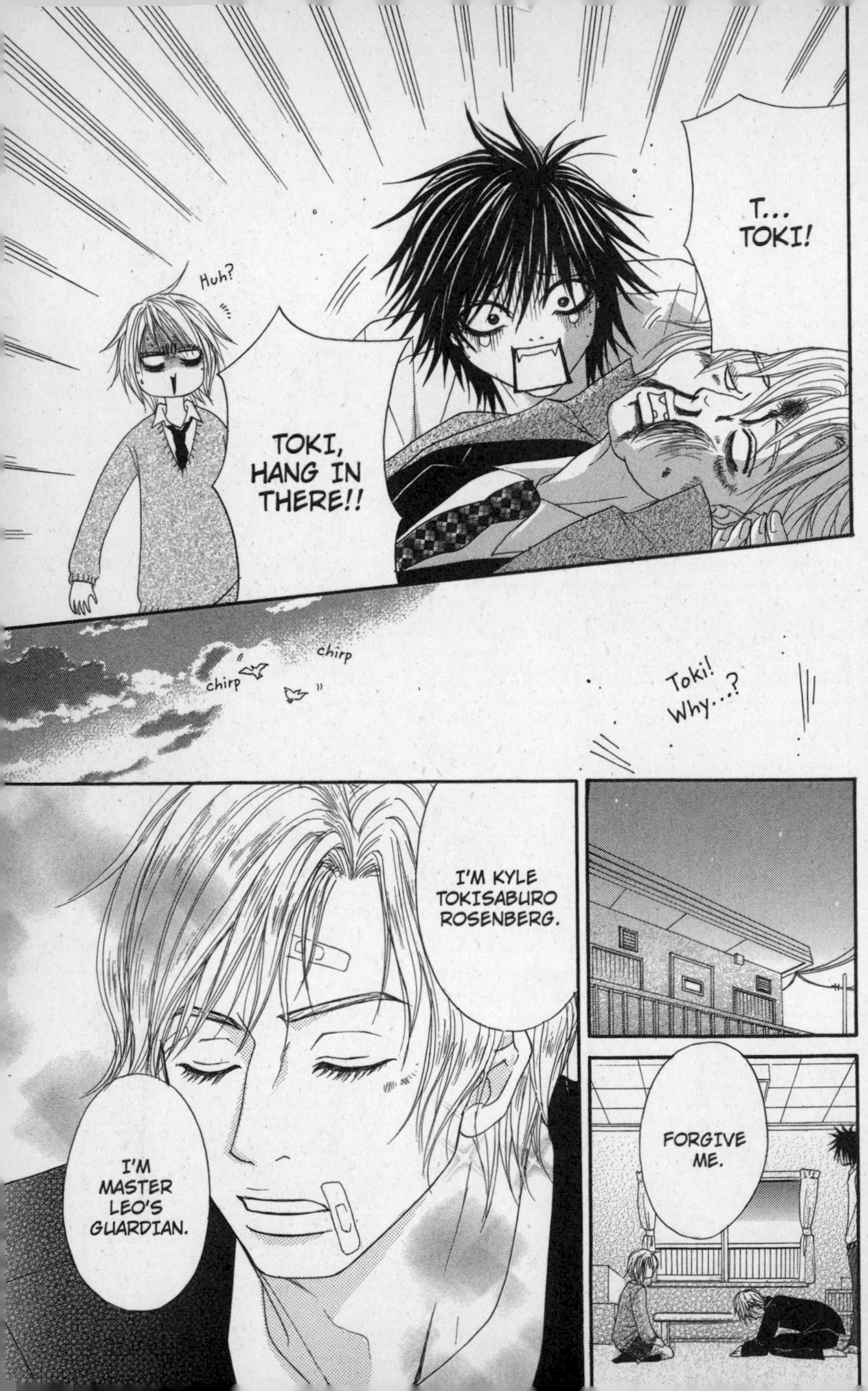
T... TOKI!
TOKI, HANG IN THERE!!
Huh?
Toki! Why...?
chirp
chirp
FORGIVE ME.
I'M KYLE TOKISABURO ROSENBERG.
I'M MASTER LEO'S GUARDIAN.

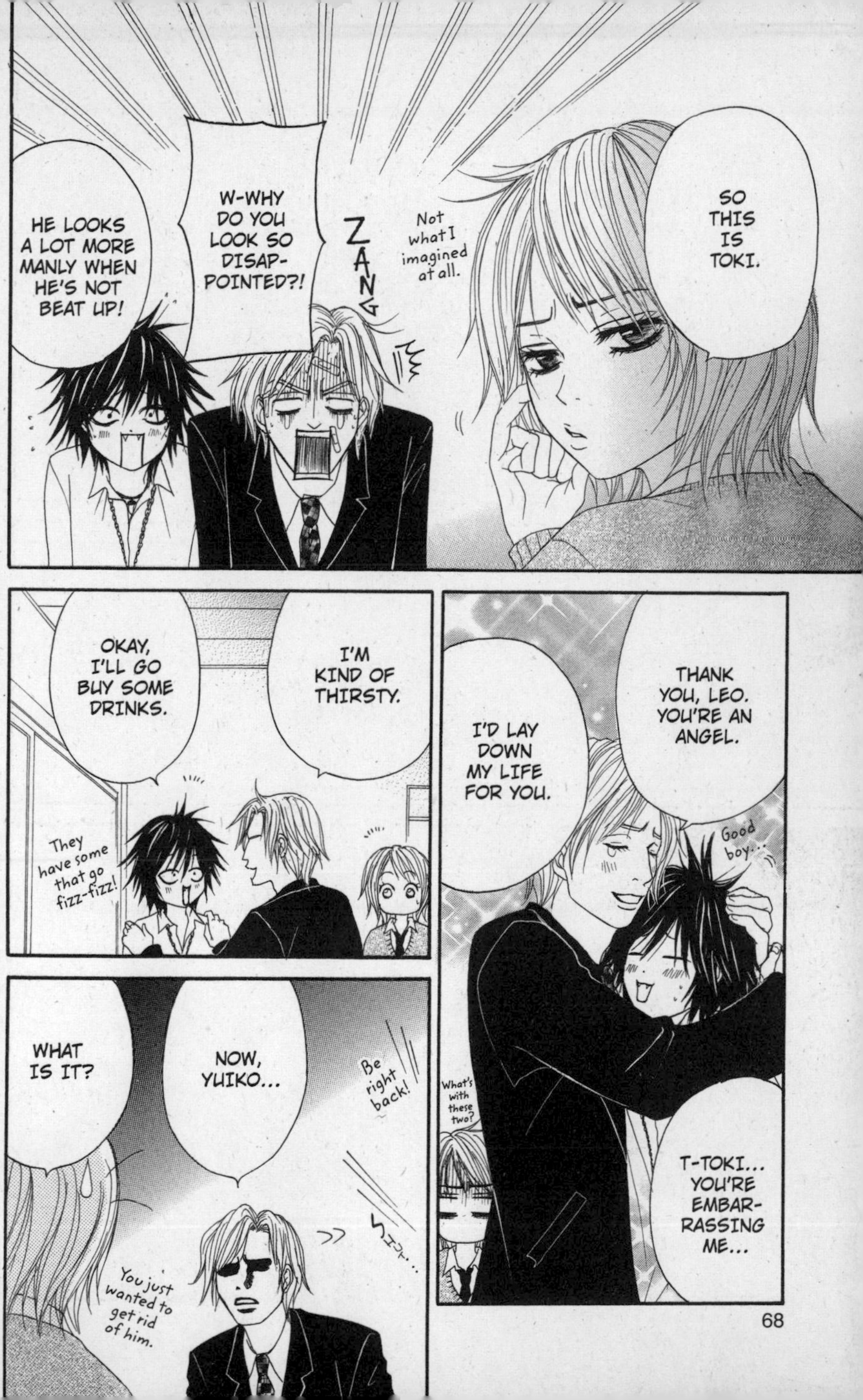
SO THIS IS TOKI.
Not what I imagined at all.
ZANG
W-WHY DO YOU LOOK SO DISAP-POINTED?!
HE LOOKS A LOT MORE MANLY WHEN HE'S NOT BEAT UP!
THANK YOU, LEO. YOU'RE AN ANGEL.
I'D LAY DOWN MY LIFE FOR YOU.
Good boy...
What's with these two?
T-TOKI... YOU'RE EMBAR-RASSING ME...
I'M KIND OF THIRSTY.
OKAY, I'LL GO BUY SOME DRINKS.
They have some that go fizz-fizz!
NOW, YUIKO...
WHAT IS IT?
Be right back!
You just wanted to get rid of him.

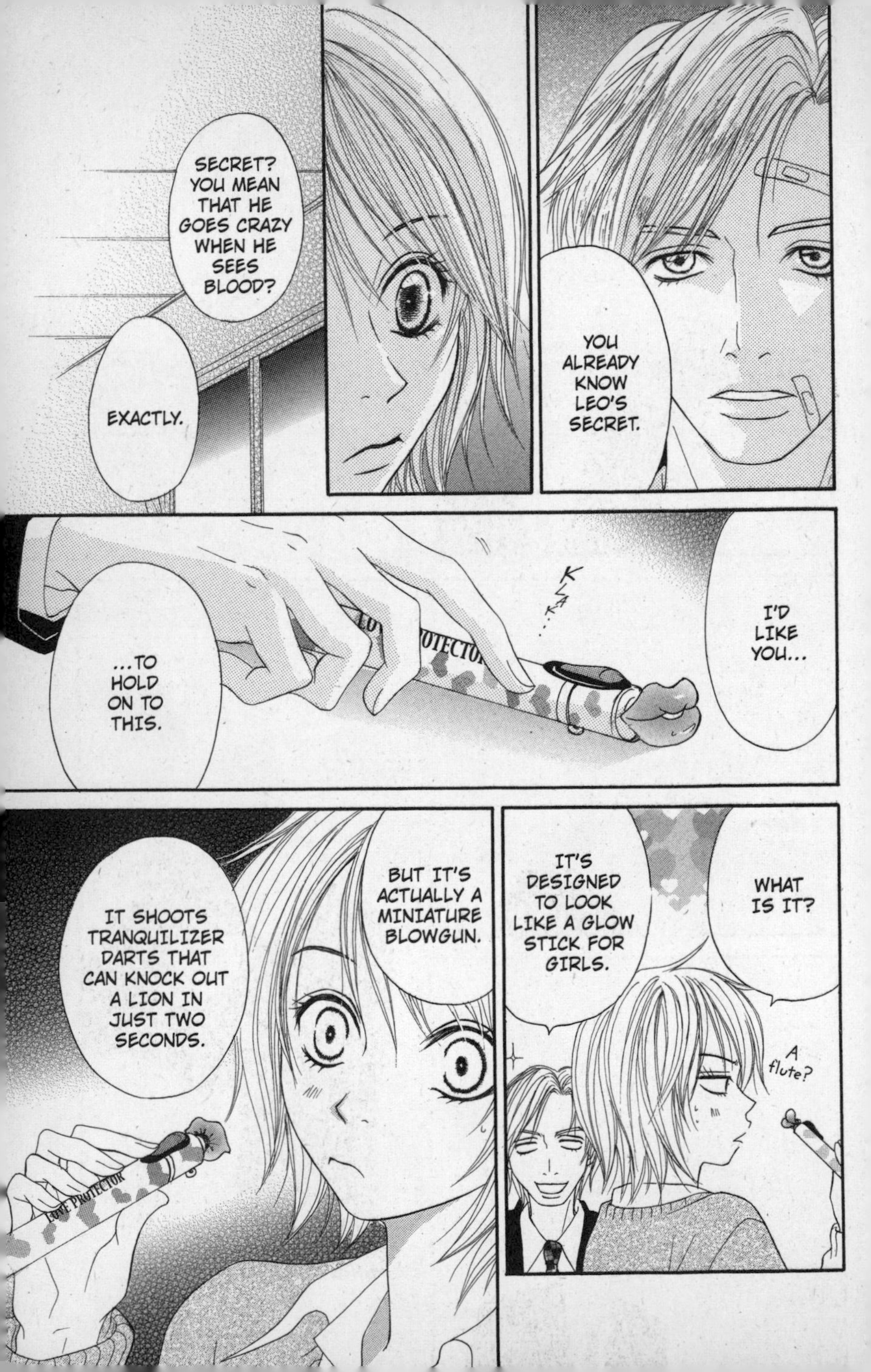
YOU ALREADY KNOW LEO'S SECRET.
SECRET? YOU MEAN THAT HE GOES CRAZY WHEN HE SEES BLOOD?
EXACTLY.
I'D LIKE YOU...
KLAK...
LOVE PROTECTOR
...TO HOLD ON TO THIS.
WHAT IS IT?
A flute?
IT'S DESIGNED TO LOOK LIKE A GLOW STICK FOR GIRLS.
BUT IT'S ACTUALLY A MINIATURE BLOWGUN.
IT SHOOTS TRANQUILIZER DARTS THAT CAN KNOCK OUT A LION IN JUST TWO SECONDS.
LOVE PROTECTOR

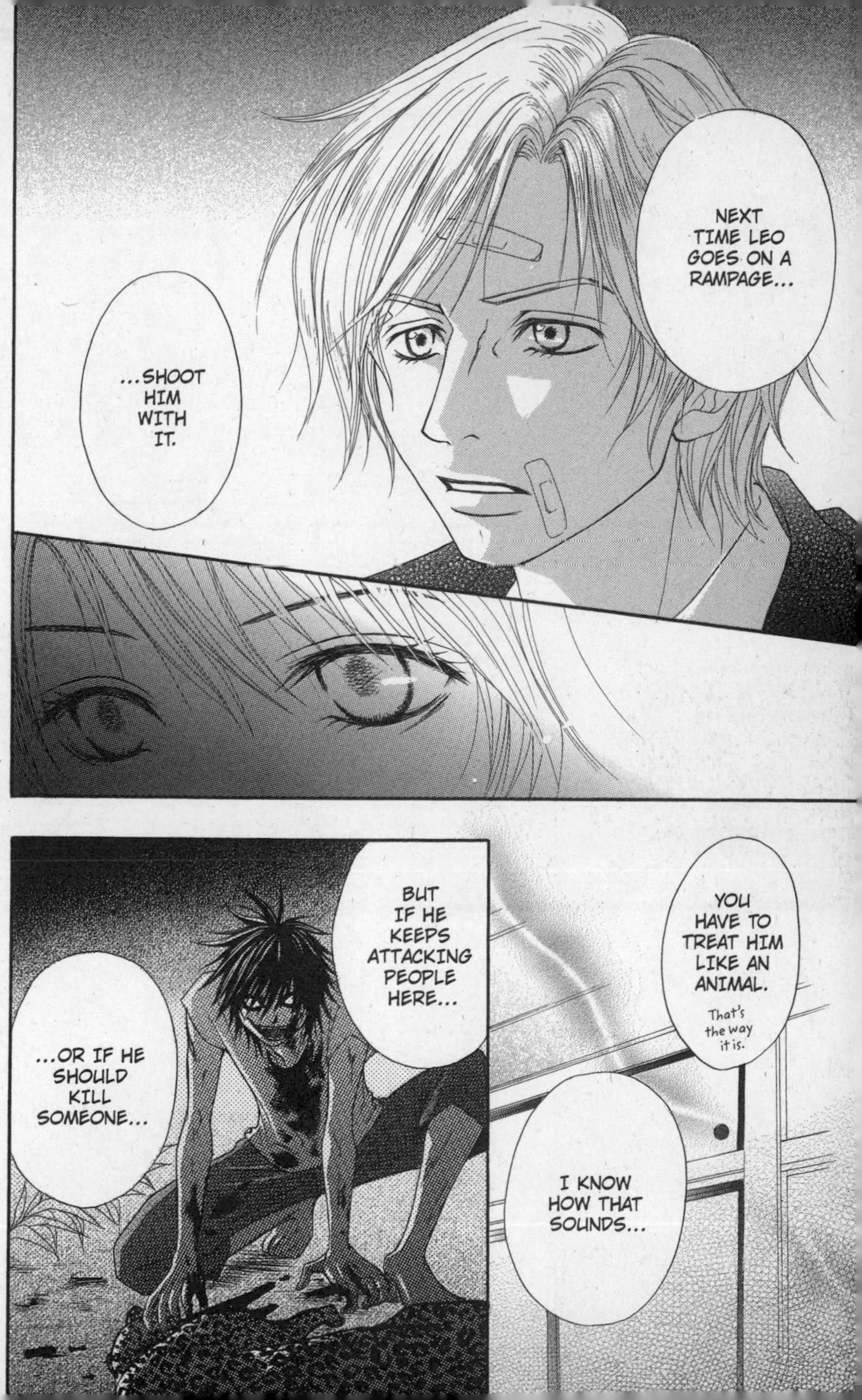
NEXT TIME LEO GOES ON A RAMPAGE...
...SHOOT HIM WITH IT.
YOU HAVE TO TREAT HIM LIKE AN ANIMAL.
That's the way it is.
I KNOW HOW THAT SOUNDS...
BUT IF HE KEEPS ATTACKING PEOPLE HERE...
...OR IF HE SHOULD KILL SOMEONE...

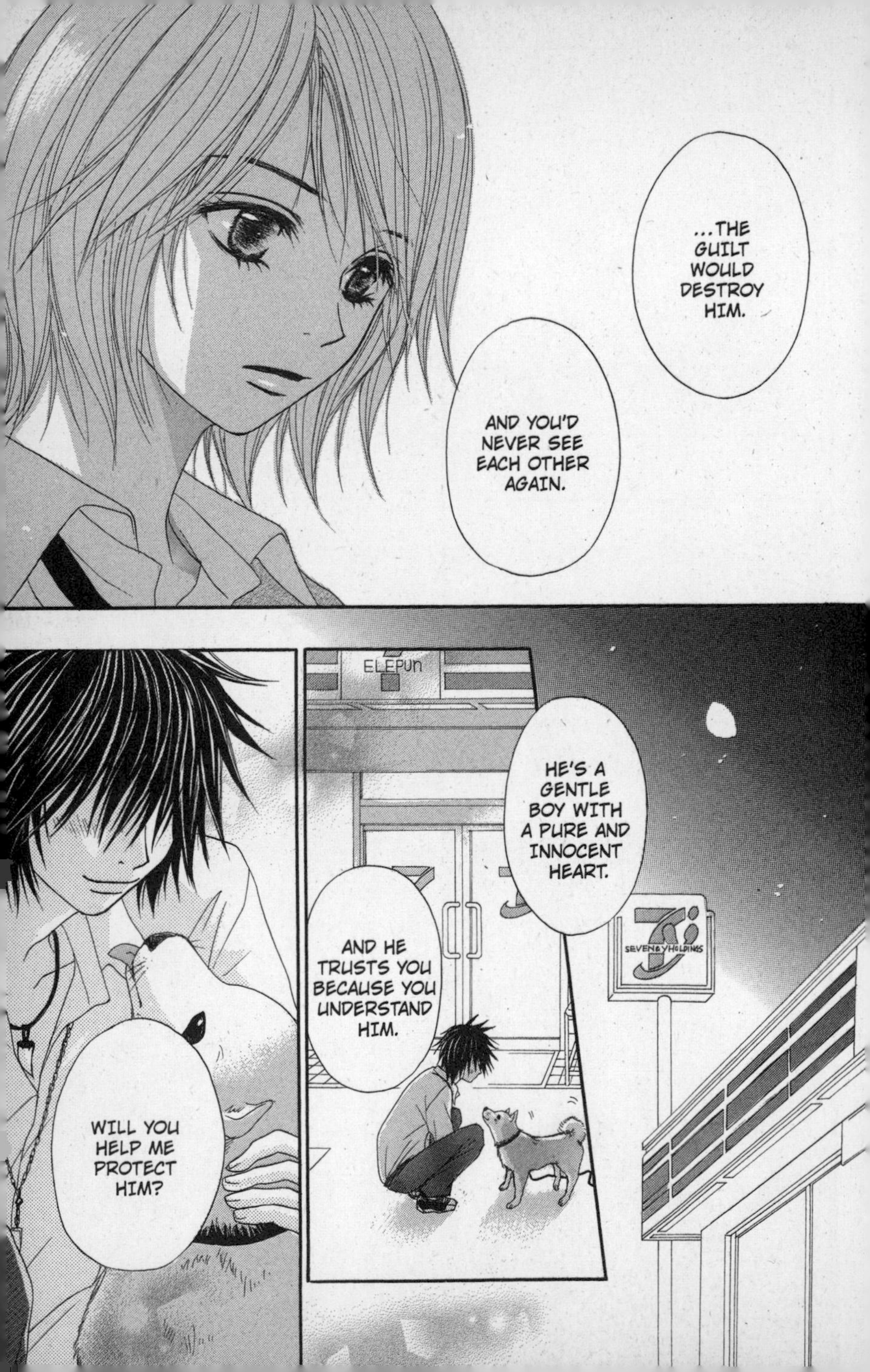
...THE GUILT WOULD DESTROY HIM.
AND YOU'D NEVER SEE EACH OTHER AGAIN.
HE'S A GENTLE BOY WITH A PURE AND INNOCENT HEART.
AND HE TRUSTS YOU BECAUSE YOU UNDERSTAND HIM.
WILL YOU HELP ME PROTECT HIM?

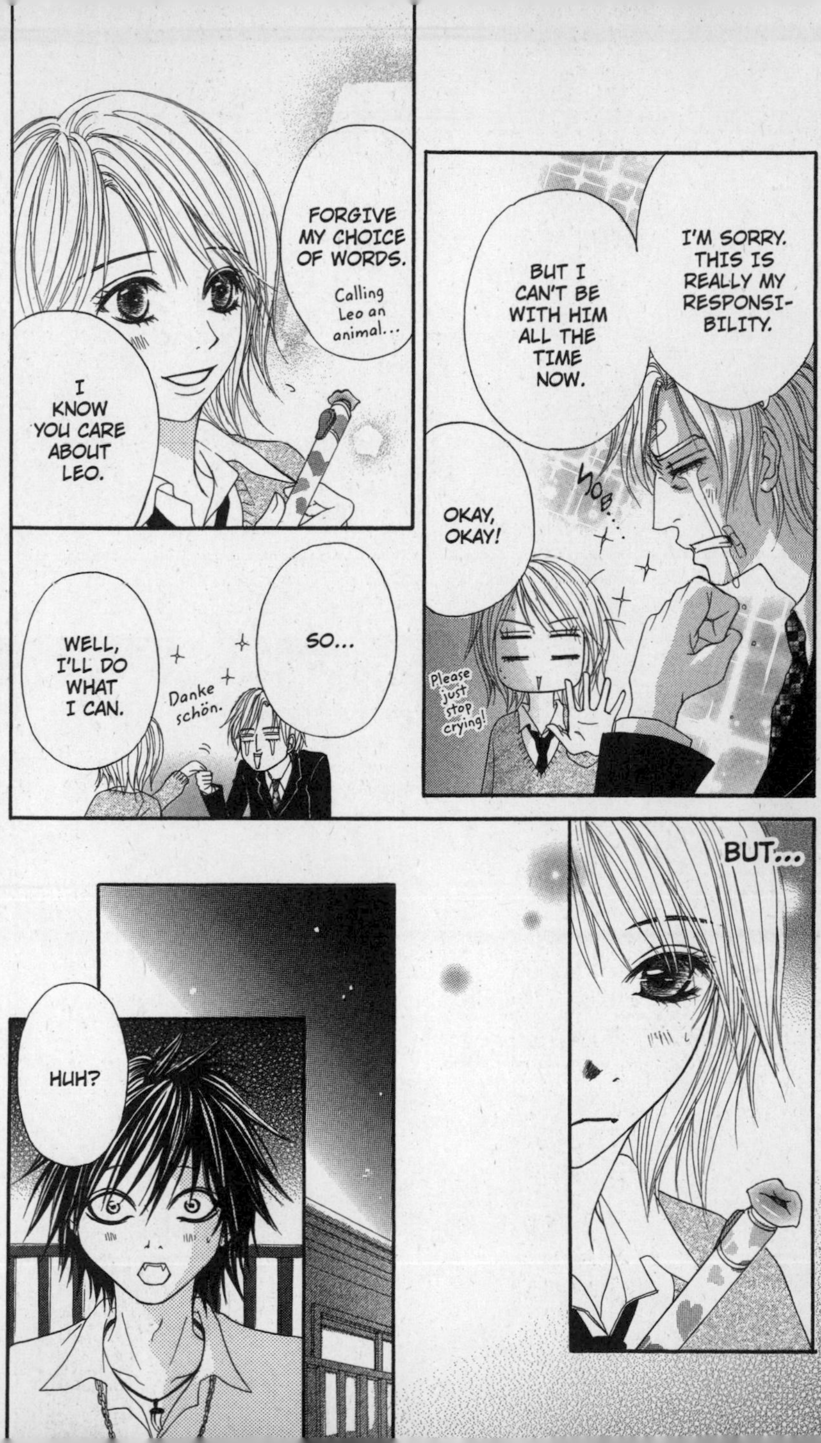
I'M SORRY. THIS IS REALLY MY RESPONSI-BILITY.
BUT I CAN'T BE WITH HIM ALL THE TIME NOW.
SOB...
OKAY, OKAY!
Please just stop crying!
FORGIVE MY CHOICE OF WORDS.
Calling Leo an animal...
I KNOW YOU CARE ABOUT LEO.
SO...
Danke schön.
WELL, I'LL DO WHAT I CAN.
BUT...
HUH?

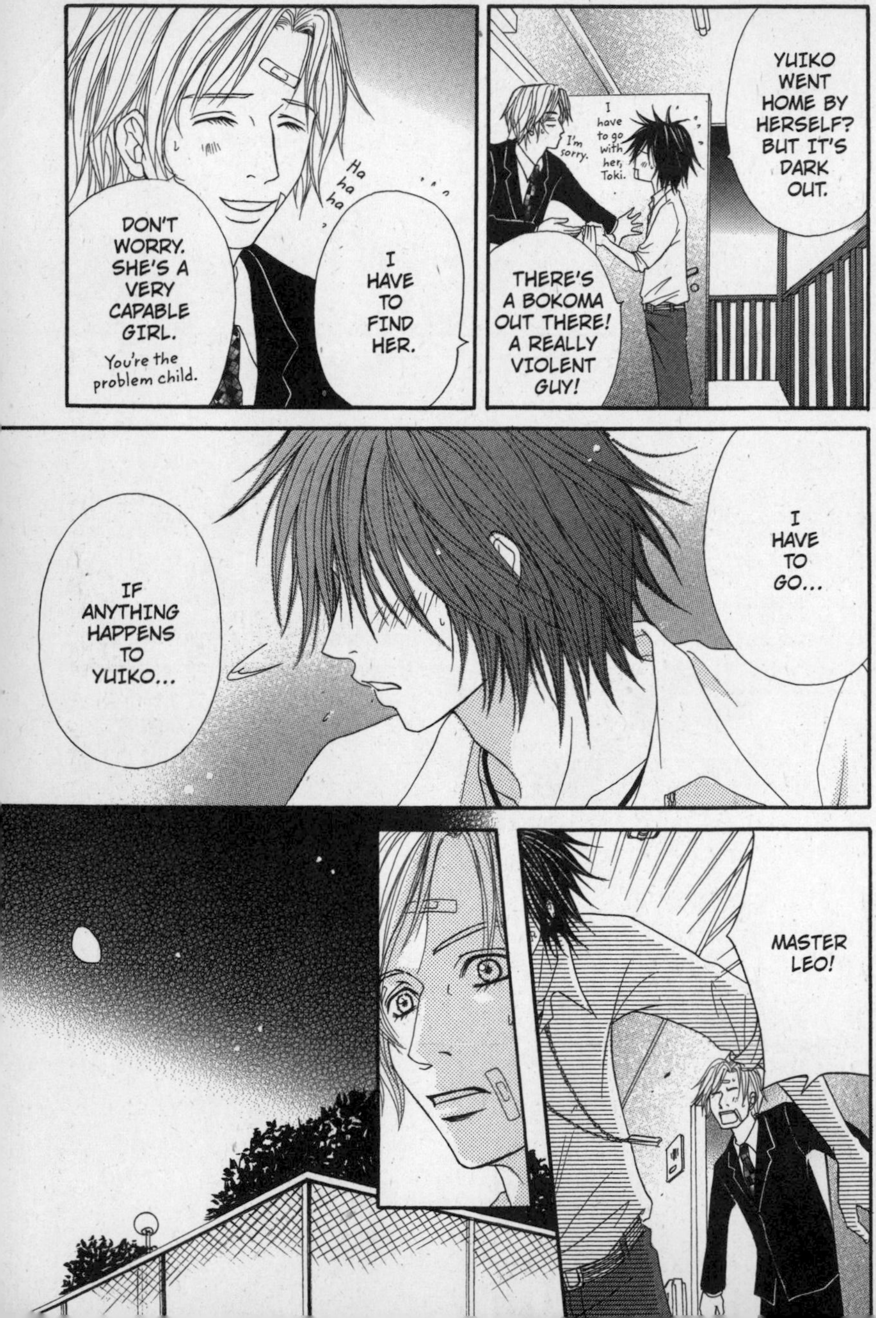
YUIKO WENT HOME BY HERSELF? BUT IT'S DARK OUT.
I have to go with her, Toki.
I'm sorry.
THERE'S A BOKOMA OUT THERE! A REALLY VIOLENT GUY!
I HAVE TO FIND HER.
Ha ha ha
DON'T WORRY. SHE'S A VERY CAPABLE GIRL.
You're the problem child.
I HAVE TO GO...
IF ANYTHING HAPPENS TO YUIKO...
MASTER LEO!

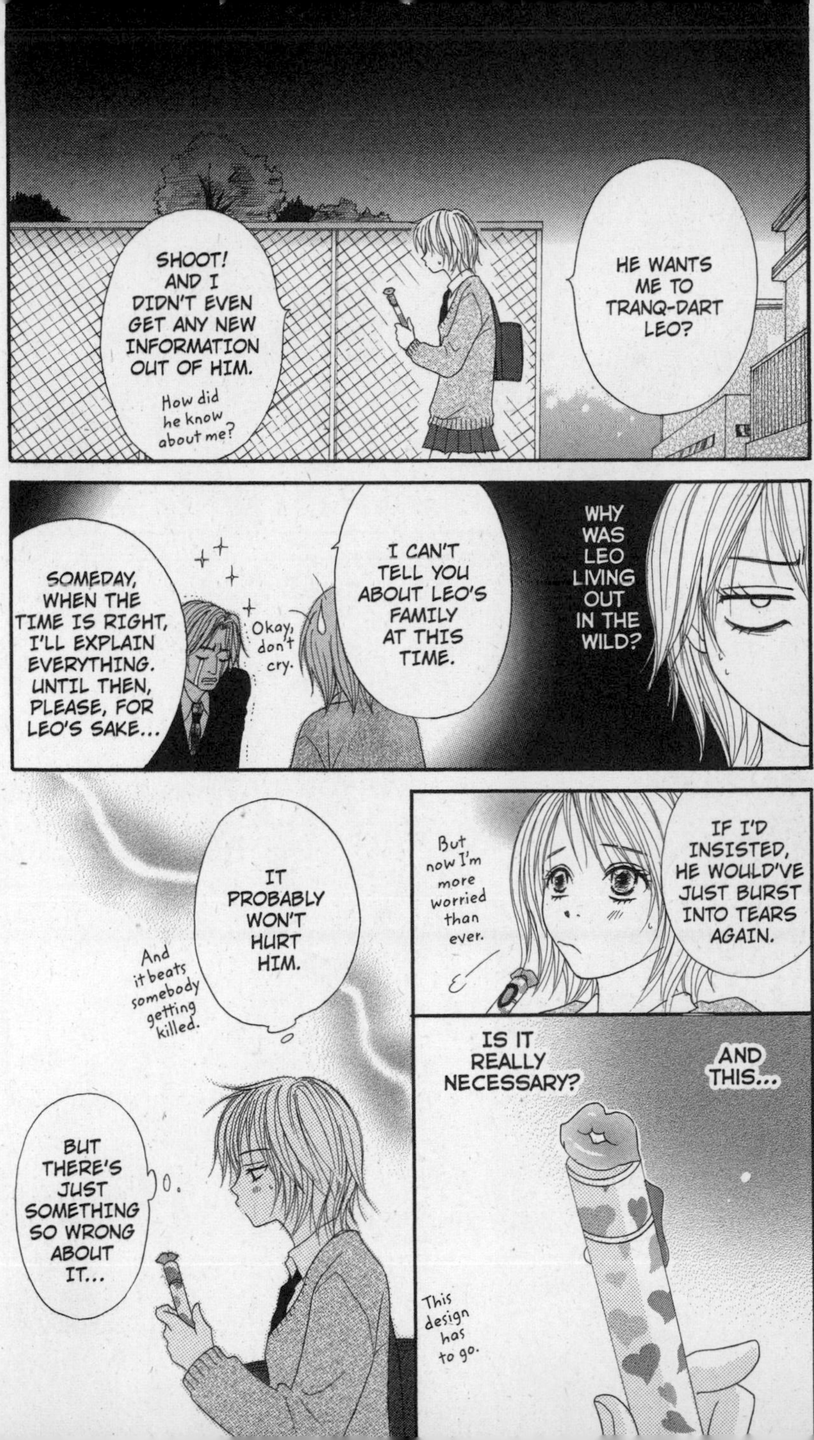
HE WANTS ME TO TRANQ-DART LEO?
SHOOT! AND I DIDN'T EVEN GET ANY NEW INFORMATION OUT OF HIM.
How did he know about me?
WHY WAS LEO LIVING OUT IN THE WILD?
I CAN'T TELL YOU ABOUT LEO'S FAMILY AT THIS TIME.
Okay, don't cry.
SOMEDAY, WHEN THE TIME IS RIGHT, I'LL EXPLAIN EVERYTHING. UNTIL THEN, PLEASE, FOR LEO'S SAKE...
IF I'D INSISTED, HE WOULD'VE JUST BURST INTO TEARS AGAIN.
But now I'm more worried than ever.
AND THIS...
IS IT REALLY NECESSARY?
This design has to go.
IT PROBABLY WON'T HURT HIM.
And it beats somebody getting killed.
BUT THERE'S JUST SOMETHING SO WRONG ABOUT IT...

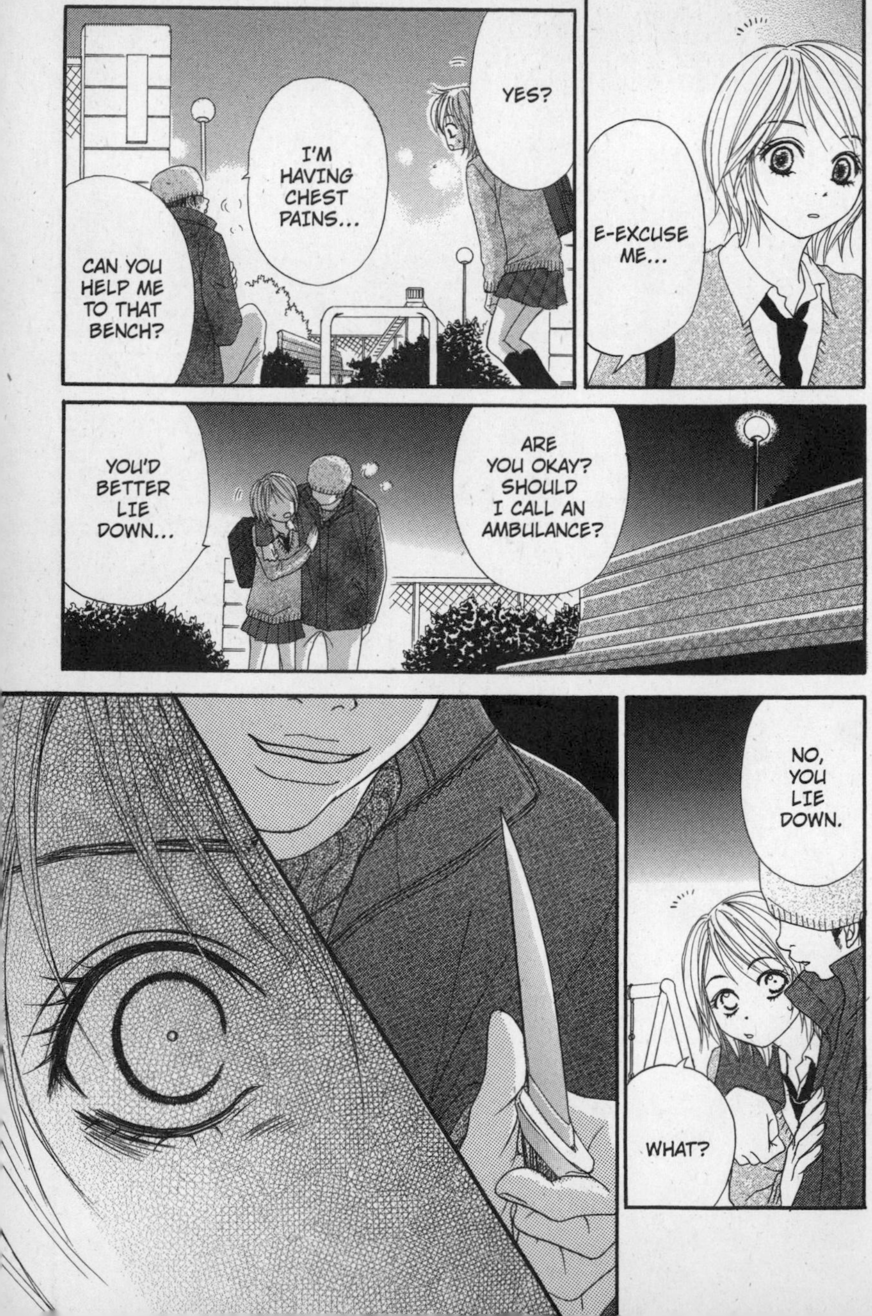
E-EXCUSE ME...
YES?
I'M HAVING CHEST PAINS...
CAN YOU HELP ME TO THAT BENCH?
ARE YOU OKAY? SHOULD I CALL AN AMBULANCE?
YOU'D BETTER LIE DOWN...
NO, YOU LIE DOWN.
WHAT?

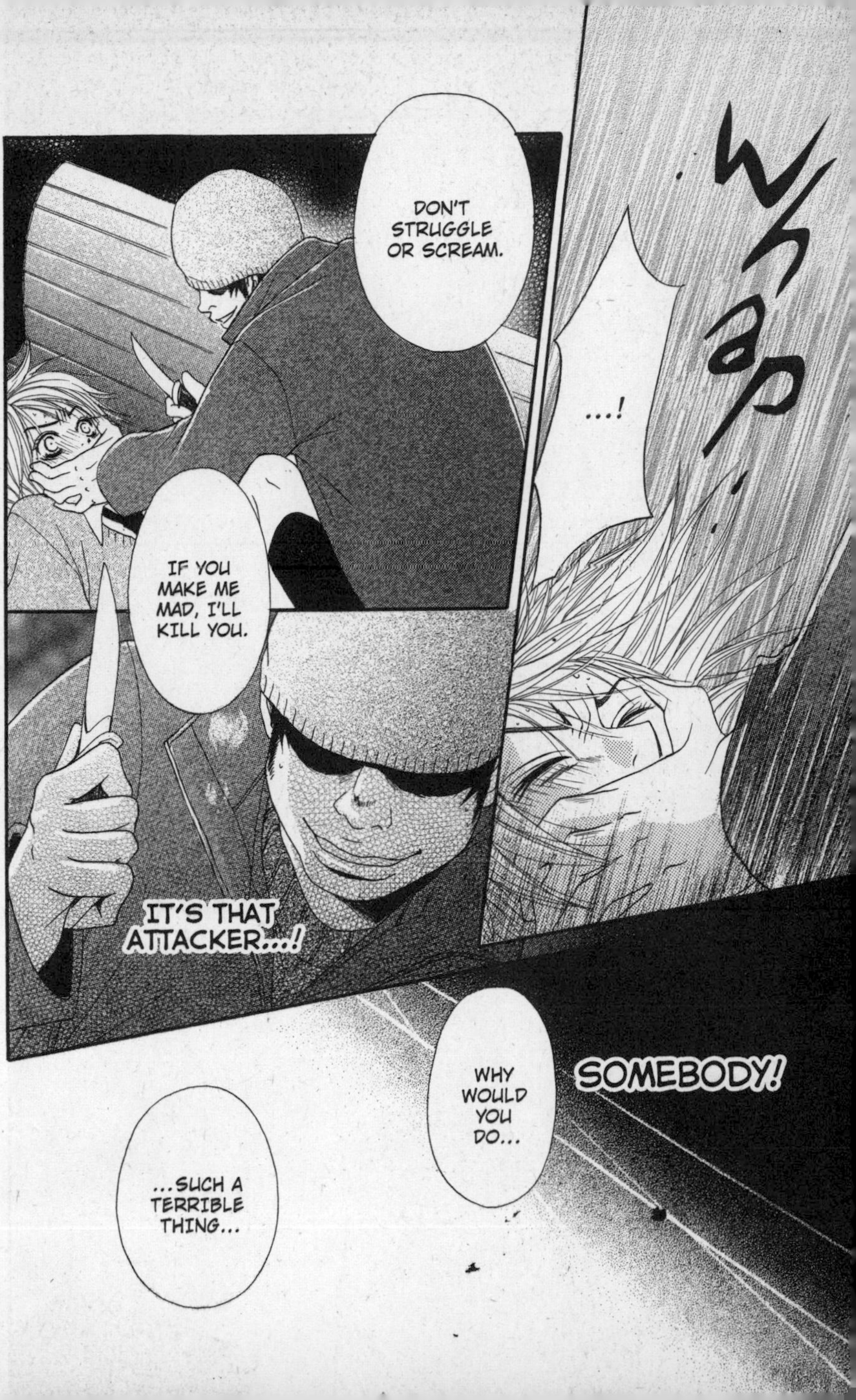
WHAP!
...!
DON'T STRUGGLE OR SCREAM.
IF YOU MAKE ME MAD, I'LL KILL YOU.
IT'S THAT ATTACKER...!
SOMEBODY!
WHY WOULD YOU DO...
...SUCH A TERRIBLE THING...

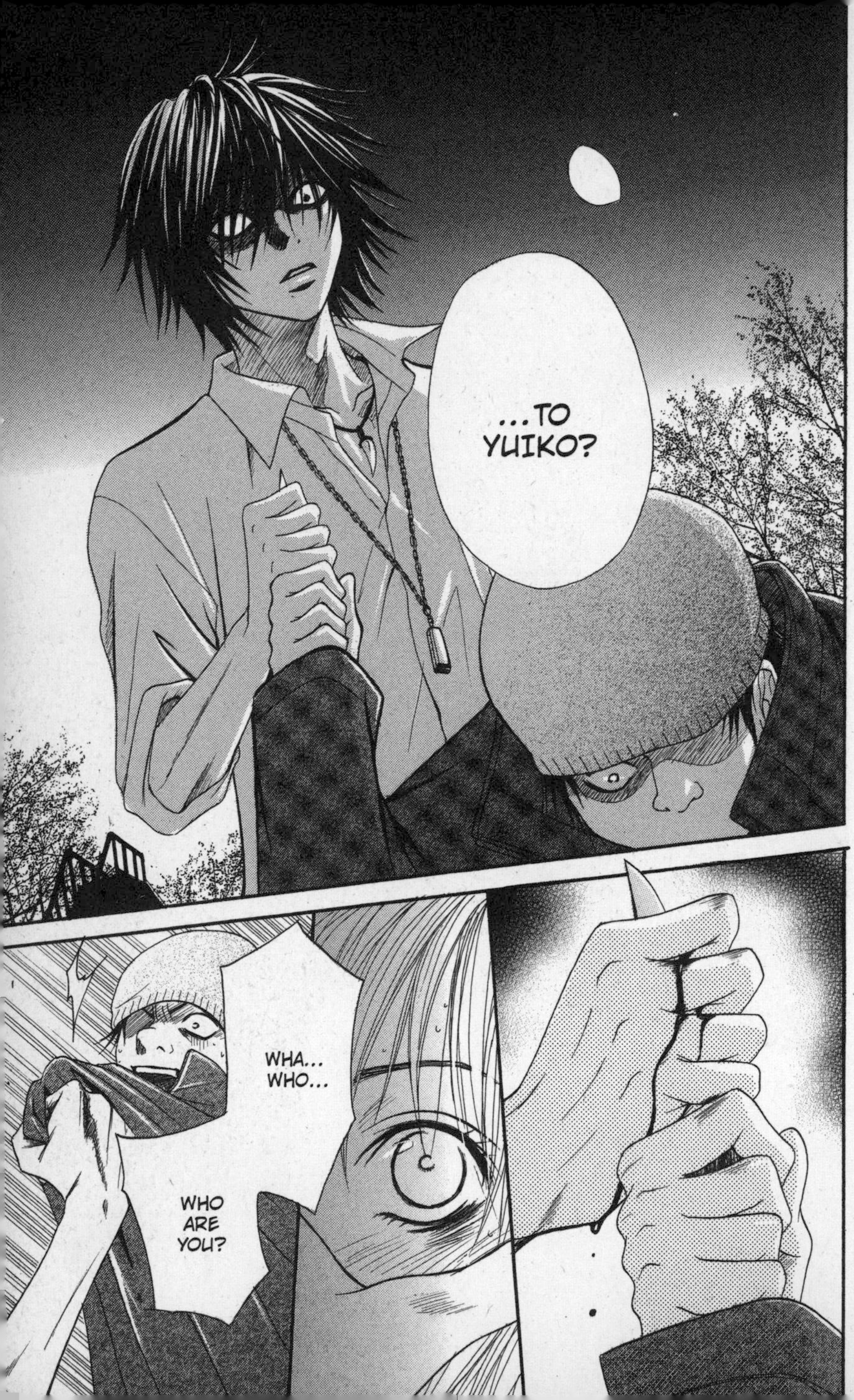
...TO YUIKO?
WHA... WHO...
WHO ARE YOU?

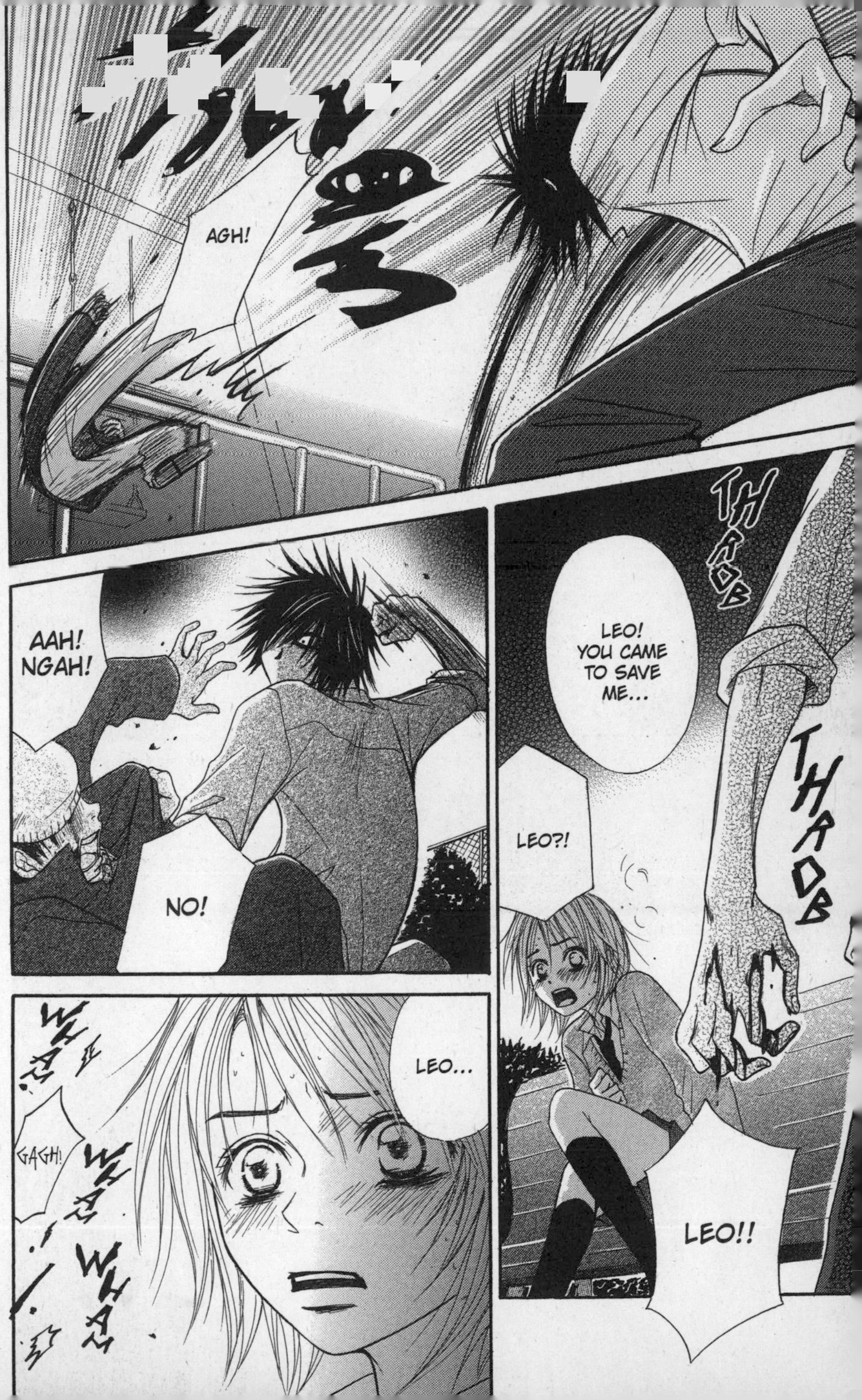
AGH!
THROB
LEO! YOU CAME TO SAVE ME...
THROB
LEO?!
LEO!!
AAH! NGAH!
NO!
LEO...
WHAM
GAGH!
WHAM
WHAM

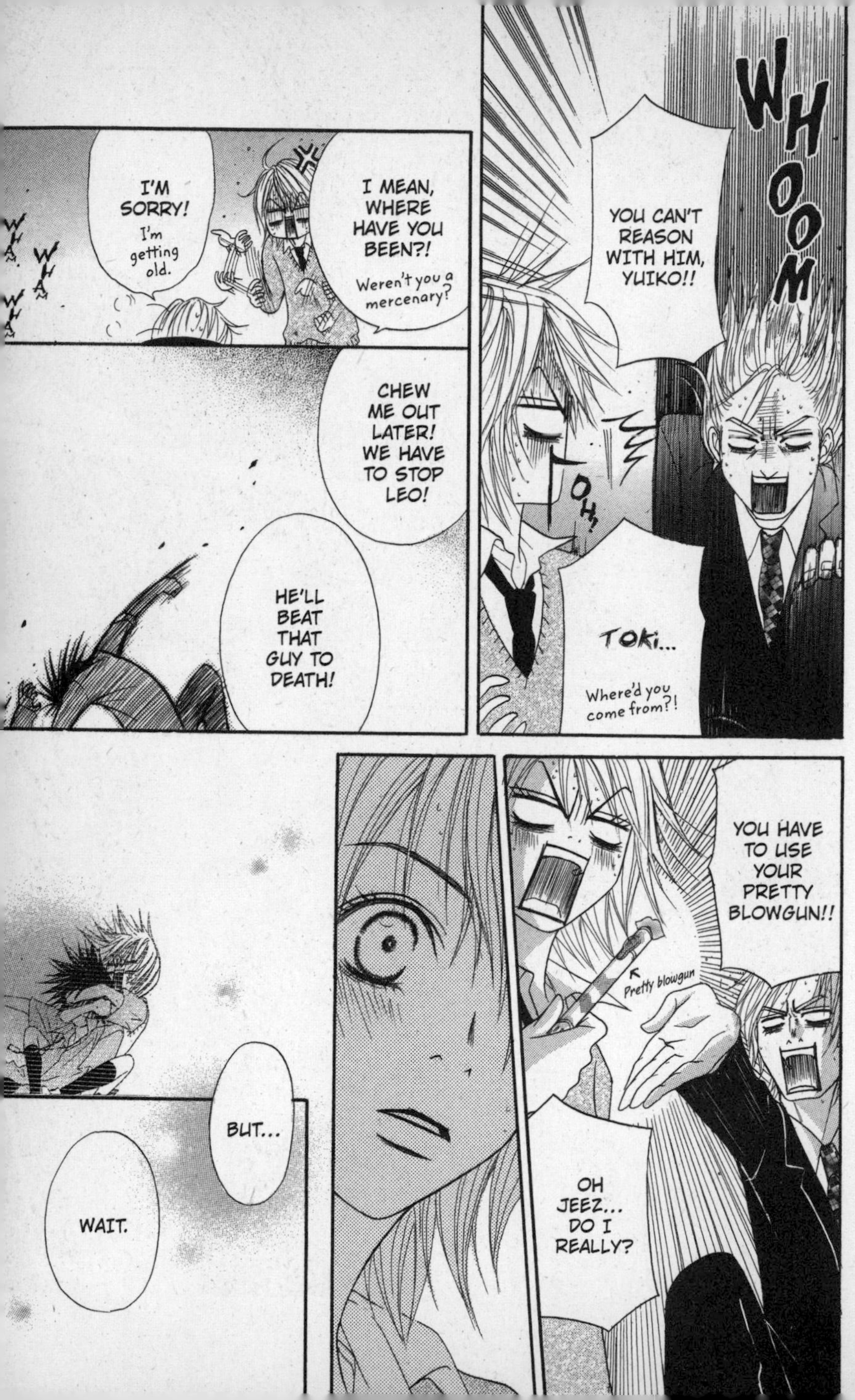
WHOOM
YOU CAN'T REASON WITH HIM, YUIKO!!
OH!
TOKI...
Where'd you come from?!
I MEAN, WHERE HAVE YOU BEEN?!
Weren't you a mercenary?
I'M SORRY!
I'm getting old.
WHAM WHAM WHAM
CHEW ME OUT LATER! WE HAVE TO STOP LEO!
HE'LL BEAT THAT GUY TO DEATH!
YOU HAVE TO USE YOUR PRETTY BLOWGUN!!
Pretty blowgun
OH JEEZ... DO I REALLY?
BUT...
WAIT.

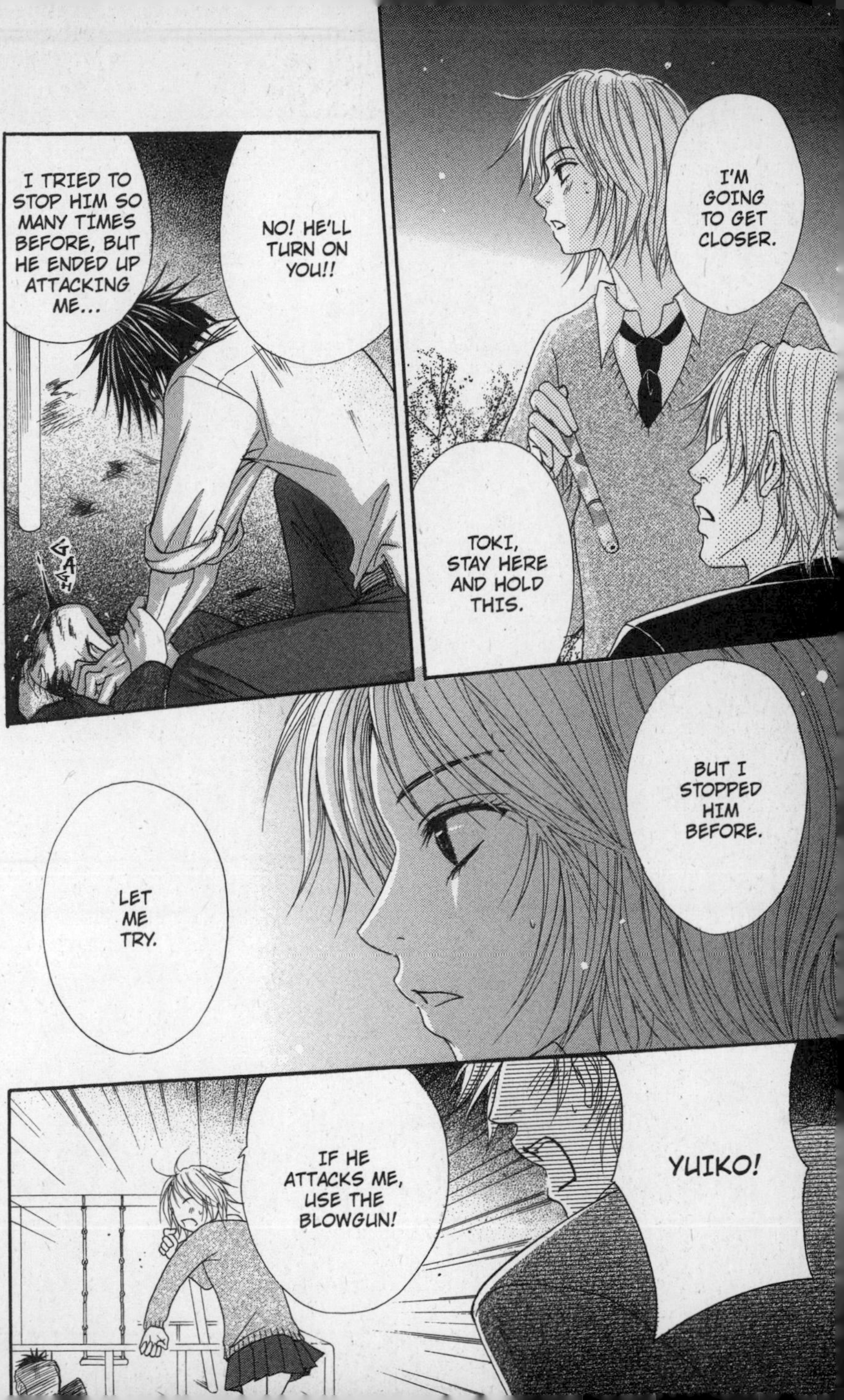
I'M GOING TO GET CLOSER.
TOKI, STAY HERE AND HOLD THIS.
NO! HE'LL TURN ON YOU!!
I TRIED TO STOP HIM SO MANY TIMES BEFORE, BUT HE ENDED UP ATTACKING ME...
GAGH
BUT I STOPPED HIM BEFORE.
LET ME TRY.
YUIKO!
IF HE ATTACKS ME, USE THE BLOWGUN!

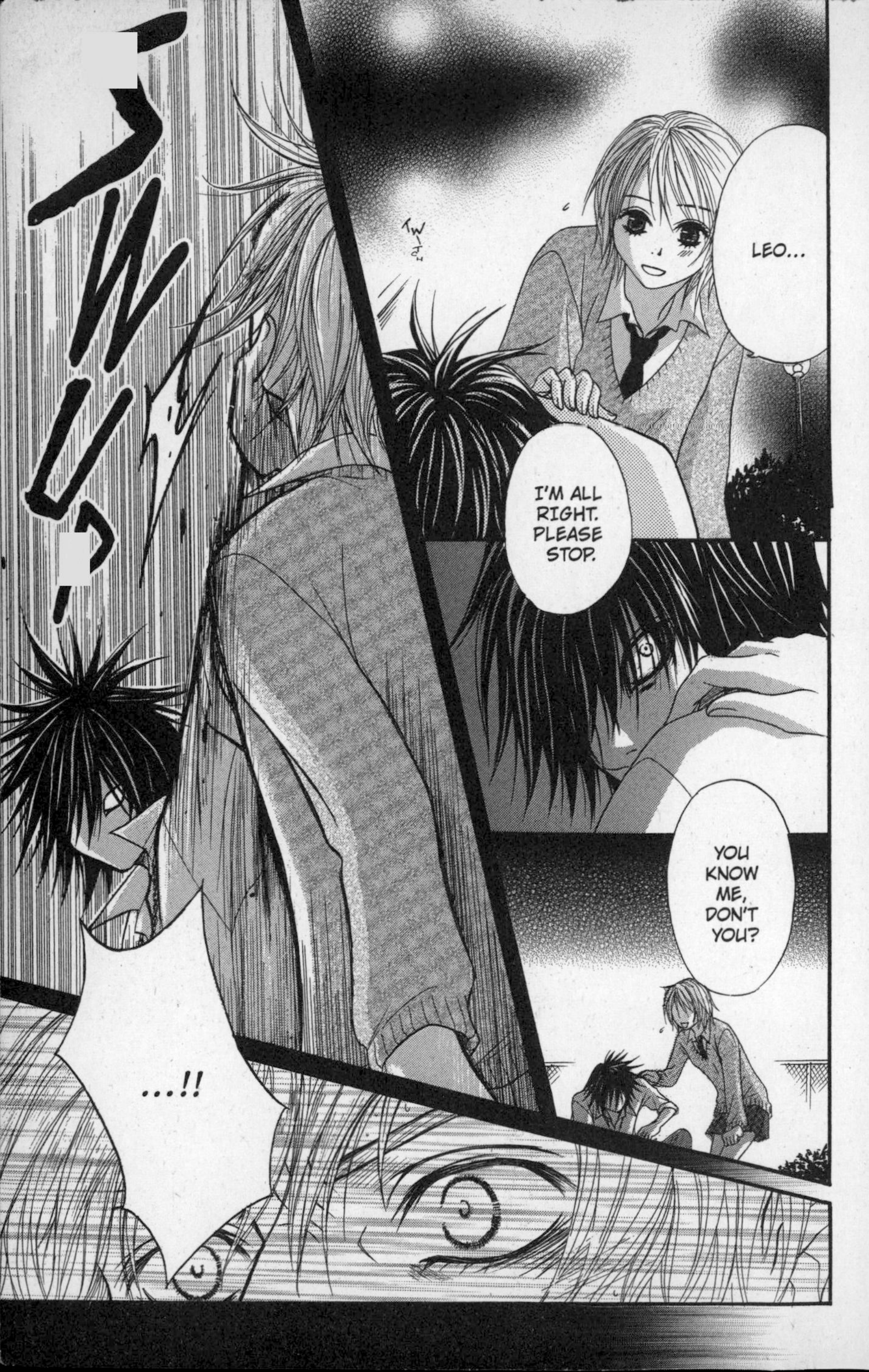
LEO...
TWITCH
I'M ALL RIGHT. PLEASE STOP.
YOU KNOW ME, DON'T YOU?
...!!

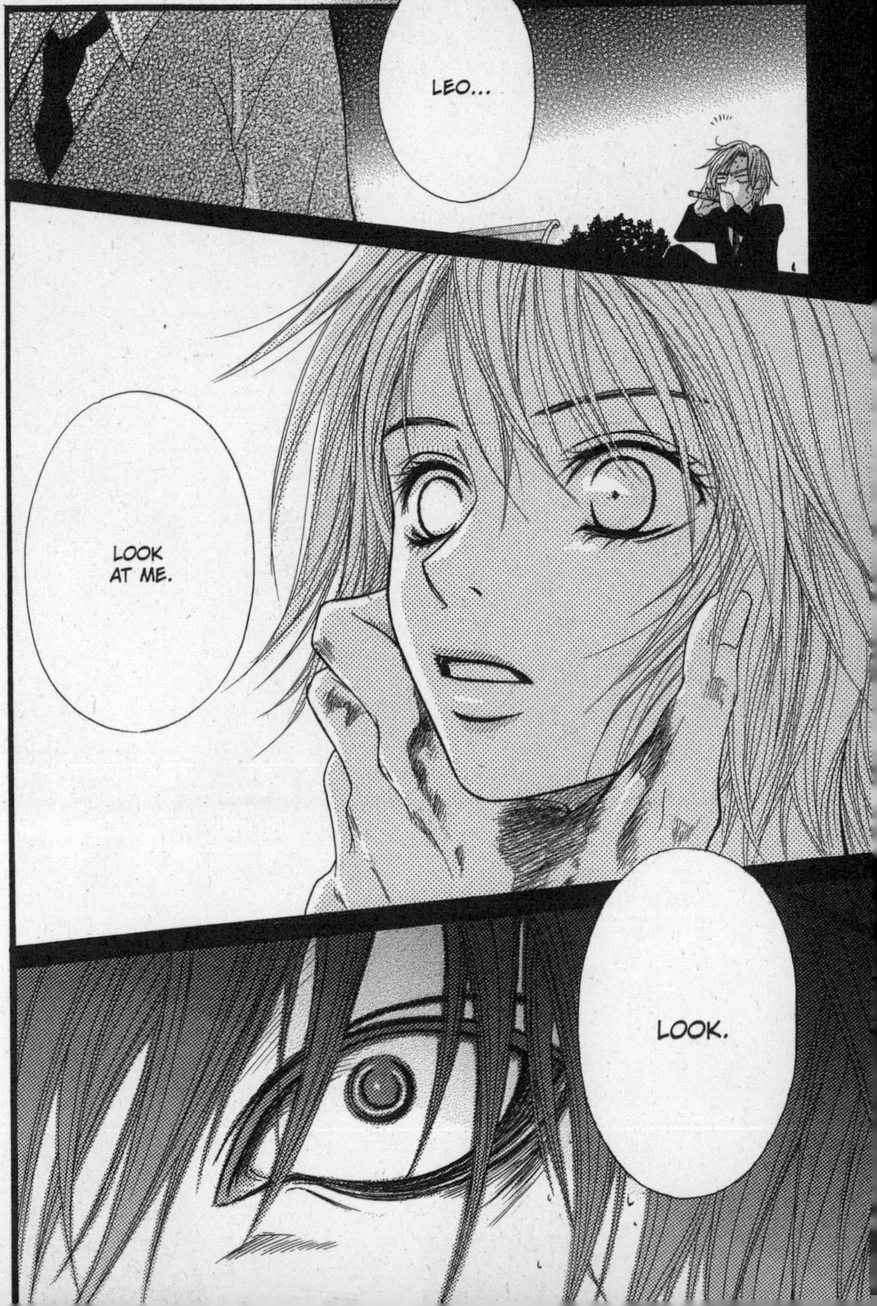
LEO...
LOOK AT ME.
LOOK.

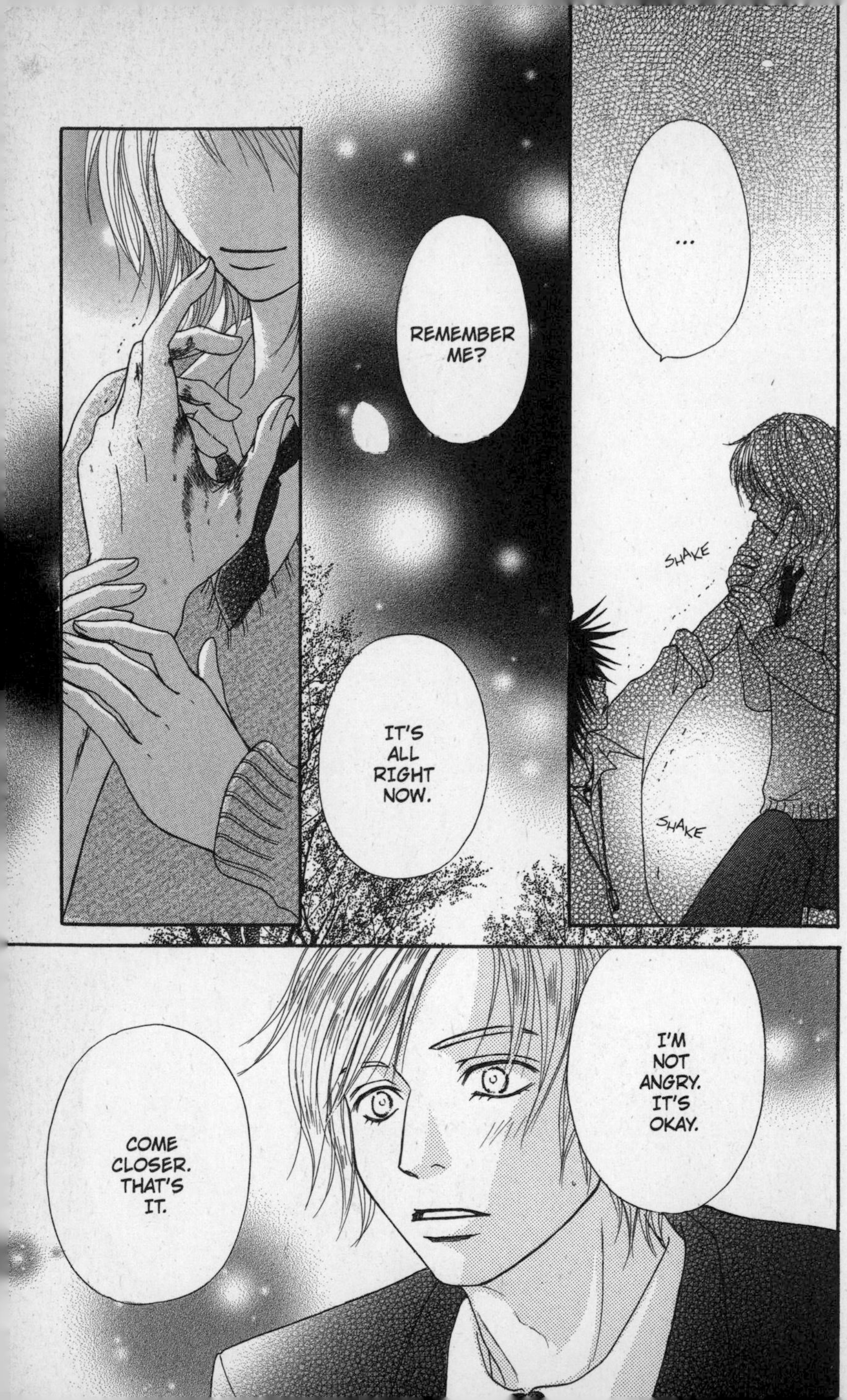
...
SHAKE
SHAKE
REMEMBER ME?
IT'S ALL RIGHT NOW.
I'M NOT ANGRY. IT'S OKAY.
COME CLOSER. THAT'S IT.

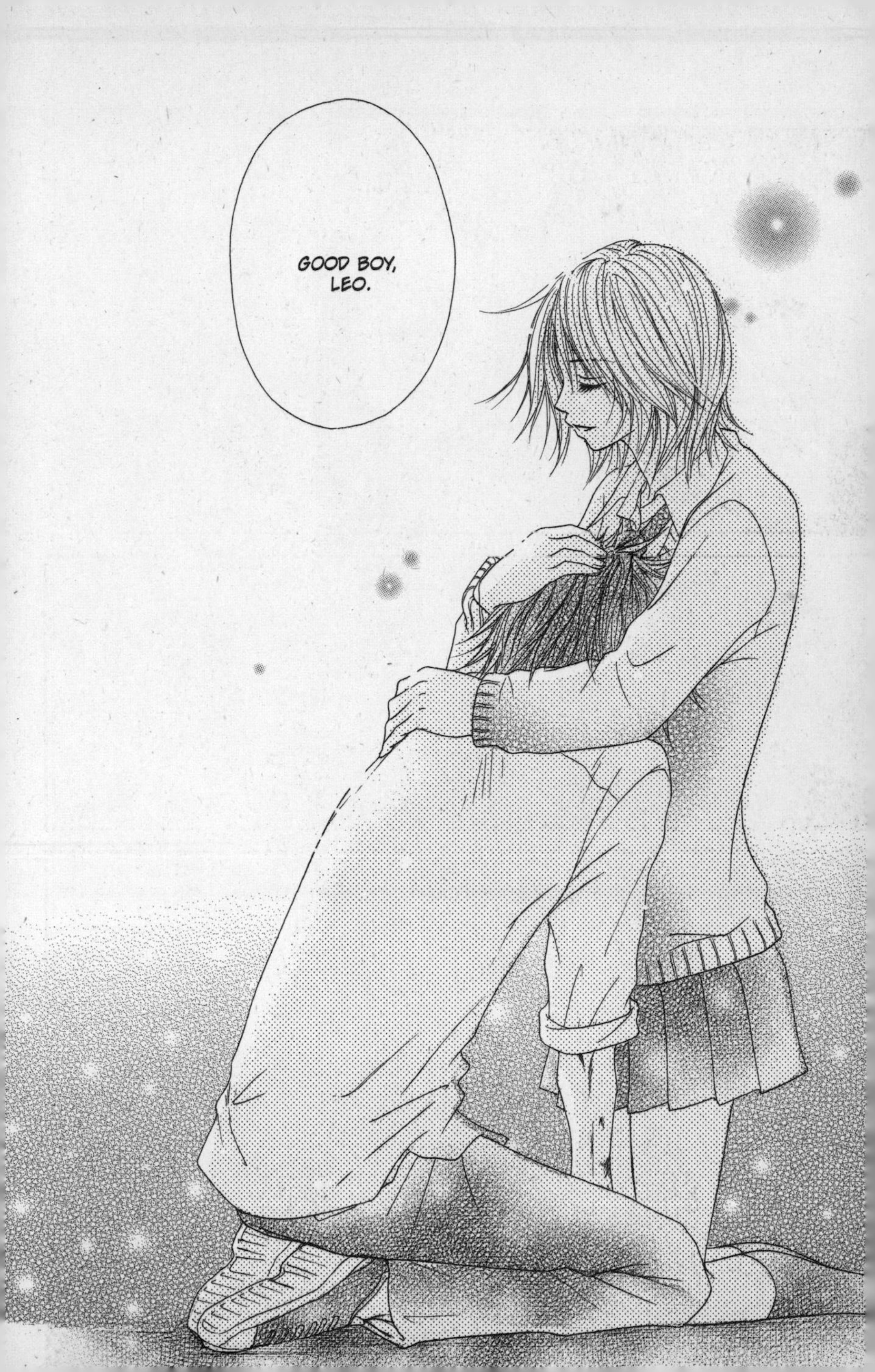
GOOD BOY, LEO.

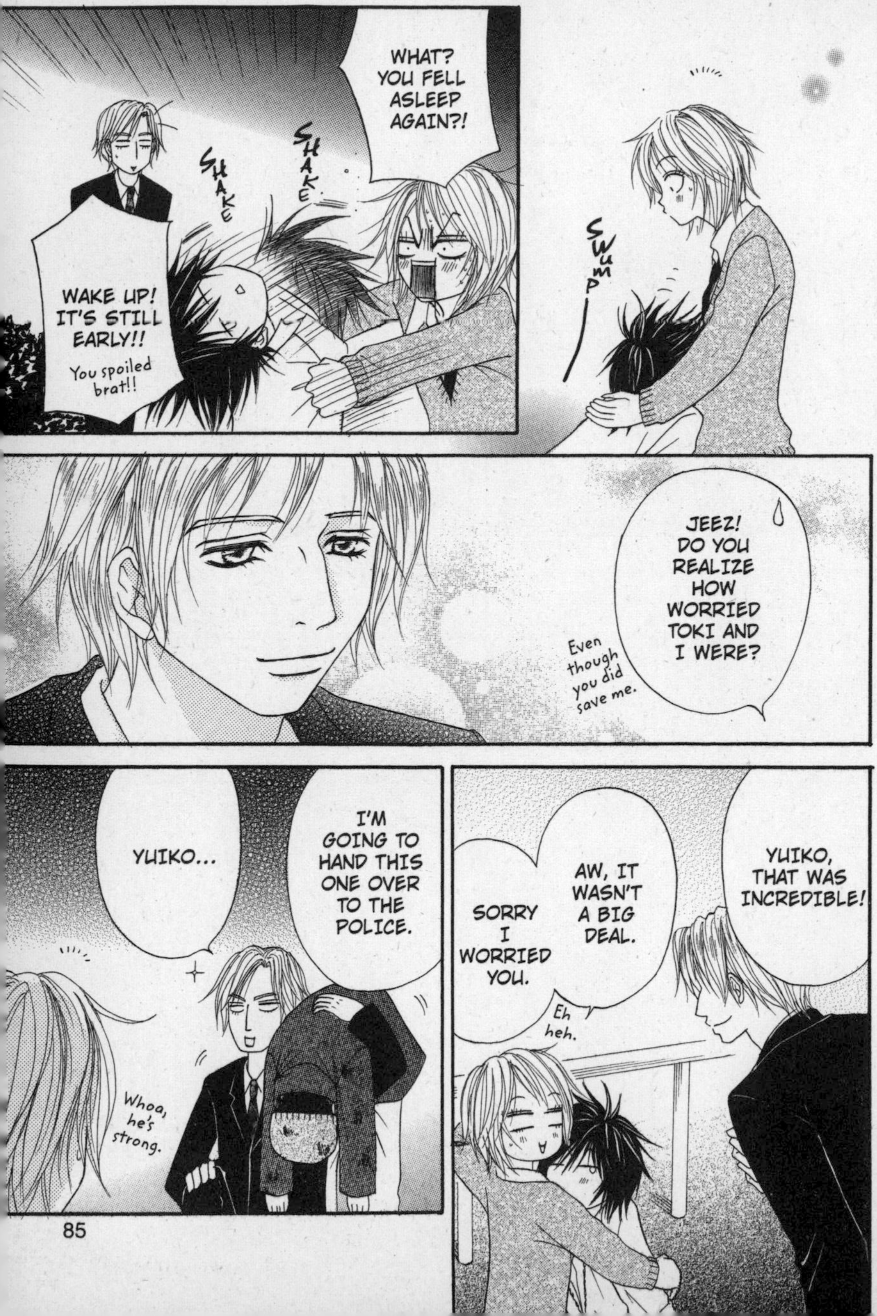
SWUMP
WHAT? YOU FELL ASLEEP AGAIN?!
SHAKE
SHAKE
WAKE UP! IT'S STILL EARLY!!
You spoiled brat!!
JEEZ! DO YOU REALIZE HOW WORRIED TOKI AND I WERE?
Even though you did save me.
YUIKO, THAT WAS INCREDIBLE!
AW, IT WASN'T A BIG DEAL.
SORRY I WORRIED YOU.
Eh heh.
I'M GOING TO HAND THIS ONE OVER TO THE POLICE.
YUIKO...
Whoa, he's strong.

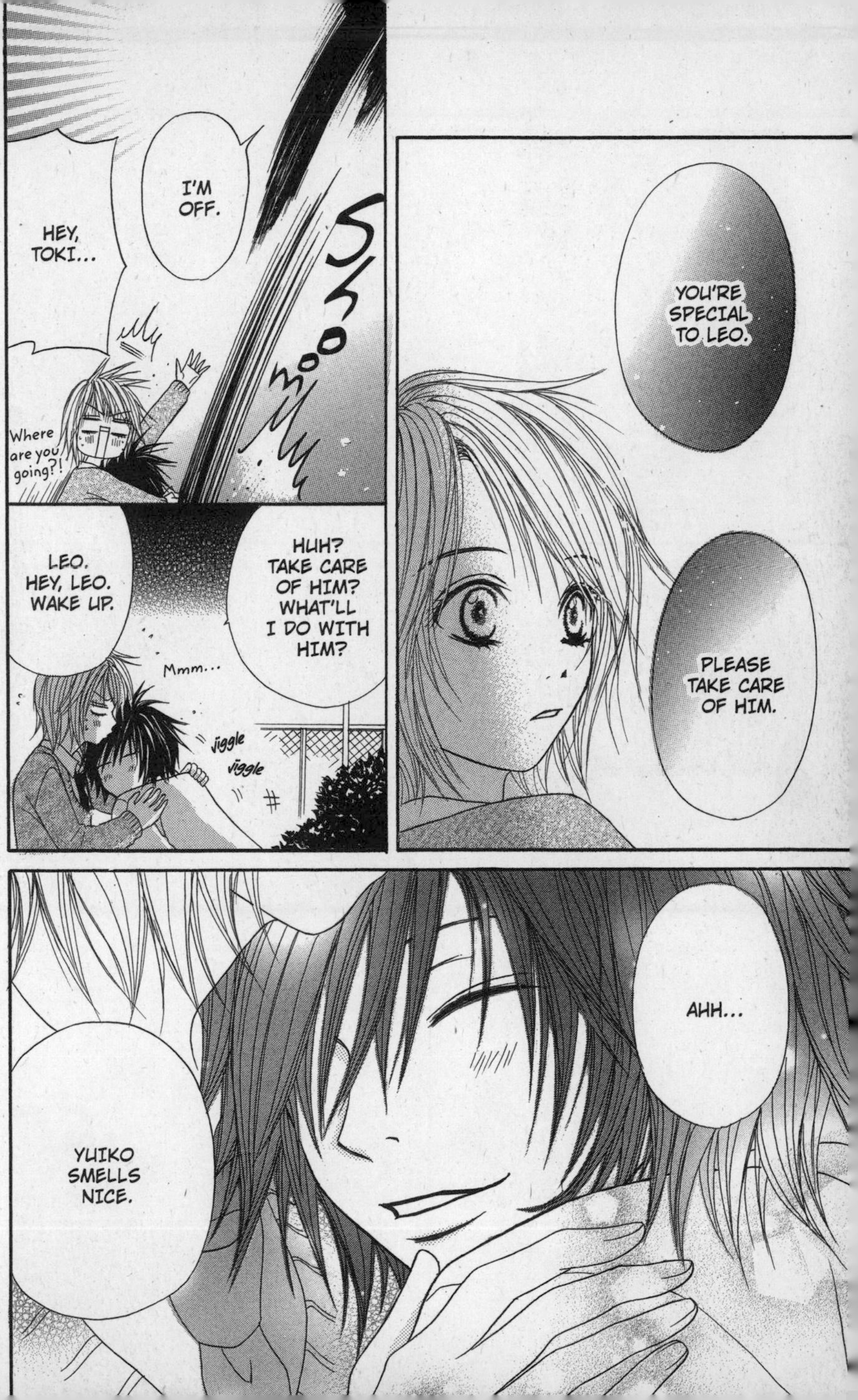
YOU'RE SPECIAL TO LEO.
PLEASE TAKE CARE OF HIM.
SHOOM
I'M OFF.
HEY, TOKI...
Where are you going?!
HUH? TAKE CARE OF HIM? WHAT'LL I DO WITH HIM?
LEO. HEY, LEO. WAKE UP.
Mmm...
jiggle jiggle
AHH...
YUIKO SMELLS NICE.

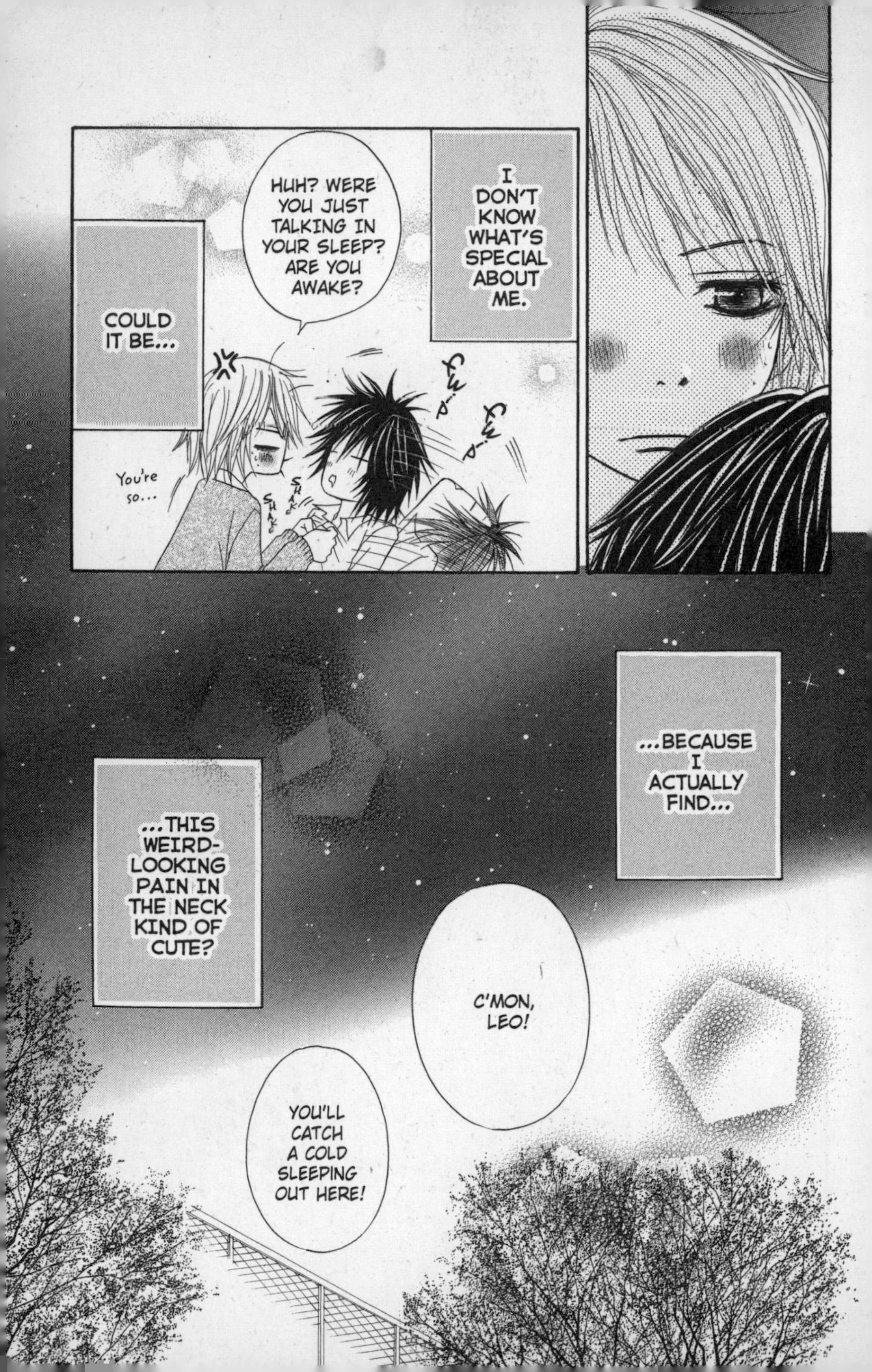
I DON'T KNOW WHAT'S SPECIAL ABOUT ME.
HUH? WERE YOU JUST TALKING IN YOUR SLEEP? ARE YOU AWAKE?
FWIP
FWIP
COULD IT BE...
SHAKE
SHAKE
You're so...
...BECAUSE I ACTUALLY FIND...
...THIS WEIRD-LOOKING PAIN IN THE NECK KIND OF CUTE?
C'MON, LEO!
YOU'LL CATCH A COLD SLEEPING OUT HERE!

CHAPTER 2: THE STORY BEHIND THE PICTURE

YUIKO: LEO, YOU ATE MY
OMELET, DIDN'T YOU?
THAT WAS MY LUNCH!

LEO: NO, I DIDN'T!
REALLY!

YUIKO: LIAR! THEN WHY IS
THERE KETCHUP ALL
OVER YOUR LIPS?

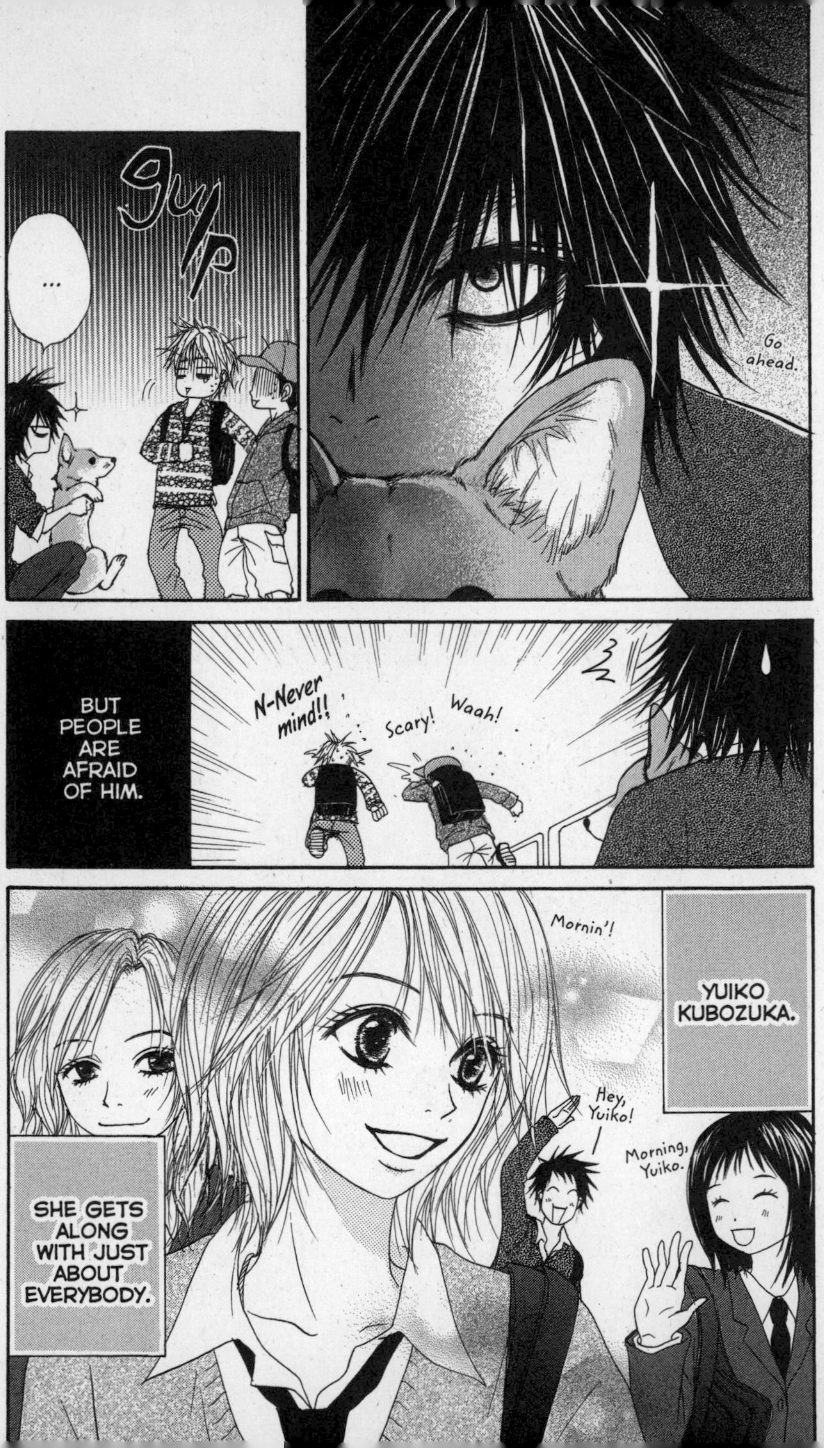
Go ahead.
gulp
...
N-Never mind!!
Waah!
Scary!
BUT PEOPLE ARE AFRAID OF HIM.
YUIKO KUBOZUKA.
Mornin'!
Hey, Yuiko!
Morning, Yuiko.
SHE GETS ALONG WITH JUST ABOUT EVERYBODY.

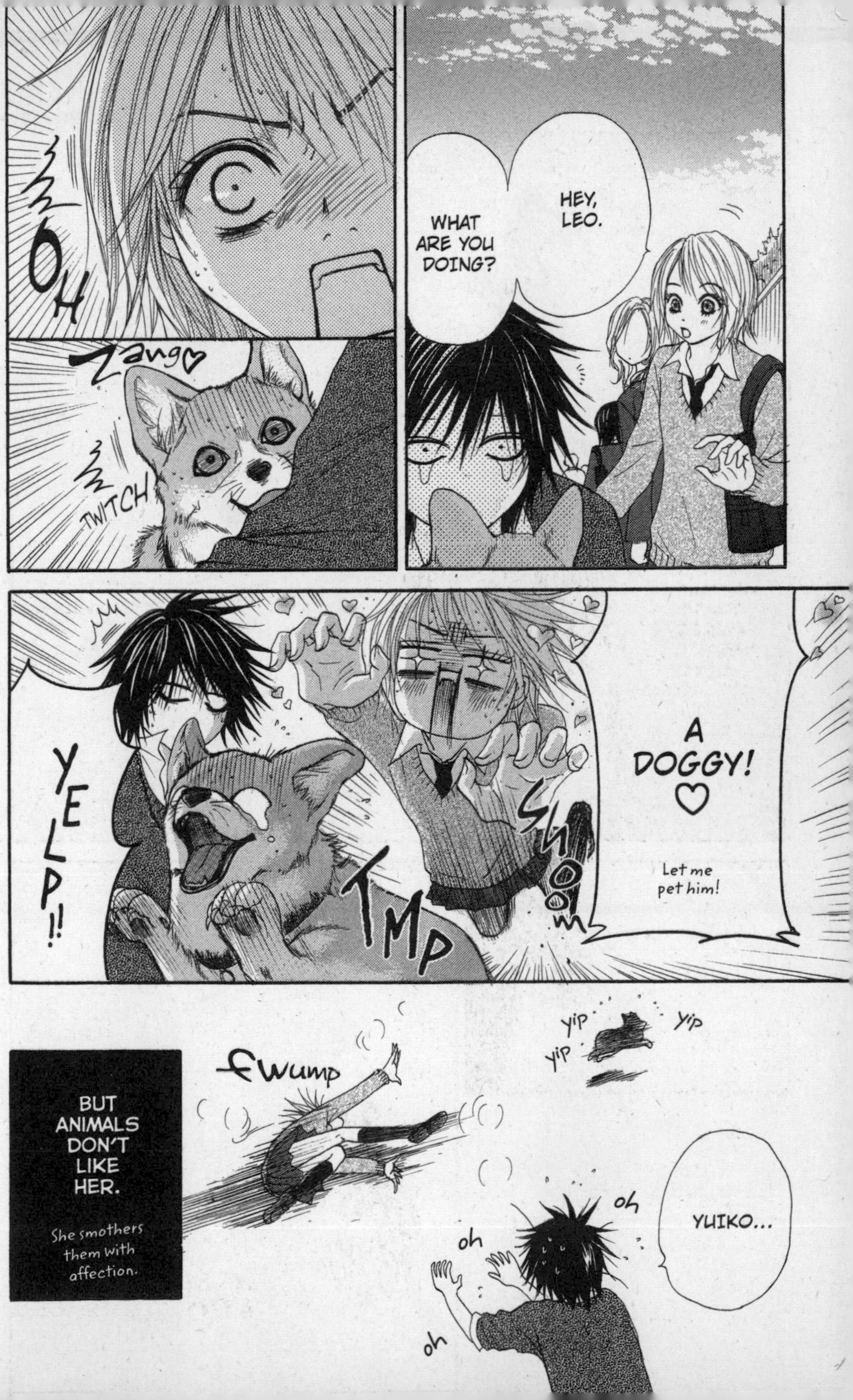
HEY, LEO.
WHAT ARE YOU DOING?
OH
Zang♡
TWITCH
A DOGGY! ♡
Let me pet him!
SHOOM
TMP
YELP!!
YUIKO...
oh
oh
oh
yip
yip
yip
fwump
BUT ANIMALS DON'T LIKE HER.
She smothers them with affection.

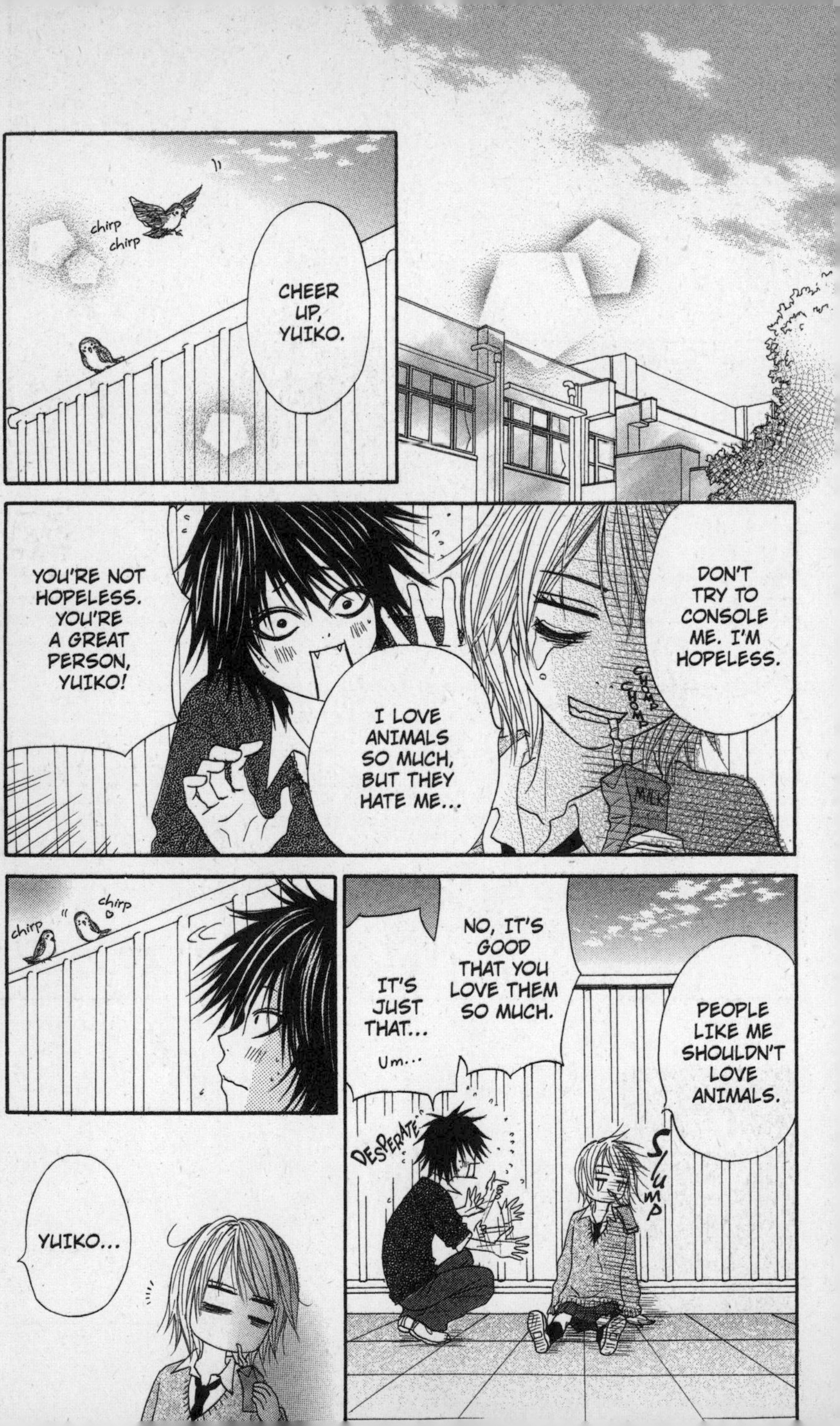
chirp
chirp
CHEER UP, YUIKO.
DON'T TRY TO CONSOLE ME. I'M HOPELESS.
CHOMP CHOMP
MILK
I LOVE ANIMALS SO MUCH, BUT THEY HATE ME...
YOU'RE NOT HOPELESS. YOU'RE A GREAT PERSON, YUIKO!
PEOPLE LIKE ME SHOULDN'T LOVE ANIMALS.
SLUMP
NO, IT'S GOOD THAT YOU LOVE THEM SO MUCH.
IT'S JUST THAT...
Um...
DESPERATE
chirp
chirp
YUIKO...

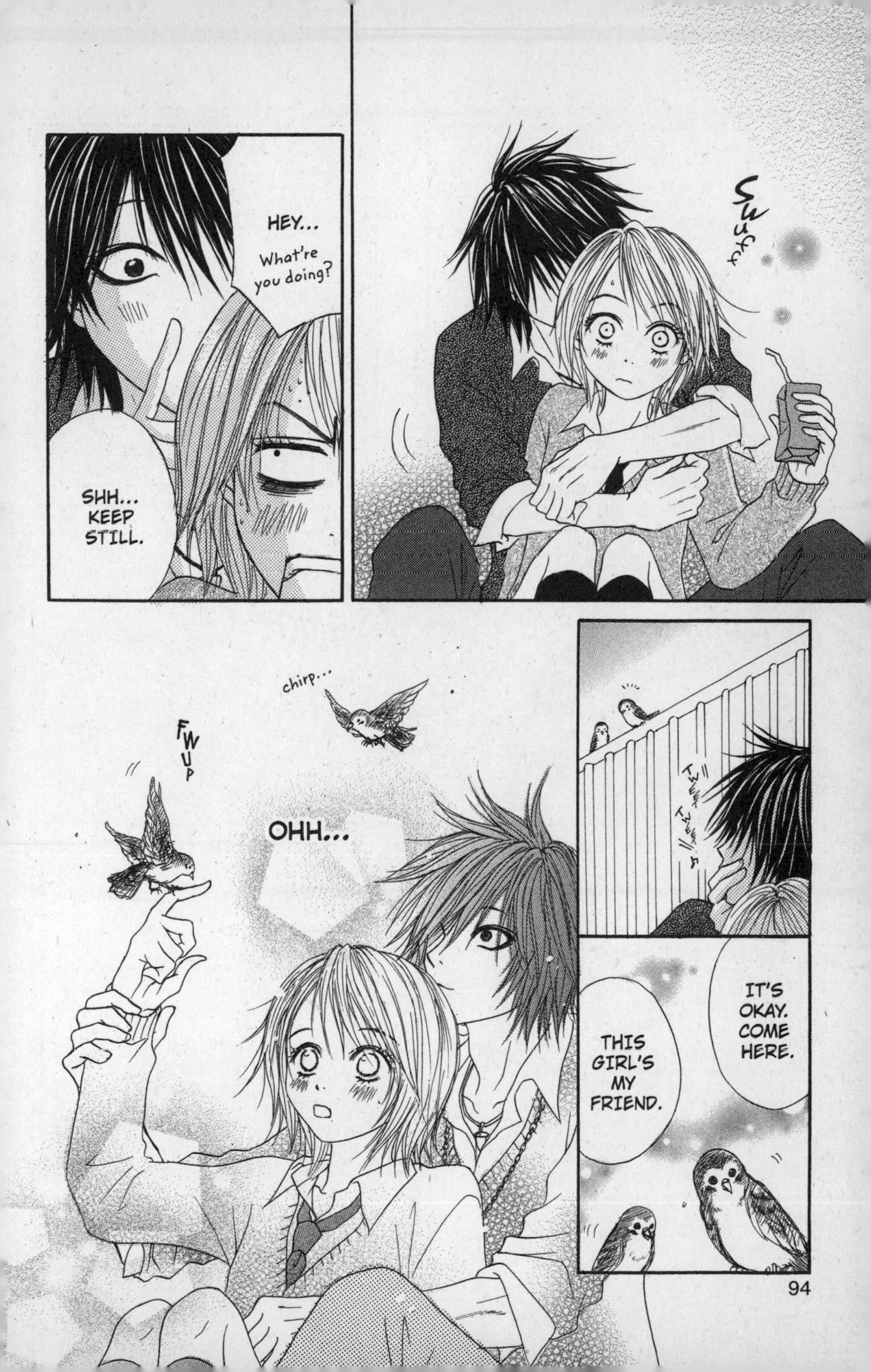
Swuff
HEY... What're you doing?
SHH... KEEP STILL.
TWEET TWEET
IT'S OKAY. COME HERE.
THIS GIRL'S MY FRIEND.
chirp...
FWUP
OHH...

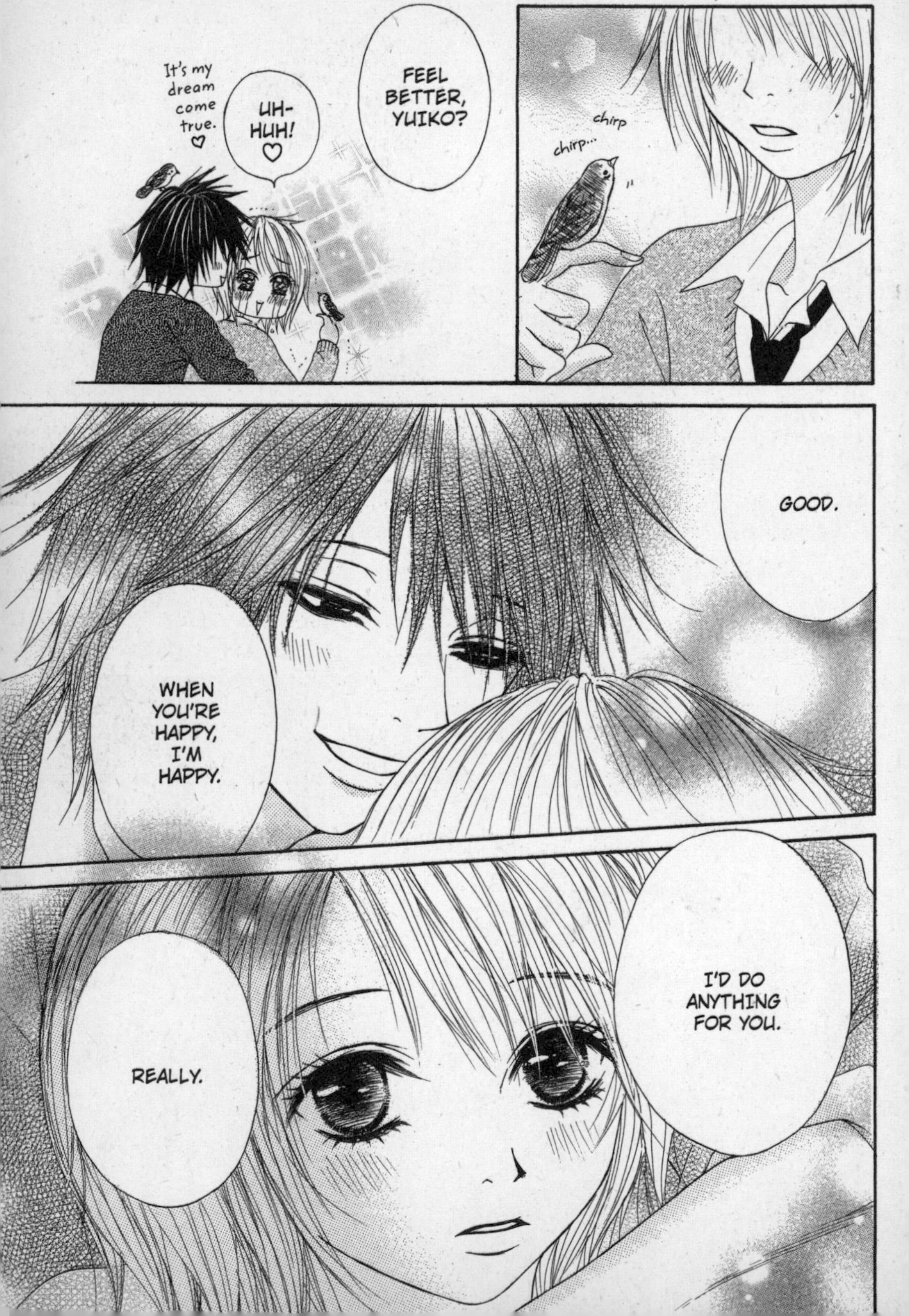
chirp
chirp...
FEEL BETTER, YUIKO?
UH-HUH! ♡
It's my dream come true. ♡
GOOD.
WHEN YOU'RE HAPPY, I'M HAPPY.
I'D DO ANYTHING FOR YOU.
REALLY.

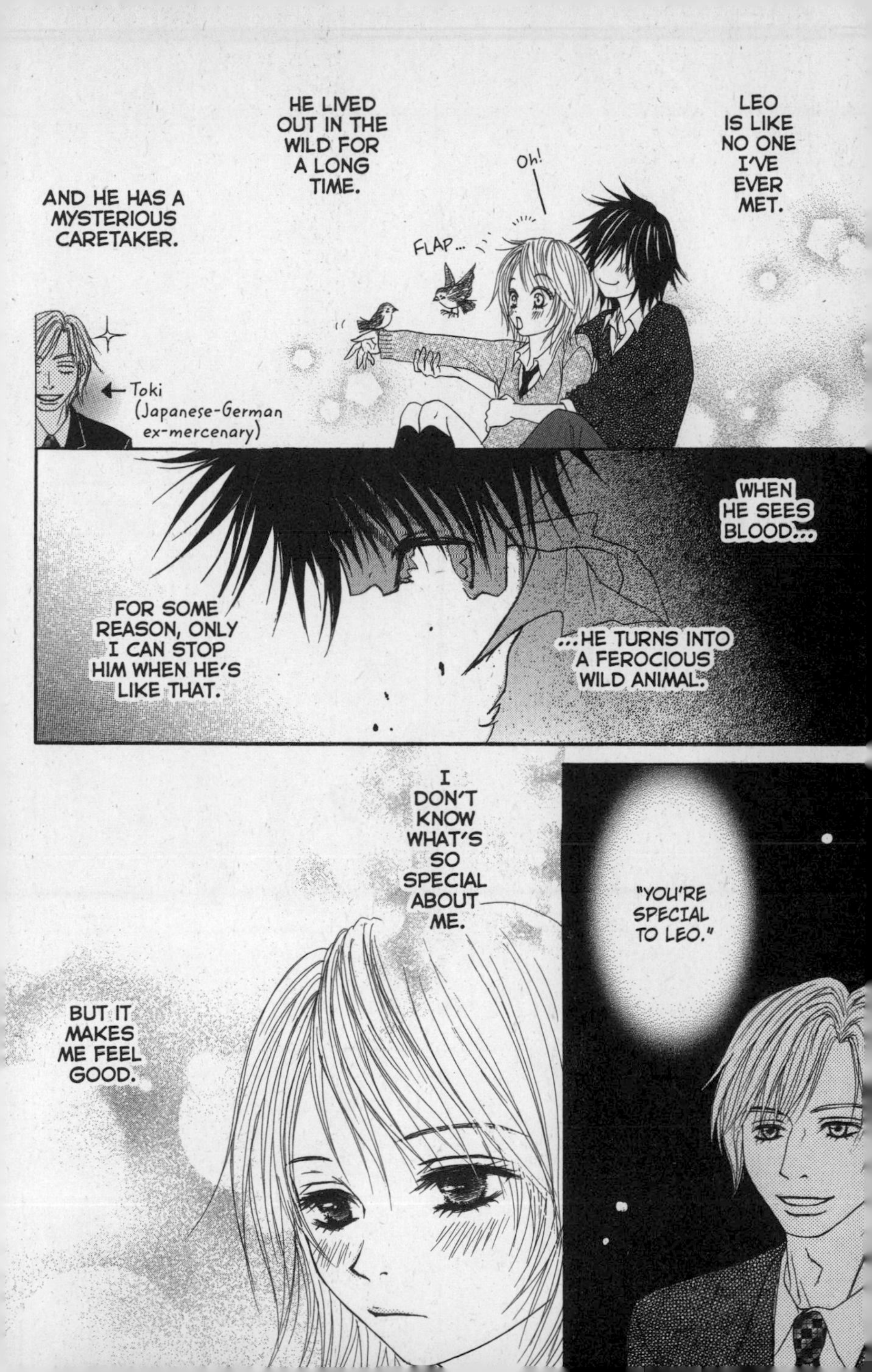
LEO IS LIKE NO ONE I'VE EVER MET.
Oh!
FLAP...
HE LIVED OUT IN THE WILD FOR A LONG TIME.
AND HE HAS A MYSTERIOUS CARETAKER.
Toki (Japanese-German ex-mercenary)
WHEN HE SEES BLOOD...
...HE TURNS INTO A FEROCIOUS WILD ANIMAL.
FOR SOME REASON, ONLY I CAN STOP HIM WHEN HE'S LIKE THAT.
"YOU'RE SPECIAL TO LEO."
I DON'T KNOW WHAT'S SO SPECIAL ABOUT ME.
BUT IT MAKES ME FEEL GOOD.

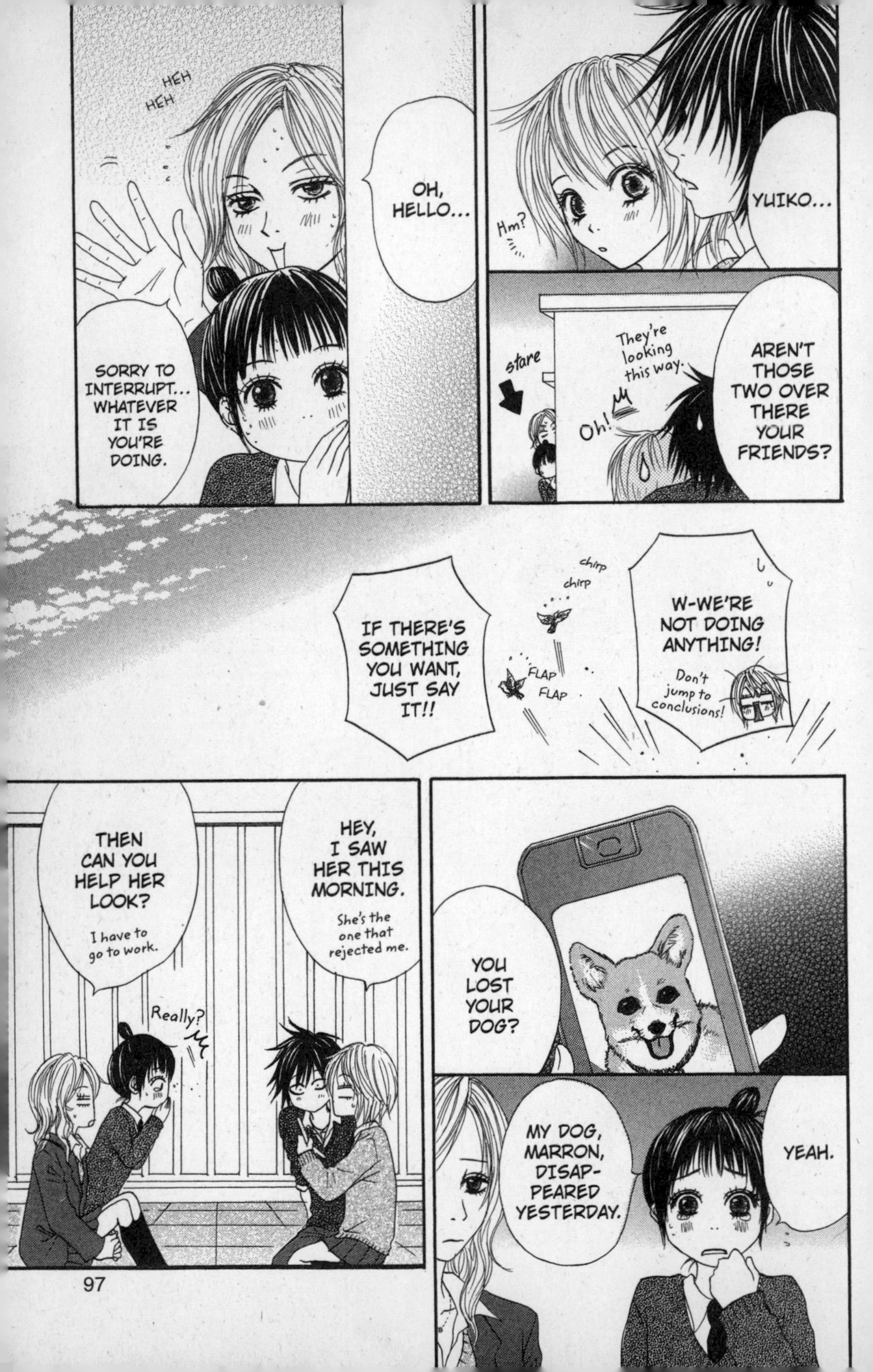
YUIKO...
Hm?
AREN'T THOSE TWO OVER THERE YOUR FRIENDS?
They're looking this way.
stare
Oh!
OH, HELLO...
HEH HEH
SORRY TO INTERRUPT... WHATEVER IT IS YOU'RE DOING.
W-WE'RE NOT DOING ANYTHING!
Don't jump to conclusions!
chirp
chirp
FLAP
FLAP
IF THERE'S SOMETHING YOU WANT, JUST SAY IT!!
YOU LOST YOUR DOG?
YEAH.
MY DOG, MARRON, DISAP-PEARED YESTERDAY.
HEY, I SAW HER THIS MORNING.
She's the one that rejected me.
THEN CAN YOU HELP HER LOOK?
I have to go to work.
Really?

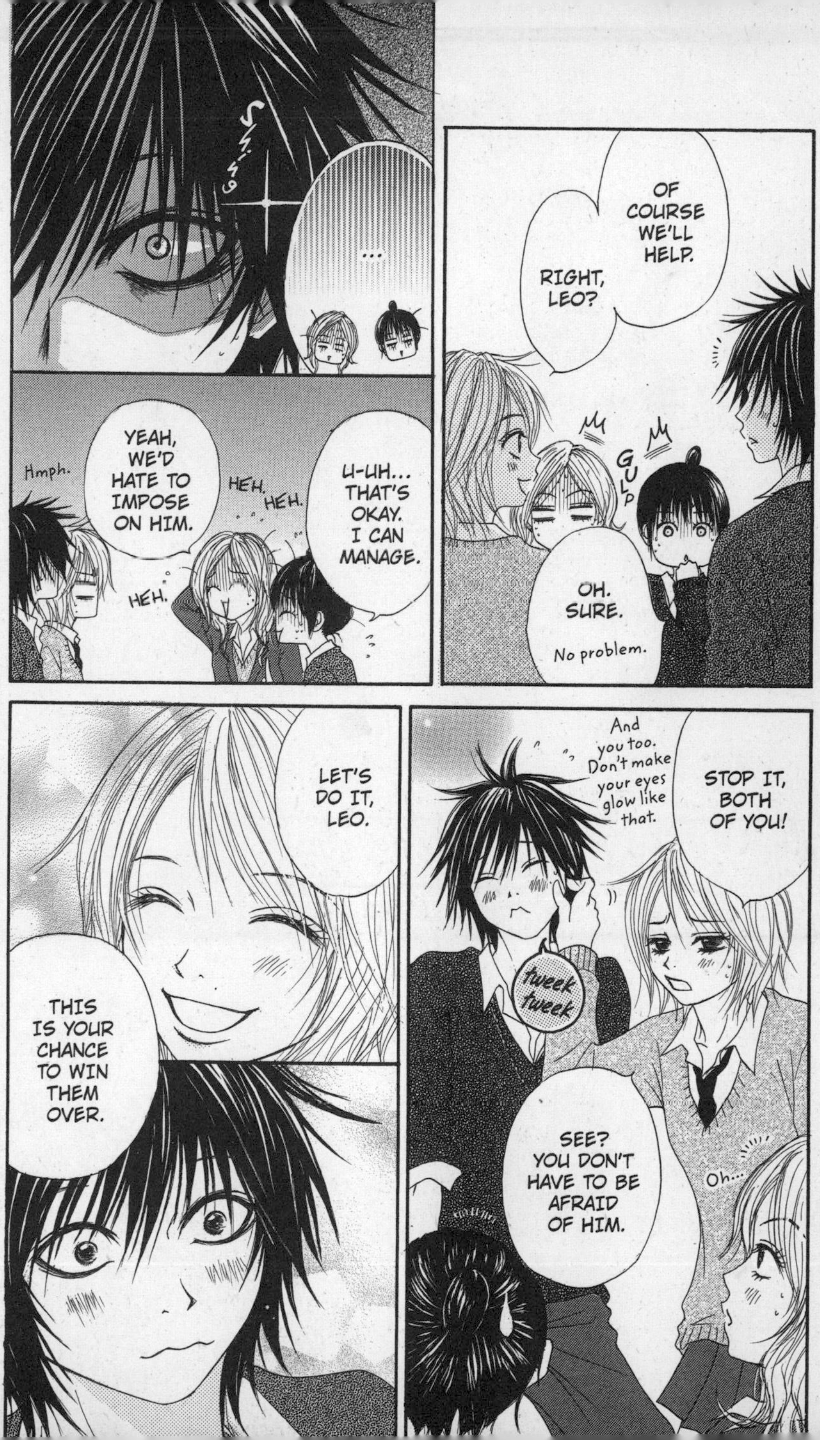
OF COURSE WE'LL HELP.
RIGHT, LEO?
GULP
OH. SURE.
No problem.
Swing
...
U-UH... THAT'S OKAY. I CAN MANAGE.
HEH. HEH.
YEAH, WE'D HATE TO IMPOSE ON HIM.
Hmph.
HEH.
STOP IT, BOTH OF YOU!
And you too. Don't make your eyes glow like that.
tweek tweek
Oh...
SEE? YOU DON'T HAVE TO BE AFRAID OF HIM.
LET'S DO IT, LEO.
THIS IS YOUR CHANCE TO WIN THEM OVER.

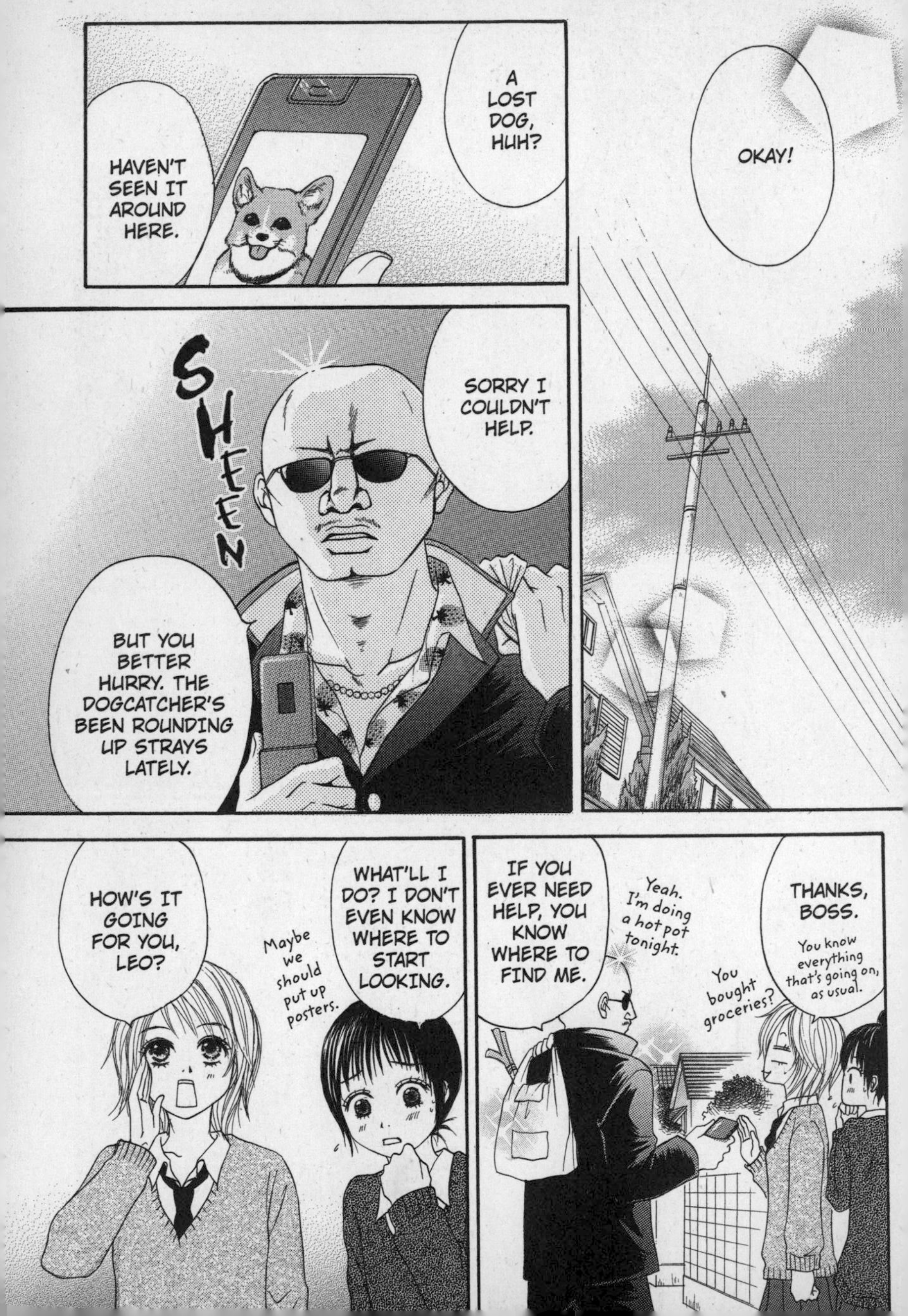
A LOST DOG, HUH?
HAVEN'T SEEN IT AROUND HERE.
SORRY I COULDN'T HELP.
SHEEN
BUT YOU BETTER HURRY. THE DOGCATCHER'S BEEN ROUNDING UP STRAYS LATELY.
OKAY!
THANKS, BOSS.
You know everything that's going on, as usual.
You bought groceries?
Yeah. I'm doing a hot pot tonight.
IF YOU EVER NEED HELP, YOU KNOW WHERE TO FIND ME.
WHAT'LL I DO? I DON'T EVEN KNOW WHERE TO START LOOKING.
Maybe we should put up posters.
HOW'S IT GOING FOR YOU, LEO?

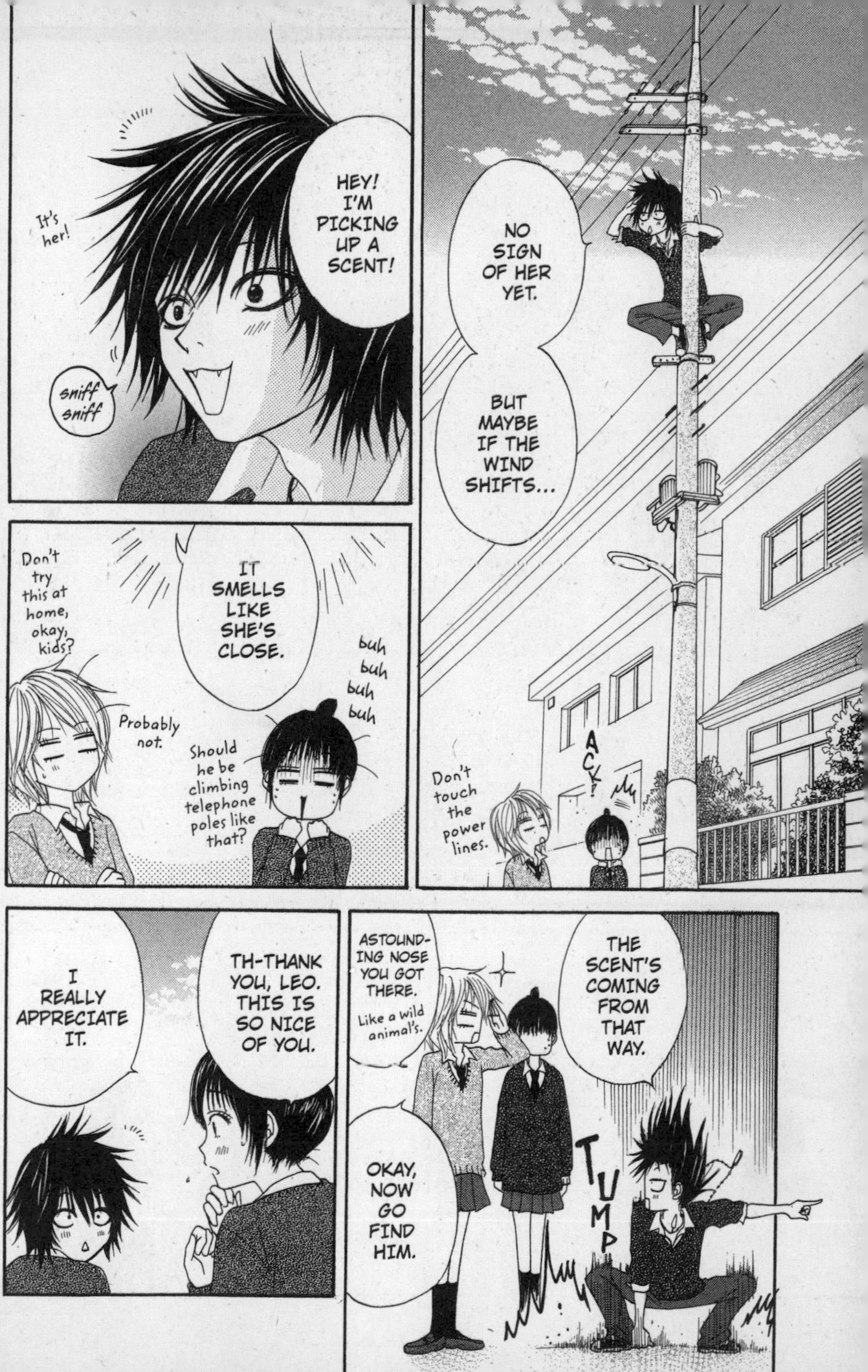
NO SIGN OF HER YET.
BUT MAYBE IF THE WIND SHIFTS...
ACK!
Don't touch the power lines.
HEY! I'M PICKING UP A SCENT!
It's her!
sniff sniff
IT SMELLS LIKE SHE'S CLOSE.
buh buh buh buh
Should he be climbing telephone poles like that?
Probably not.
Don't try this at home, okay, kids?
THE SCENT'S COMING FROM THAT WAY.
TUMP
ASTOUND-ING NOSE YOU GOT THERE.
Like a wild animal's.
OKAY, NOW GO FIND HIM.
TH-THANK YOU, LEO. THIS IS SO NICE OF YOU.
I REALLY APPRECIATE IT.

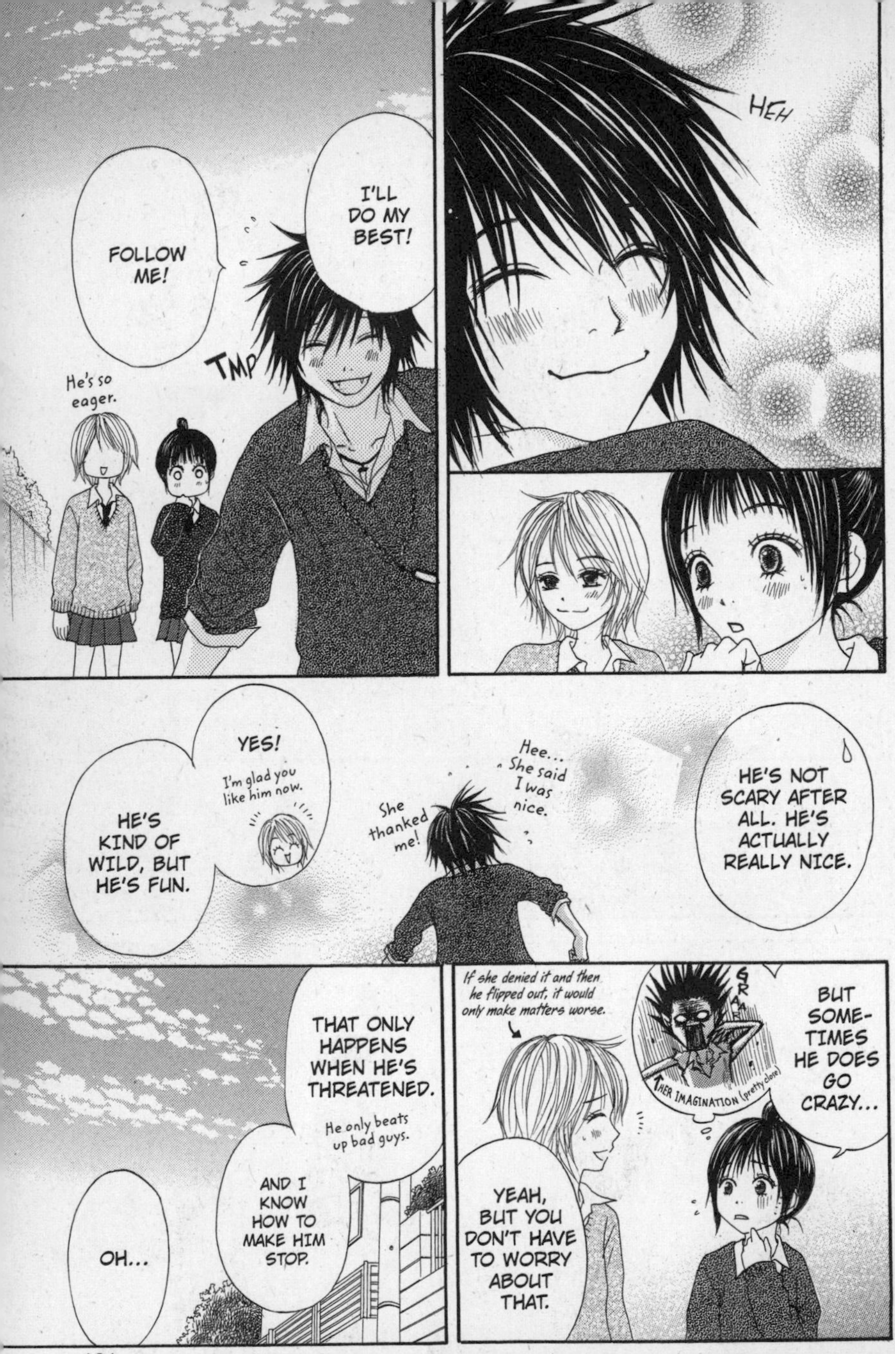
HEH
I'LL DO MY BEST!
FOLLOW ME!
TMP
He's so eager.
HE'S NOT SCARY AFTER ALL. HE'S ACTUALLY REALLY NICE.
Hee... She said I was nice.
She thanked me!
YES!
I'm glad you like him now.
HE'S KIND OF WILD, BUT HE'S FUN.
BUT SOME-TIMES HE DOES GO CRAZY...
HER IMAGINATION (pretty close)
If she denied it and then he flipped out, it would only make matters worse.
YEAH, BUT YOU DON'T HAVE TO WORRY ABOUT THAT.
THAT ONLY HAPPENS WHEN HE'S THREATENED.
He only beats up bad guys.
AND I KNOW HOW TO MAKE HIM STOP.
OH...

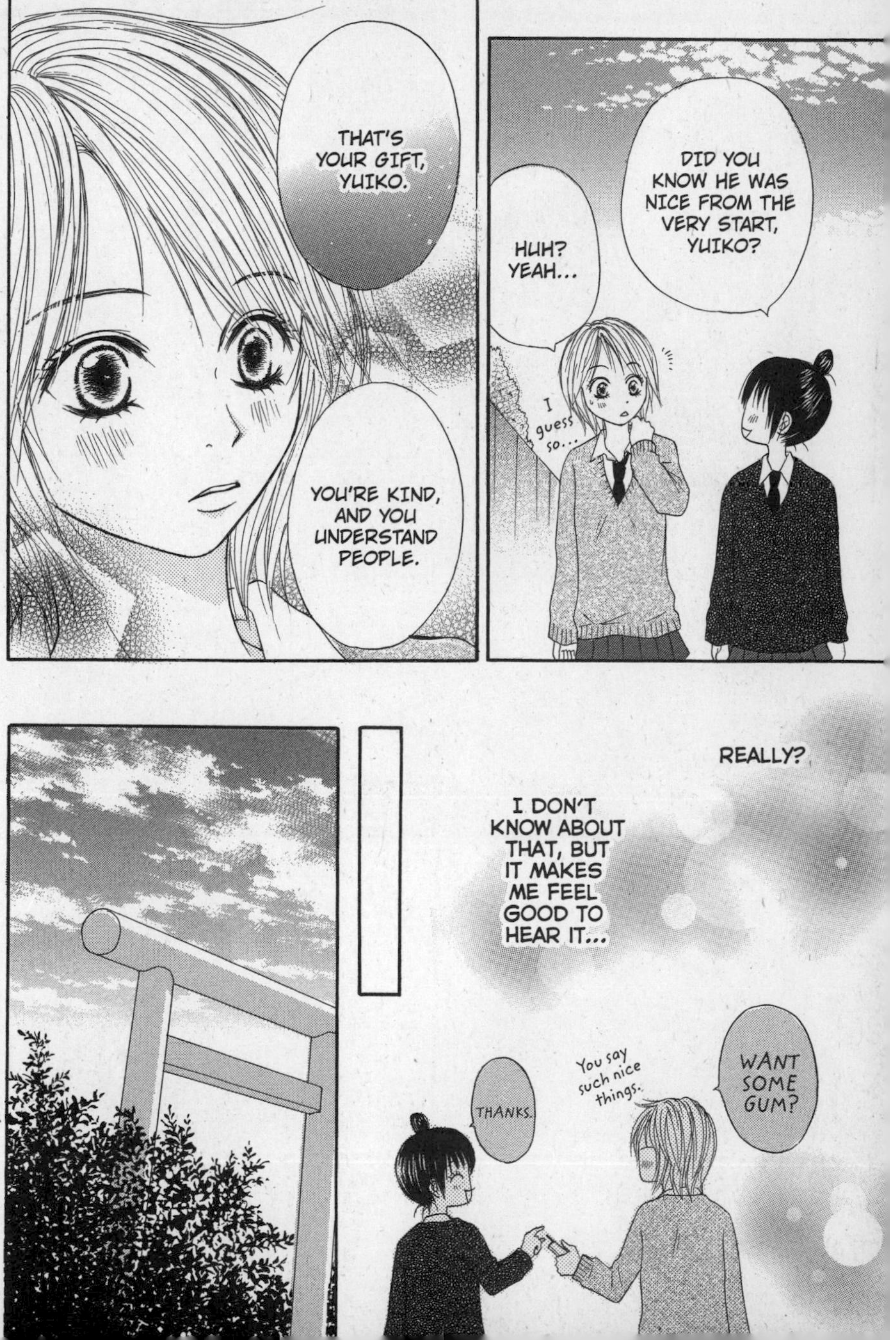
DID YOU KNOW HE WAS NICE FROM THE VERY START, YUIKO?
HUH? YEAH...
I guess so...
THAT'S YOUR GIFT, YUIKO.
YOU'RE KIND, AND YOU UNDERSTAND PEOPLE.
REALLY?
I DON'T KNOW ABOUT THAT, BUT IT MAKES ME FEEL GOOD TO HEAR IT...
WANT SOME GUM?
You say such nice things.
THANKS.

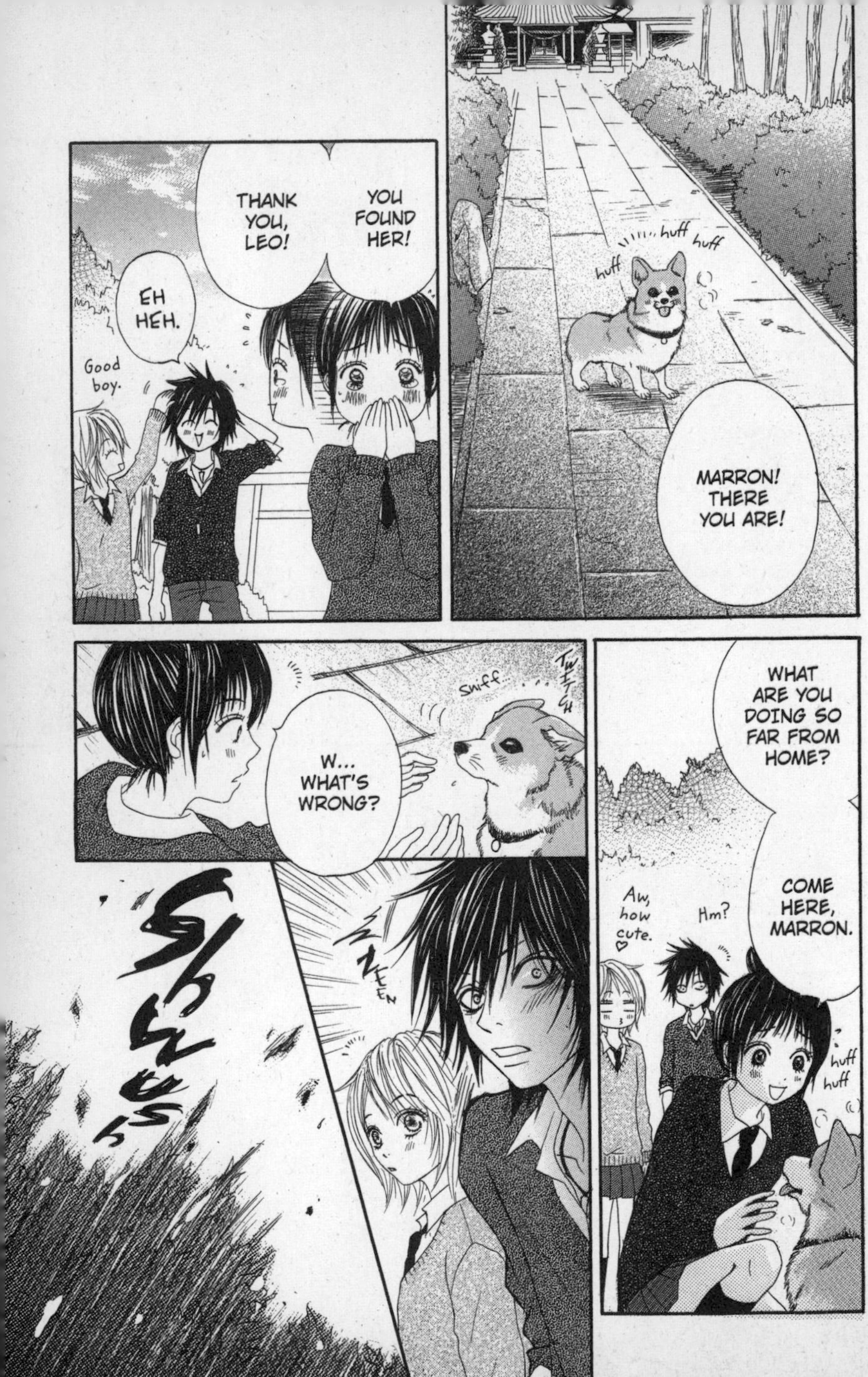
huff huff
huff
MARRON! THERE YOU ARE!
YOU FOUND HER!
THANK YOU, LEO!
EH HEH.
Good boy.
WHAT ARE YOU DOING SO FAR FROM HOME?
COME HERE, MARRON.
huff huff
Hm?
Aw, how cute.
TWITCH
Sniff...
W... WHAT'S WRONG?

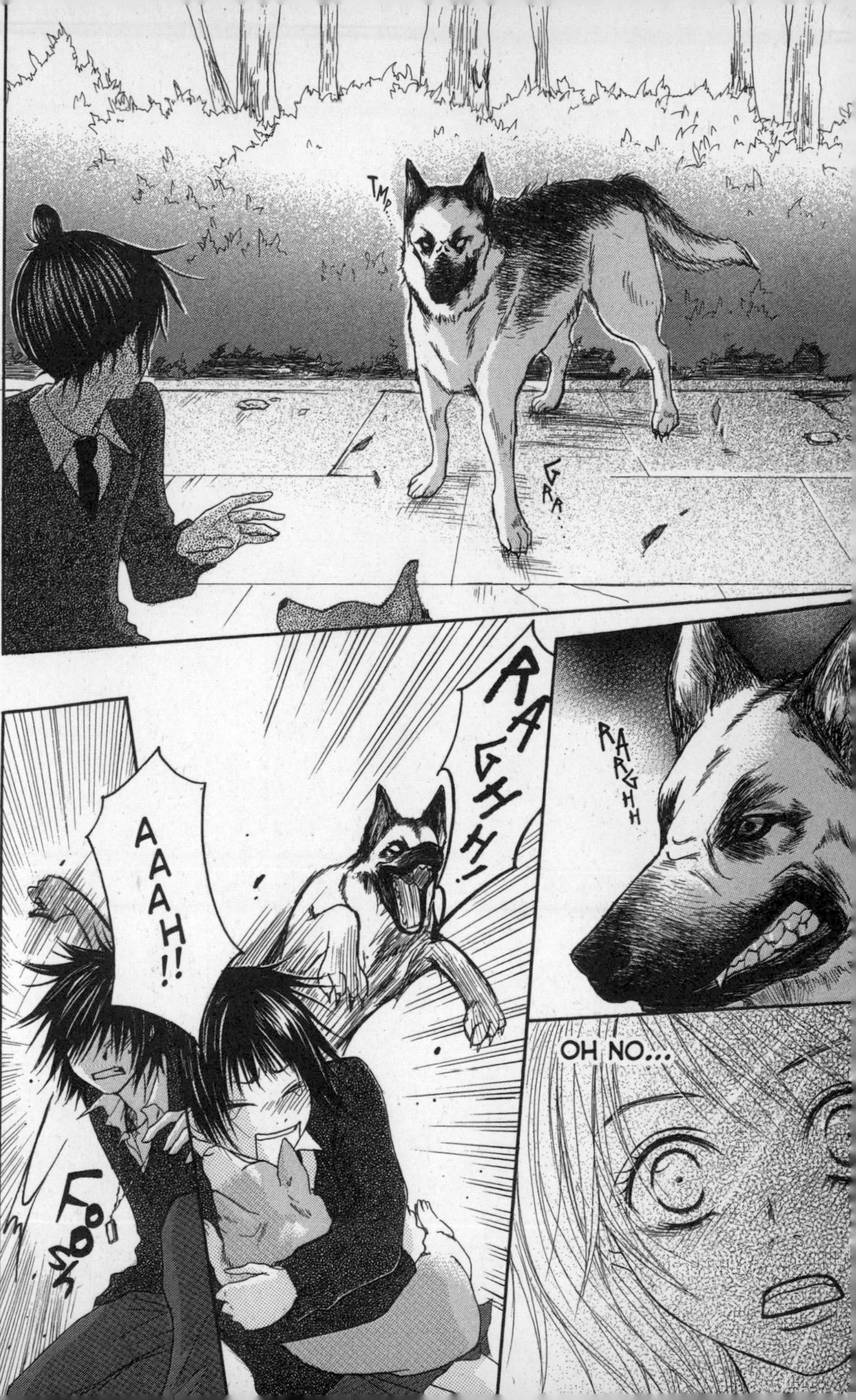
TMP...
GRR...
RARGHH
OH NO...
RAGHH!
AAAH!!

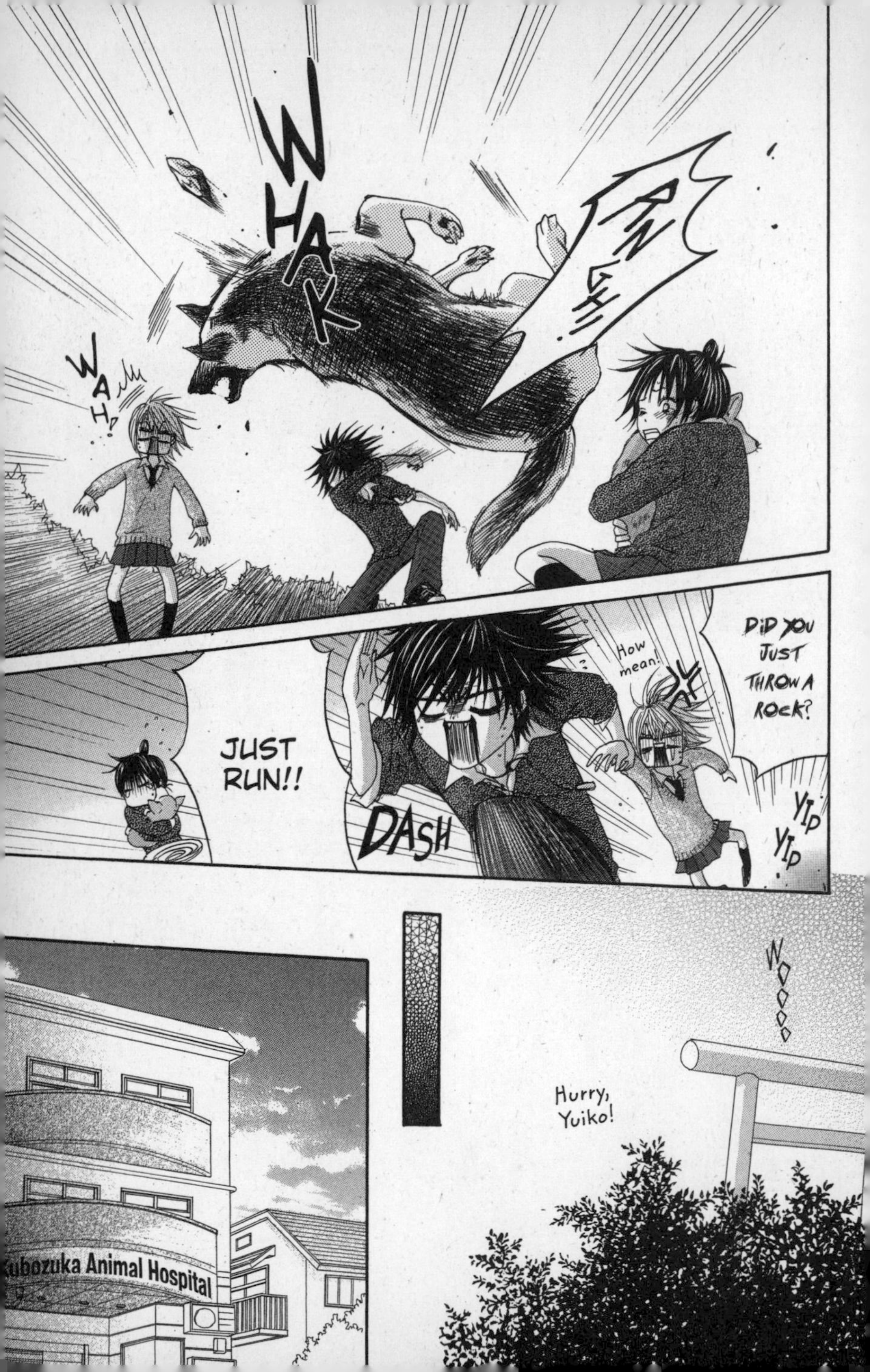
WHAK
ANGH!!
WAH
DID YOU JUST THROW A ROCK?
YIP YIP
How mean!
DASH
JUST RUN!!
WOOOOO
Hurry, Yuiko!
Kubozuka Animal Hospital

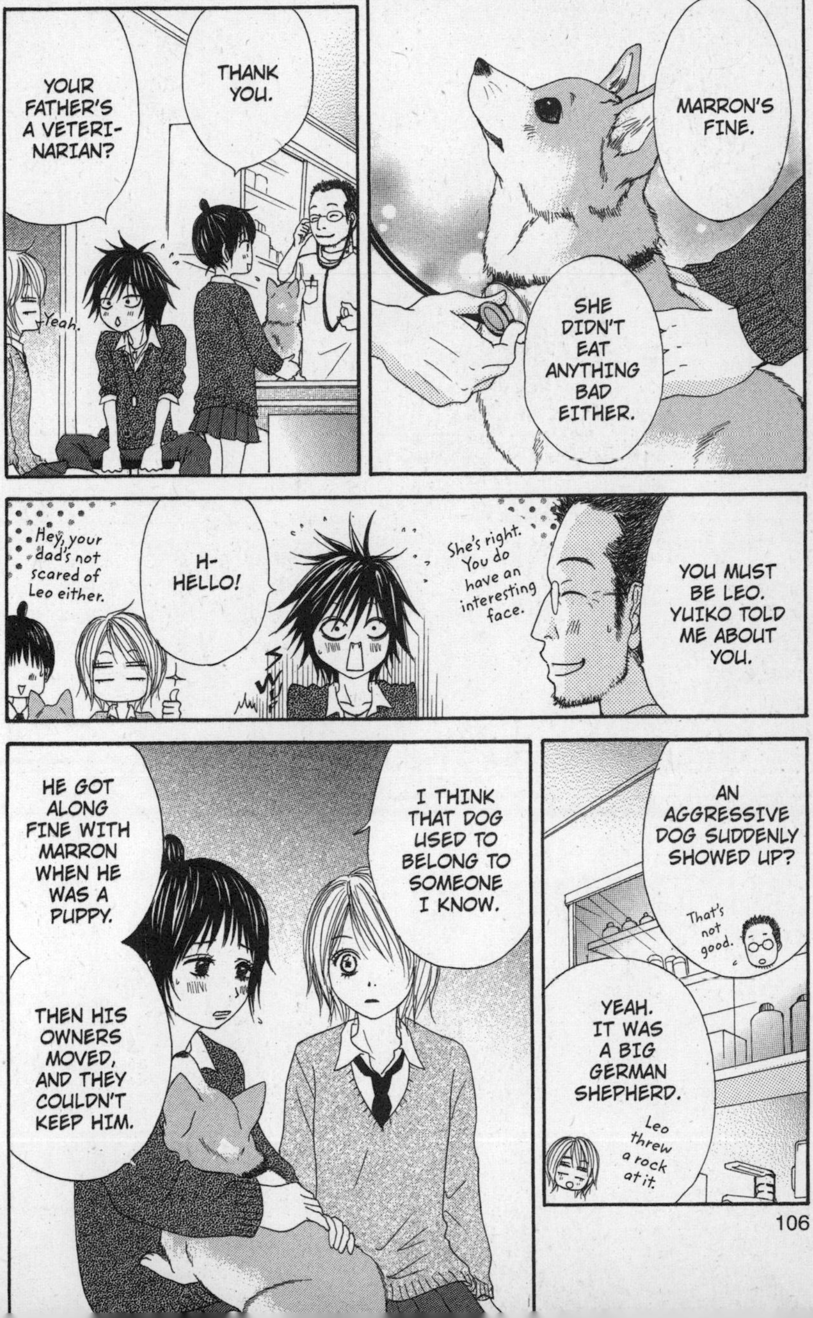
MARRON'S FINE.
SHE DIDN'T EAT ANYTHING BAD EITHER.
THANK YOU.
YOUR FATHER'S A VETERI-NARIAN?
Yeah.
YOU MUST BE LEO. YUIKO TOLD ME ABOUT YOU.
She's right. You do have an interesting face.
H-HELLO!
Hey, your dad's not scared of Leo either.
AN AGGRESSIVE DOG SUDDENLY SHOWED UP?
That's not good.
YEAH. IT WAS A BIG GERMAN SHEPHERD.
Leo threw a rock at it.
I THINK THAT DOG USED TO BELONG TO SOMEONE I KNOW.
HE GOT ALONG FINE WITH MARRON WHEN HE WAS A PUPPY.
THEN HIS OWNERS MOVED, AND THEY COULDN'T KEEP HIM.

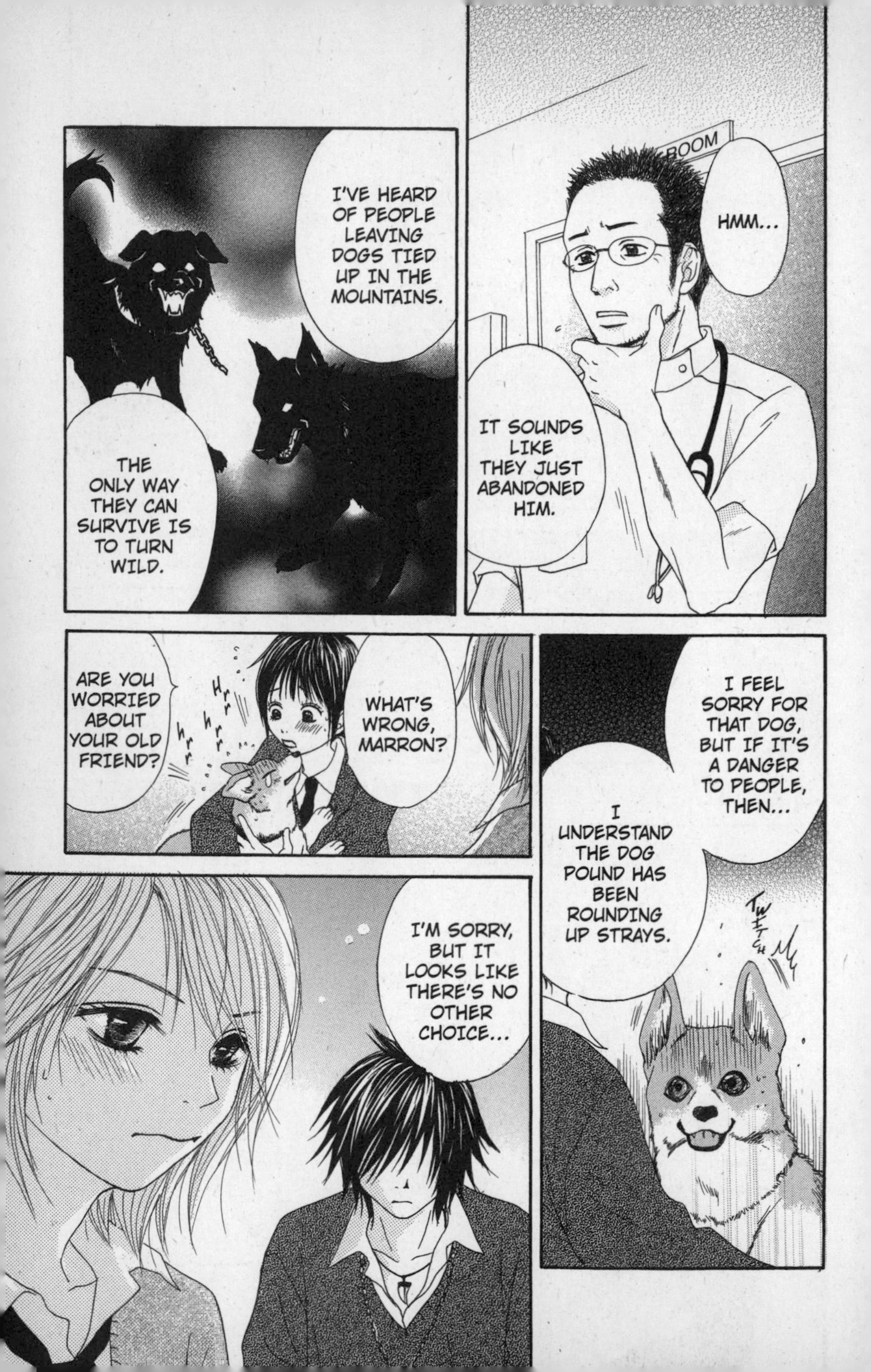
ROOM
HMM...
IT SOUNDS LIKE THEY JUST ABANDONED HIM.
I'VE HEARD OF PEOPLE LEAVING DOGS TIED UP IN THE MOUNTAINS.
THE ONLY WAY THEY CAN SURVIVE IS TO TURN WILD.
I FEEL SORRY FOR THAT DOG, BUT IF IT'S A DANGER TO PEOPLE, THEN...
I UNDERSTAND THE DOG POUND HAS BEEN ROUNDING UP STRAYS.
TWITCH
WHAT'S WRONG, MARRON?
Hrr hrr hrr
ARE YOU WORRIED ABOUT YOUR OLD FRIEND?
I'M SORRY, BUT IT LOOKS LIKE THERE'S NO OTHER CHOICE...

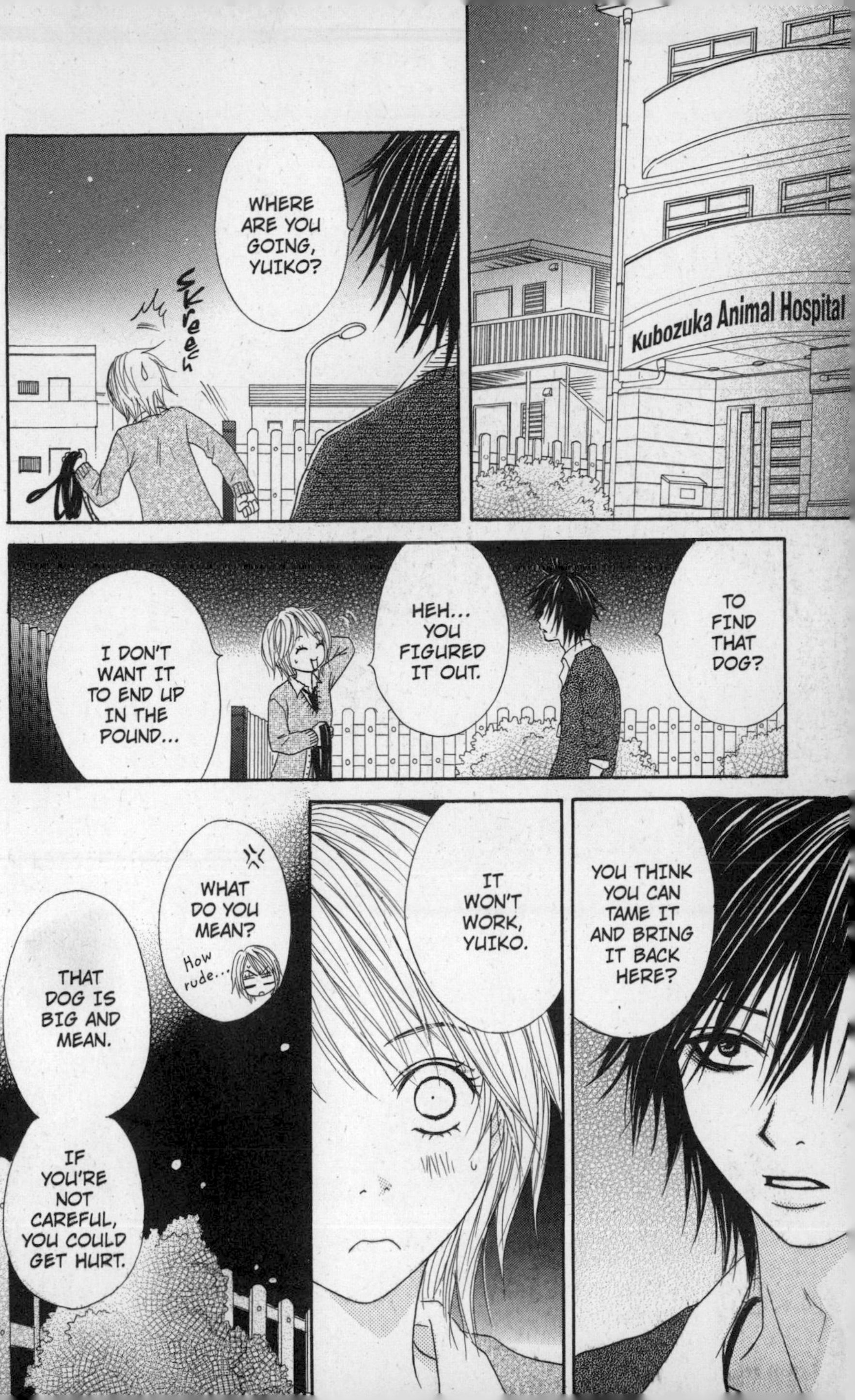
Kubozuka Animal Hospital
WHERE ARE YOU GOING, YUIKO?
SKreech
TO FIND THAT DOG?
HEH... YOU FIGURED IT OUT.
I DON'T WANT IT TO END UP IN THE POUND...
YOU THINK YOU CAN TAME IT AND BRING IT BACK HERE?
IT WON'T WORK, YUIKO.
WHAT DO YOU MEAN?
How rude...
THAT DOG IS BIG AND MEAN.
IF YOU'RE NOT CAREFUL, YOU COULD GET HURT.

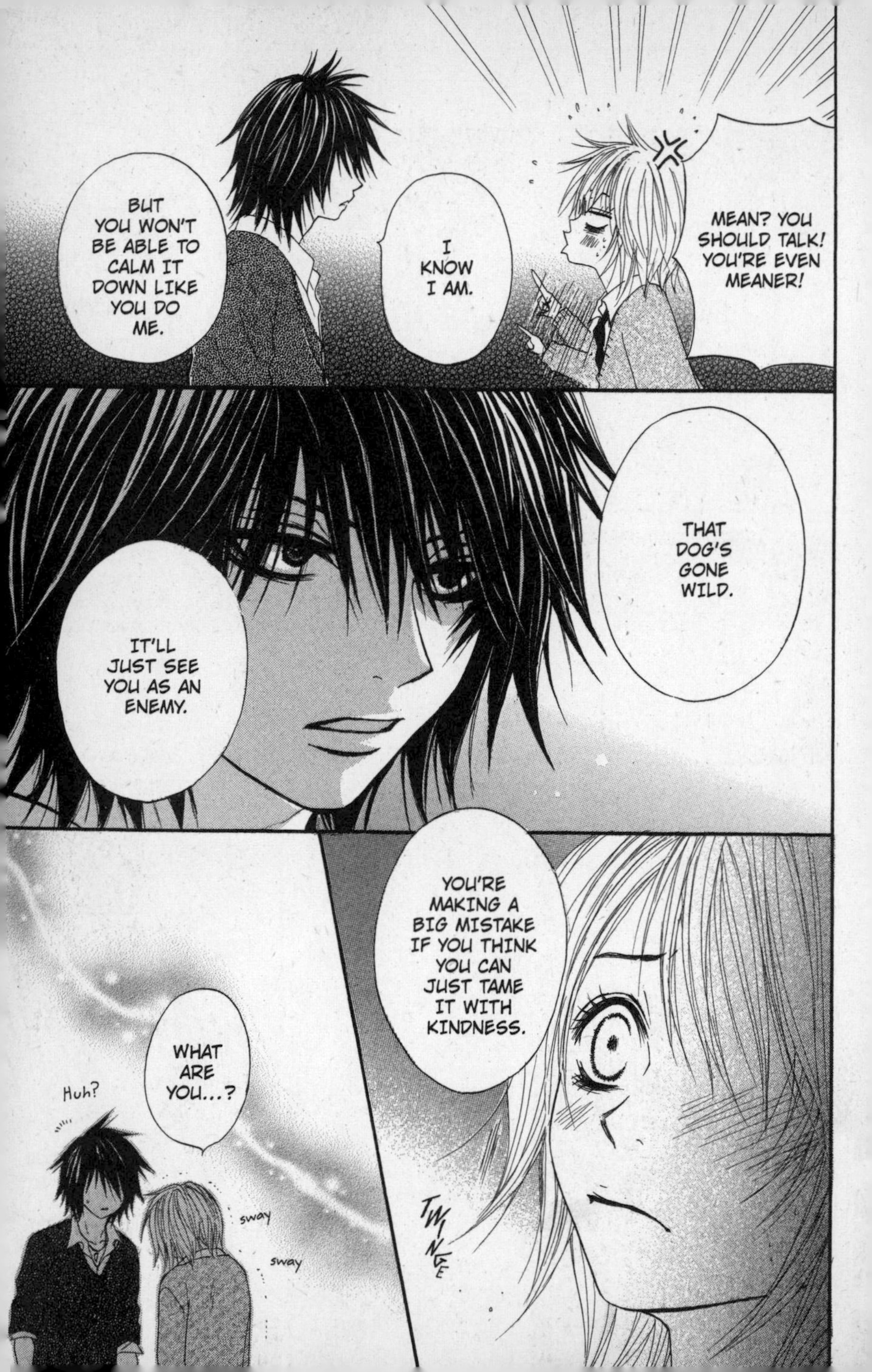
MEAN? YOU SHOULD TALK! YOU'RE EVEN MEANER!
I KNOW I AM.
BUT YOU WON'T BE ABLE TO CALM IT DOWN LIKE YOU DO ME.
THAT DOG'S GONE WILD.
IT'LL JUST SEE YOU AS AN ENEMY.
YOU'RE MAKING A BIG MISTAKE IF YOU THINK YOU CAN JUST TAME IT WITH KINDNESS.
TWINGE
WHAT ARE YOU...?
Huh?
sway
sway

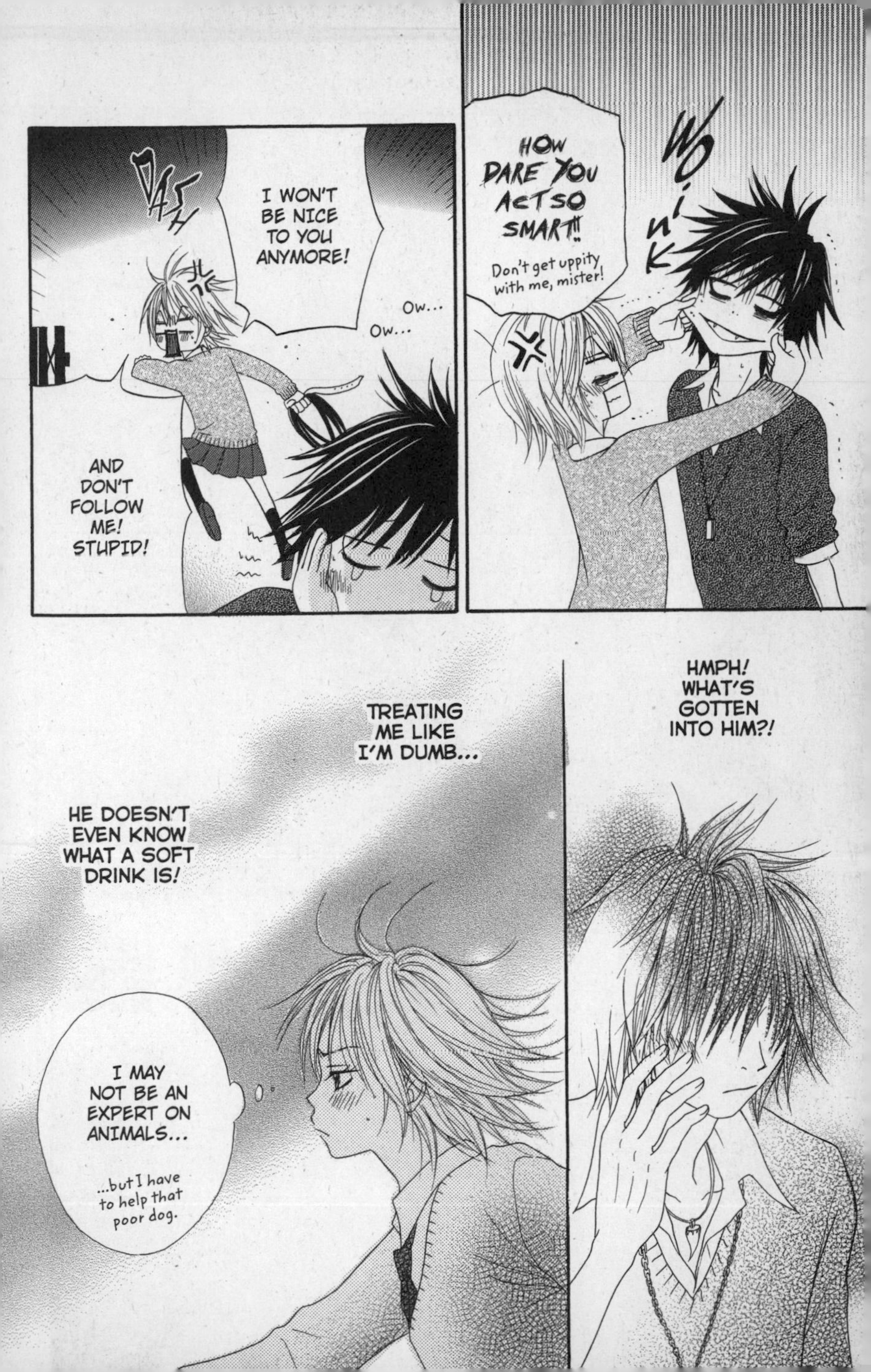
WOINK
HOW DARE YOU ACT SO SMART!!
Don't get uppity with me, mister!
DASH
I WON'T BE NICE TO YOU ANYMORE!
OW... OW...
AND DON'T FOLLOW ME! STUPID!
HMPH! WHAT'S GOTTEN INTO HIM?!
TREATING ME LIKE I'M DUMB...
HE DOESN'T EVEN KNOW WHAT A SOFT DRINK IS!
I MAY NOT BE AN EXPERT ON ANIMALS...
...but I have to help that poor dog.

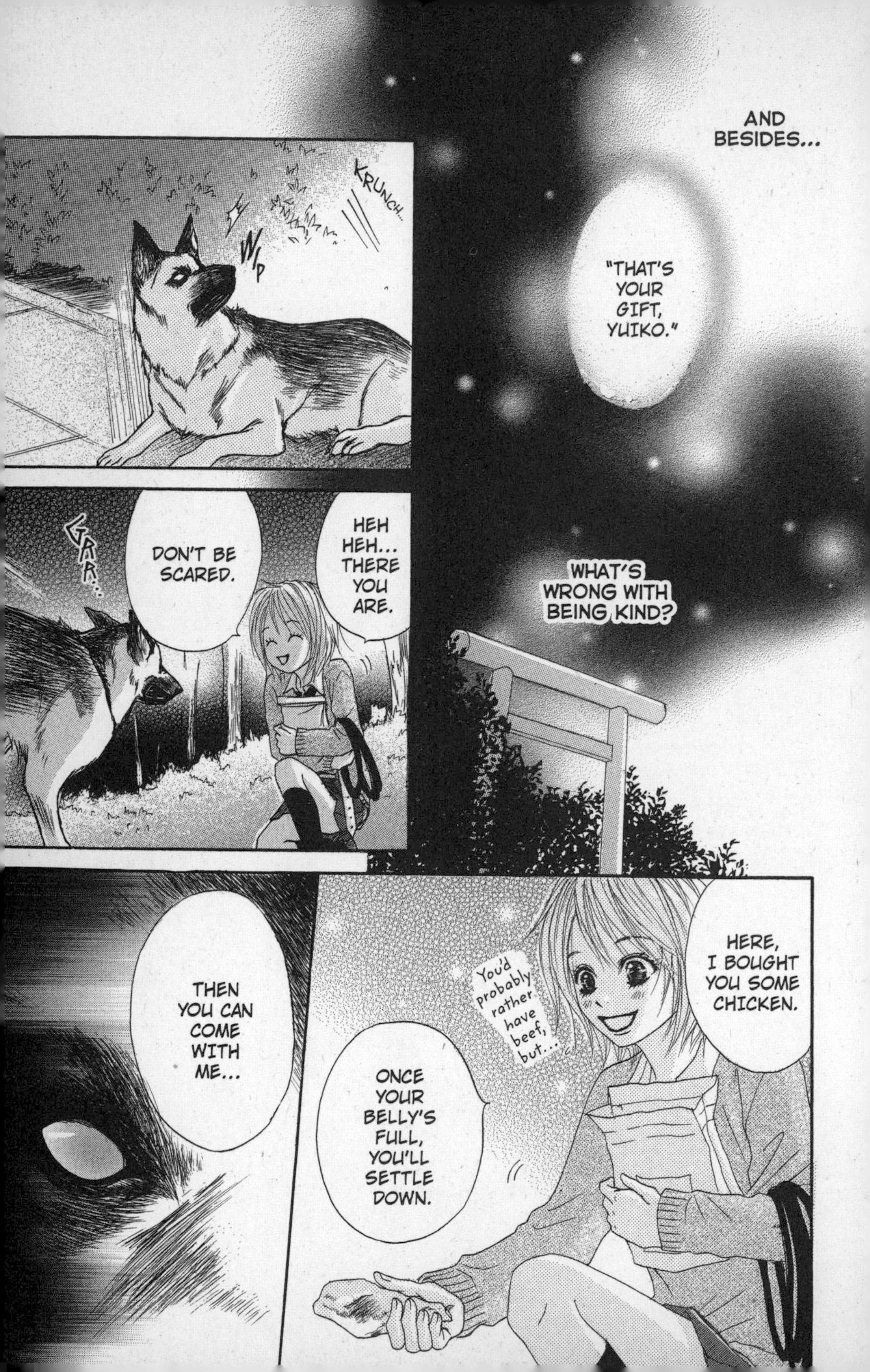
AND BESIDES...
"THAT'S YOUR GIFT, YUIKO."
WHAT'S WRONG WITH BEING KIND?
KRUNCH...
WIP
HEH HEH... THERE YOU ARE.
DON'T BE SCARED.
GRR...
HERE, I BOUGHT YOU SOME CHICKEN.
You'd probably rather have beef, but...
ONCE YOUR BELLY'S FULL, YOU'LL SETTLE DOWN.
THEN YOU CAN COME WITH ME...

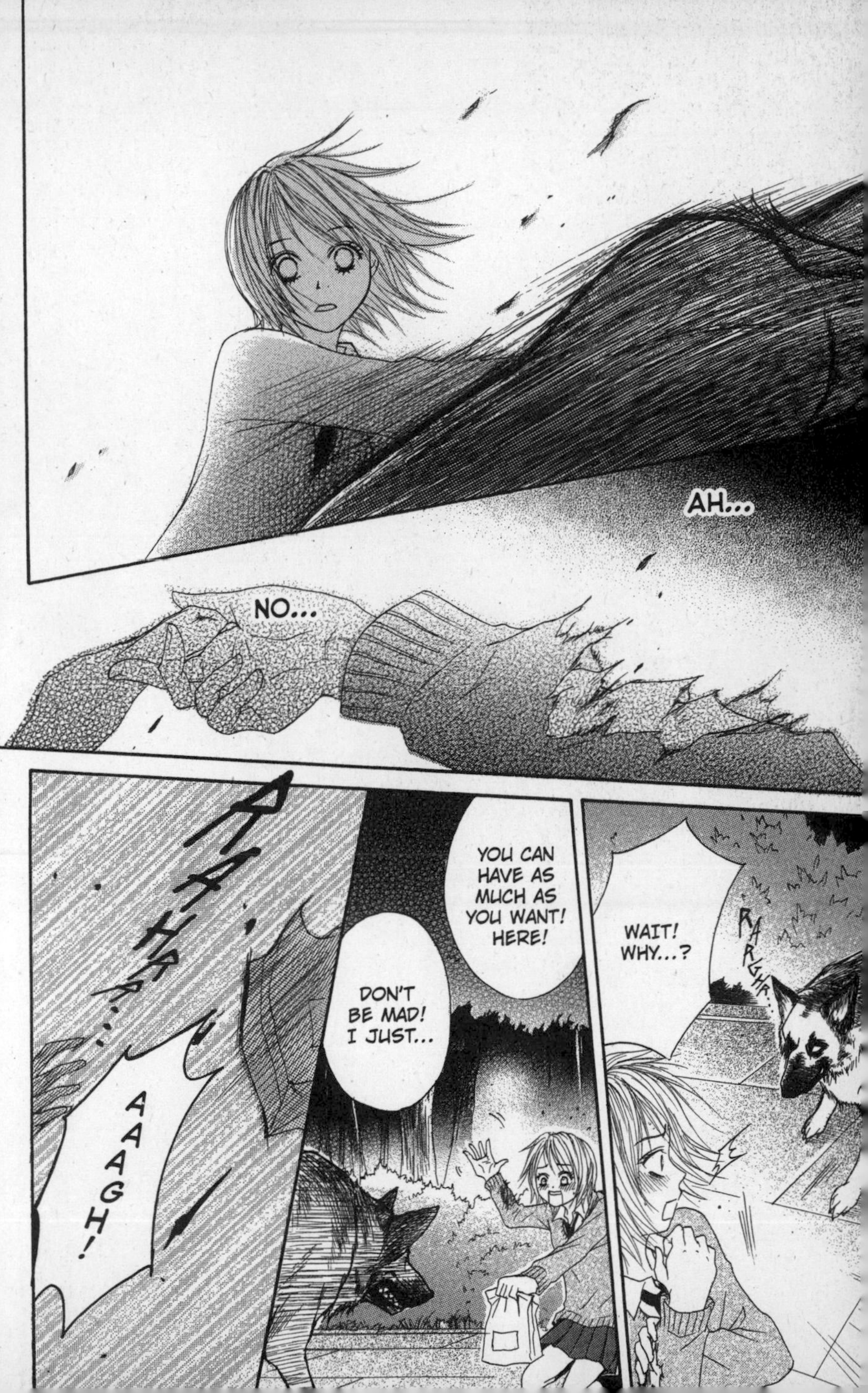
AH...
NO...
WAIT! WHY...?
RARGHR
YOU CAN HAVE AS MUCH AS YOU WANT! HERE!
DON'T BE MAD! I JUST...
RAHRR...
AAAGH!

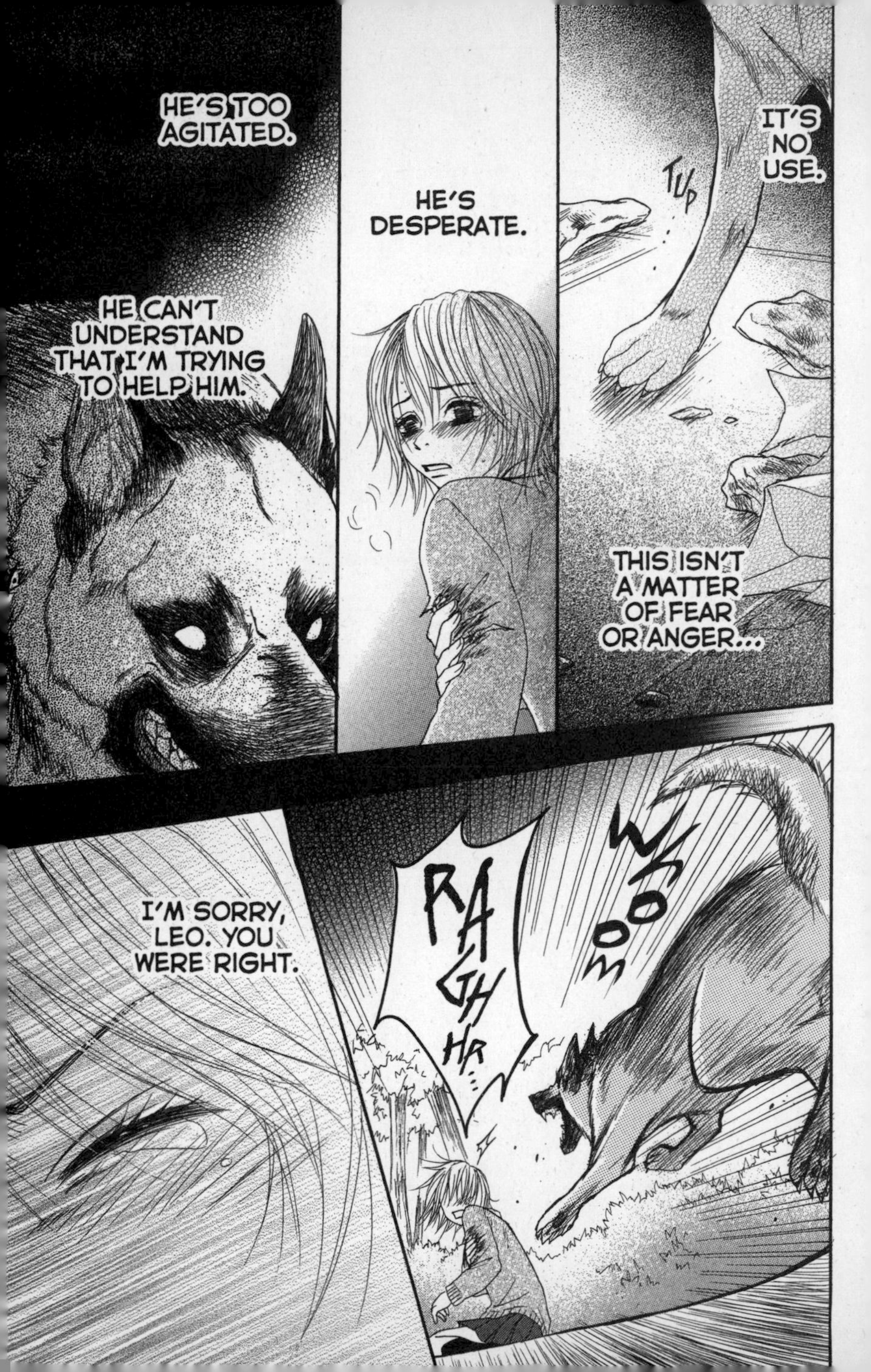
IT'S NO USE.
TUP
THIS ISN'T A MATTER OF FEAR OR ANGER...
HE'S DESPERATE.
HE'S TOO AGITATED.
HE CAN'T UNDERSTAND THAT I'M TRYING TO HELP HIM.
WHOOOM
RAGHHR...
I'M SORRY, LEO. YOU WERE RIGHT.

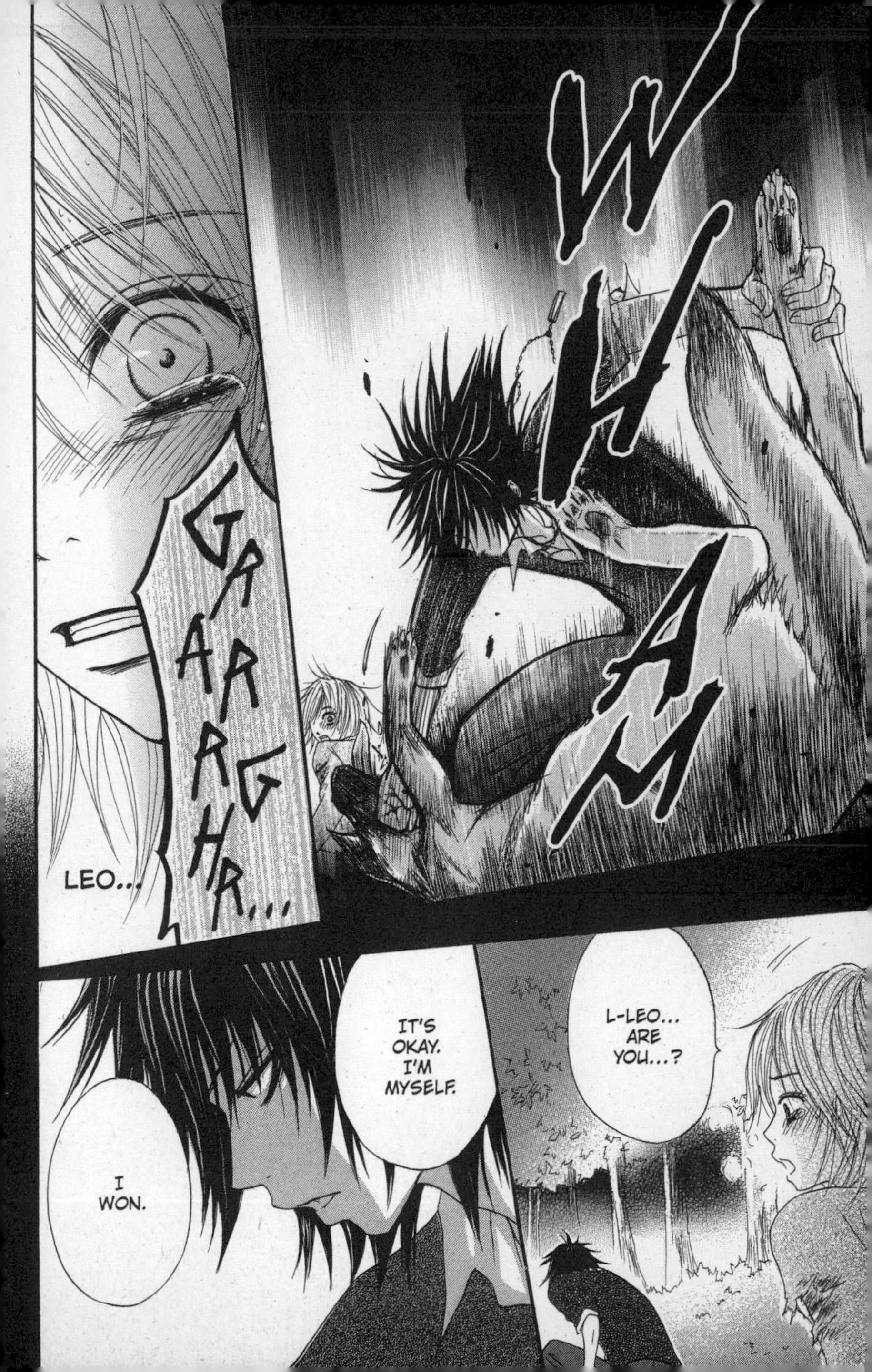
WHAM
GRARRGHR...
LEO...
L-LEO... ARE YOU...?
IT'S OKAY. I'M MYSELF.
I WON.

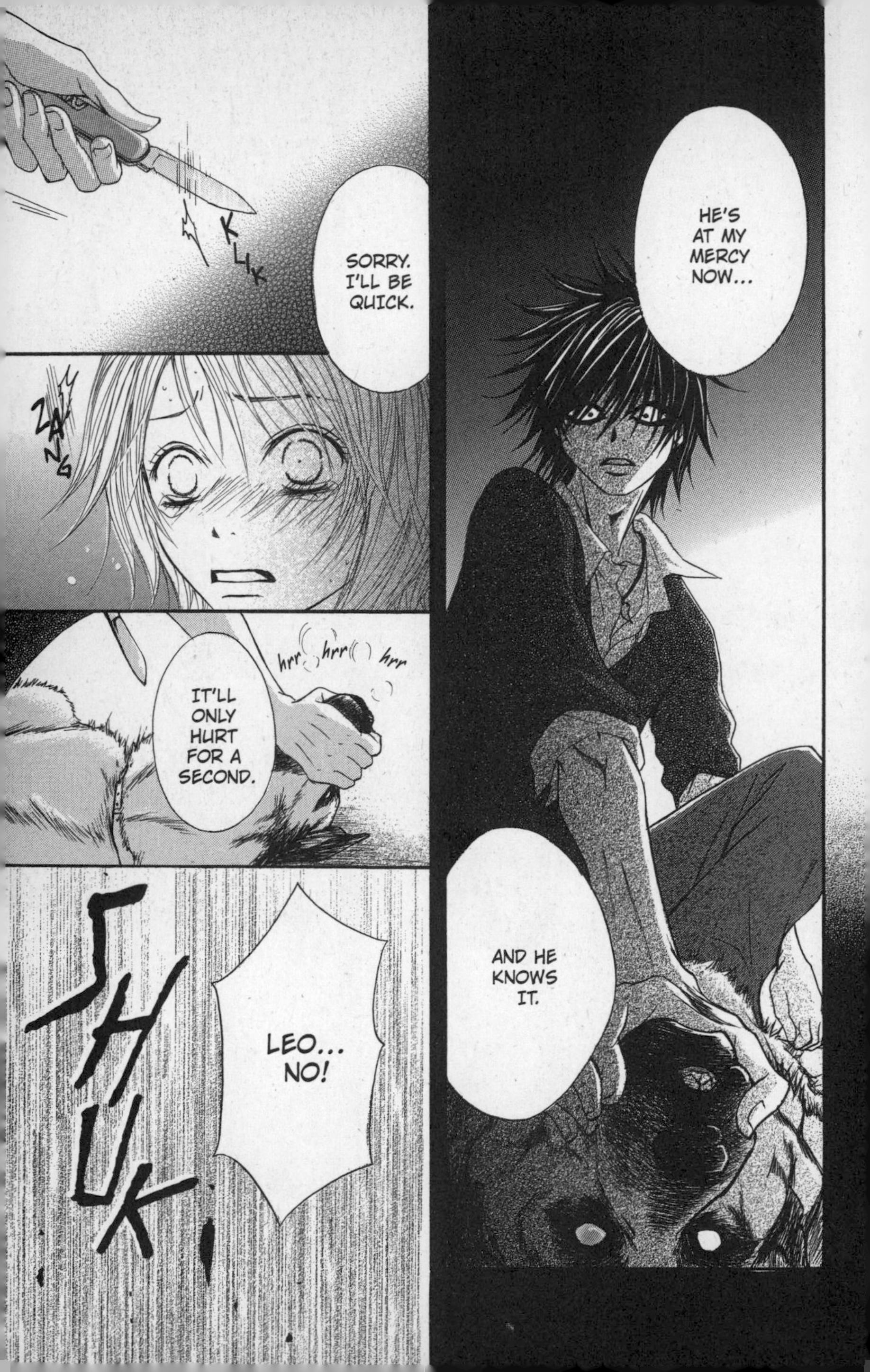
HE'S AT MY MERCY NOW...
AND HE KNOWS IT.
SORRY. I'LL BE QUICK.
KLIK
ZANG
IT'LL ONLY HURT FOR A SECOND.
hrr hrr hrr
LEO... NO!
SHUK!

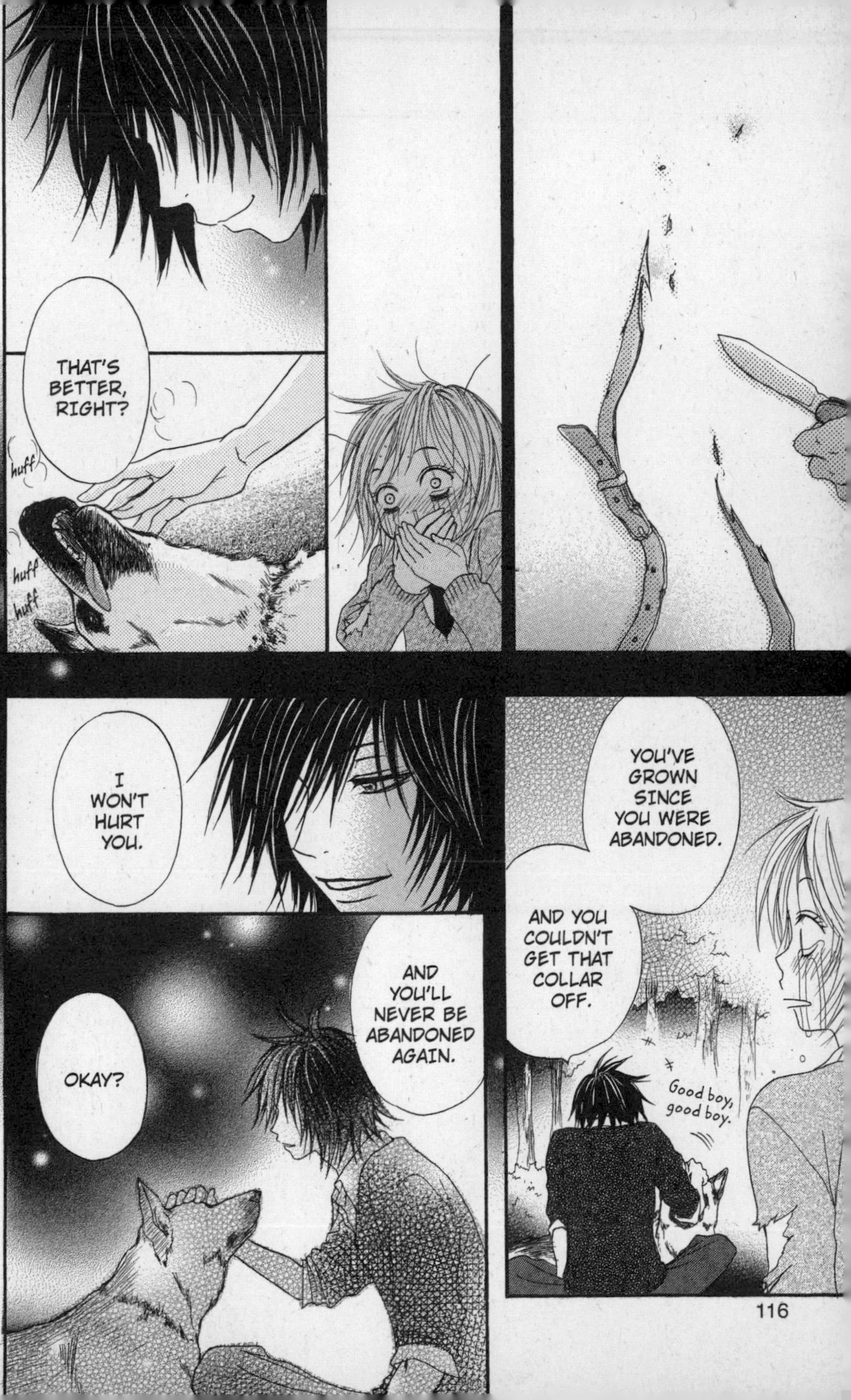
THAT'S BETTER, RIGHT?
huff
huff
huff
YOU'VE GROWN SINCE YOU WERE ABANDONED.
AND YOU COULDN'T GET THAT COLLAR OFF.
Good boy, good boy.
I WON'T HURT YOU.
AND YOU'LL NEVER BE ABANDONED AGAIN.
OKAY?

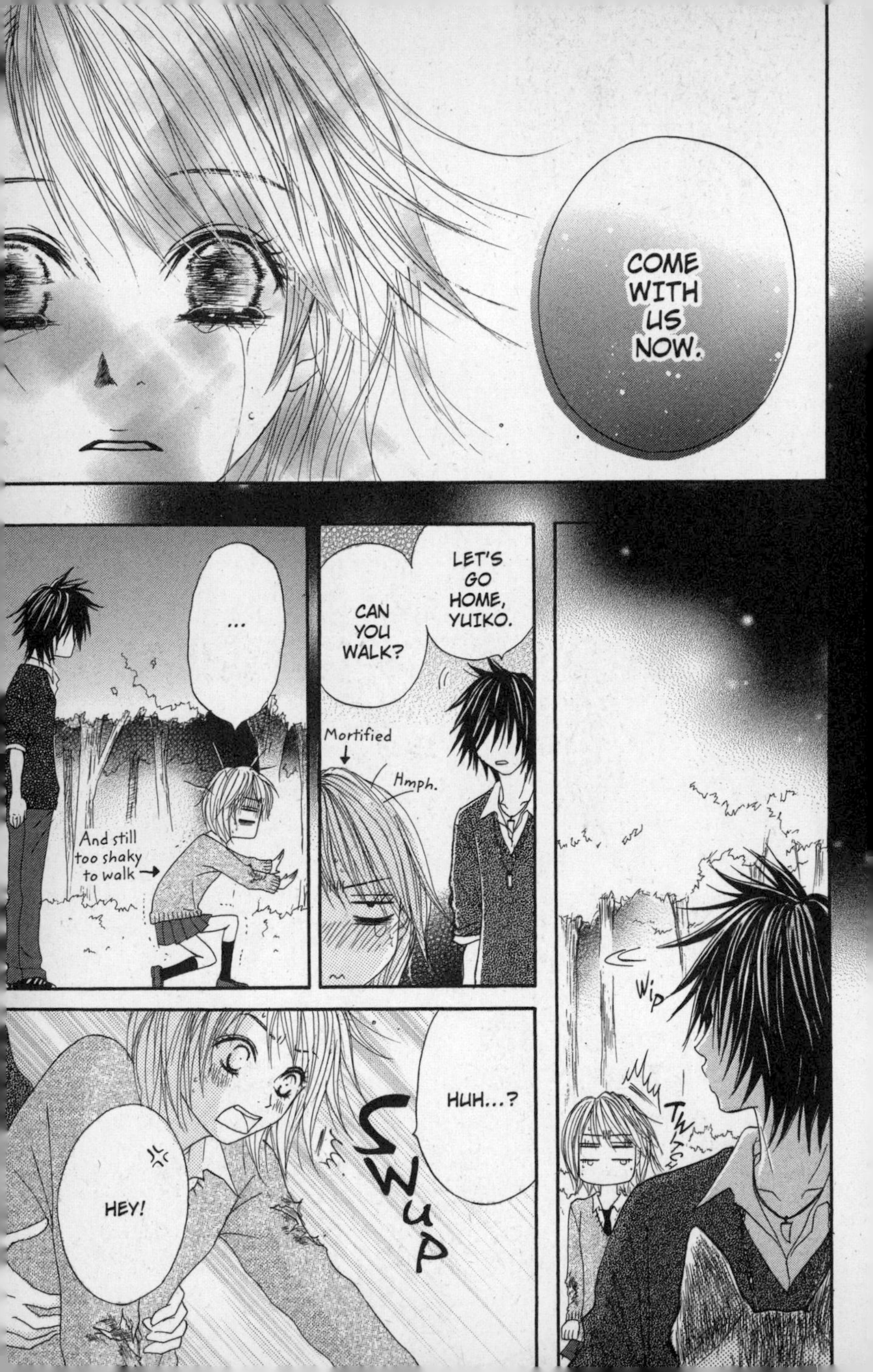

COME WITH US NOW.
Wip
TWITCH
LET'S GO HOME, YUIKO.
CAN YOU WALK?
Mortified
Hmph.
...
And still too shaky to walk
HUH...?
SWUP
HEY!

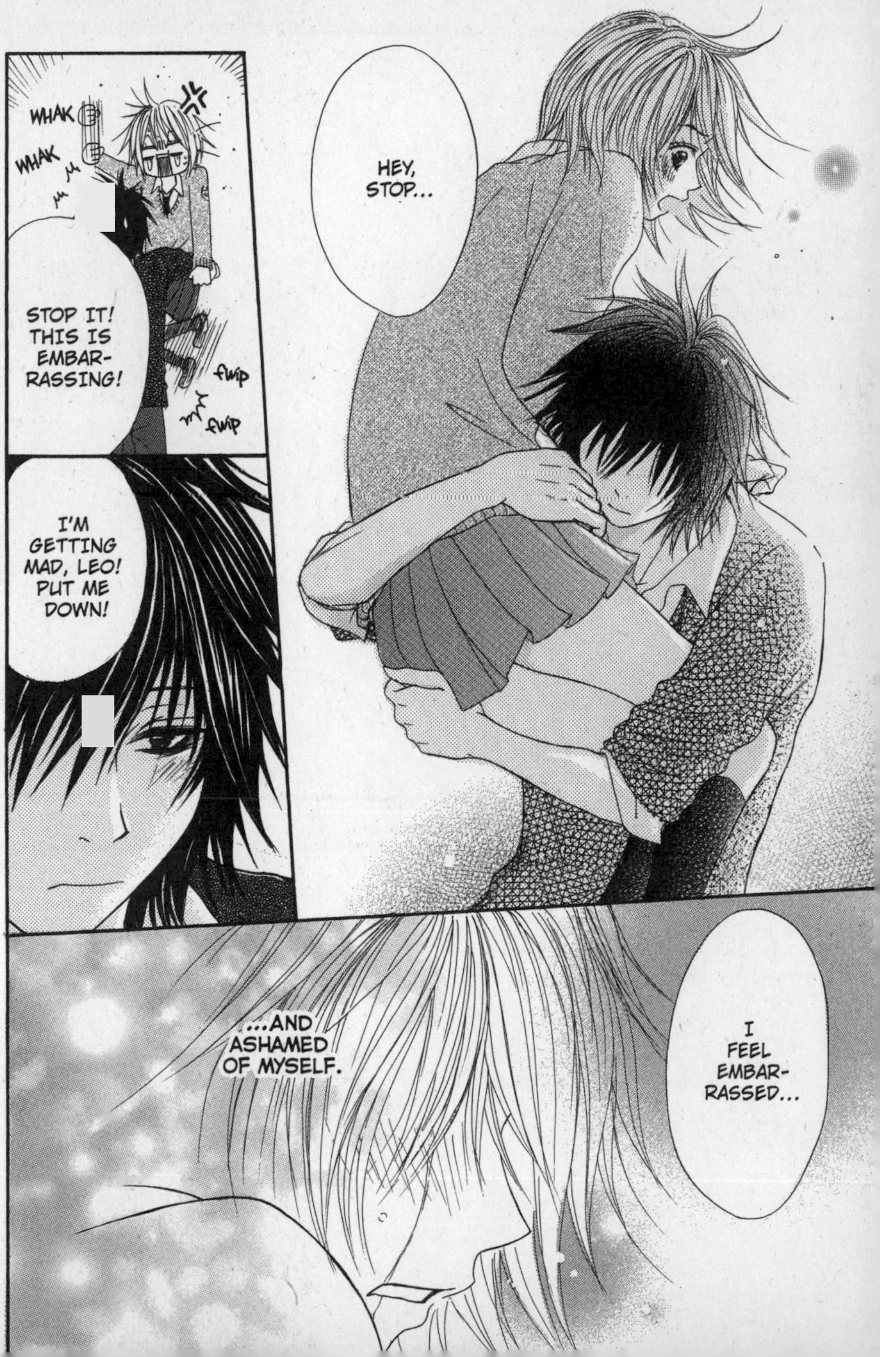
HEY, STOP...
WHAK
WHAK
STOP IT! THIS IS EMBARRASSING!
fwip
fwip
I'M GETTING MAD, LEO! PUT ME DOWN!
I FEEL EMBARRASSED...
...AND ASHAMED OF MYSELF.

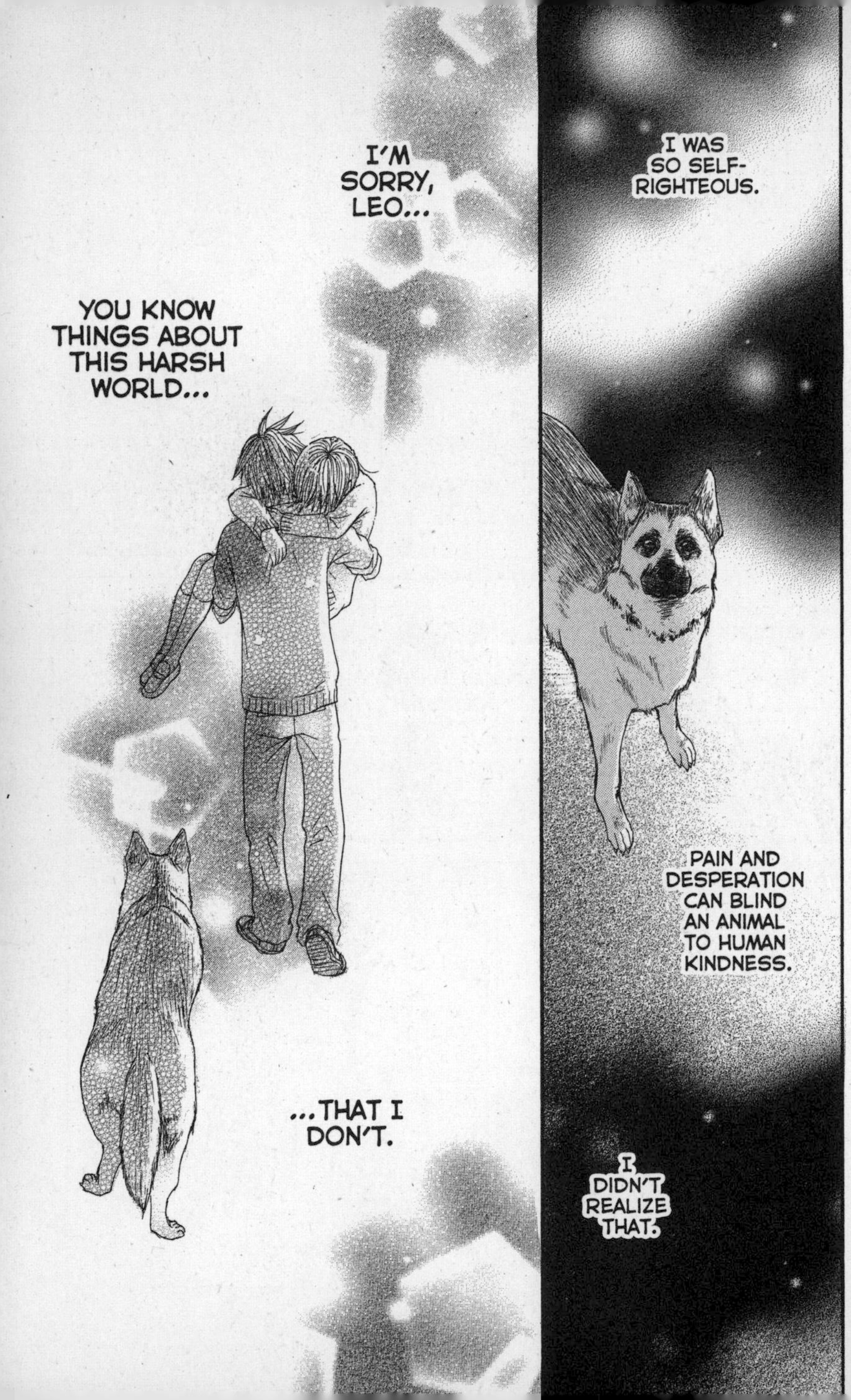
I WAS SO SELF-RIGHTEOUS.
PAIN AND DESPERATION CAN BLIND AN ANIMAL TO HUMAN KINDNESS.
I DIDN'T REALIZE THAT.
I'M SORRY, LEO...
YOU KNOW THINGS ABOUT THIS HARSH WORLD...
...THAT I DON'T.

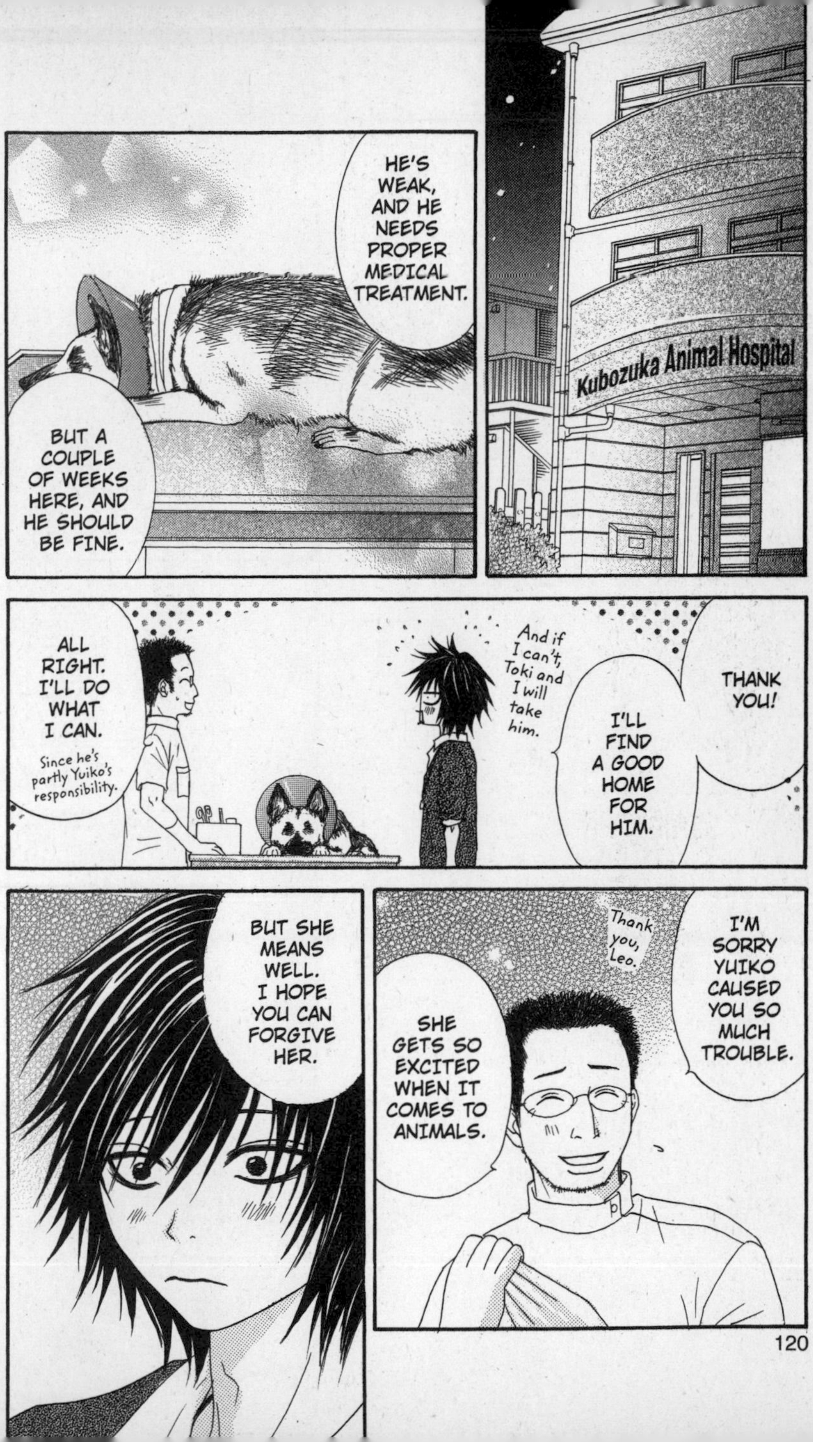
Kubozuka Animal Hospital
HE'S WEAK, AND HE NEEDS PROPER MEDICAL TREATMENT.
BUT A COUPLE OF WEEKS HERE, AND HE SHOULD BE FINE.
THANK YOU!
I'LL FIND A GOOD HOME FOR HIM.
And if I can't, Toki and I will take him.
ALL RIGHT. I'LL DO WHAT I CAN.
Since he's partly Yuiko's responsibility.
I'M SORRY YUIKO CAUSED YOU SO MUCH TROUBLE.
Thank you, Leo.
SHE GETS SO EXCITED WHEN IT COMES TO ANIMALS.
BUT SHE MEANS WELL. I HOPE YOU CAN FORGIVE HER.

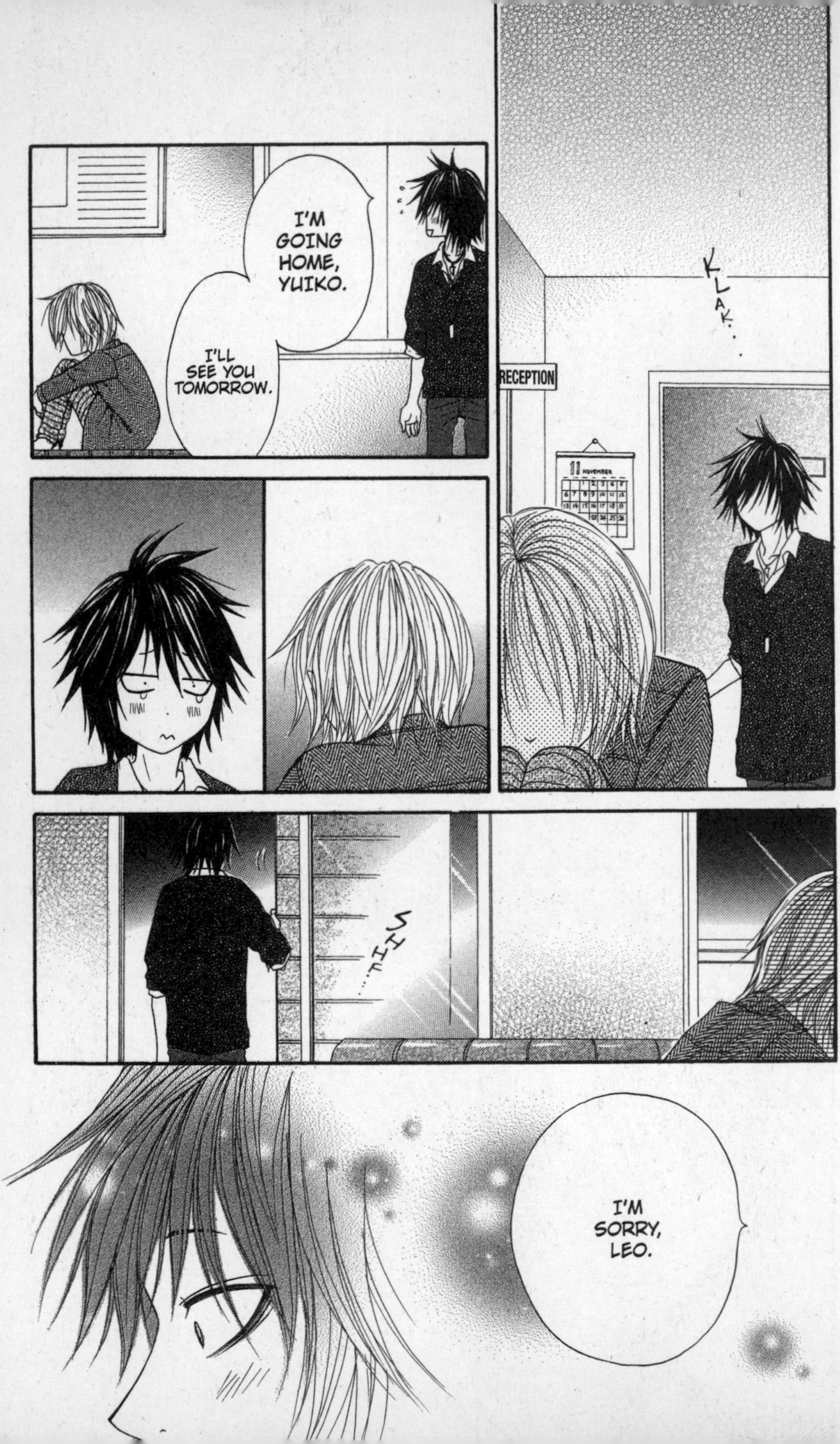
KLAK..
RECEPTION
I'M GOING HOME, YUIKO.
I'LL SEE YOU TOMORROW.
SHHF...
I'M SORRY, LEO.

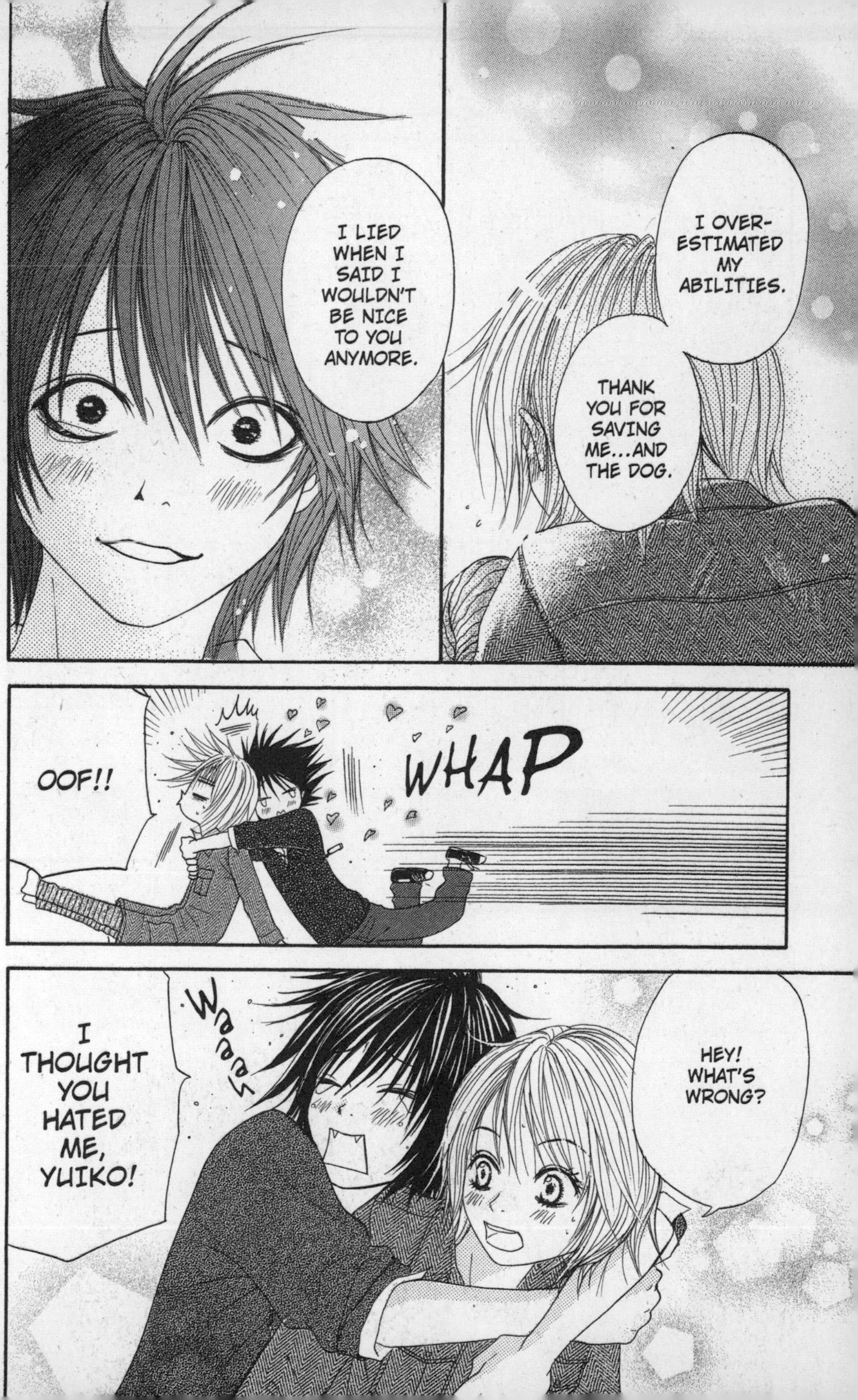
I OVER-ESTIMATED MY ABILITIES.
THANK YOU FOR SAVING ME...AND THE DOG.
I LIED WHEN I SAID I WOULDN'T BE NICE TO YOU ANYMORE.
WHAP
OOF!!
HEY! WHAT'S WRONG?
I THOUGHT YOU HATED ME, YUIKO!

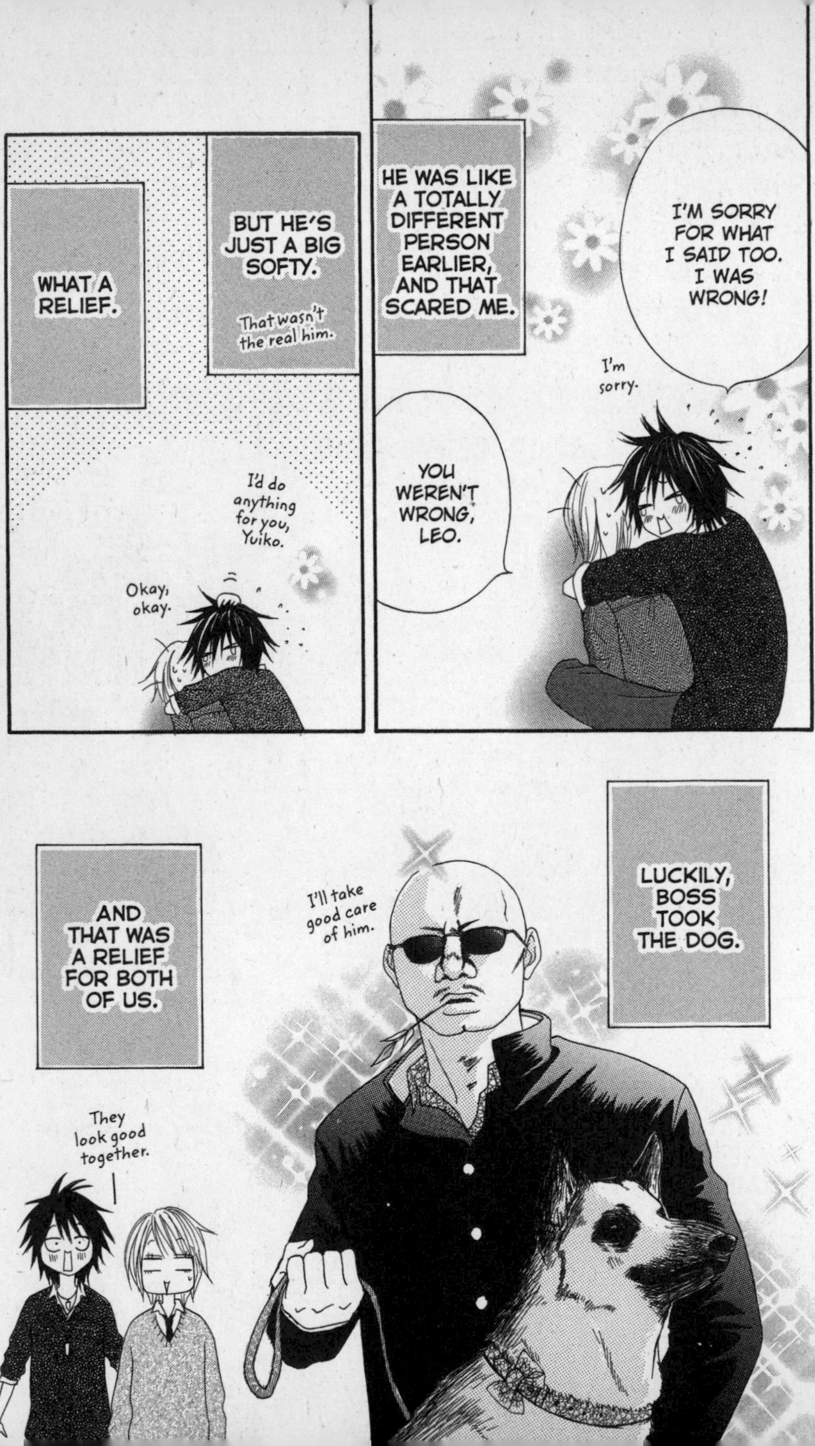
I'M SORRY FOR WHAT I SAID TOO. I WAS WRONG!
HE WAS LIKE A TOTALLY DIFFERENT PERSON EARLIER, AND THAT SCARED ME.
I'm sorry.
YOU WEREN'T WRONG, LEO.
BUT HE'S JUST A BIG SOFTY.
That wasn't the real him.
WHAT A RELIEF.
I'd do anything for you, Yuiko.
Okay, okay.
LUCKILY, BOSS TOOK THE DOG.
I'll take good care of him.
AND THAT WAS A RELIEF FOR BOTH OF US.
They look good together.

I'D LIKE TO USE THIS EXTRA PAGE TO SAY GOODBYE FOR NOW. THIS VOLUME OF *BEAST MASTER* ENDS WITH CHAPTER 4, WHICH STARTS ON THE NEXT PAGE, BUT THE STORY CONTINUES.

I HOPE TO SEE YOU AGAIN IN THE NEXT VOLUME. MAY YOUR LIVES BE FILLED WITH WISDOM, THE STRENGTH TO PERSEVERE AND LAUGHTER.

KYOUSUKE MOTOMI

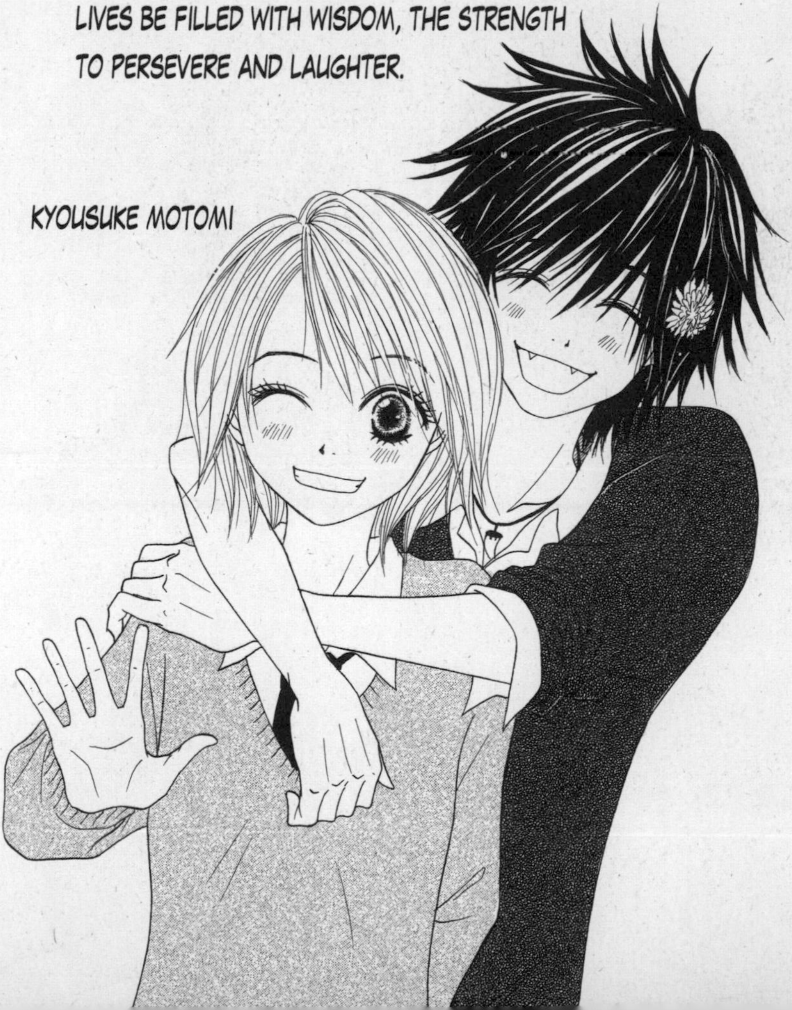

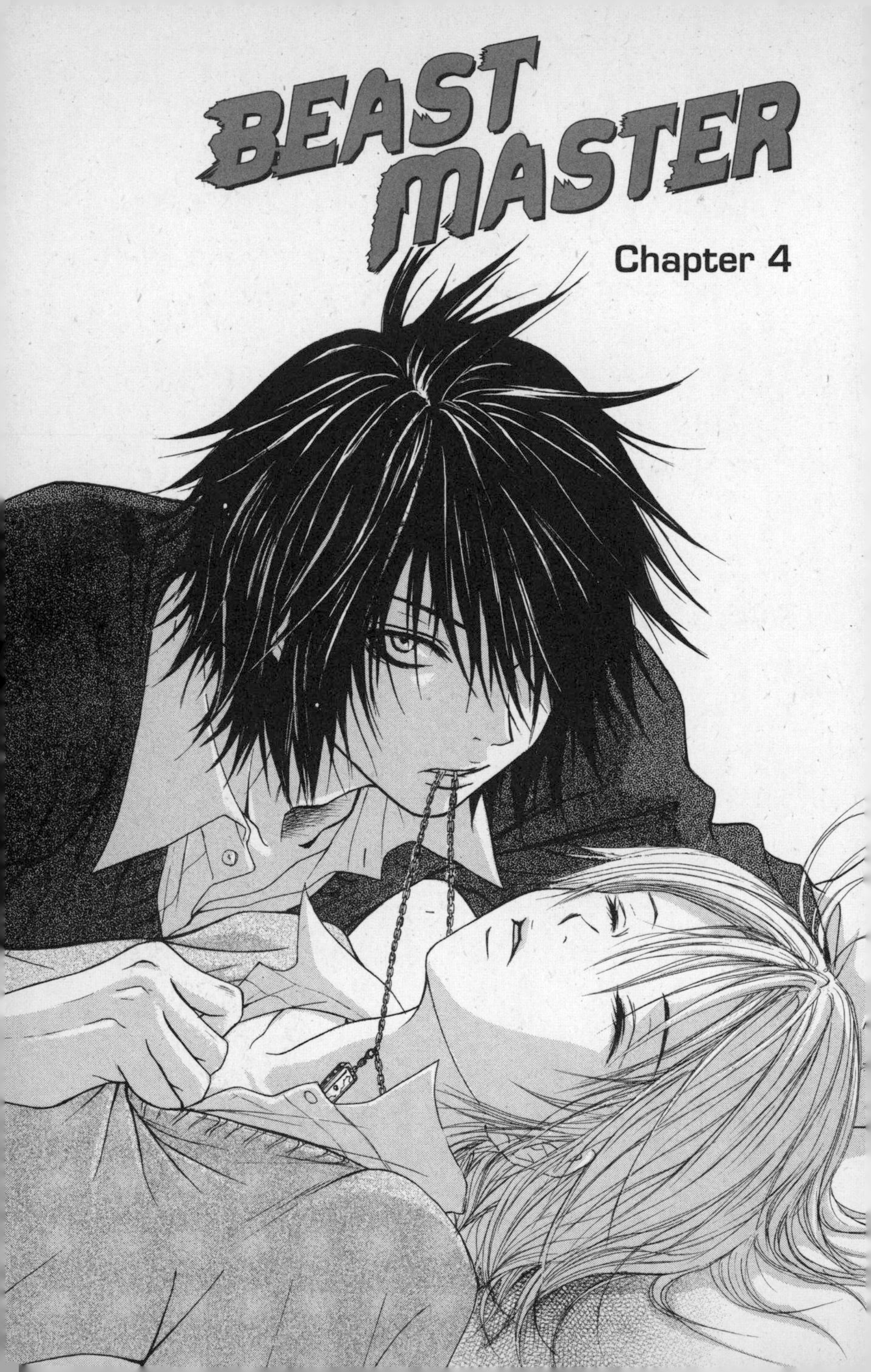
BEAST MASTER
Chapter 4

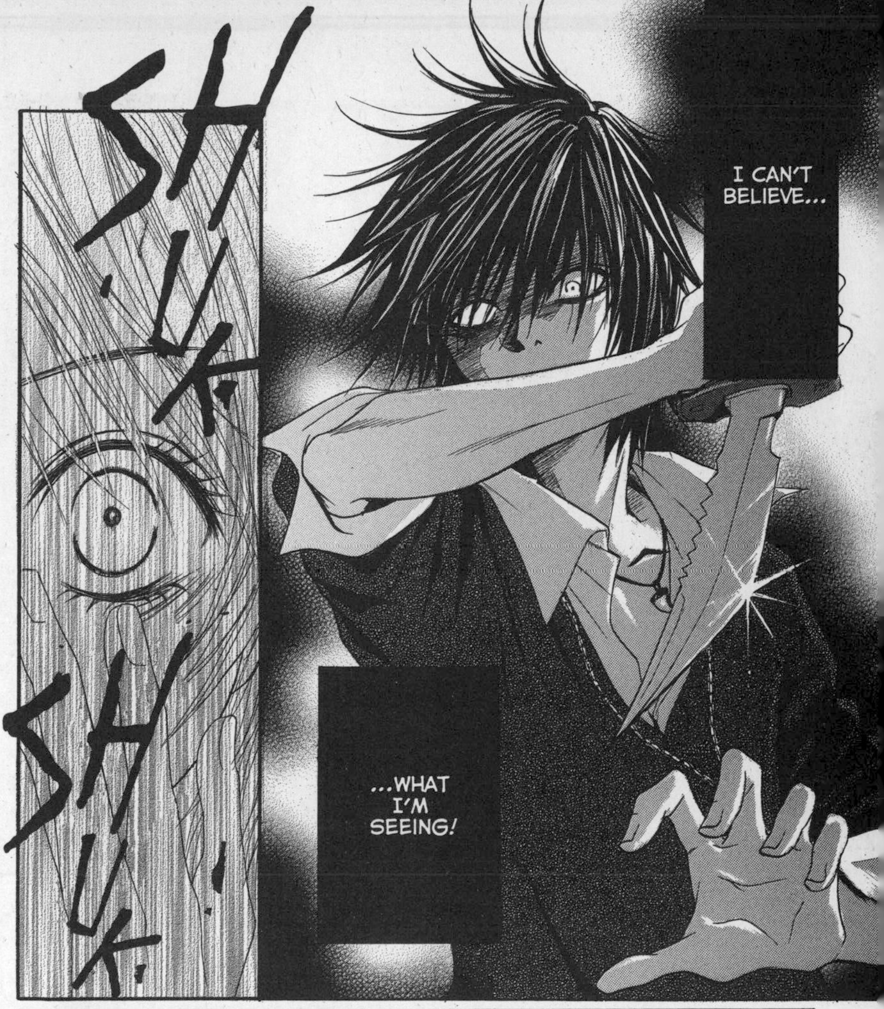
I CAN'T BELIEVE...
...WHAT I'M SEEING!
SHUK
SHUK

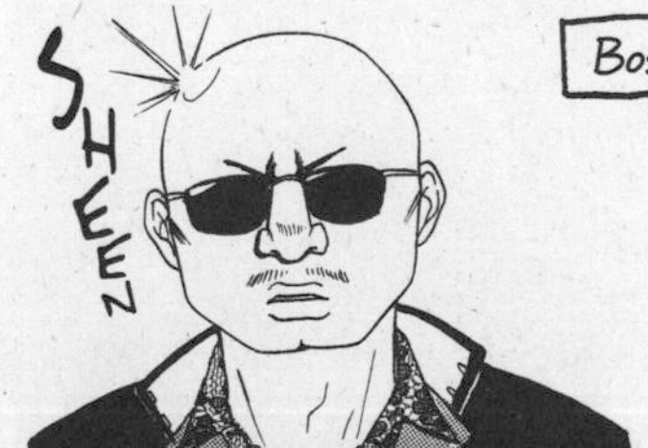
SHEEN

Boss

Frankly, he's the easiest one to draw. What kind of person is Boss? Do people like him really exist? Boss likes to think of himself as a gangster, but his biggest crime is not following school uniform regulations.

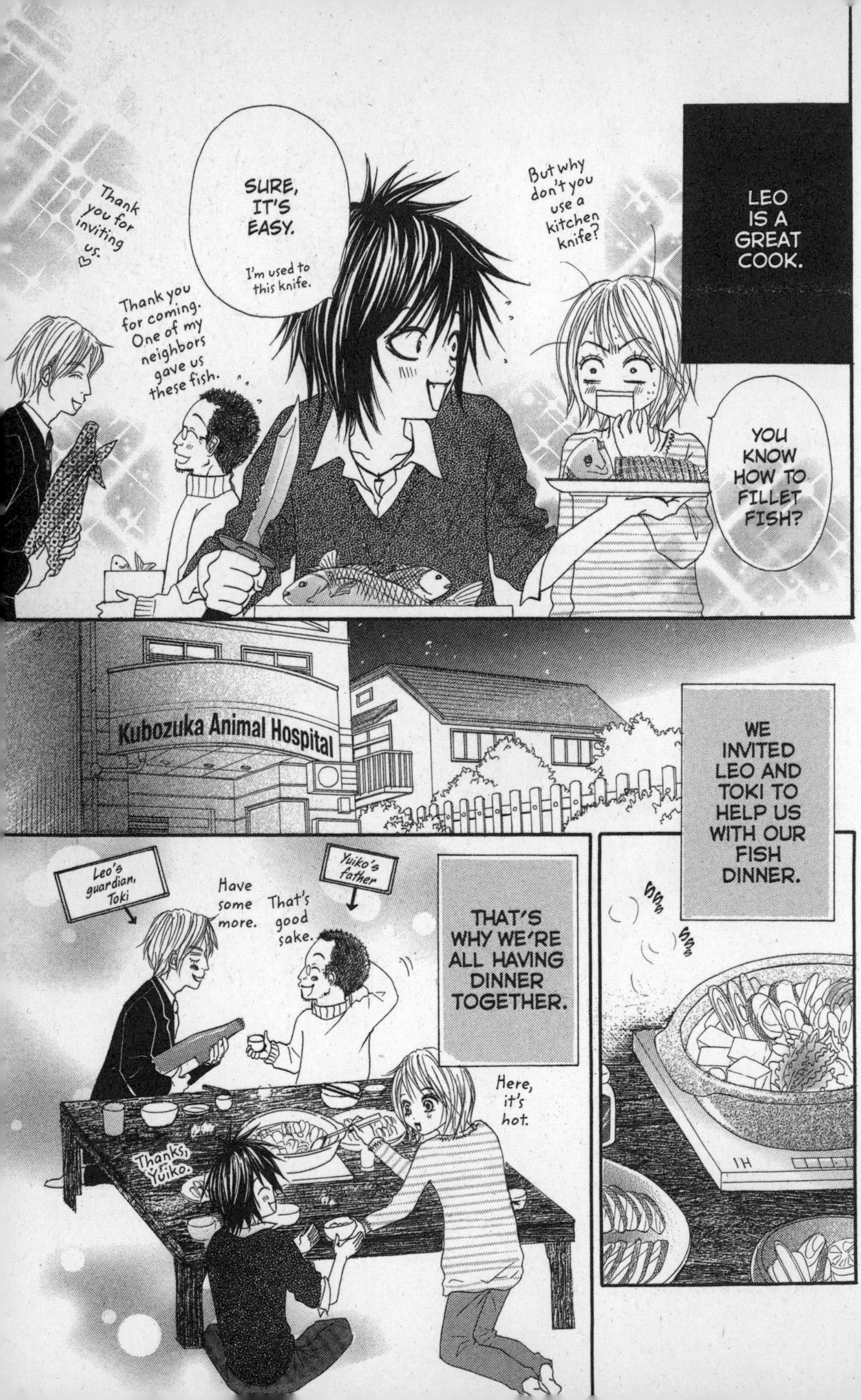
LEO IS A GREAT COOK.
YOU KNOW HOW TO FILLET FISH?
But why don't you use a kitchen knife?
SURE, IT'S EASY.
I'm used to this knife.
Thank you for inviting us. ♡
Thank you for coming. One of my neighbors gave us these fish.
WE INVITED LEO AND TOKI TO HELP US WITH OUR FISH DINNER.
Kubozuka Animal Hospital
IH
THAT'S WHY WE'RE ALL HAVING DINNER TOGETHER.
Here, it's hot.
Yuiko's father
That's good sake.
Have some more.
Leo's guardian, Toki
Thanks, Yuiko.

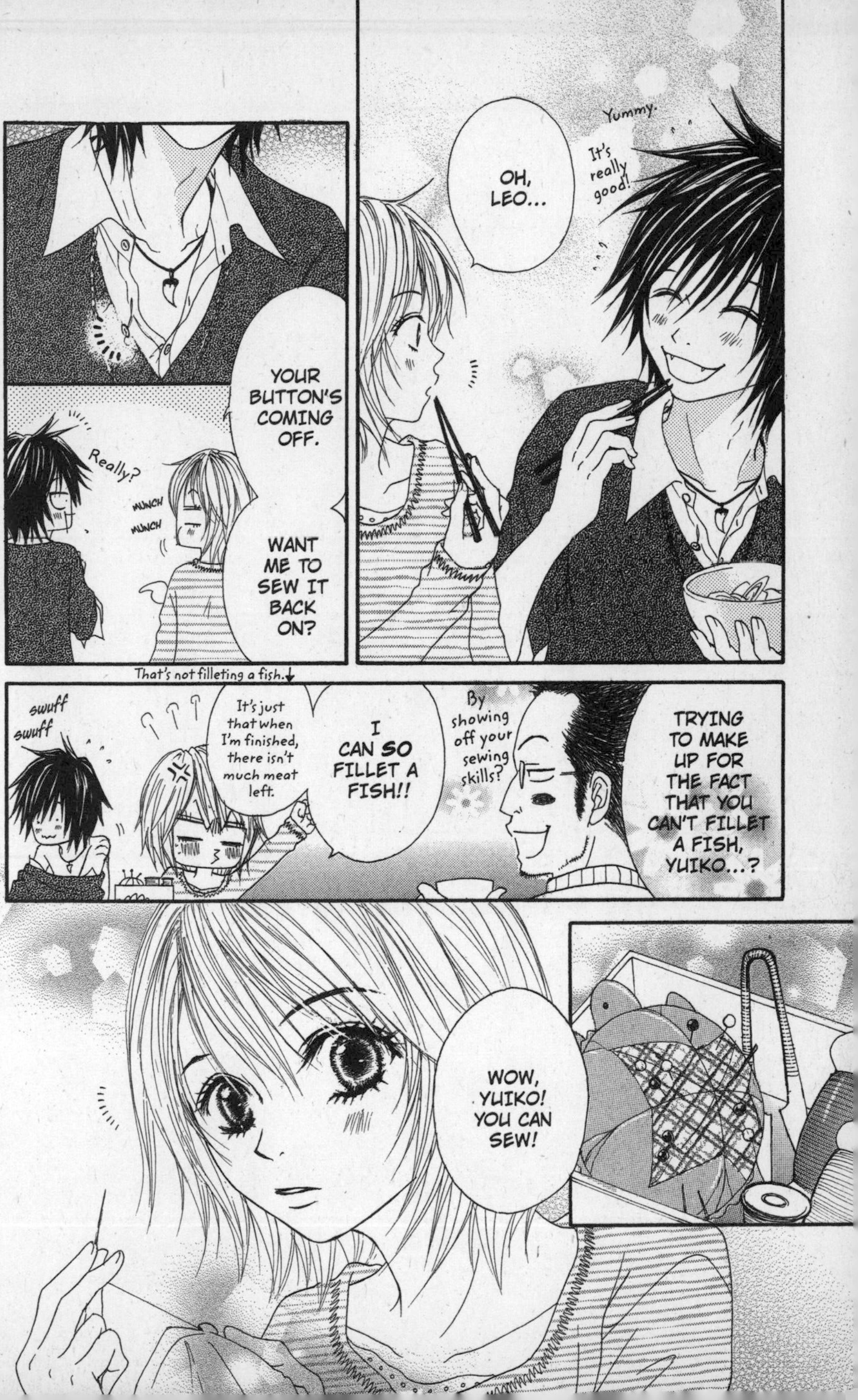
Yummy.
It's really good!
OH, LEO...
YOUR BUTTON'S COMING OFF.
WANT ME TO SEW IT BACK ON?
Really?
MUNCH MUNCH
TRYING TO MAKE UP FOR THE FACT THAT YOU CAN'T FILLET A FISH, YUIKO...?
By showing off your sewing skills?
I CAN SO FILLET A FISH!!
It's just that when I'm finished, there isn't much meat left.
That's not filleting a fish.
swuff swuff
WOW, YUIKO! YOU CAN SEW!

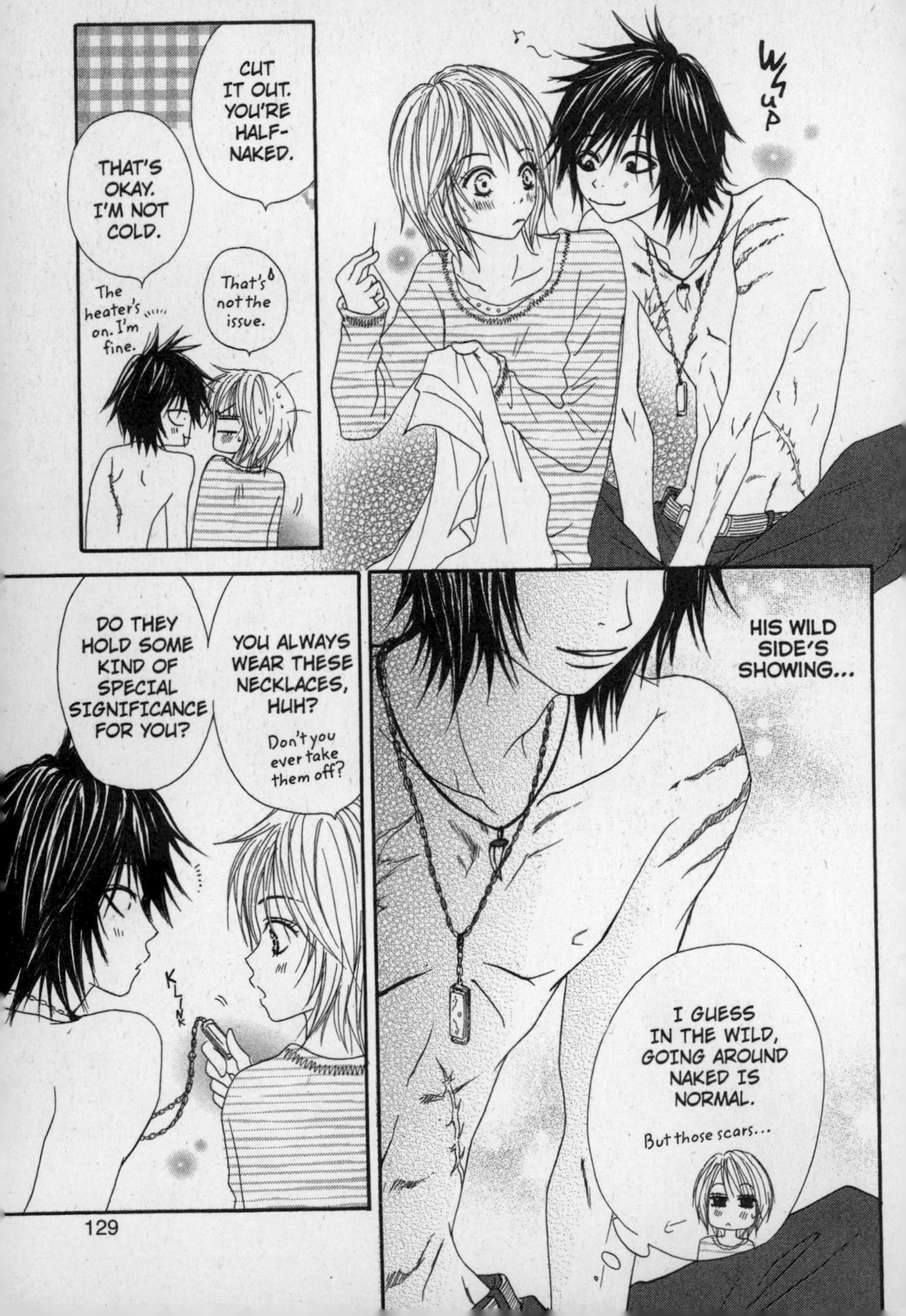
WHUP
CUT IT OUT. YOU'RE HALF-NAKED.
THAT'S OKAY. I'M NOT COLD.
That's not the issue.
The heater's on. I'm fine.
HIS WILD SIDE'S SHOWING...
I GUESS IN THE WILD, GOING AROUND NAKED IS NORMAL.
But those scars...
YOU ALWAYS WEAR THESE NECKLACES, HUH?
Don't you ever take them off?
DO THEY HOLD SOME KIND OF SPECIAL SIGNIFICANCE FOR YOU?
KLINK

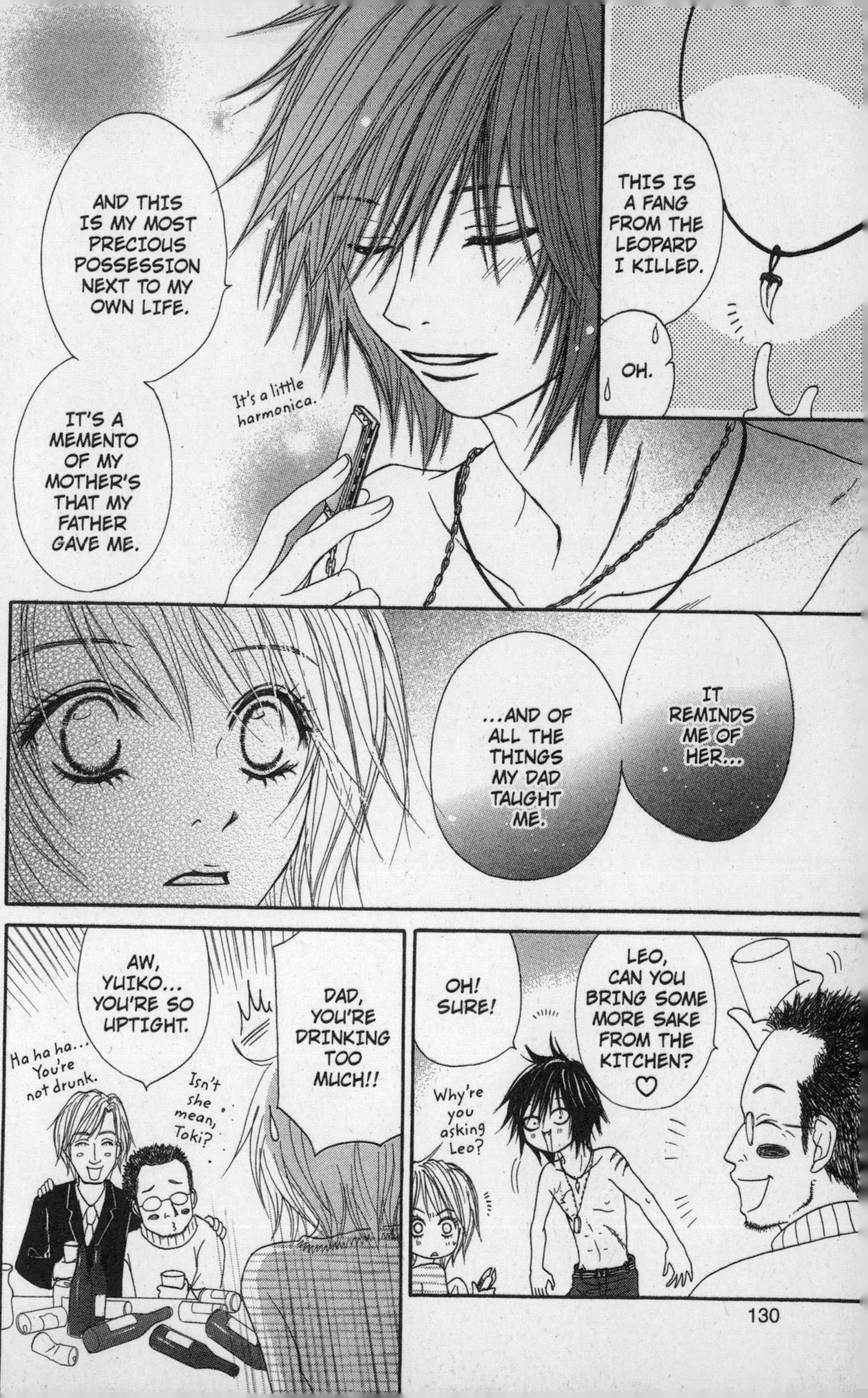
THIS IS A FANG FROM THE LEOPARD I KILLED.
OH.
AND THIS IS MY MOST PRECIOUS POSSESSION NEXT TO MY OWN LIFE.
IT'S A MEMENTO OF MY MOTHER'S THAT MY FATHER GAVE ME.
It's a little harmonica.
IT REMINDS ME OF HER...
...AND OF ALL THE THINGS MY DAD TAUGHT ME.
LEO, CAN YOU BRING SOME MORE SAKE FROM THE KITCHEN? ♡
OH! SURE!
Why're you asking Leo?
DAD, YOU'RE DRINKING TOO MUCH!!
AW, YUIKO... YOU'RE SO UPTIGHT.
Isn't she mean, Toki?
Ha ha ha... You're not drunk.

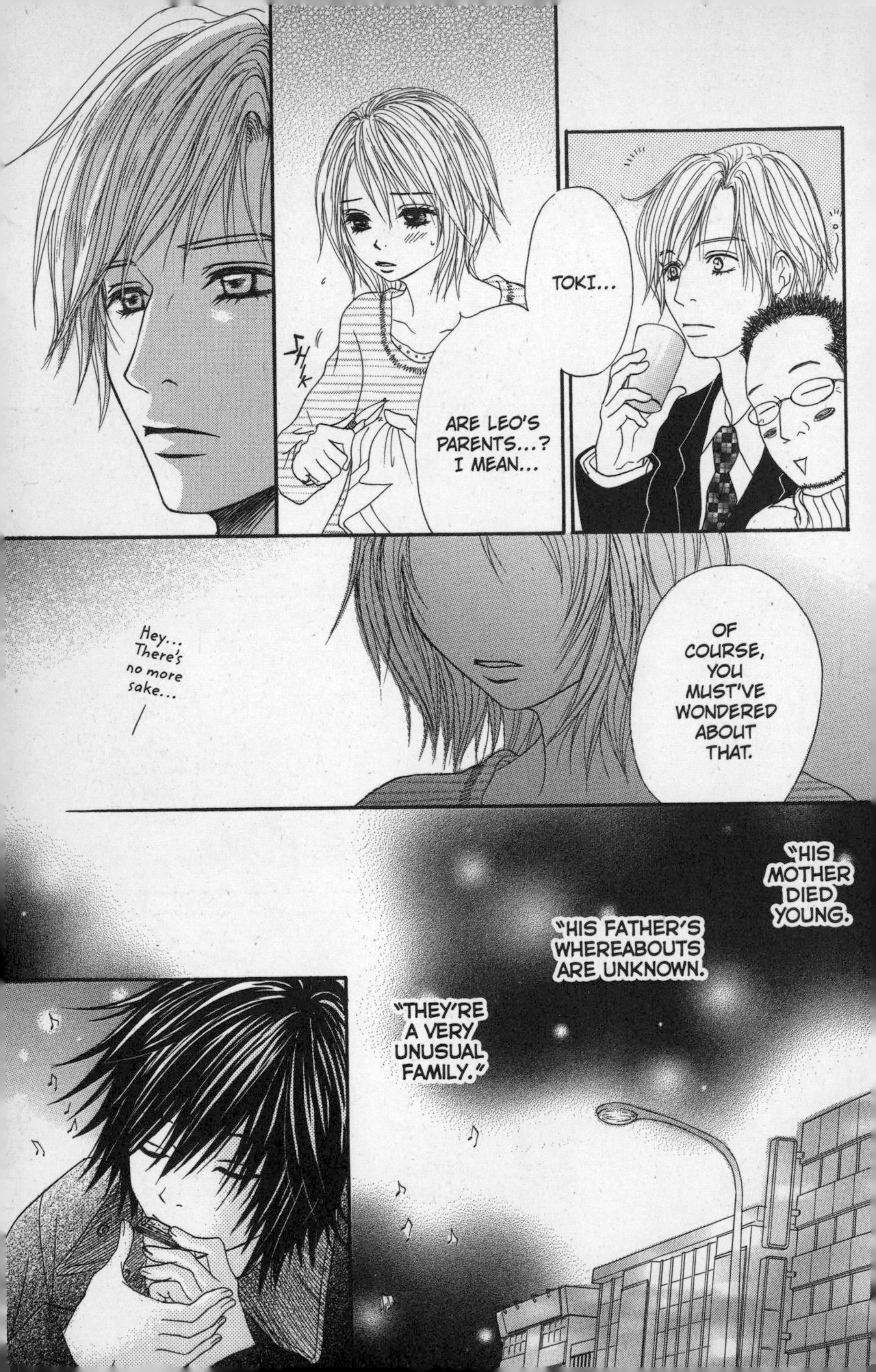
TOKI...
ARE LEO'S PARENTS...? I MEAN...
SHIK
OF COURSE, YOU MUST'VE WONDERED ABOUT THAT.
Hey... There's no more sake...
"HIS MOTHER DIED YOUNG.
"HIS FATHER'S WHEREABOUTS ARE UNKNOWN.
"THEY'RE A VERY UNUSUAL FAMILY."

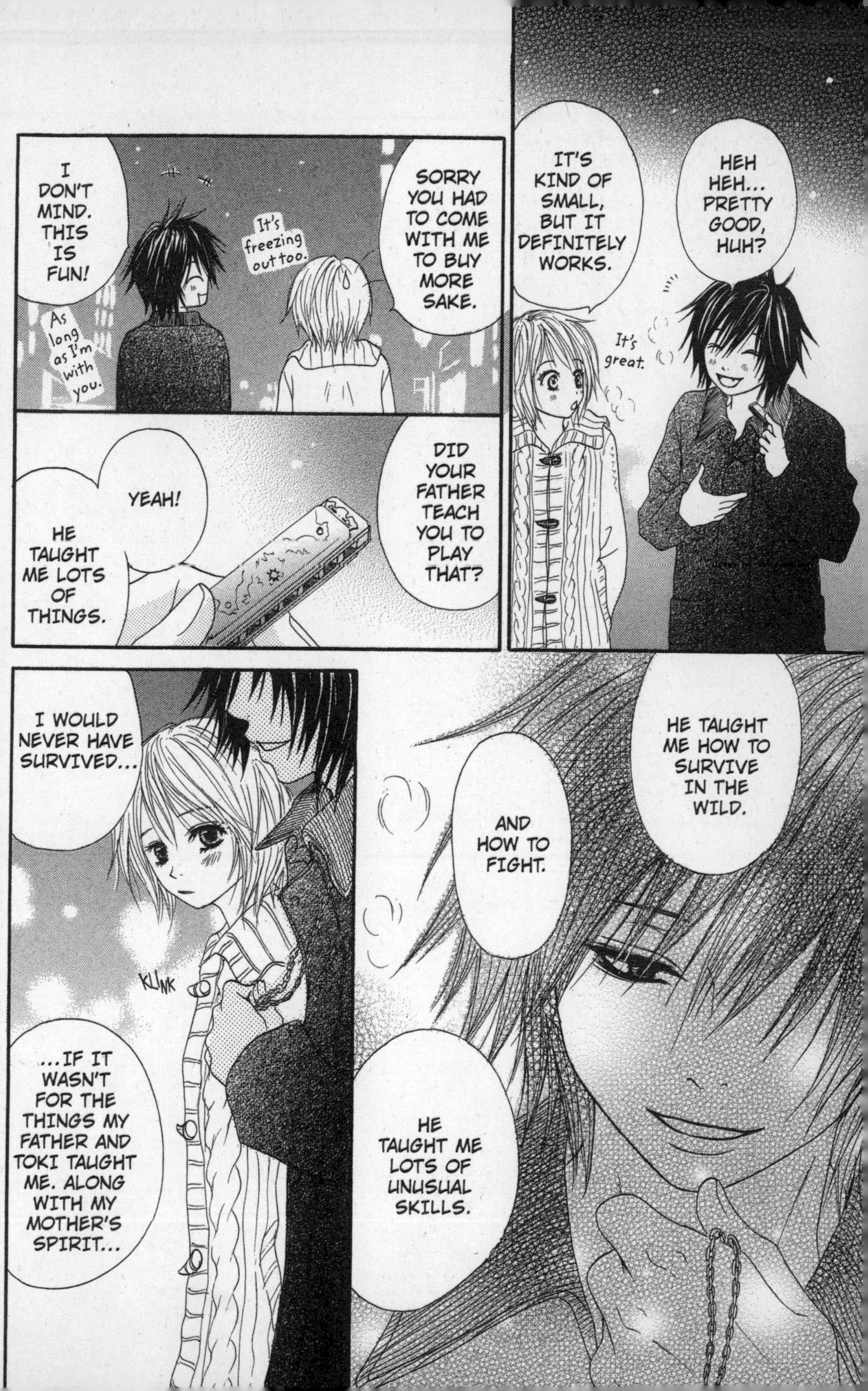
HEH HEH... PRETTY GOOD, HUH?
IT'S KIND OF SMALL, BUT IT DEFINITELY WORKS.
It's great.
SORRY YOU HAD TO COME WITH ME TO BUY MORE SAKE.
It's freezing out too.
I DON'T MIND. THIS IS FUN!
As long as I'm with you.
DID YOUR FATHER TEACH YOU TO PLAY THAT?
YEAH!
HE TAUGHT ME LOTS OF THINGS.
HE TAUGHT ME HOW TO SURVIVE IN THE WILD.
AND HOW TO FIGHT.
HE TAUGHT ME LOTS OF UNUSUAL SKILLS.
I WOULD NEVER HAVE SURVIVED...
KLINK
...IF IT WASN'T FOR THE THINGS MY FATHER AND TOKI TAUGHT ME. ALONG WITH MY MOTHER'S SPIRIT...

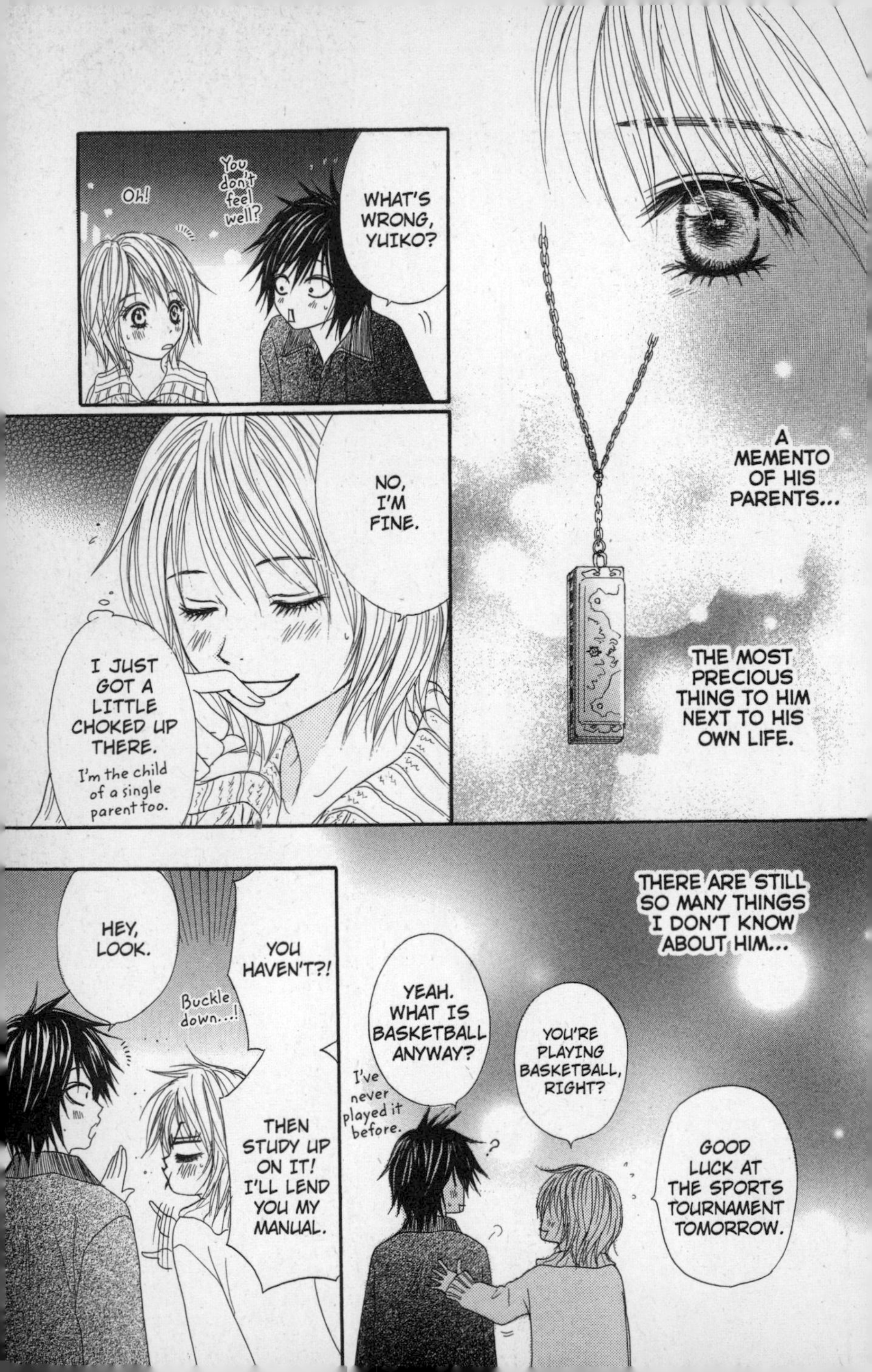
A MEMENTO OF HIS PARENTS...
THE MOST PRECIOUS THING TO HIM NEXT TO HIS OWN LIFE.
WHAT'S WRONG, YUIKO?
You don't feel well?
Oh!
NO, I'M FINE.
I JUST GOT A LITTLE CHOKED UP THERE.
I'm the child of a single parent too.
THERE ARE STILL SO MANY THINGS I DON'T KNOW ABOUT HIM...
GOOD LUCK AT THE SPORTS TOURNAMENT TOMORROW.
YOU'RE PLAYING BASKETBALL, RIGHT?
YEAH. WHAT IS BASKETBALL ANYWAY?
I've never played it before.
YOU HAVEN'T?!
Buckle down...!
HEY, LOOK.
THEN STUDY UP ON IT! I'LL LEND YOU MY MANUAL.

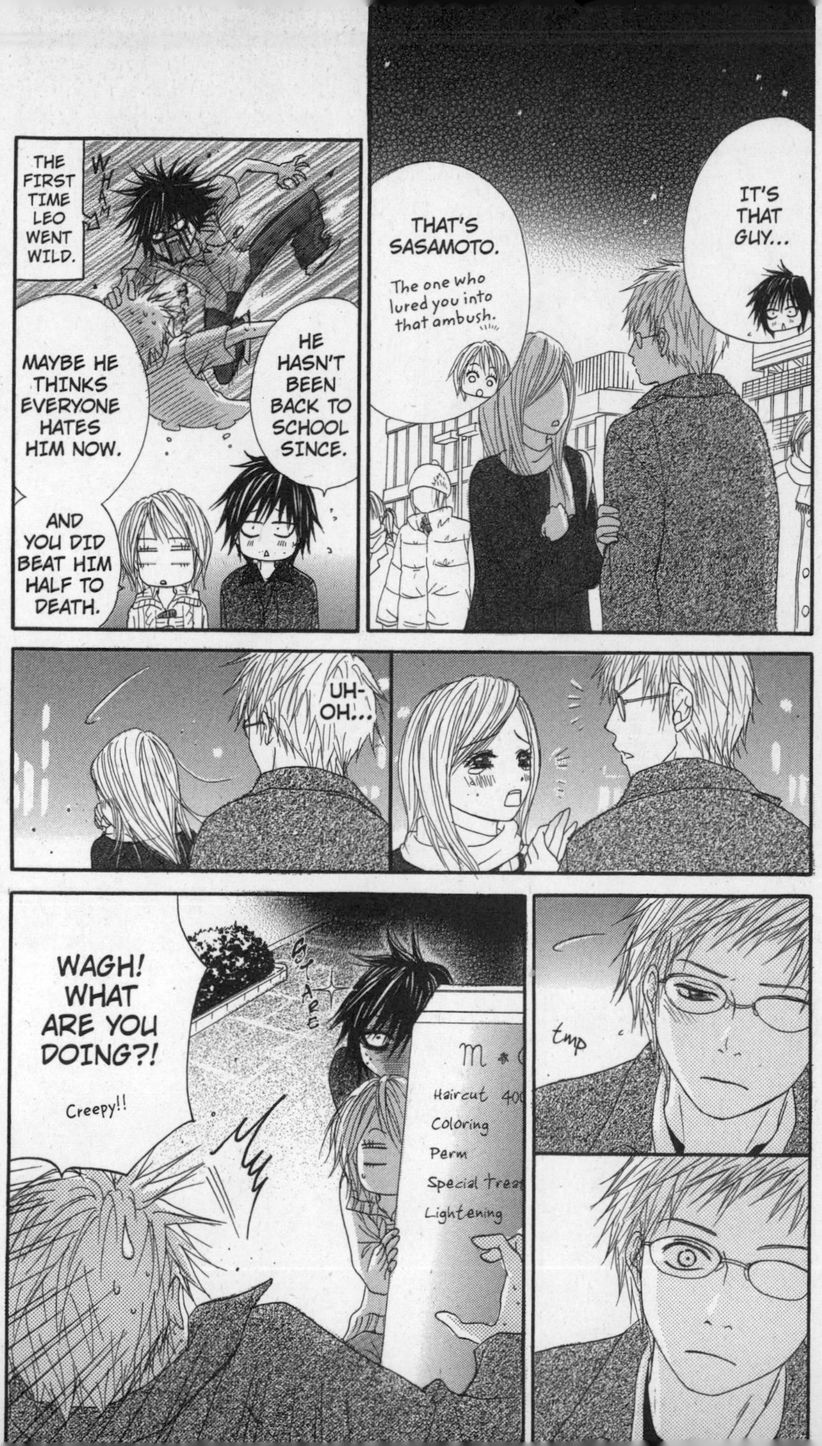
IT'S THAT GUY...
THAT'S SASAMOTO.
The one who lured you into that ambush.
THE FIRST TIME LEO WENT WILD.
WHAM
HE HASN'T BEEN BACK TO SCHOOL SINCE.
MAYBE HE THINKS EVERYONE HATES HIM NOW.
AND YOU DID BEAT HIM HALF TO DEATH.
UH-OH...
tmp
WAGH! WHAT ARE YOU DOING?!
Creepy!!
STARE
Haircut 400
Coloring
Perm
Special Trea
Lightening

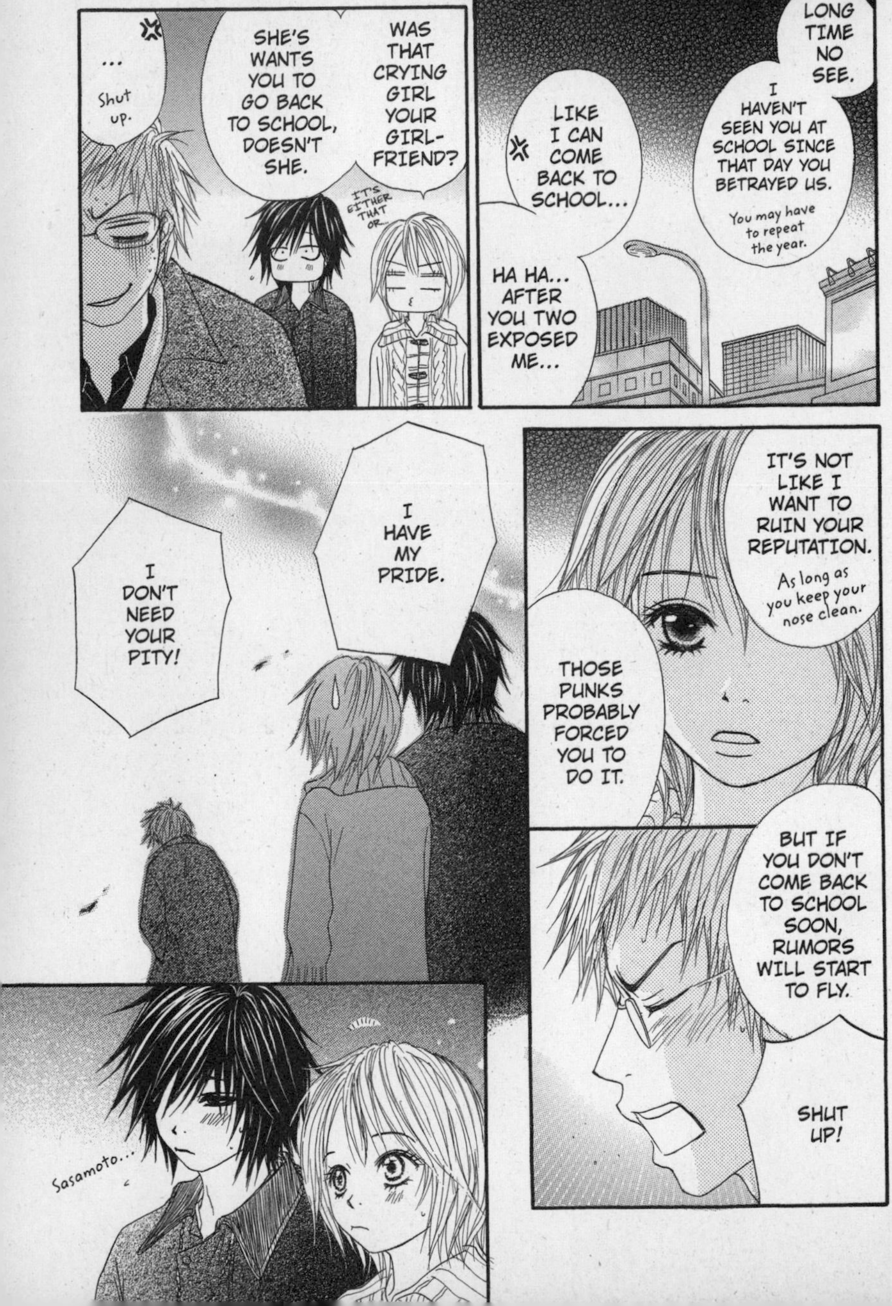
LONG TIME NO SEE.
I HAVEN'T SEEN YOU AT SCHOOL SINCE THAT DAY YOU BETRAYED US.
You may have to repeat the year.
LIKE I CAN COME BACK TO SCHOOL...
HA HA... AFTER YOU TWO EXPOSED ME...
WAS THAT CRYING GIRL YOUR GIRL-FRIEND?
IT'S EITHER THAT OR...
SHE'S WANTS YOU TO GO BACK TO SCHOOL, DOESN'T SHE.
...
Shut up.
IT'S NOT LIKE I WANT TO RUIN YOUR REPUTATION.
As long as you keep your nose clean.
THOSE PUNKS PROBABLY FORCED YOU TO DO IT.
BUT IF YOU DON'T COME BACK TO SCHOOL SOON, RUMORS WILL START TO FLY.
SHUT UP!
I HAVE MY PRIDE.
I DON'T NEED YOUR PITY!
Sasamoto...

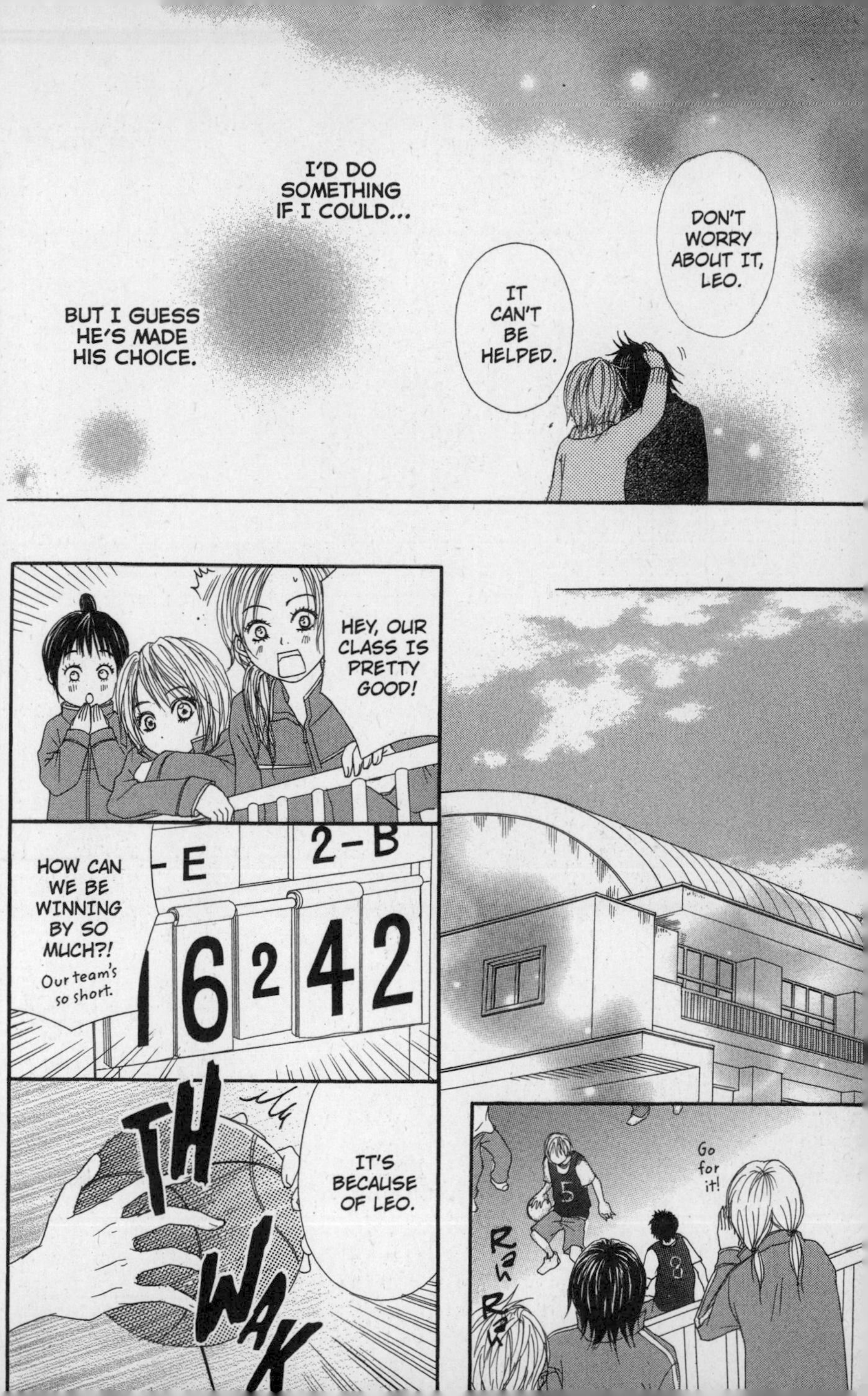
DON'T WORRY ABOUT IT, LEO.
IT CAN'T BE HELPED.
I'D DO SOMETHING IF I COULD...
BUT I GUESS HE'S MADE HIS CHOICE.
HEY, OUR CLASS IS PRETTY GOOD!
2-B
-E
16 2 42
HOW CAN WE BE WINNING BY SO MUCH?!
Our team's so short.
Go for it!
IT'S BECAUSE OF LEO.
THWAK

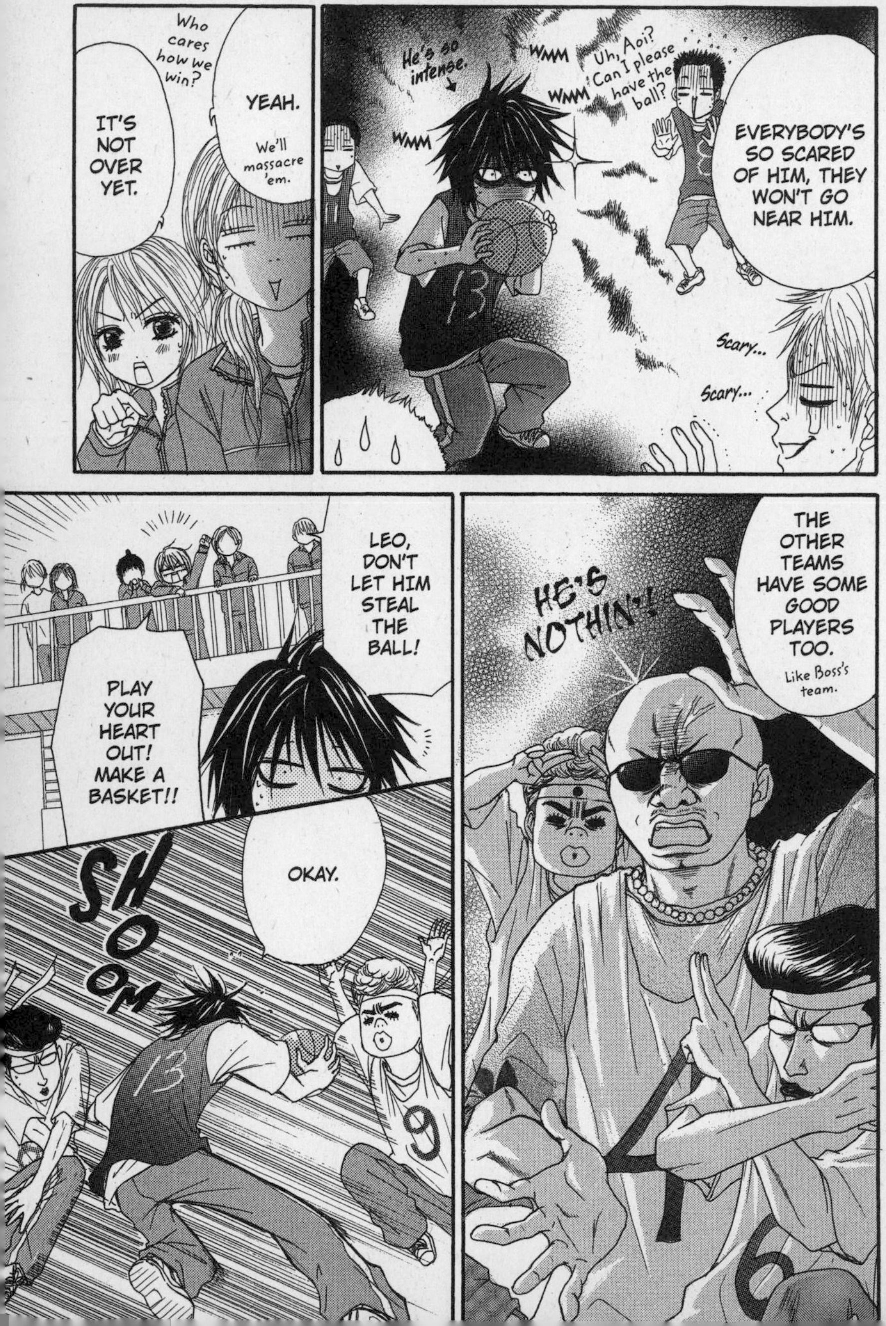
EVERYBODY'S SO SCARED OF HIM, THEY WON'T GO NEAR HIM.
Uh, Aoi? Can I please have the ball?
WMM
WMM
WMM
He's so intense.
Scary...
Scary...
YEAH.
We'll massacre 'em.
Who cares how we win?
IT'S NOT OVER YET.
THE OTHER TEAMS HAVE SOME GOOD PLAYERS TOO.
Like Boss's team.
HE'S NOTHIN'!
LEO, DON'T LET HIM STEAL THE BALL!
PLAY YOUR HEART OUT! MAKE A BASKET!!
OKAY.
SHOOOM

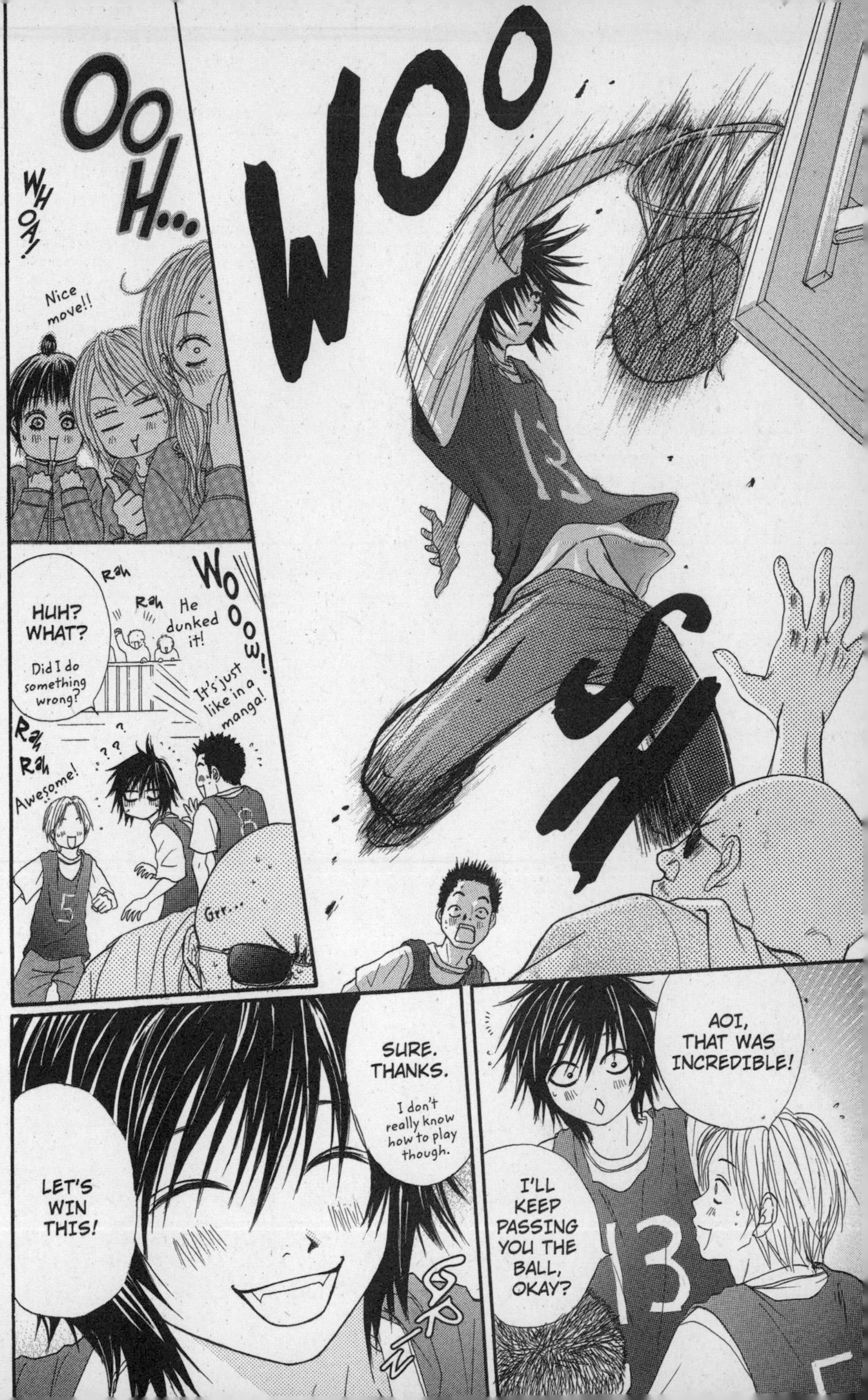
WOO
SH
OOOH...
WHOA!
Nice move!!
WOOOOW!!
It's just like in a manga!
He dunked it!
Rah
Rah
HUH? WHAT?
Did I do something wrong?
???
Rah
Rah
Awesome!
Grr...
AOI, THAT WAS INCREDIBLE!
I'LL KEEP PASSING YOU THE BALL, OKAY?
SURE. THANKS.
I don't really know how to play though.
LET'S WIN THIS!
GRIN

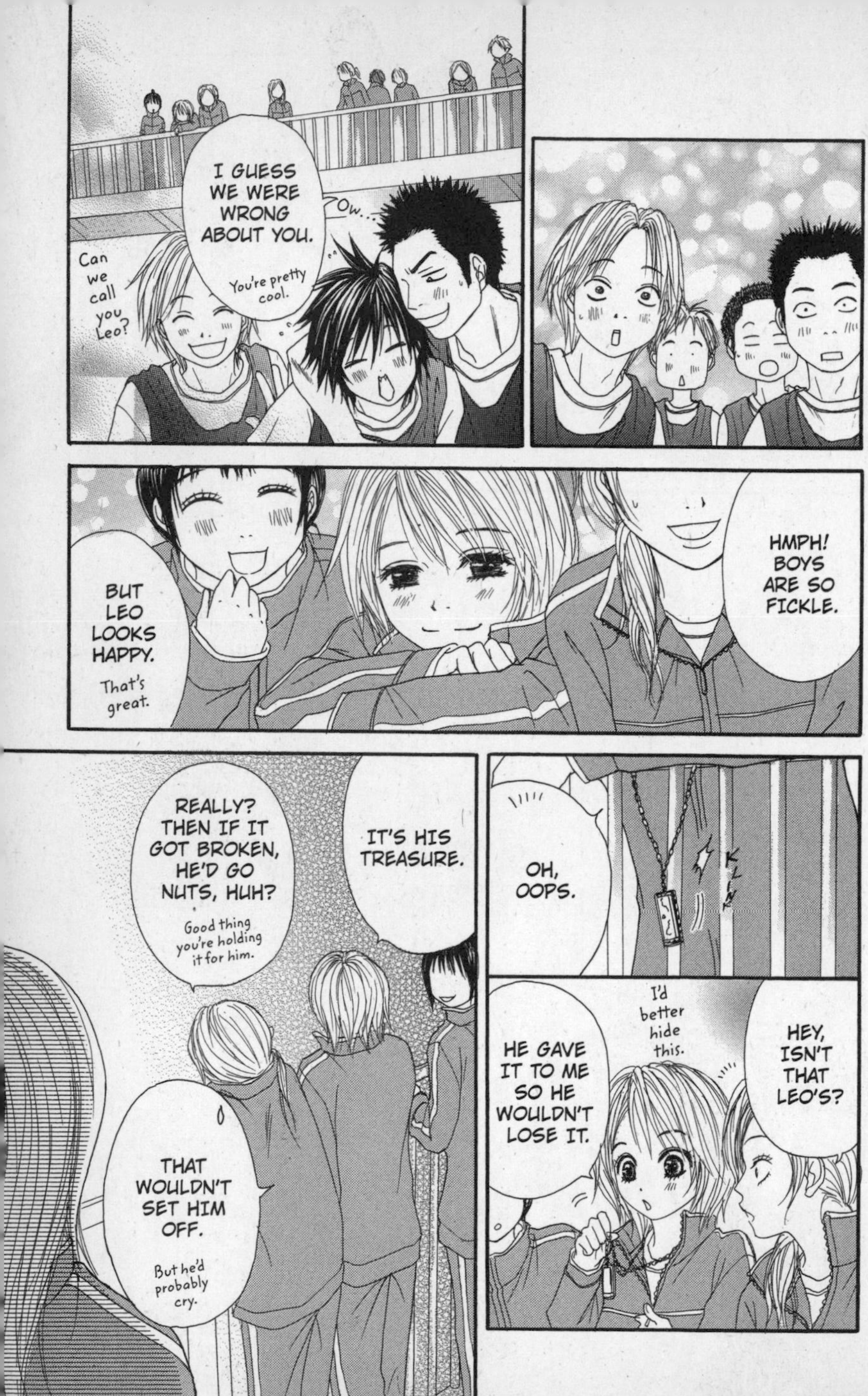
Ow...
I GUESS WE WERE WRONG ABOUT YOU.
You're pretty cool.
Can we call you Leo?
HMPH! BOYS ARE SO FICKLE.
BUT LEO LOOKS HAPPY.
That's great.
KLINK
OH, OOPS.
HEY, ISN'T THAT LEO'S?
I'd better hide this.
HE GAVE IT TO ME SO HE WOULDN'T LOSE IT.
IT'S HIS TREASURE.
REALLY? THEN IF IT GOT BROKEN, HE'D GO NUTS, HUH?
Good thing you're holding it for him.
THAT WOULDN'T SET HIM OFF.
But he'd probably cry.

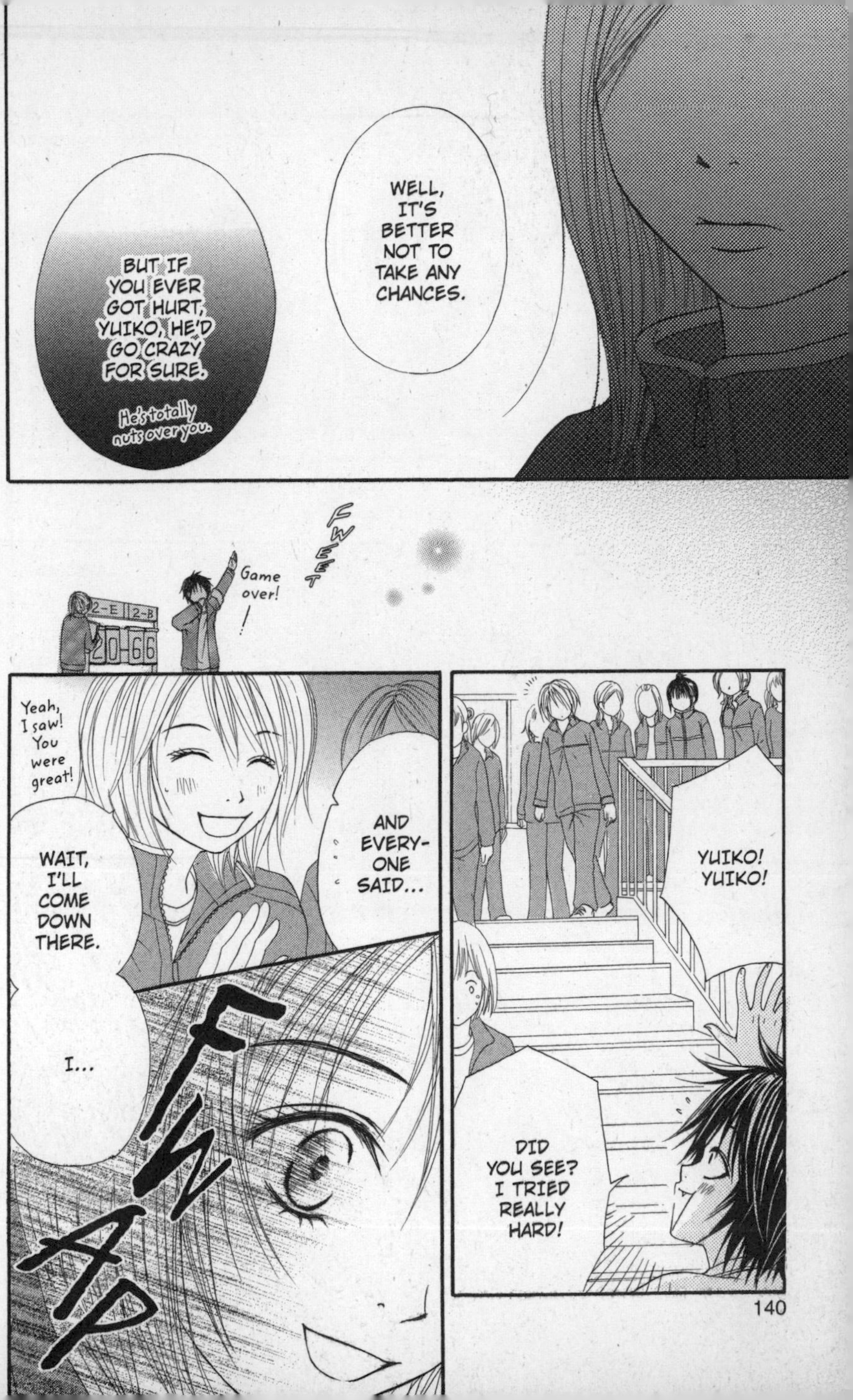
WELL, IT'S BETTER NOT TO TAKE ANY CHANCES.
BUT IF YOU EVER GOT HURT, YUIKO, HE'D GO CRAZY FOR SURE.
He's totally nuts over you.
FWEET
Game over!
2-E 2-B
20 66
YUIKO! YUIKO!
DID YOU SEE? I TRIED REALLY HARD!
AND EVERY-ONE SAID...
Yeah, I saw! You were great!
WAIT, I'LL COME DOWN THERE.
I...
FWAP

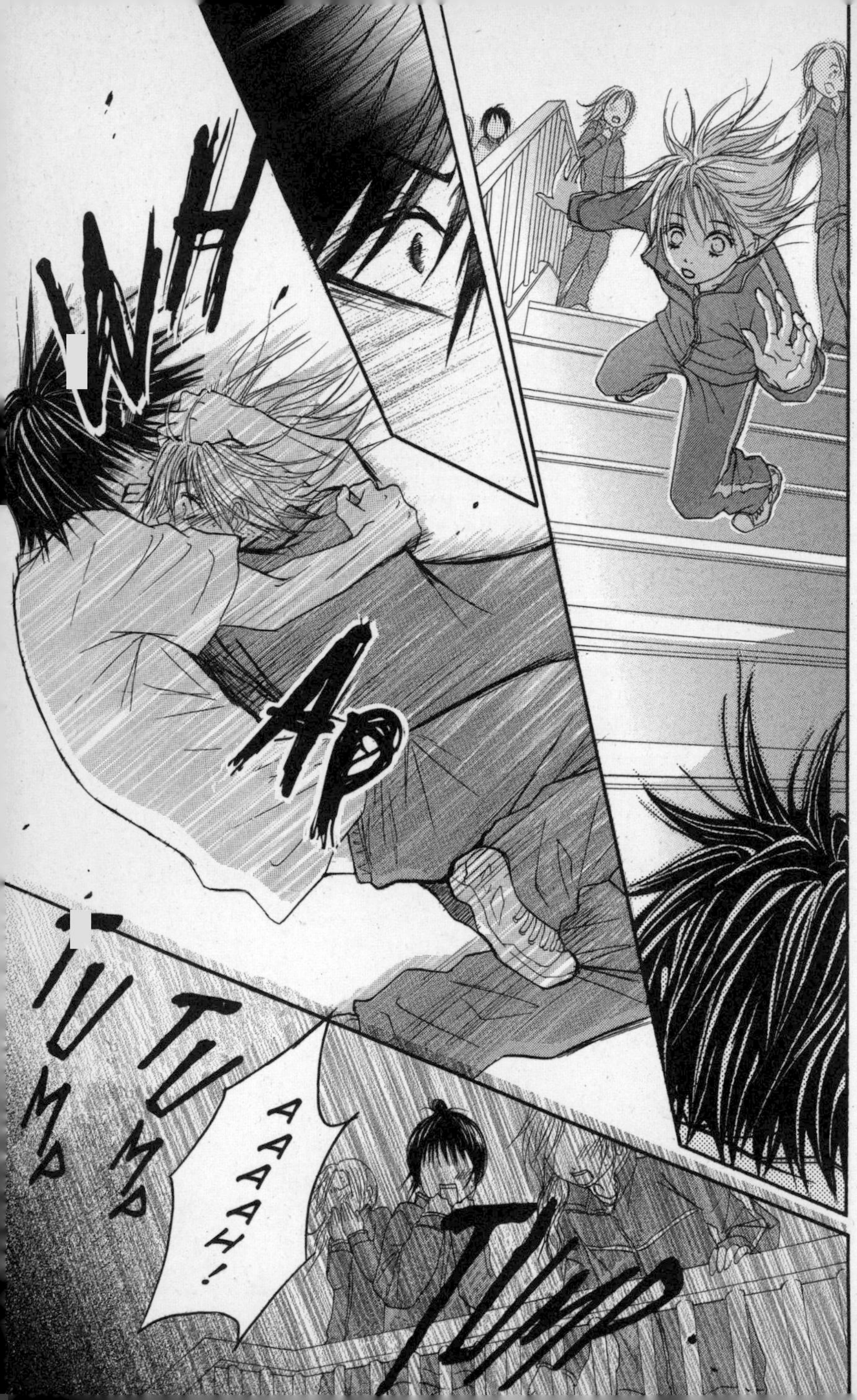
AAAAAH!
TUMP

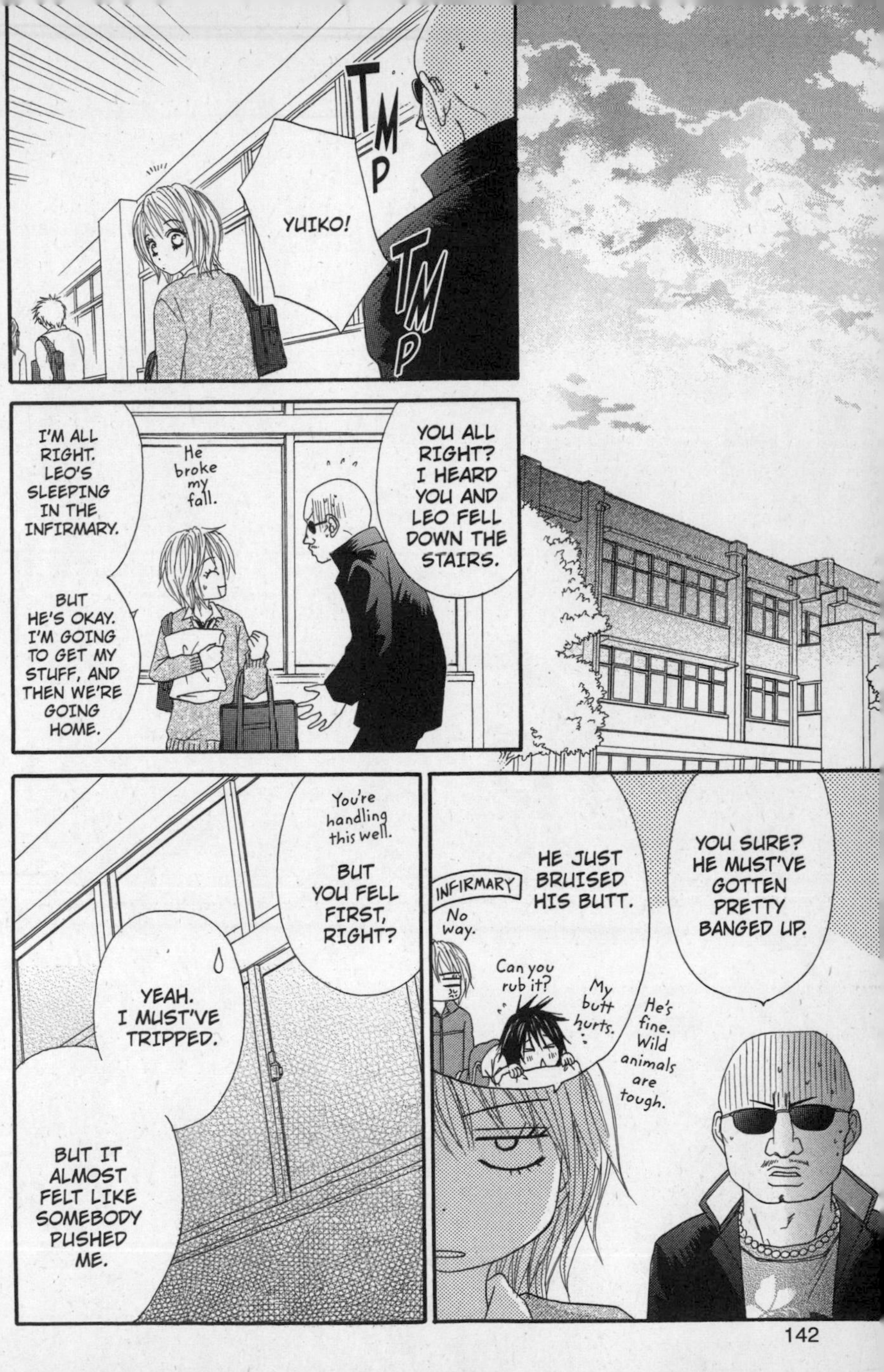
TMP
TMP
YUIKO!
YOU ALL RIGHT? I HEARD YOU AND LEO FELL DOWN THE STAIRS.
I'M ALL RIGHT. LEO'S SLEEPING IN THE INFIRMARY.
He broke my fall.
BUT HE'S OKAY. I'M GOING TO GET MY STUFF, AND THEN WE'RE GOING HOME.
YOU SURE? HE MUST'VE GOTTEN PRETTY BANGED UP.
HE JUST BRUISED HIS BUTT.
INFIRMARY
No way.
Can you rub it?
My butt hurts.
He's fine. Wild animals are tough.
You're handling this well.
BUT YOU FELL FIRST, RIGHT?
YEAH. I MUST'VE TRIPPED.
BUT IT ALMOST FELT LIKE SOMEBODY PUSHED ME.

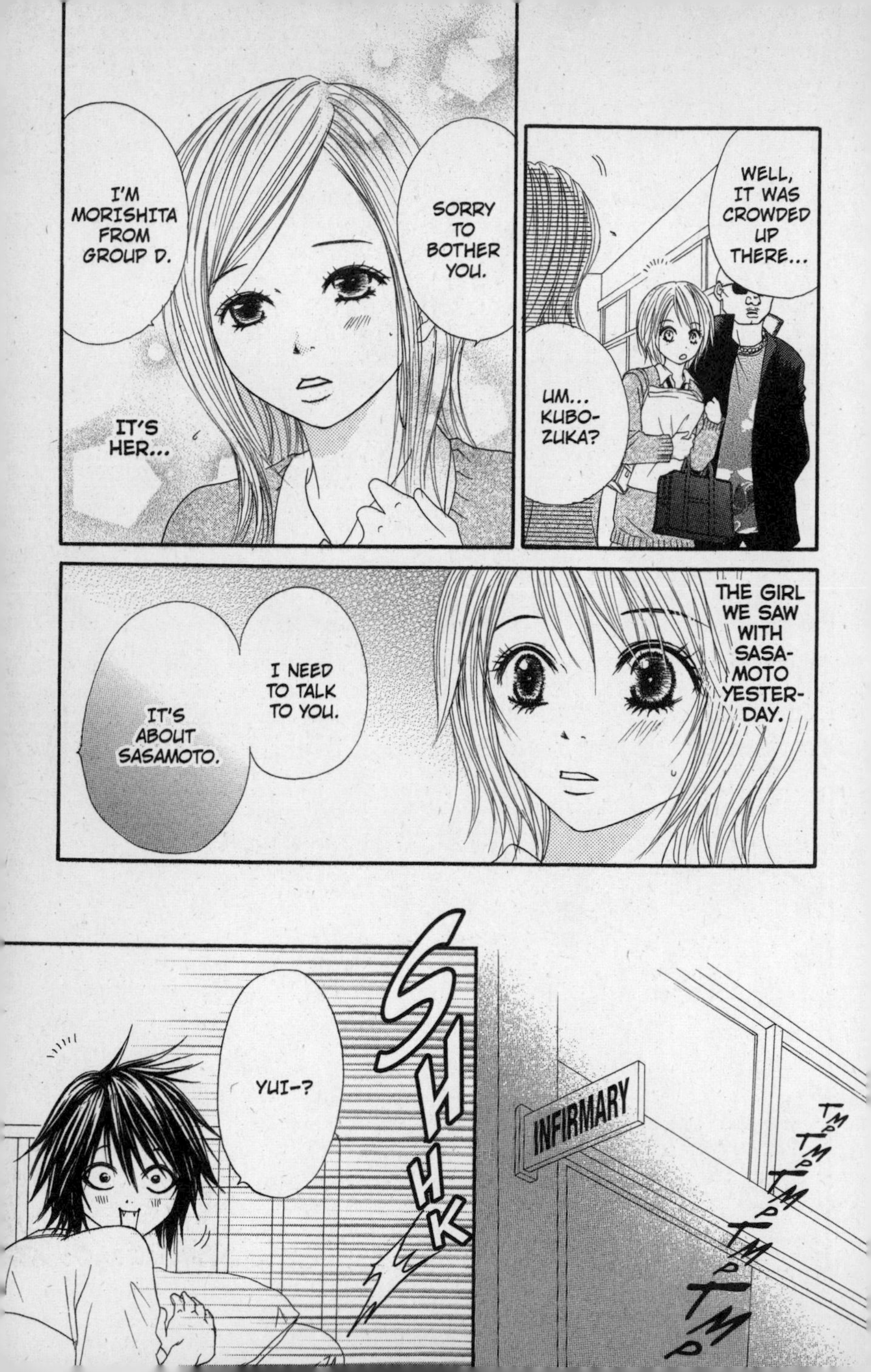
WELL, IT WAS CROWDED UP THERE...
UM... KUBO-ZUKA?
SORRY TO BOTHER YOU.
I'M MORISHITA FROM GROUP D.
IT'S HER...
THE GIRL WE SAW WITH SASA-MOTO YESTER-DAY.
I NEED TO TALK TO YOU.
IT'S ABOUT SASAMOTO.
TMP TMP TMP TMP TMP TMP
INFIRMARY
SHHK
YUI-?

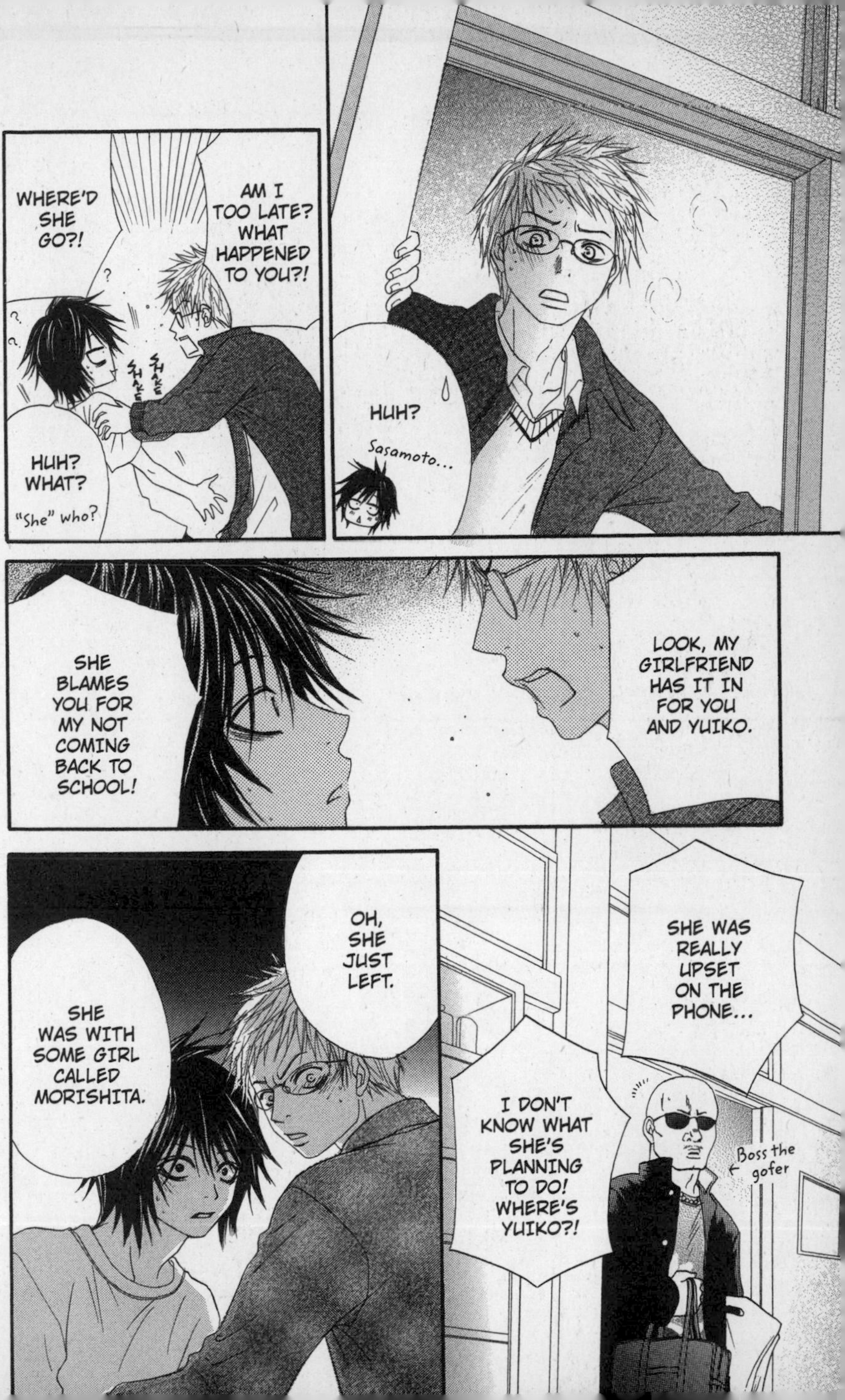
HUH?
Sasamoto...
AM I TOO LATE? WHAT HAPPENED TO YOU?!
WHERE'D SHE GO?!
SHAKE SHAKE
HUH? WHAT?
"She" who?
LOOK, MY GIRLFRIEND HAS IT IN FOR YOU AND YUIKO.
SHE BLAMES YOU FOR MY NOT COMING BACK TO SCHOOL!
SHE WAS REALLY UPSET ON THE PHONE...
I DON'T KNOW WHAT SHE'S PLANNING TO DO! WHERE'S YUIKO?!
Boss the gofer
OH, SHE JUST LEFT.
SHE WAS WITH SOME GIRL CALLED MORISHITA.

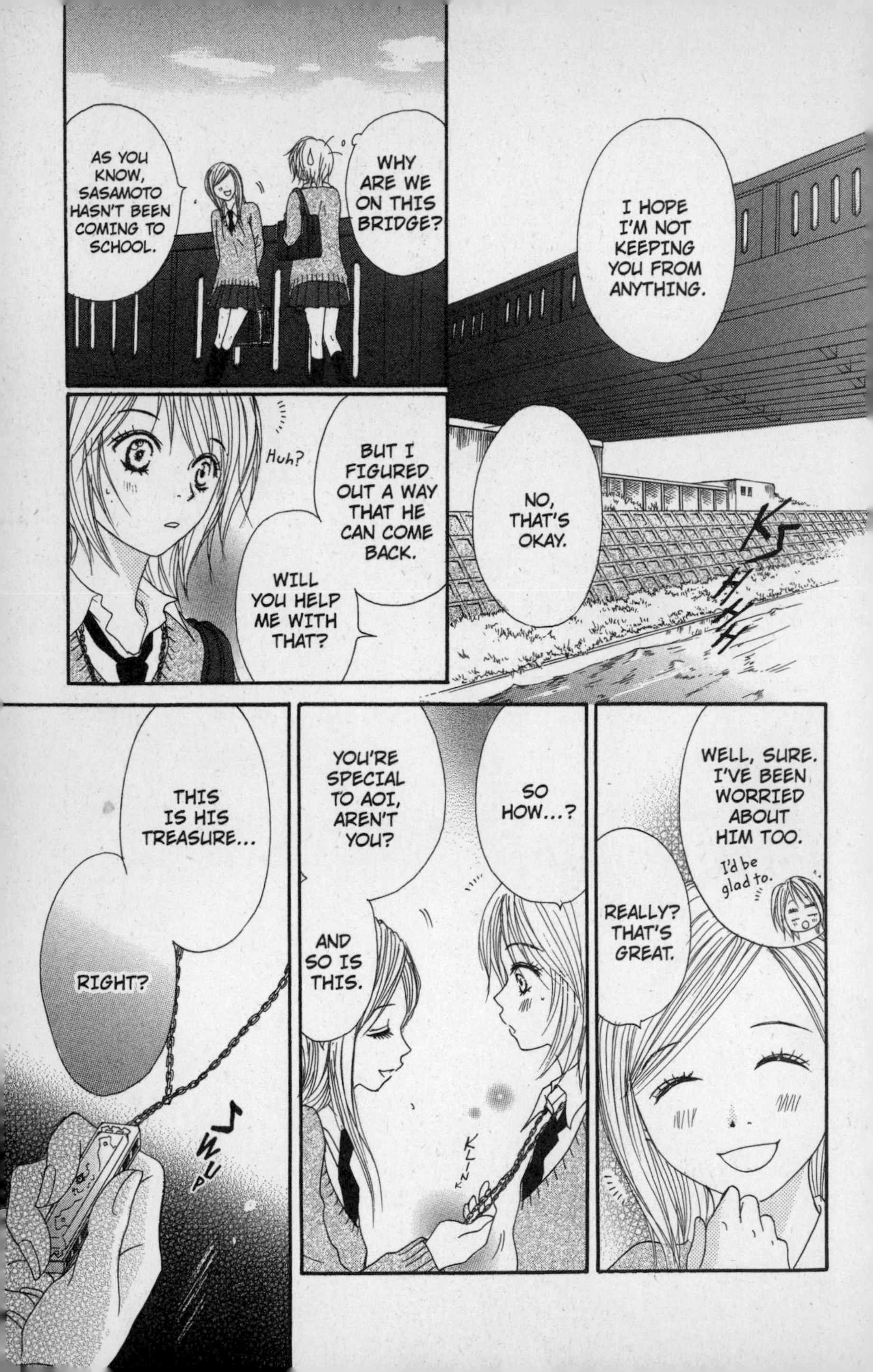
I HOPE I'M NOT KEEPING YOU FROM ANYTHING.
NO, THAT'S OKAY.
KSHHHH
WHY ARE WE ON THIS BRIDGE?
AS YOU KNOW, SASAMOTO HASN'T BEEN COMING TO SCHOOL.
BUT I FIGURED OUT A WAY THAT HE CAN COME BACK.
Huh?
WILL YOU HELP ME WITH THAT?
WELL, SURE. I'VE BEEN WORRIED ABOUT HIM TOO.
I'd be glad to.
REALLY? THAT'S GREAT.
SO HOW...?
YOU'RE SPECIAL TO AOI, AREN'T YOU?
AND SO IS THIS.
KLINK
THIS IS HIS TREASURE...
RIGHT?
SWUP

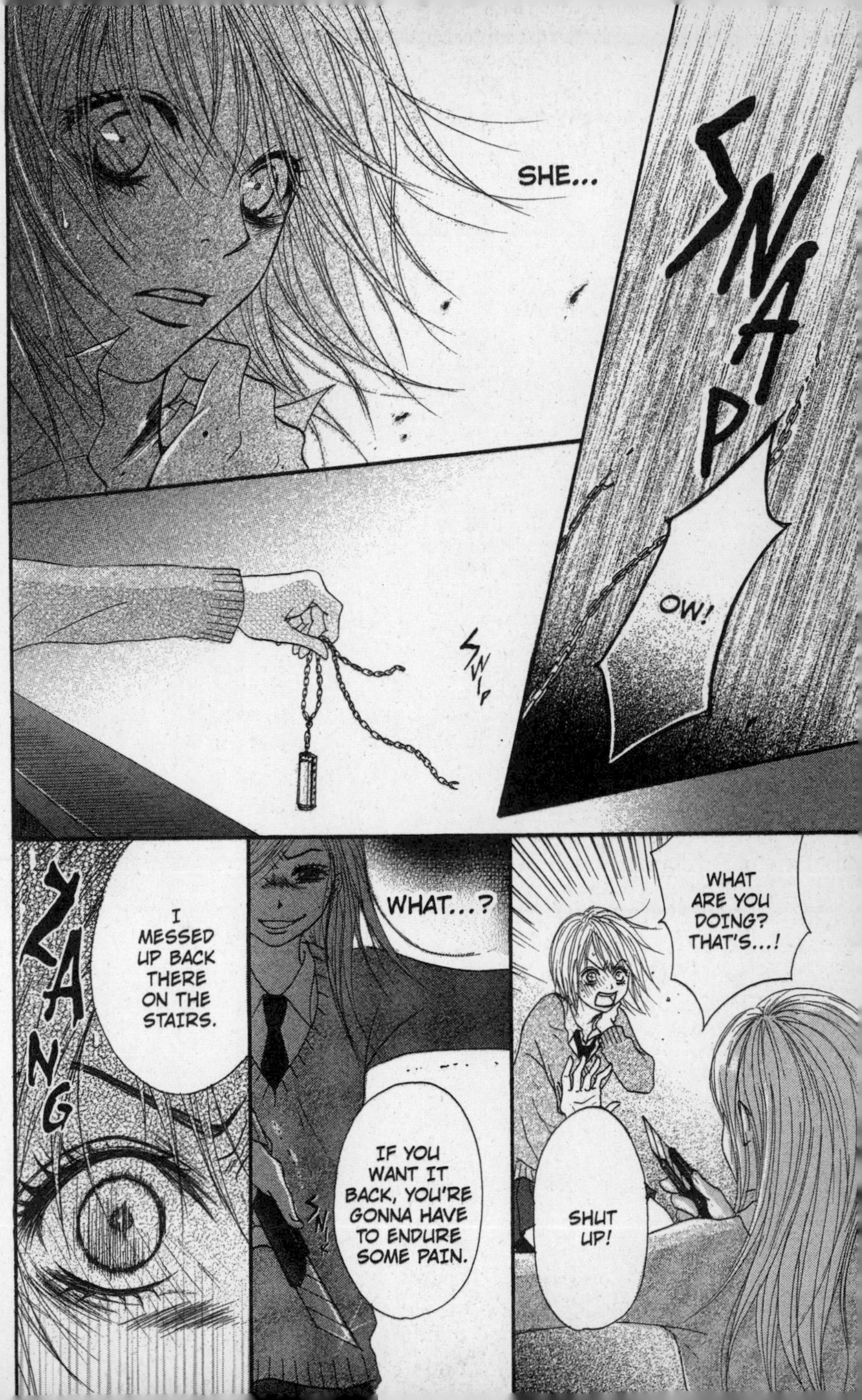
SNAP
OW!
SHE...
SNIP
WHAT ARE YOU DOING? THAT'S...!
SHUT UP!
WHAT...?
IF YOU WANT IT BACK, YOU'RE GONNA HAVE TO ENDURE SOME PAIN.
SNIK
I MESSED UP BACK THERE ON THE STAIRS.
ZANG

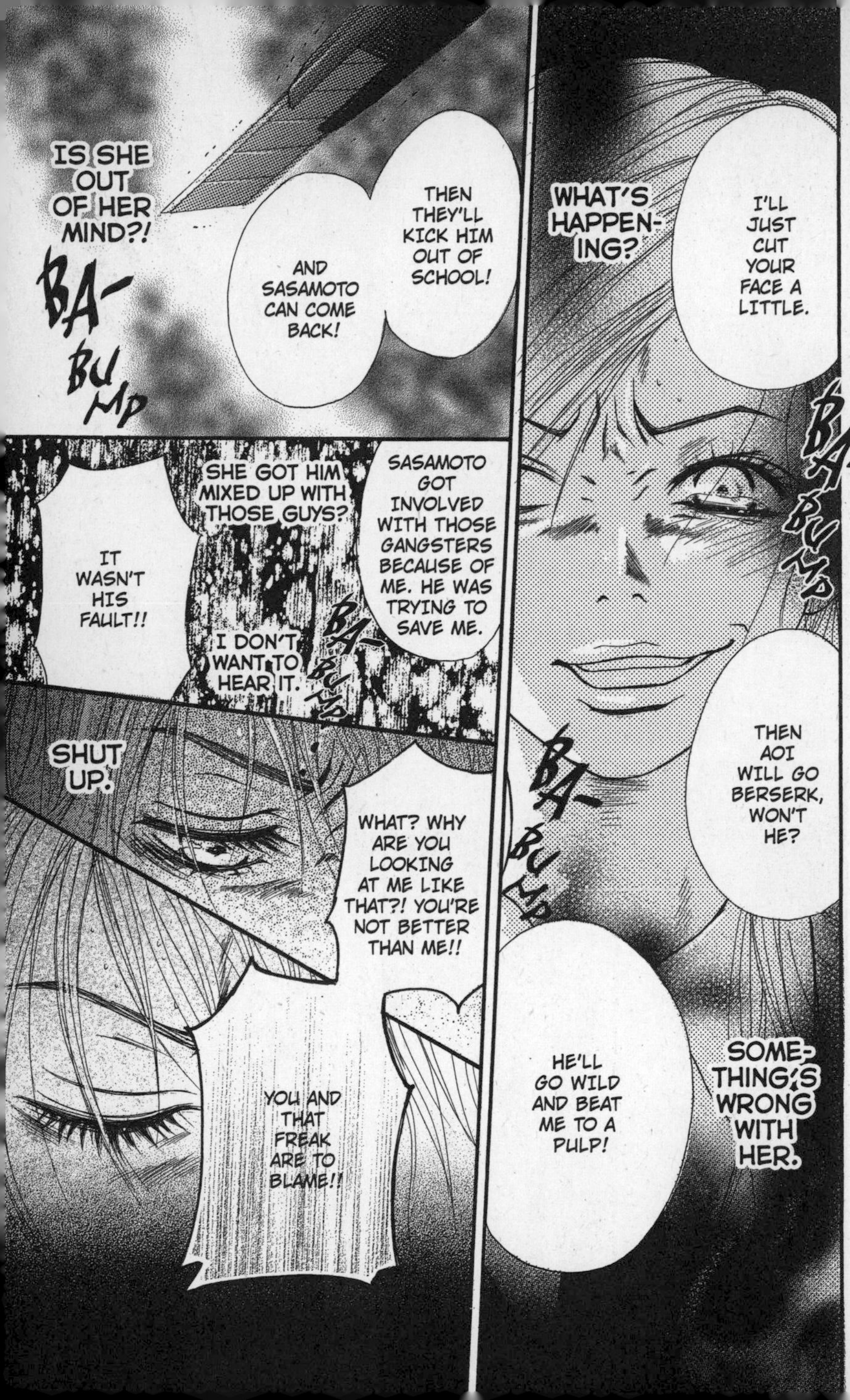
I'LL JUST CUT YOUR FACE A LITTLE.
WHAT'S HAPPENING?
BA-BUMP
THEN AOI WILL GO BERSERK, WON'T HE?
BA-BUMP
SOMETHING'S WRONG WITH HER.
HE'LL GO WILD AND BEAT ME TO A PULP!
THEN THEY'LL KICK HIM OUT OF SCHOOL!
AND SASAMOTO CAN COME BACK!
IS SHE OUT OF HER MIND?!
BA-BUMP
SASAMOTO GOT INVOLVED WITH THOSE GANGSTERS BECAUSE OF ME. HE WAS TRYING TO SAVE ME.
SHE GOT HIM MIXED UP WITH THOSE GUYS?
BA-BUMP
I DON'T WANT TO HEAR IT.
IT WASN'T HIS FAULT!!
WHAT? WHY ARE YOU LOOKING AT ME LIKE THAT?! YOU'RE NOT BETTER THAN ME!!
SHUT UP.
YOU AND THAT FREAK ARE TO BLAME!!

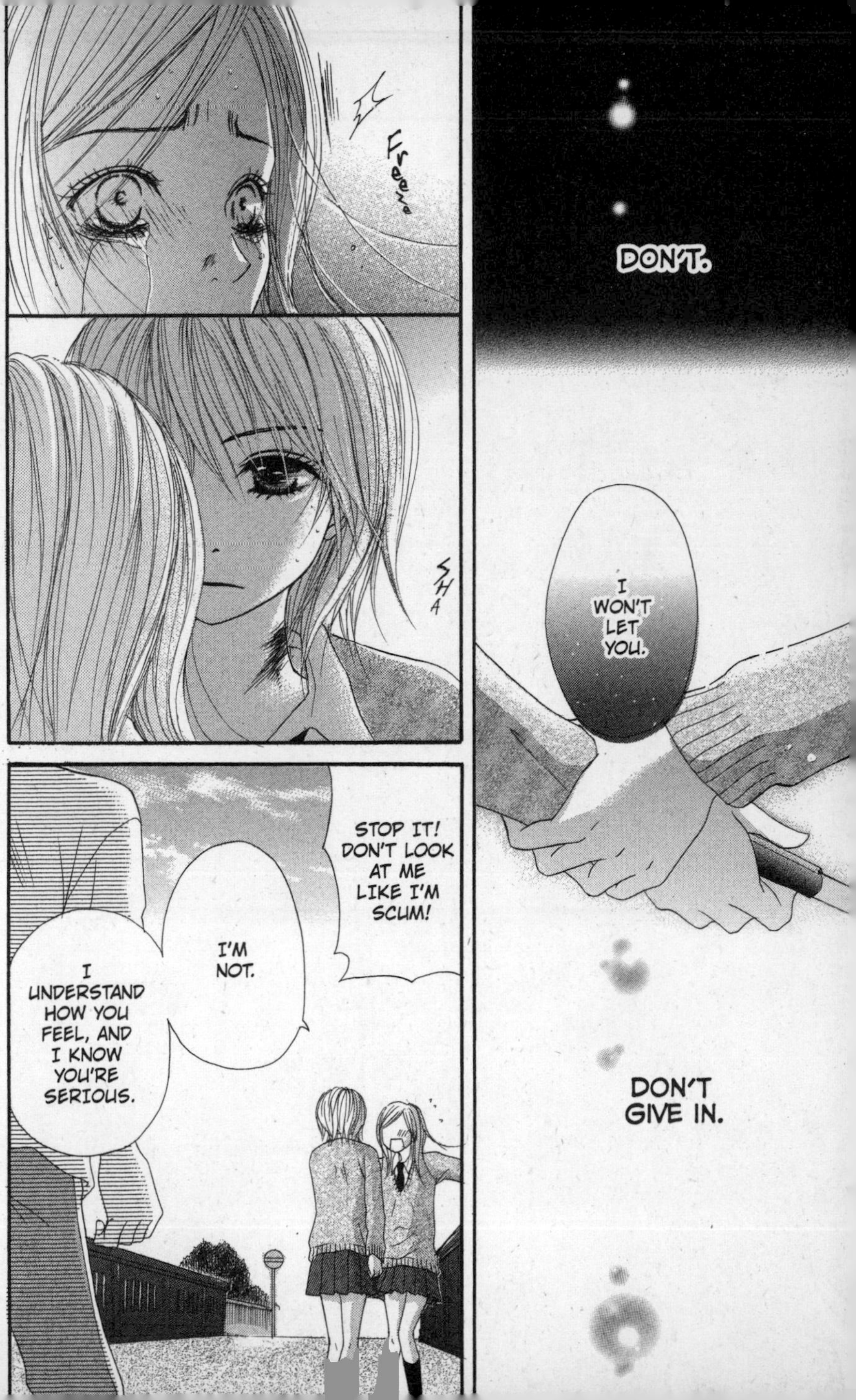
DON'T.
I WON'T LET YOU.
DON'T GIVE IN.
Freeze
SHA
STOP IT! DON'T LOOK AT ME LIKE I'M SCUM!
I'M NOT.
I UNDERSTAND HOW YOU FEEL, AND I KNOW YOU'RE SERIOUS.

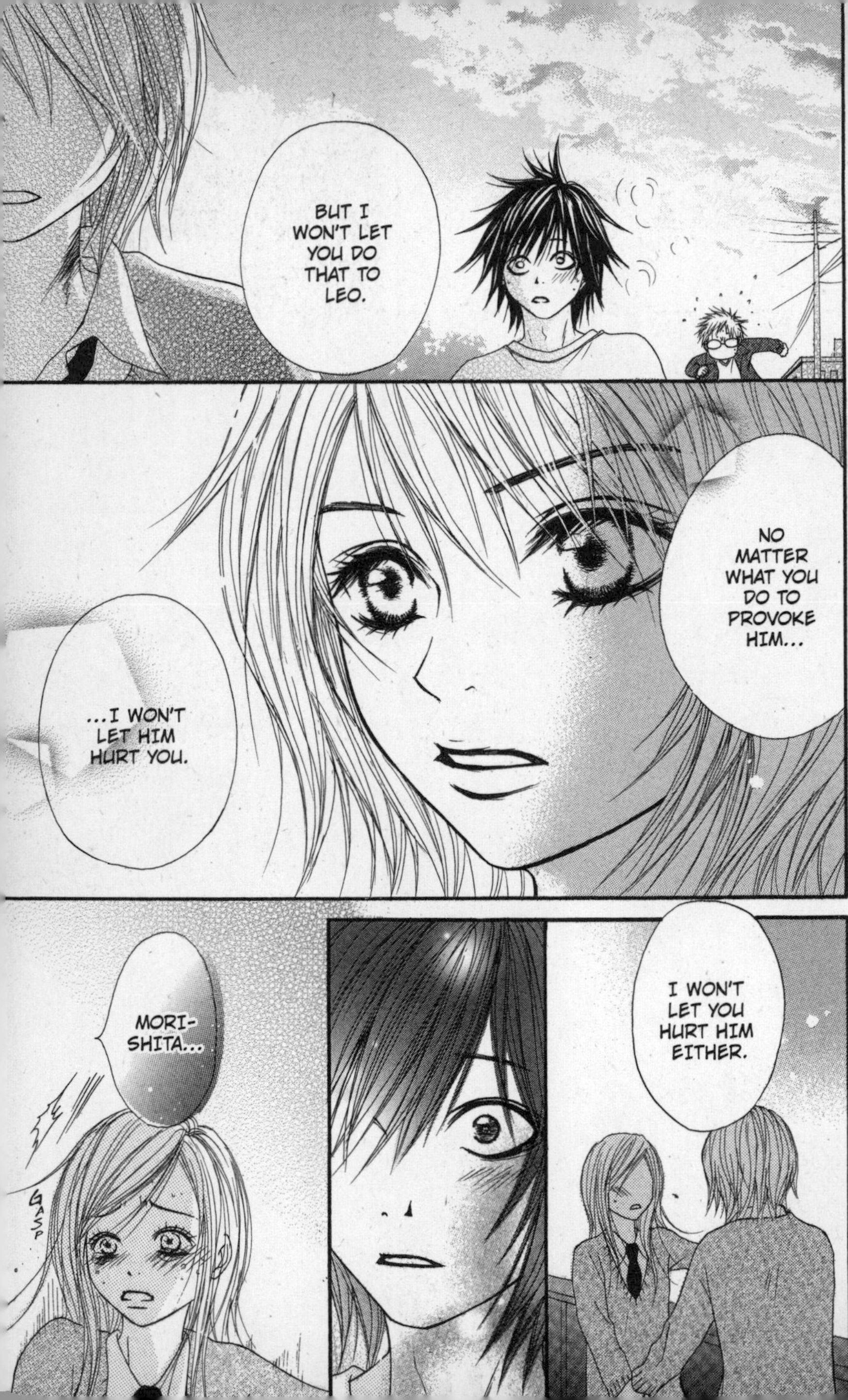
BUT I WON'T LET YOU DO THAT TO LEO.
NO MATTER WHAT YOU DO TO PROVOKE HIM...
...I WON'T LET HIM HURT YOU.
I WON'T LET YOU HURT HIM EITHER.
MORI-SHITA...
GASP

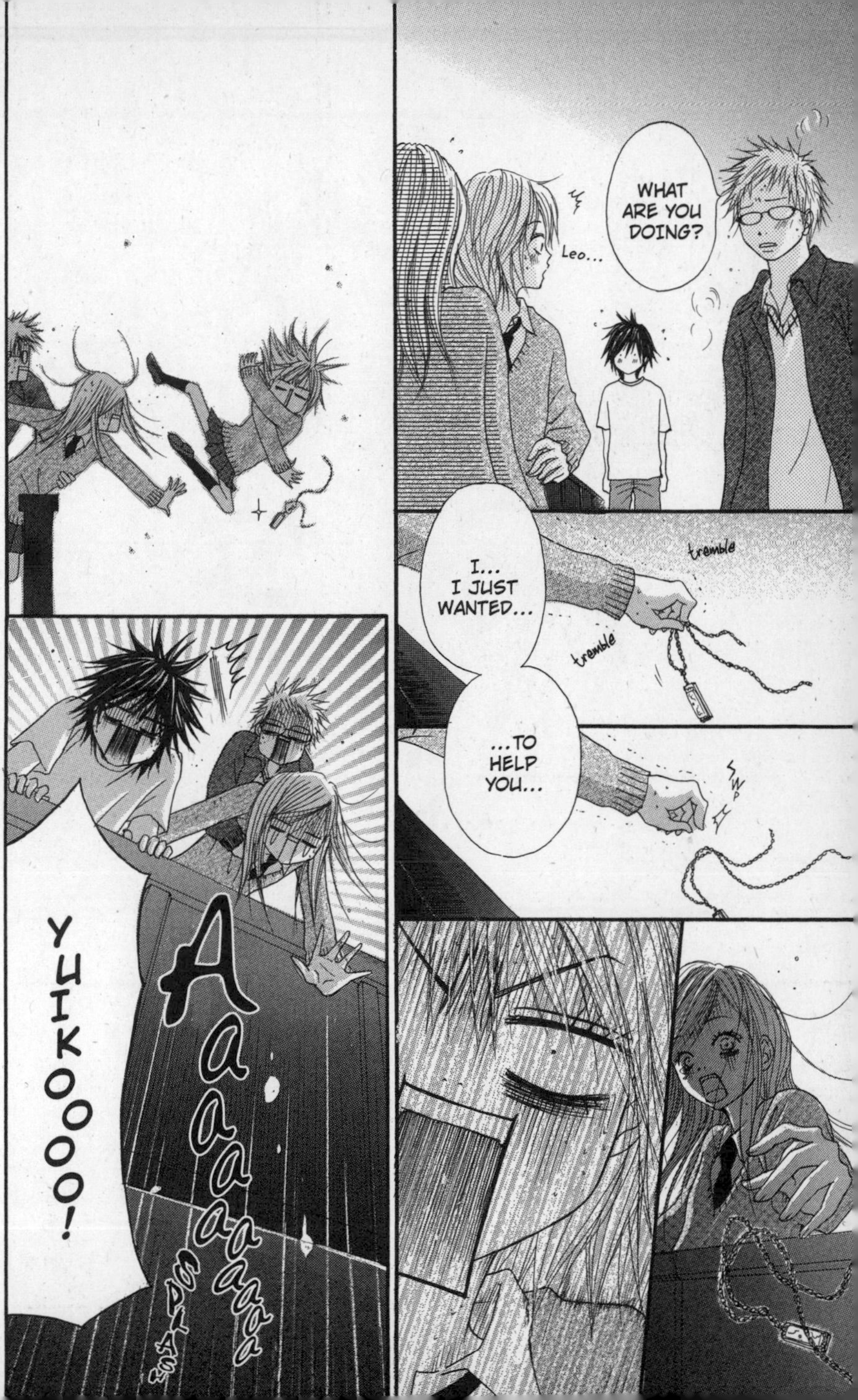
WHAT ARE YOU DOING?
Leo...
I... I JUST WANTED...
tremble
tremble
...TO HELP YOU...
SWP
Aaaaaaaaaaa
YUIKOOOOO!

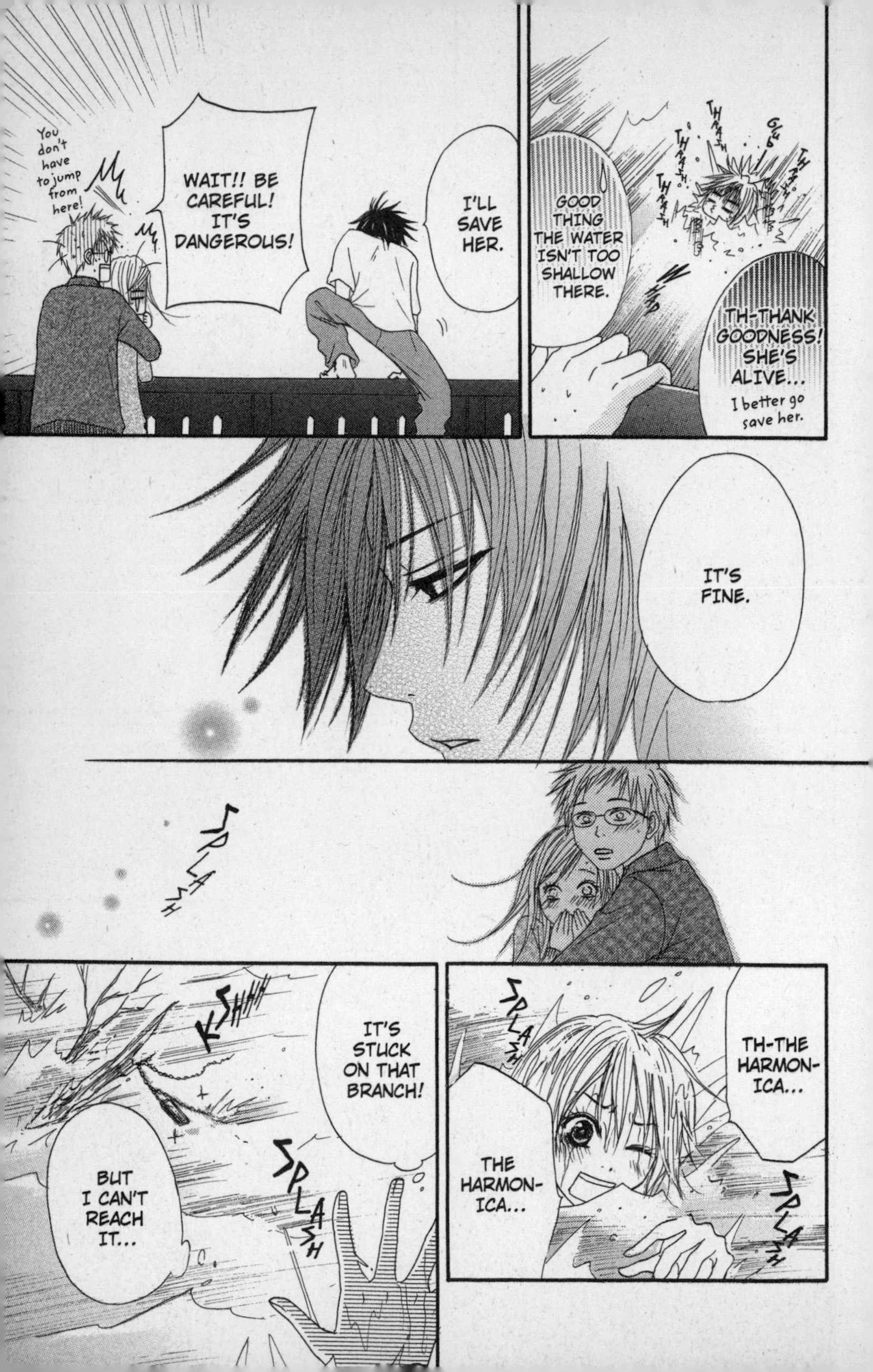
THRASH
GLUB
THRASH
THRASH
THRASH
GOOD THING THE WATER ISN'T TOO SHALLOW THERE.
TH-THANK GOODNESS! SHE'S ALIVE...
I better go save her.
I'LL SAVE HER.
WAIT!! BE CAREFUL! IT'S DANGEROUS!
You don't have to jump from here!
IT'S FINE.
SPLASH
SPLASH
TH-THE HARMONICA...
THE HARMONICA...
SPLASH
IT'S STUCK ON THAT BRANCH!
KSHHH
SPLASH
BUT I CAN'T REACH IT...

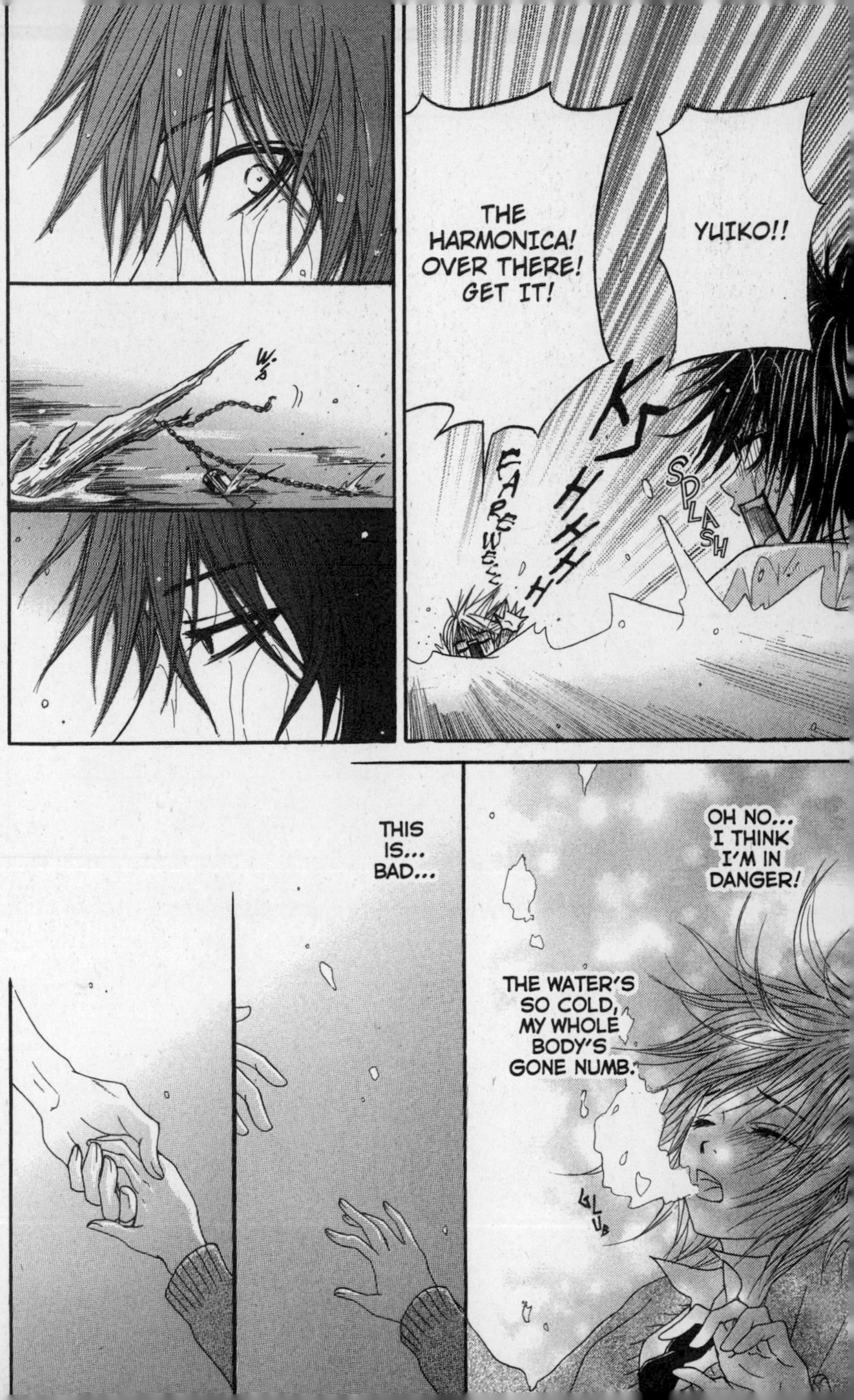
YUIKO!!
THE HARMONICA! OVER THERE! GET IT!
KSHHHHH
FAREWELL
SPLASH
OH NO... I THINK I'M IN DANGER!
THE WATER'S SO COLD, MY WHOLE BODY'S GONE NUMB.
GLUB
THIS IS... BAD...

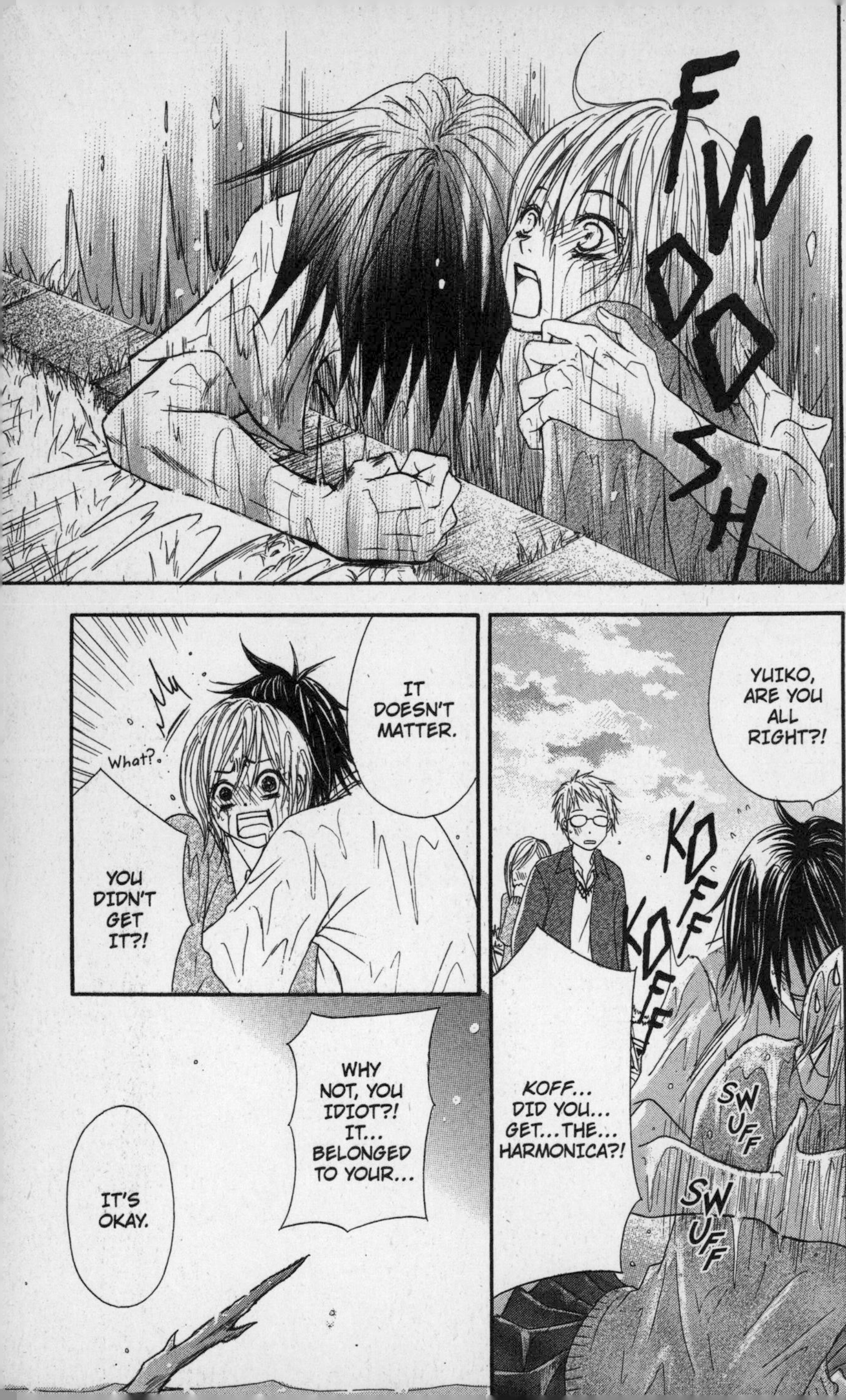
FWOOSH
YUIKO, ARE YOU ALL RIGHT?!
KOFF
KOFF
KOFF... DID YOU... GET...THE... HARMONICA?!
SWUFF
SWUFF
IT DOESN'T MATTER.
What?
YOU DIDN'T GET IT?!
WHY NOT, YOU IDIOT?! IT... BELONGED TO YOUR...
IT'S OKAY.

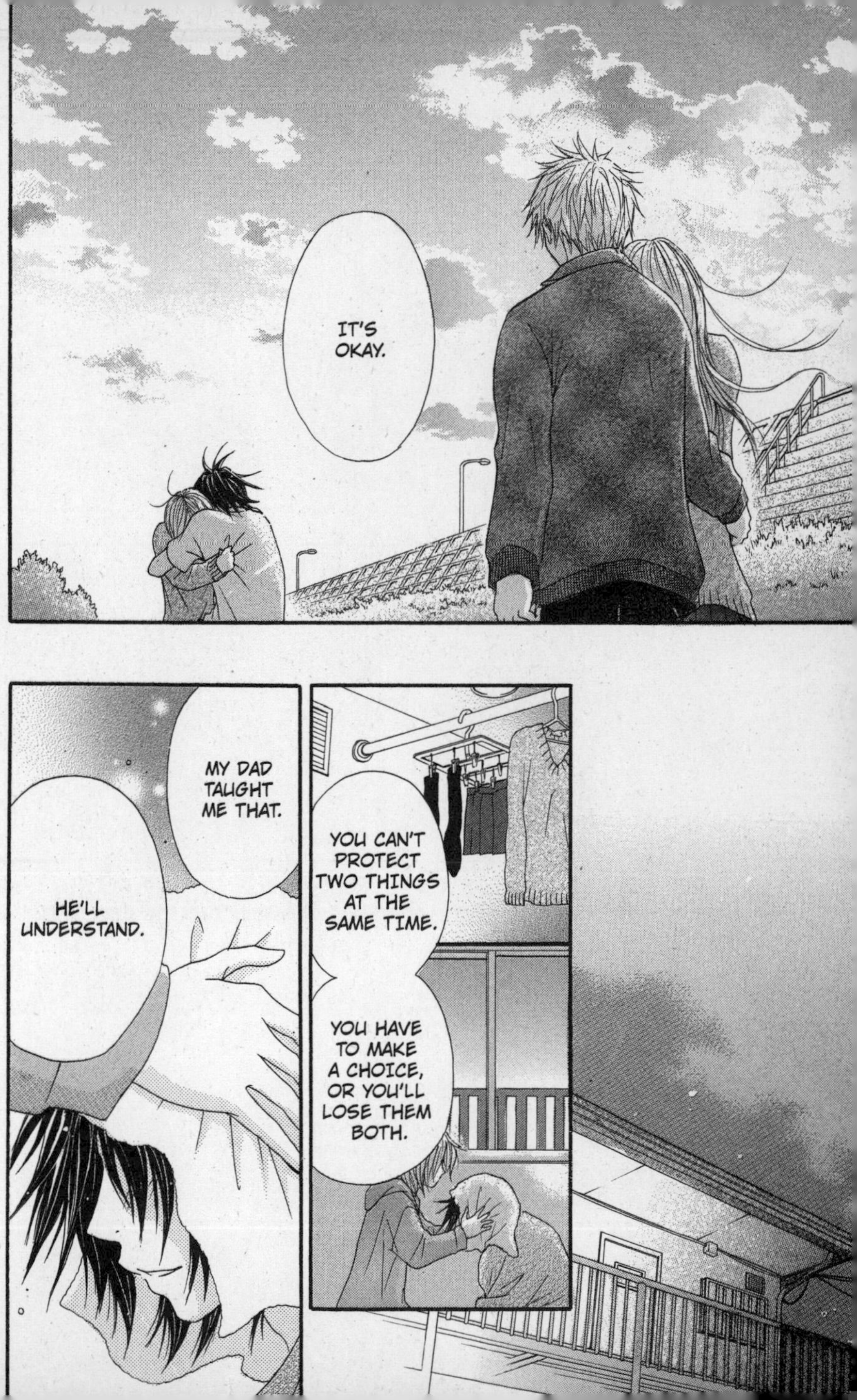
IT'S OKAY.
YOU CAN'T PROTECT TWO THINGS AT THE SAME TIME.
YOU HAVE TO MAKE A CHOICE, OR YOU'LL LOSE THEM BOTH.
MY DAD TAUGHT ME THAT.
HE'LL UNDERSTAND.

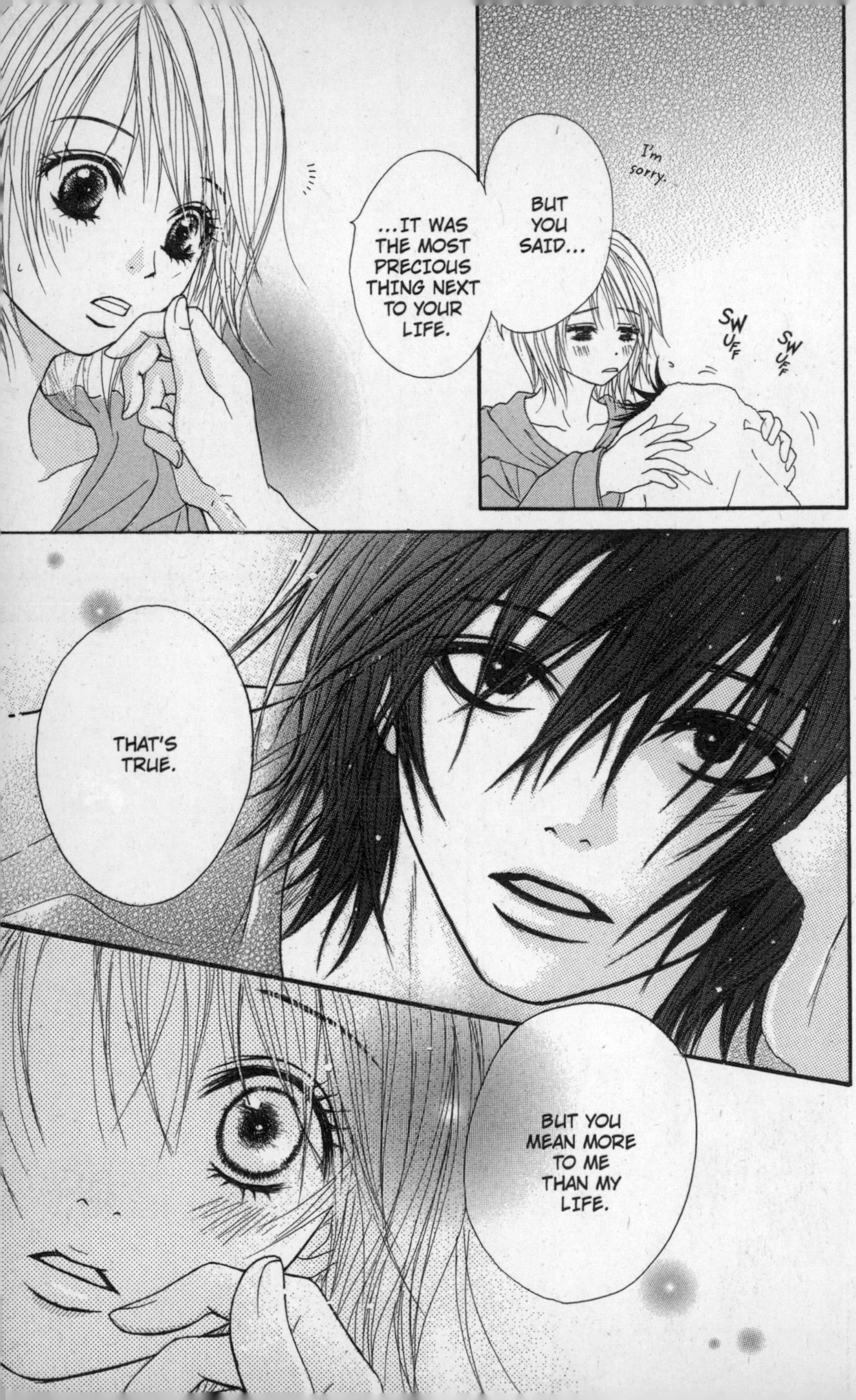
I'm sorry.
BUT YOU SAID...
...IT WAS THE MOST PRECIOUS THING NEXT TO YOUR LIFE.
SWUFF
SWUFF
THAT'S TRUE.
BUT YOU MEAN MORE TO ME THAN MY LIFE.

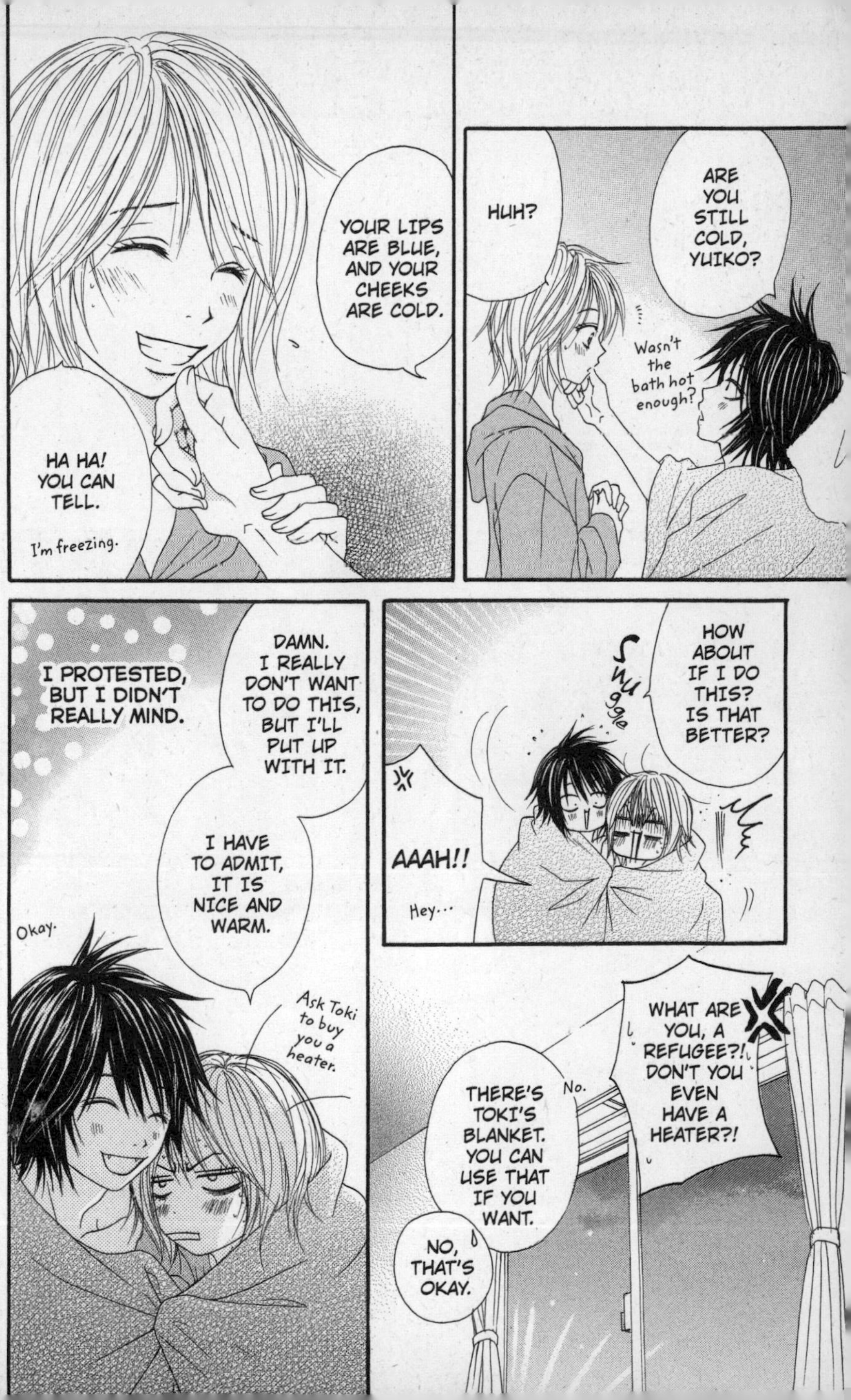
ARE YOU STILL COLD, YUIKO?
HUH?
Wasn't the bath hot enough?
YOUR LIPS ARE BLUE, AND YOUR CHEEKS ARE COLD.
HA HA! YOU CAN TELL.
I'm freezing.
HOW ABOUT IF I DO THIS? IS THAT BETTER?
Snuggle
AAAH!!
Hey...
WHAT ARE YOU, A REFUGEE?! DON'T YOU EVEN HAVE A HEATER?!
No.
THERE'S TOKI'S BLANKET. YOU CAN USE THAT IF YOU WANT.
NO, THAT'S OKAY.
I PROTESTED, BUT I DIDN'T REALLY MIND.
DAMN. I REALLY DON'T WANT TO DO THIS, BUT I'LL PUT UP WITH IT.
I HAVE TO ADMIT, IT IS NICE AND WARM.
Okay.
Ask Toki to buy you a heater.

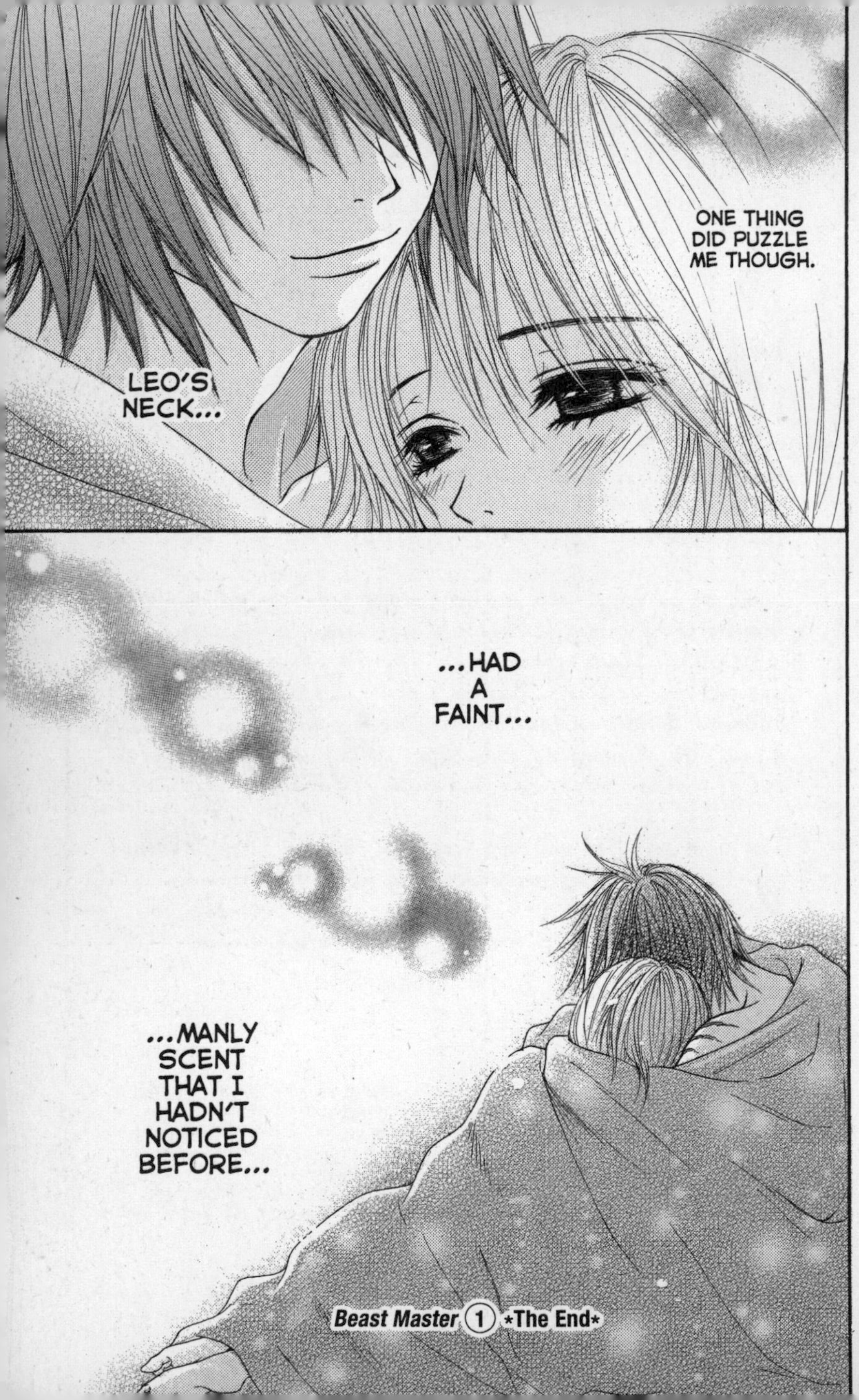
ONE THING DID PUZZLE ME THOUGH.
LEO'S NECK...
...HAD A FAINT...
...MANLY SCENT THAT I HADN'T NOTICED BEFORE...
Beast Master 1 *The End*

About "Fly"

Well, the short story "Fly" begins on the next page. I wrote it some time ago. That in itself is embarrassing, but on top of that, in a readers' survey done by the magazine it was first published in, it almost came in last. Actually, it's one of my most memorable works—but not in a good way. Hee hee... I'm laughing, but tears are running down my cheeks. Hee hee hee...

Now, as to why such a short story got printed... Well, maybe they thought it would get some laughs since it's so bad. I guess you could say it's about making grown-up decisions. But this story is special to me because it helped launch my career. And the passion I put into developing this story and the love that grew out of it has influenced me in many ways.

I'm sure some of you are working toward your dreams right now and are encountering heavy resistance. Maybe it seems like there's a huge wall between you and your dreams. This story is dedicated to you.

A few of the elements of this story may remind you of Beast Master, like the name of the heroine and the jumping-into-the-river part, but they're not connected. That's just my lack of creativity. Hee hee... There I go, disparaging myself to the very end...

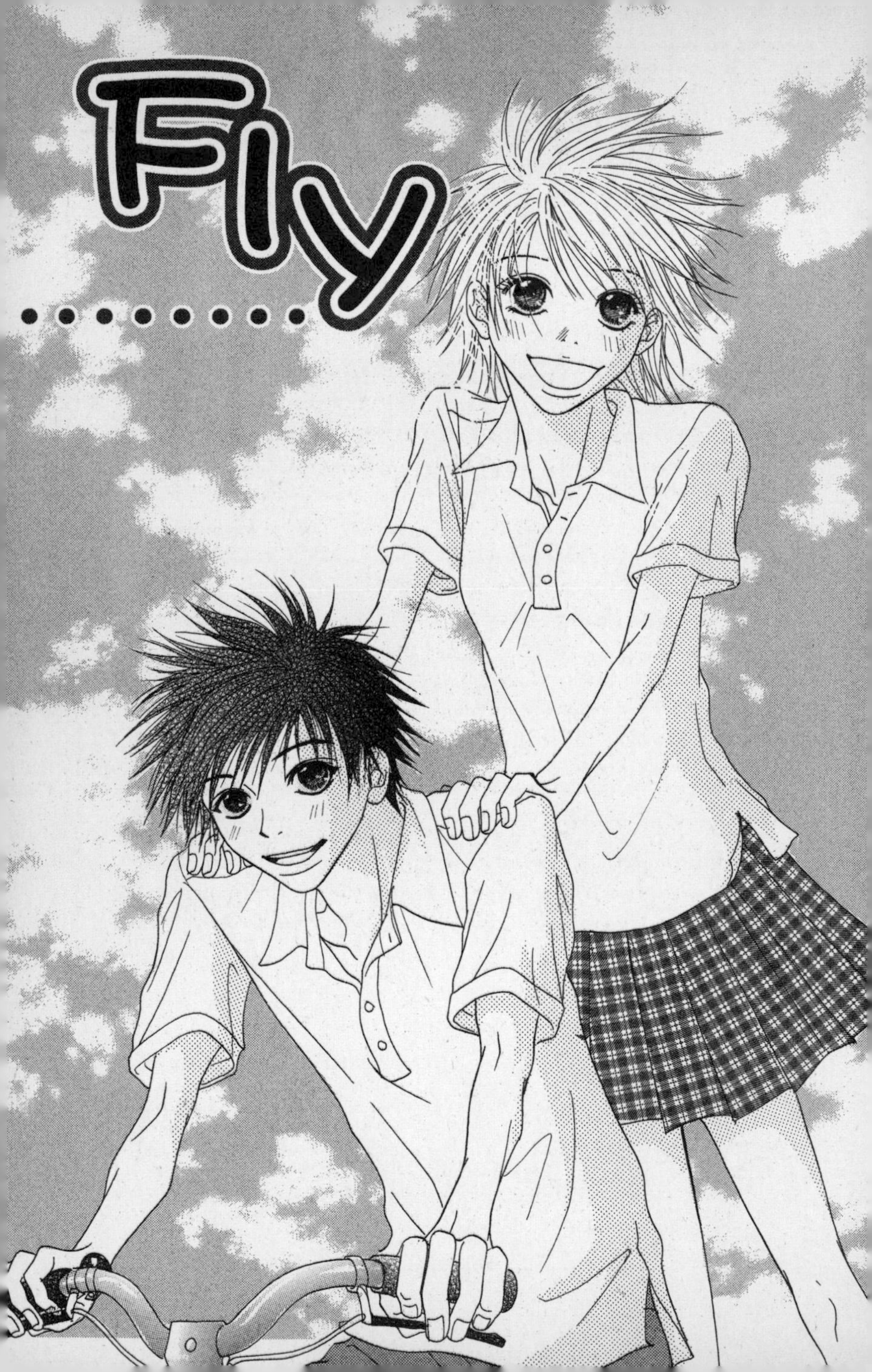
Fly

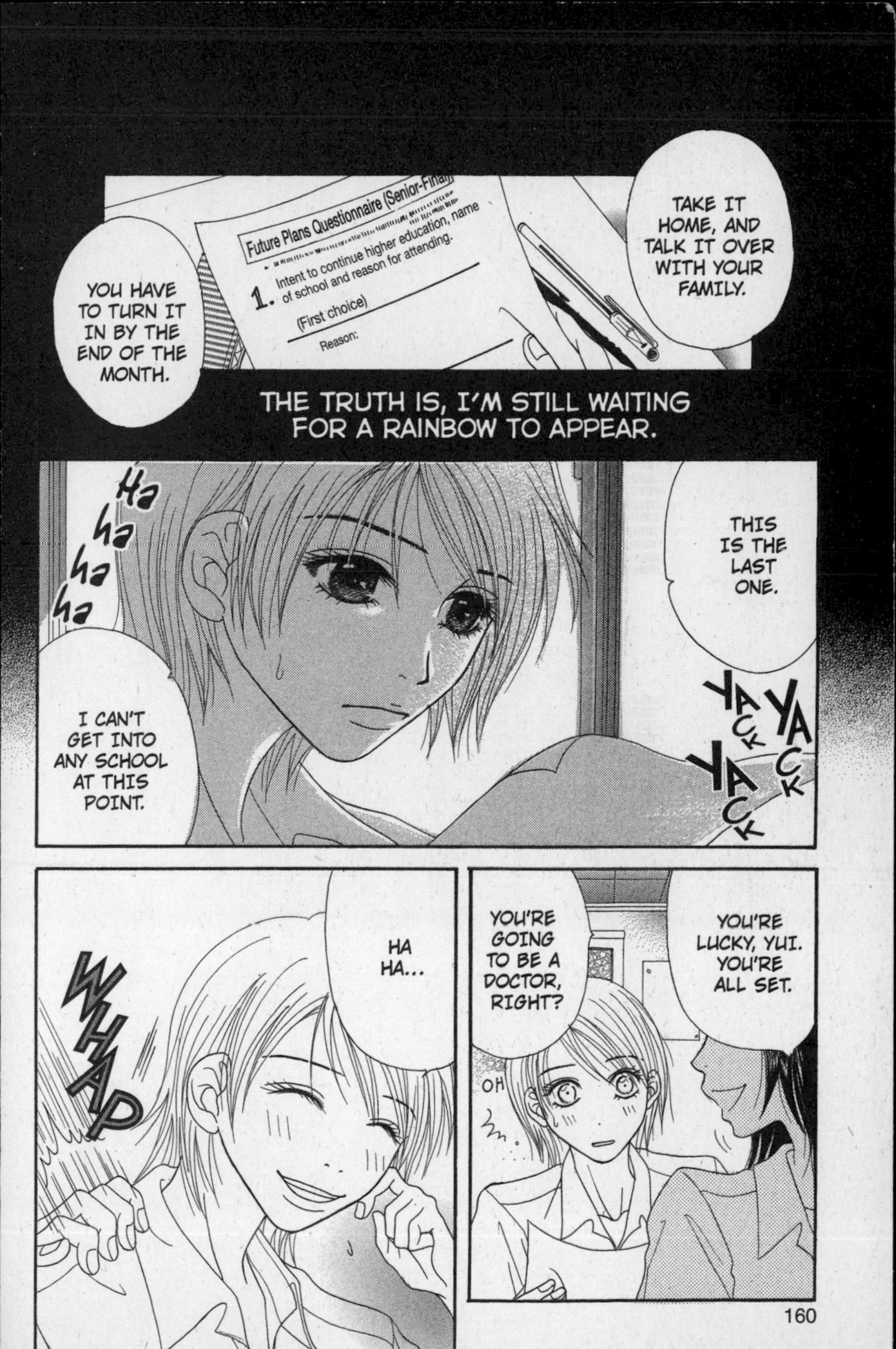
TAKE IT HOME, AND TALK IT OVER WITH YOUR FAMILY.
Future Plans Questionnaire (Senior-Final)
1. Intent to continue higher education, name of school and reason for attending.
(First choice)
Reason:
YOU HAVE TO TURN IT IN BY THE END OF THE MONTH.
THE TRUTH IS, I'M STILL WAITING FOR A RAINBOW TO APPEAR.
THIS IS THE LAST ONE.
YACK YACK YACK
Ha ha ha ha
I CAN'T GET INTO ANY SCHOOL AT THIS POINT.
YOU'RE LUCKY, YUI. YOU'RE ALL SET.
YOU'RE GOING TO BE A DOCTOR, RIGHT?
OH
HA HA...
WHAP

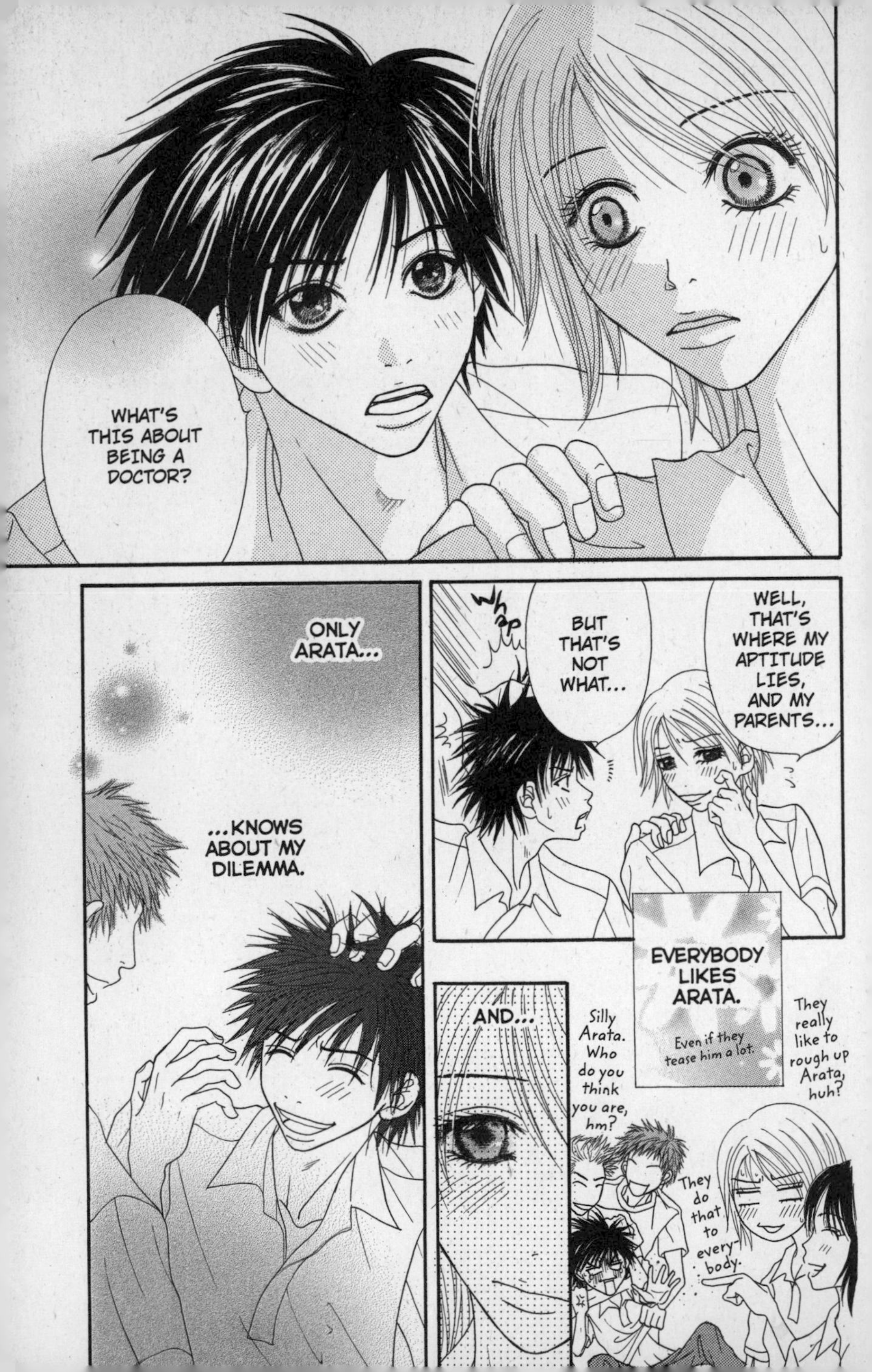
WHAT'S THIS ABOUT BEING A DOCTOR?
WELL, THAT'S WHERE MY APTITUDE LIES, AND MY PARENTS...
BUT THAT'S NOT WHAT...
Whap
EVERYBODY LIKES ARATA.
Even if they tease him a lot.
They really like to rough up Arata, huh?
Silly Arata. Who do you think you are, hm?
They do that to every-body.
AND...
ONLY ARATA...
...KNOWS ABOUT MY DILEMMA.

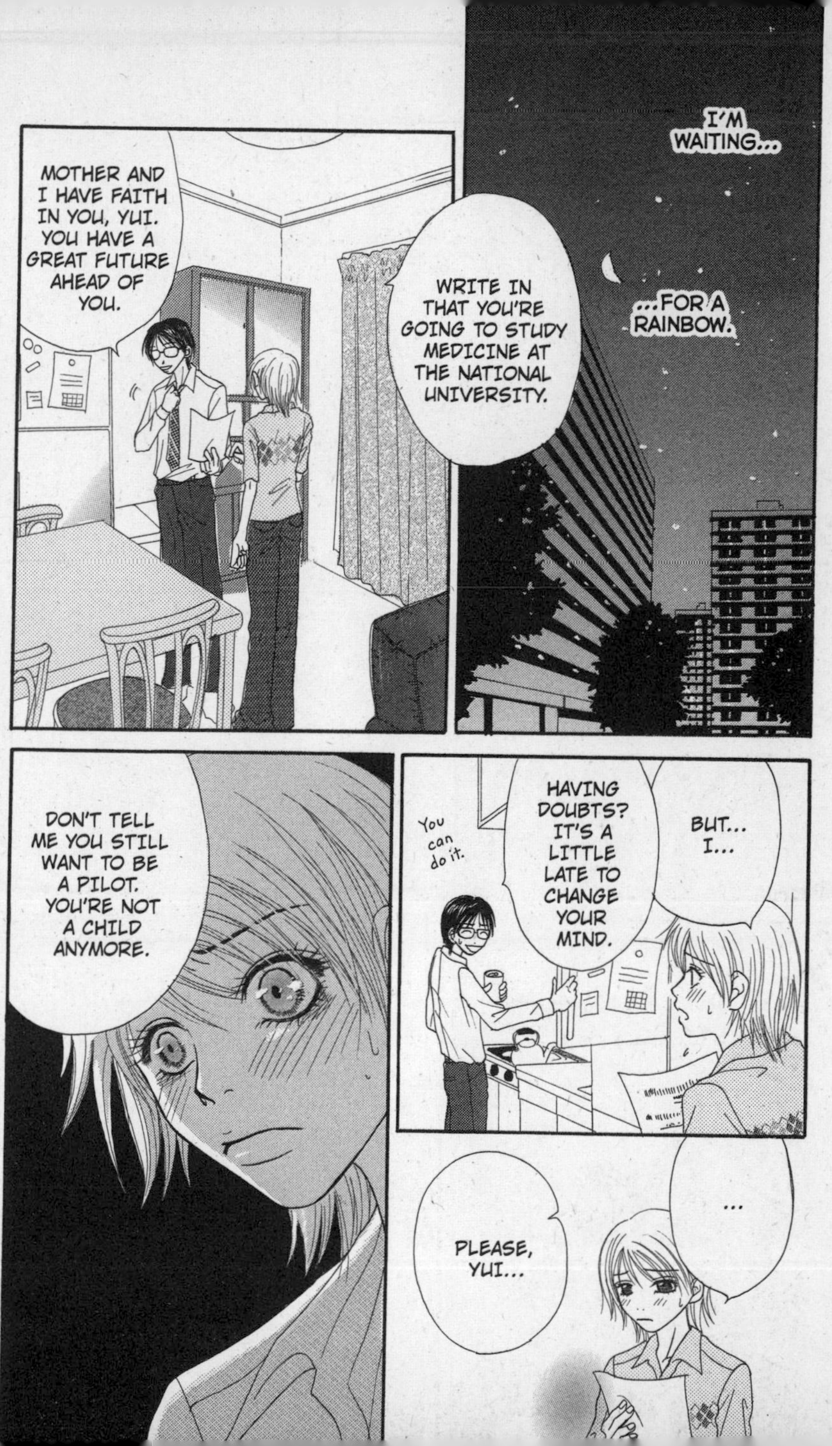
I'M WAITING...
...FOR A RAINBOW.
MOTHER AND I HAVE FAITH IN YOU, YUI. YOU HAVE A GREAT FUTURE AHEAD OF YOU.
WRITE IN THAT YOU'RE GOING TO STUDY MEDICINE AT THE NATIONAL UNIVERSITY.
BUT... I...
HAVING DOUBTS? IT'S A LITTLE LATE TO CHANGE YOUR MIND.
You can do it.
...
PLEASE, YUI...
DON'T TELL ME YOU STILL WANT TO BE A PILOT. YOU'RE NOT A CHILD ANYMORE.

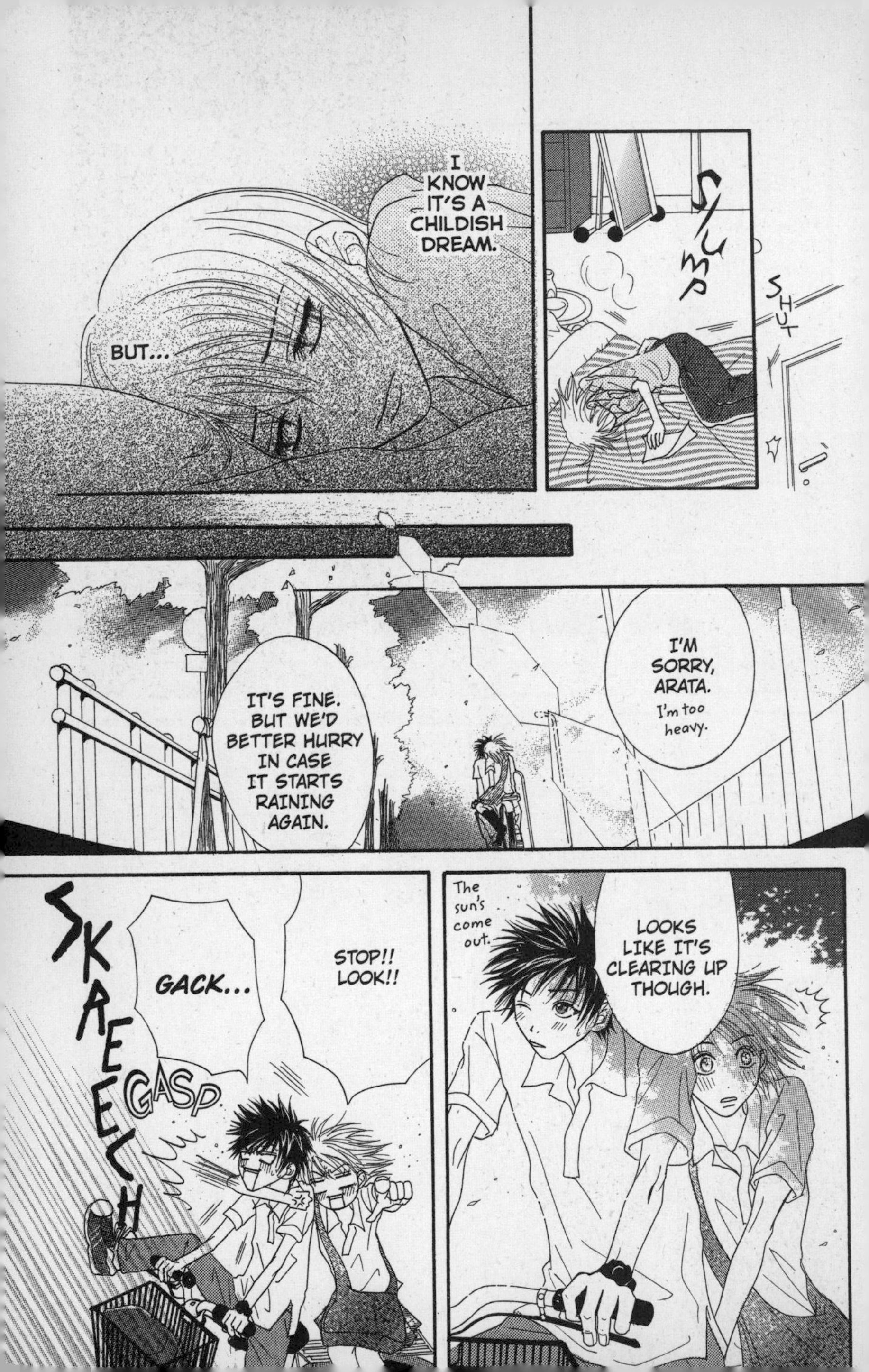
SLUMP
SHUT
I KNOW IT'S A CHILDISH DREAM.
BUT...
I'M SORRY, ARATA.
I'm too heavy.
IT'S FINE. BUT WE'D BETTER HURRY IN CASE IT STARTS RAINING AGAIN.
The sun's come out.
LOOKS LIKE IT'S CLEARING UP THOUGH.
STOP!! LOOK!!
GACK...
SKREECH
GASP

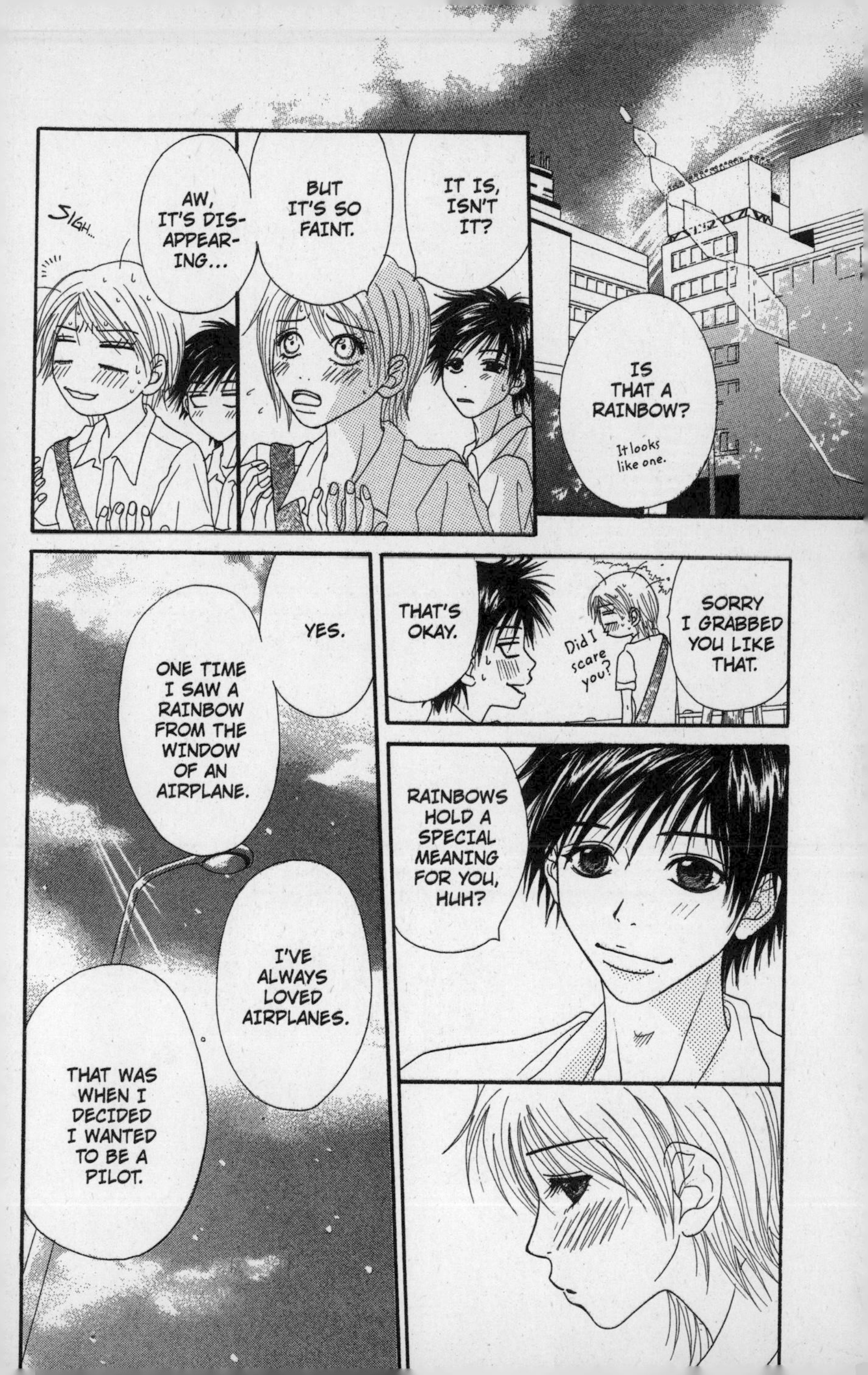
IS THAT A RAINBOW?
It looks like one.
IT IS, ISN'T IT?
BUT IT'S SO FAINT.
AW, IT'S DIS-APPEAR-ING...
SIGH...
SORRY I GRABBED YOU LIKE THAT.
Did I scare you?
THAT'S OKAY.
RAINBOWS HOLD A SPECIAL MEANING FOR YOU, HUH?
YES.
ONE TIME I SAW A RAINBOW FROM THE WINDOW OF AN AIRPLANE.
I'VE ALWAYS LOVED AIRPLANES.
THAT WAS WHEN I DECIDED I WANTED TO BE A PILOT.

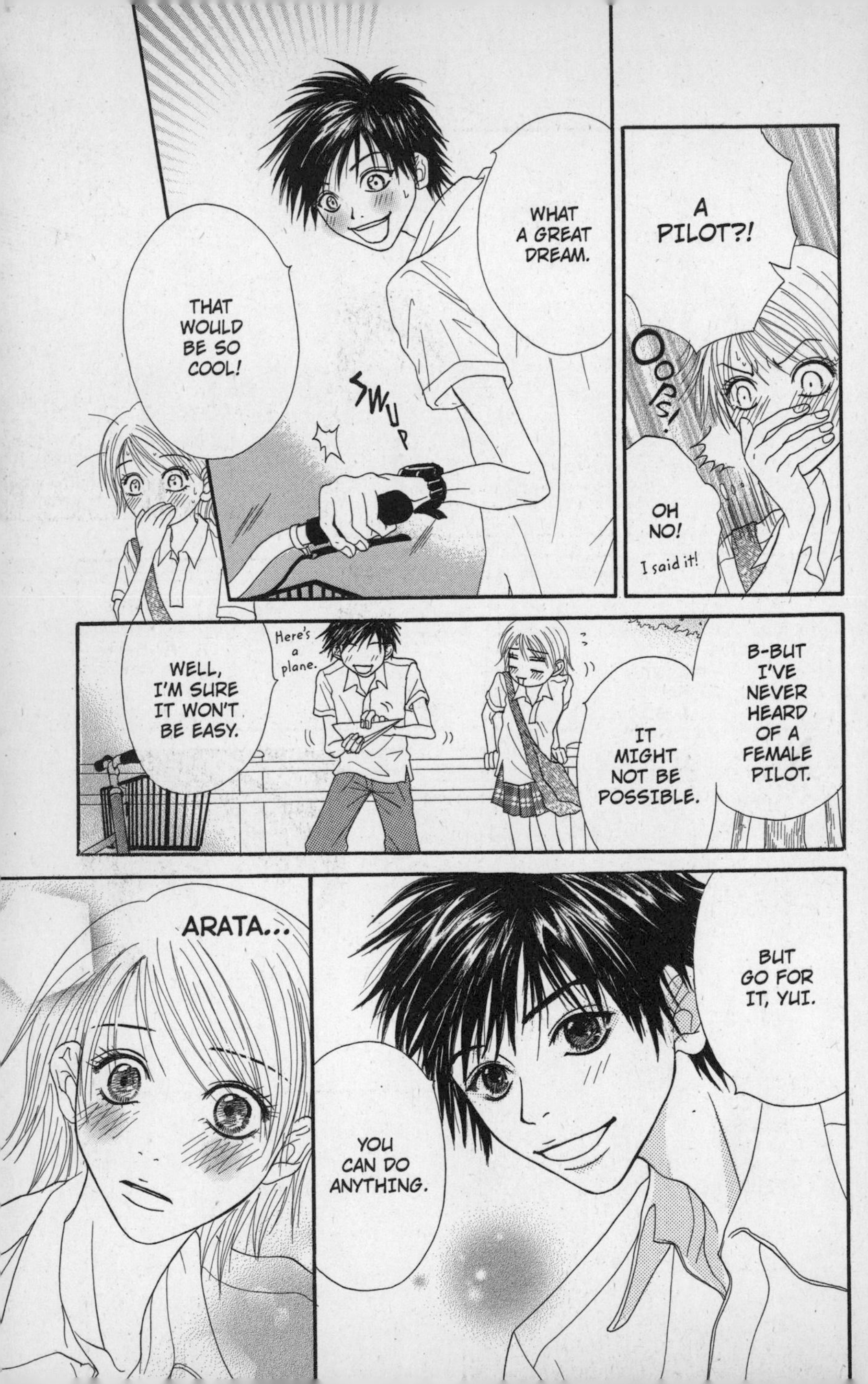
A PILOT?!
OOPS!
OH NO!
I said it!
WHAT A GREAT DREAM.
THAT WOULD BE SO COOL!
SWUP
B-BUT I'VE NEVER HEARD OF A FEMALE PILOT.
IT MIGHT NOT BE POSSIBLE.
Here's a plane.
WELL, I'M SURE IT WON'T BE EASY.
BUT GO FOR IT, YUI.
YOU CAN DO ANYTHING.
ARATA...

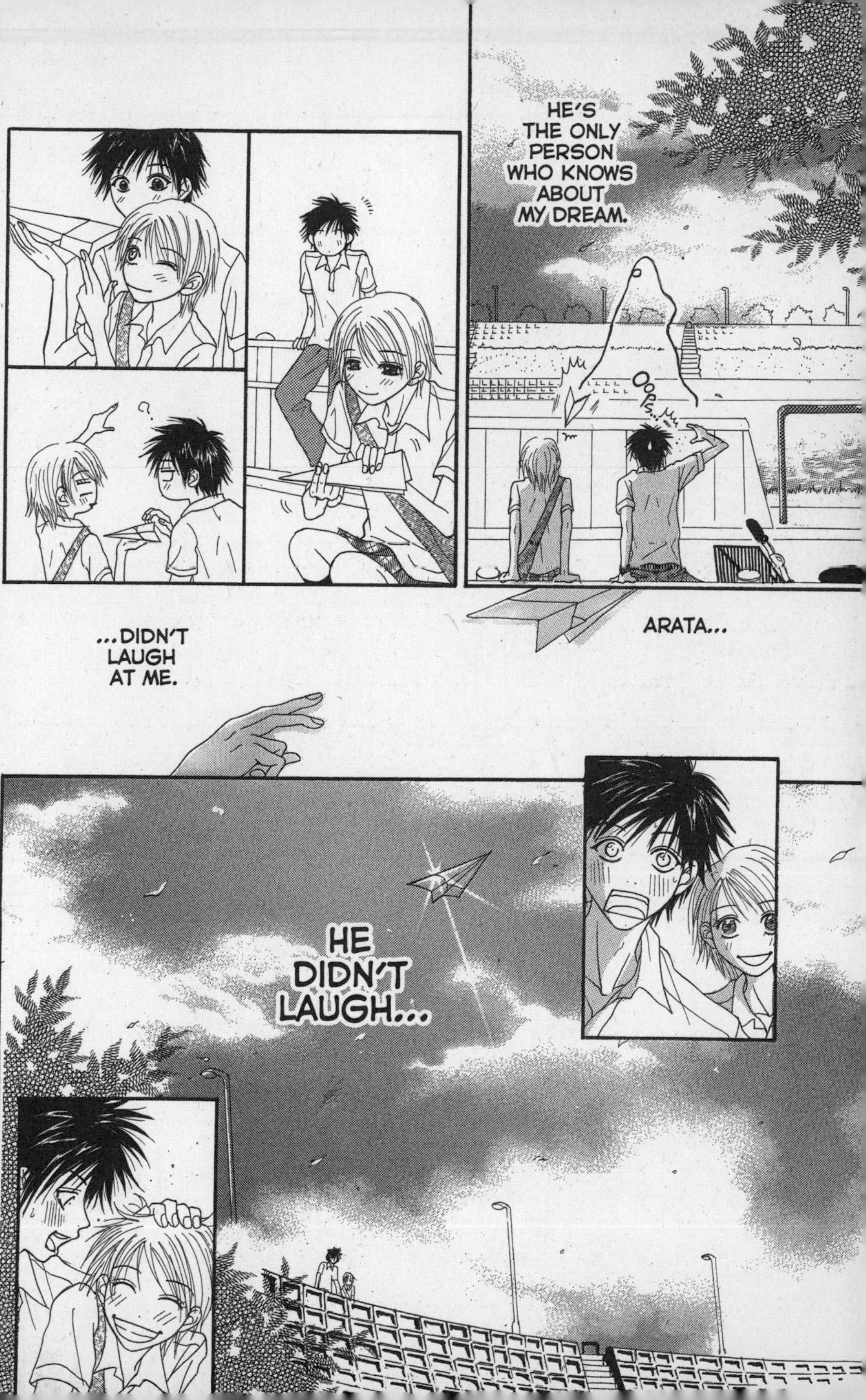
HE'S THE ONLY PERSON WHO KNOWS ABOUT MY DREAM.
OOPS...
ARATA...
...DIDN'T LAUGH AT ME.
HE DIDN'T LAUGH...

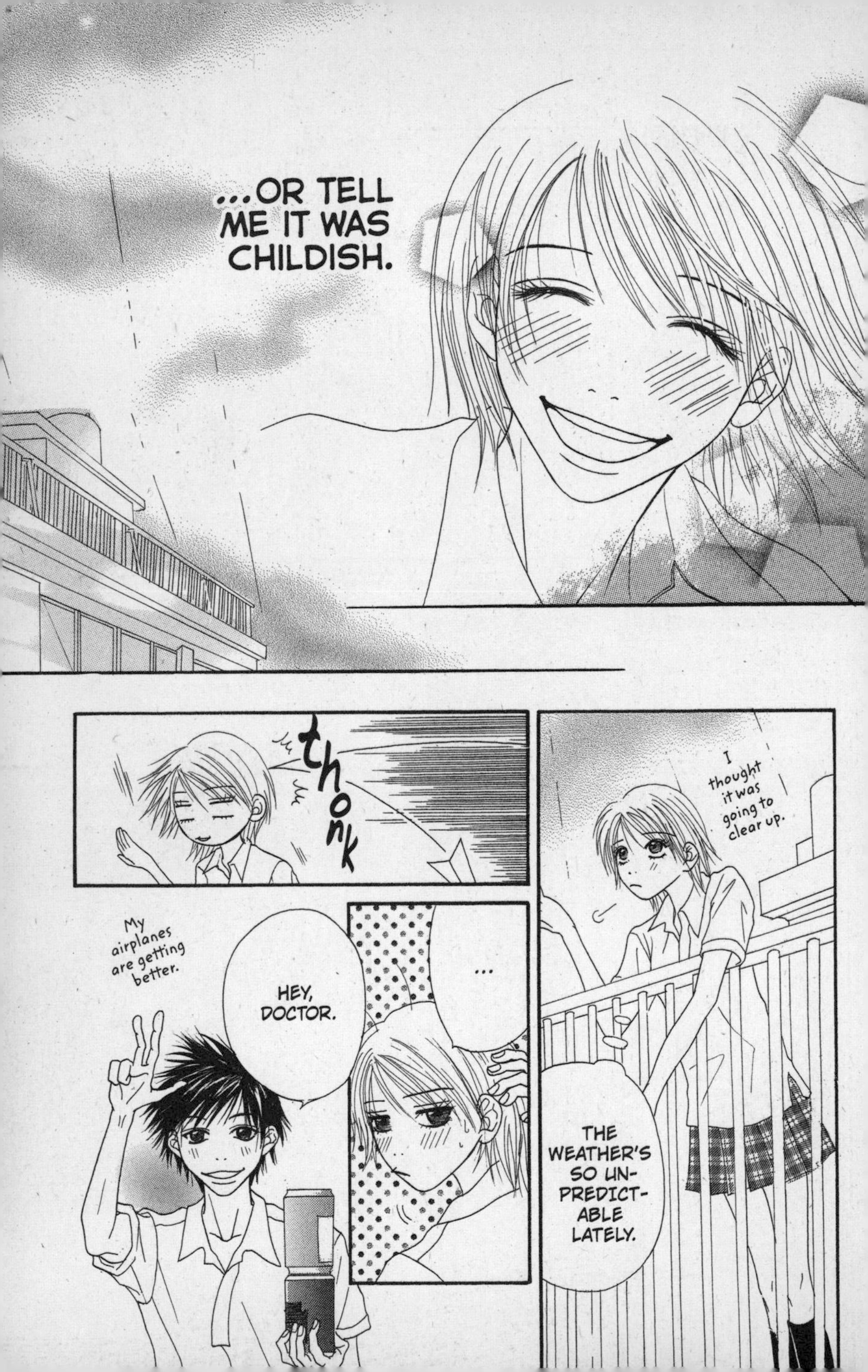
...OR TELL ME IT WAS CHILDISH.
I thought it was going to clear up.
THE WEATHER'S SO UN-PREDICT-ABLE LATELY.
thonk
...
My airplanes are getting better.
HEY, DOCTOR.

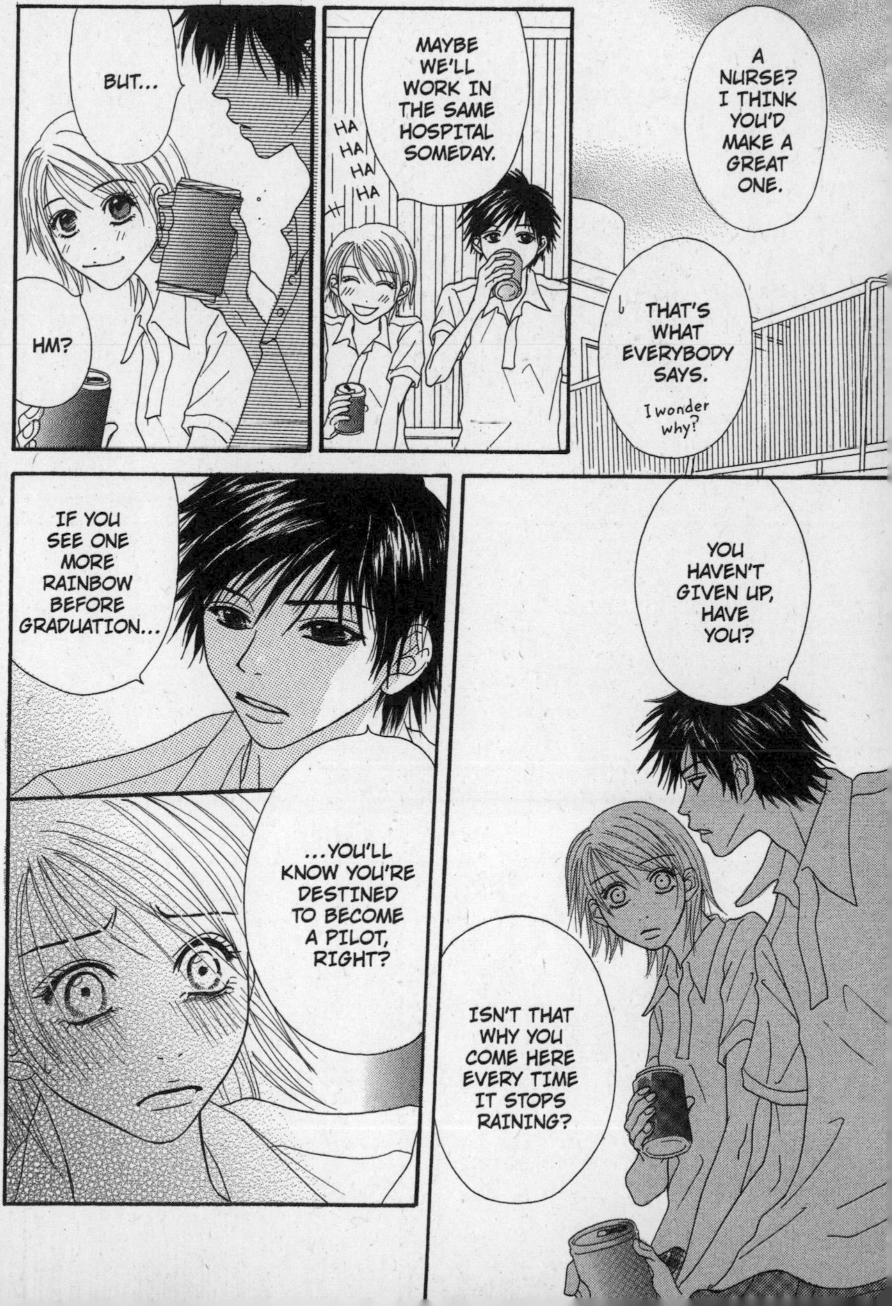
A NURSE? I THINK YOU'D MAKE A GREAT ONE.
THAT'S WHAT EVERYBODY SAYS.
I wonder why?
MAYBE WE'LL WORK IN THE SAME HOSPITAL SOMEDAY.
HA HA HA HA
BUT...
HM?
YOU HAVEN'T GIVEN UP, HAVE YOU?
ISN'T THAT WHY YOU COME HERE EVERY TIME IT STOPS RAINING?
IF YOU SEE ONE MORE RAINBOW BEFORE GRADUATION...
...YOU'LL KNOW YOU'RE DESTINED TO BECOME A PILOT, RIGHT?

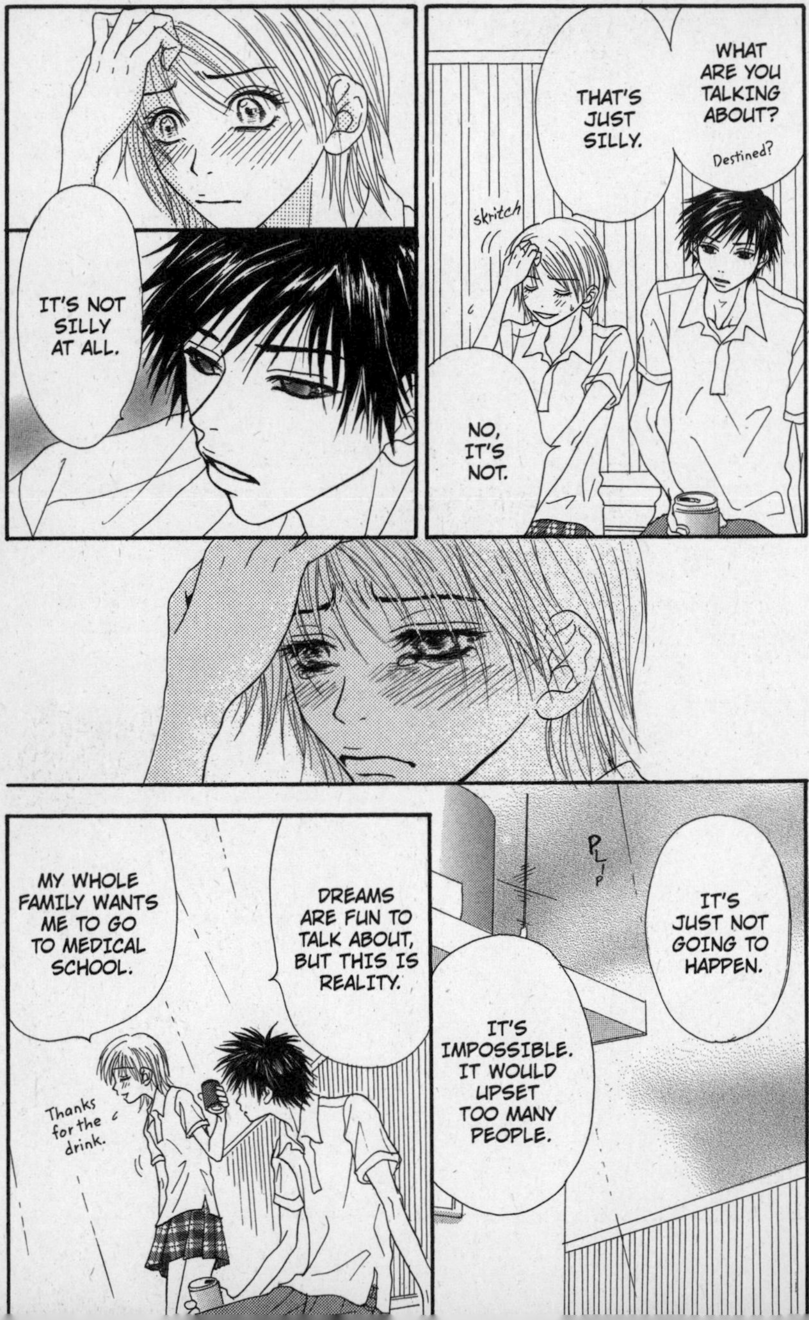
WHAT ARE YOU TALKING ABOUT?
Destined?
THAT'S JUST SILLY.
skritch
NO, IT'S NOT.
IT'S NOT SILLY AT ALL.
PLIP
IT'S JUST NOT GOING TO HAPPEN.
IT'S IMPOSSIBLE. IT WOULD UPSET TOO MANY PEOPLE.
DREAMS ARE FUN TO TALK ABOUT, BUT THIS IS REALITY.
MY WHOLE FAMILY WANTS ME TO GO TO MEDICAL SCHOOL.
Thanks for the drink.

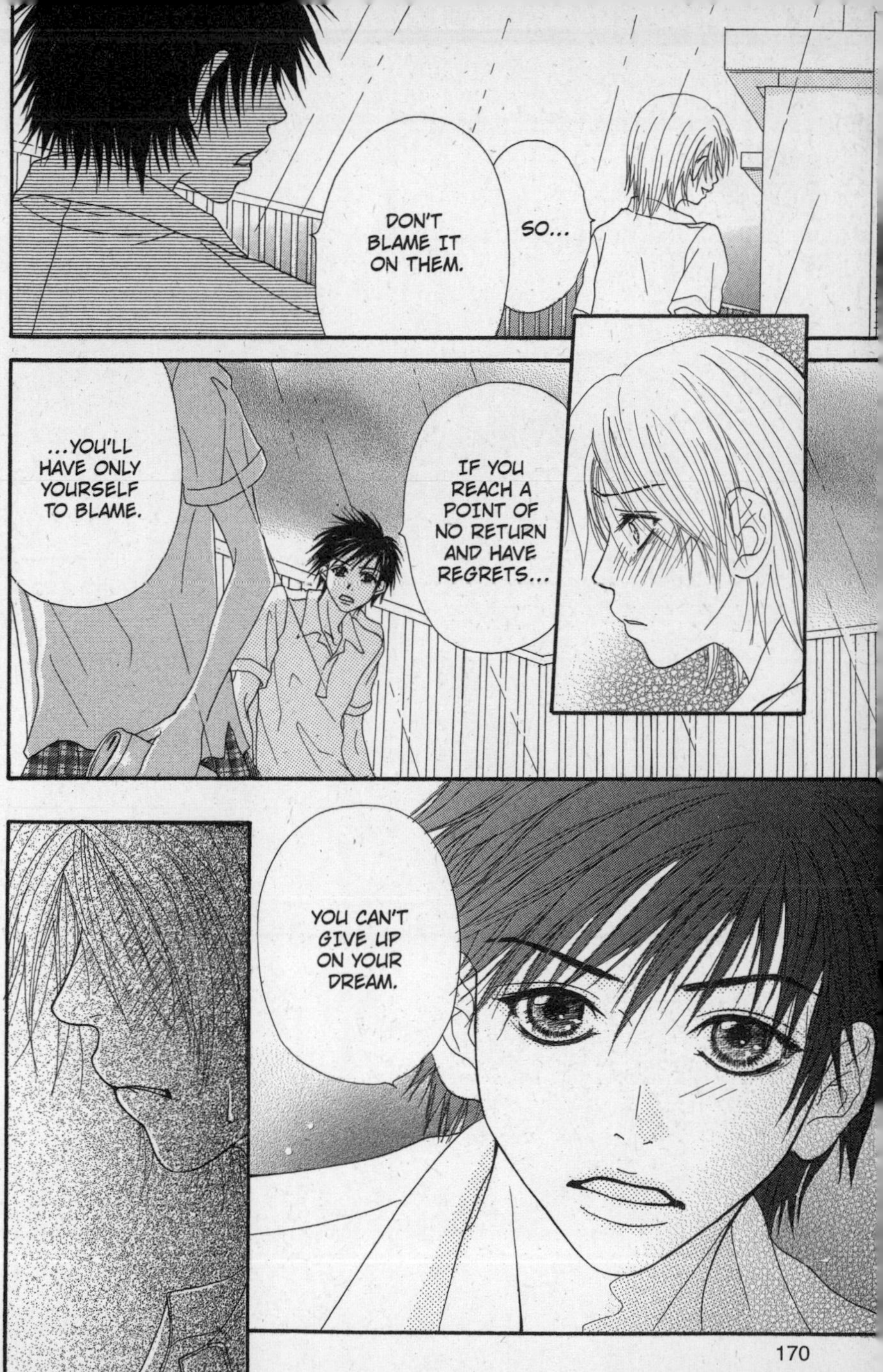
SO...
DON'T BLAME IT ON THEM.
IF YOU REACH A POINT OF NO RETURN AND HAVE REGRETS...
...YOU'LL HAVE ONLY YOURSELF TO BLAME.
YOU CAN'T GIVE UP ON YOUR DREAM.

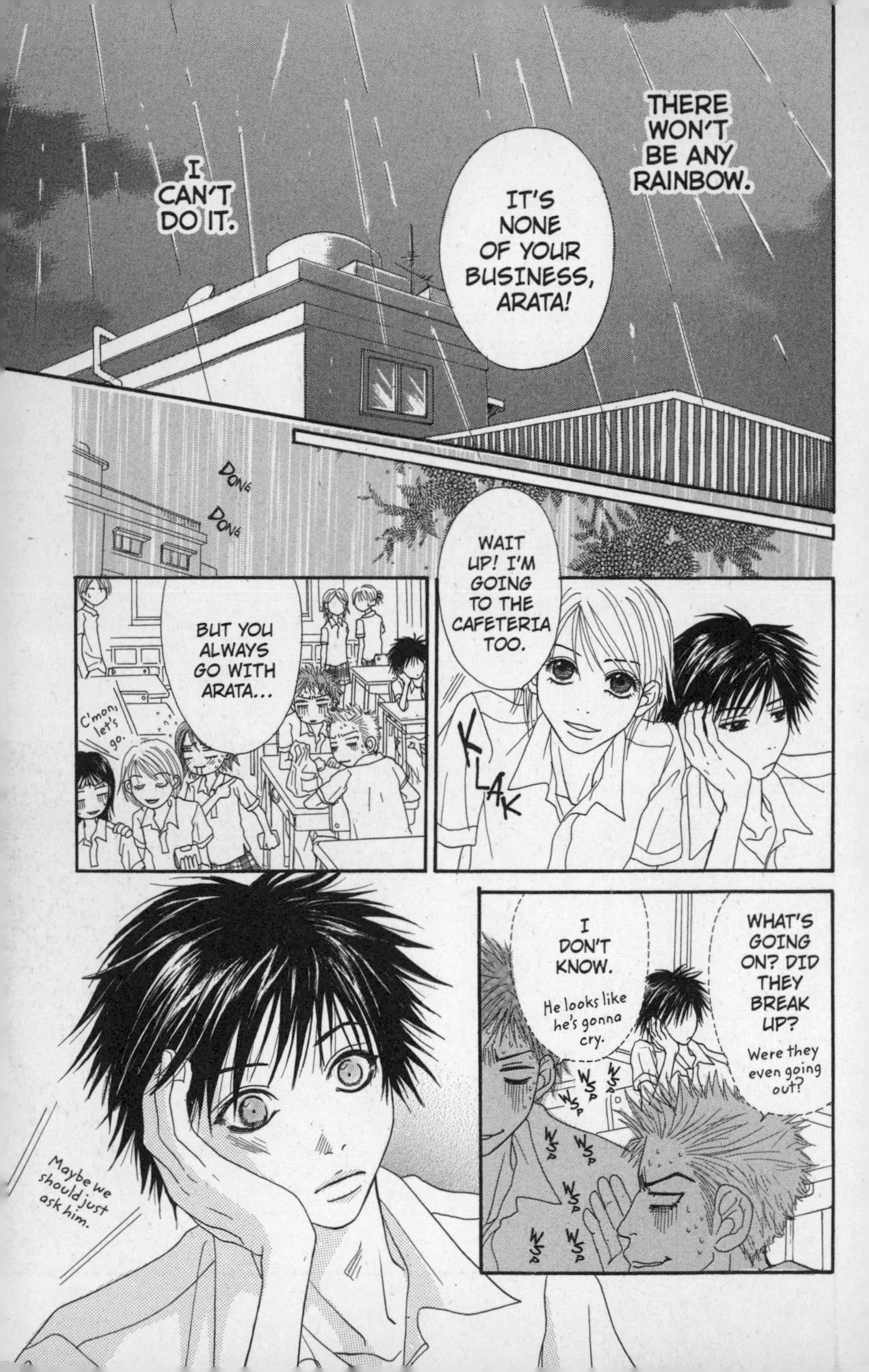
THERE WON'T BE ANY RAINBOW.
IT'S NONE OF YOUR BUSINESS, ARATA!
I CAN'T DO IT.
DONG
DONG
WAIT UP! I'M GOING TO THE CAFETERIA TOO.
KLAK
BUT YOU ALWAYS GO WITH ARATA...
C'mon, let's go.
WHAT'S GOING ON? DID THEY BREAK UP?
Were they even going out?
I DON'T KNOW.
He looks like he's gonna cry.
WSP WSP WSP WSP WSP WSP WSP WSP
Maybe we should just ask him.

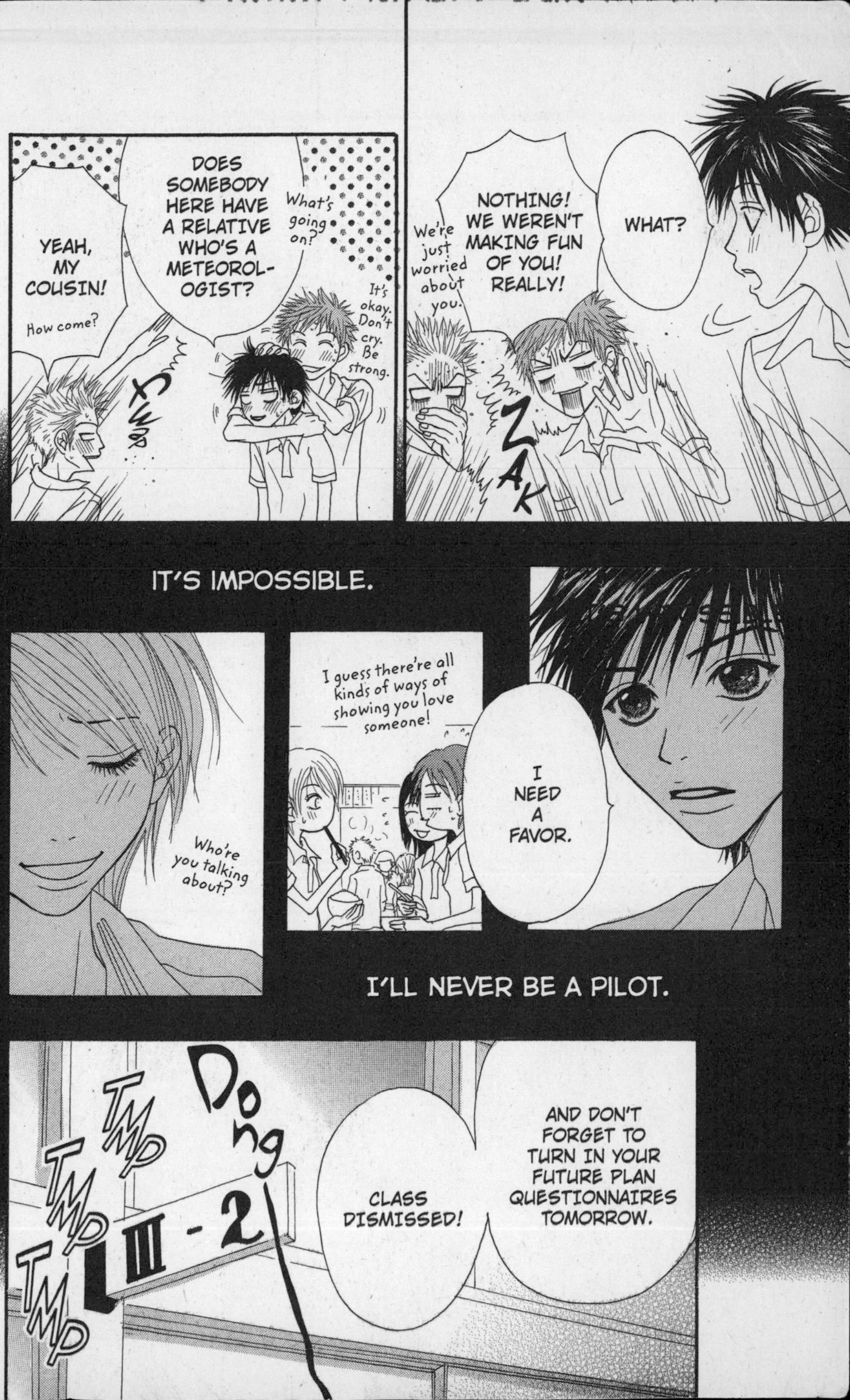
WHAT?
NOTHING! WE WEREN'T MAKING FUN OF YOU! REALLY!
We're just worried about you.
ZAK
DOES SOMEBODY HERE HAVE A RELATIVE WHO'S A METEOROLOGIST?
What's going on?
It's okay. Don't cry. Be strong.
YEAH, MY COUSIN!
How come?
IT'S IMPOSSIBLE.
I NEED A FAVOR.
I guess there're all kinds of ways of showing you love someone!
Who're you talking about?
I'LL NEVER BE A PILOT.
AND DON'T FORGET TO TURN IN YOUR FUTURE PLAN QUESTIONNAIRES TOMORROW.
CLASS DISMISSED!
Dong
III - 2
TMP
TMP
TMP
TMP

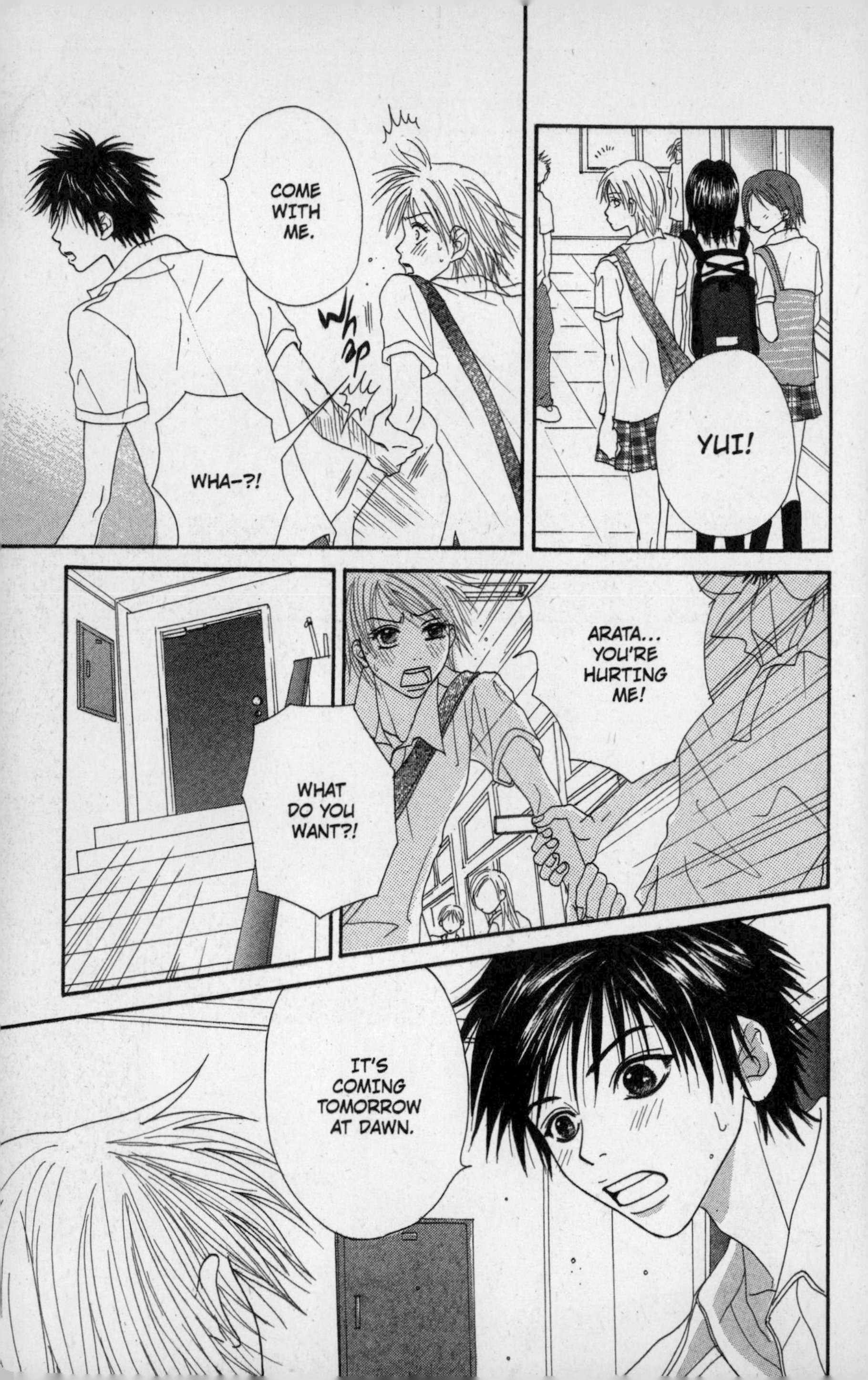
YUI!
COME WITH ME.
WHAP
WHA-?!
ARATA... YOU'RE HURTING ME!
WHAT DO YOU WANT?!
IT'S COMING TOMORROW AT DAWN.

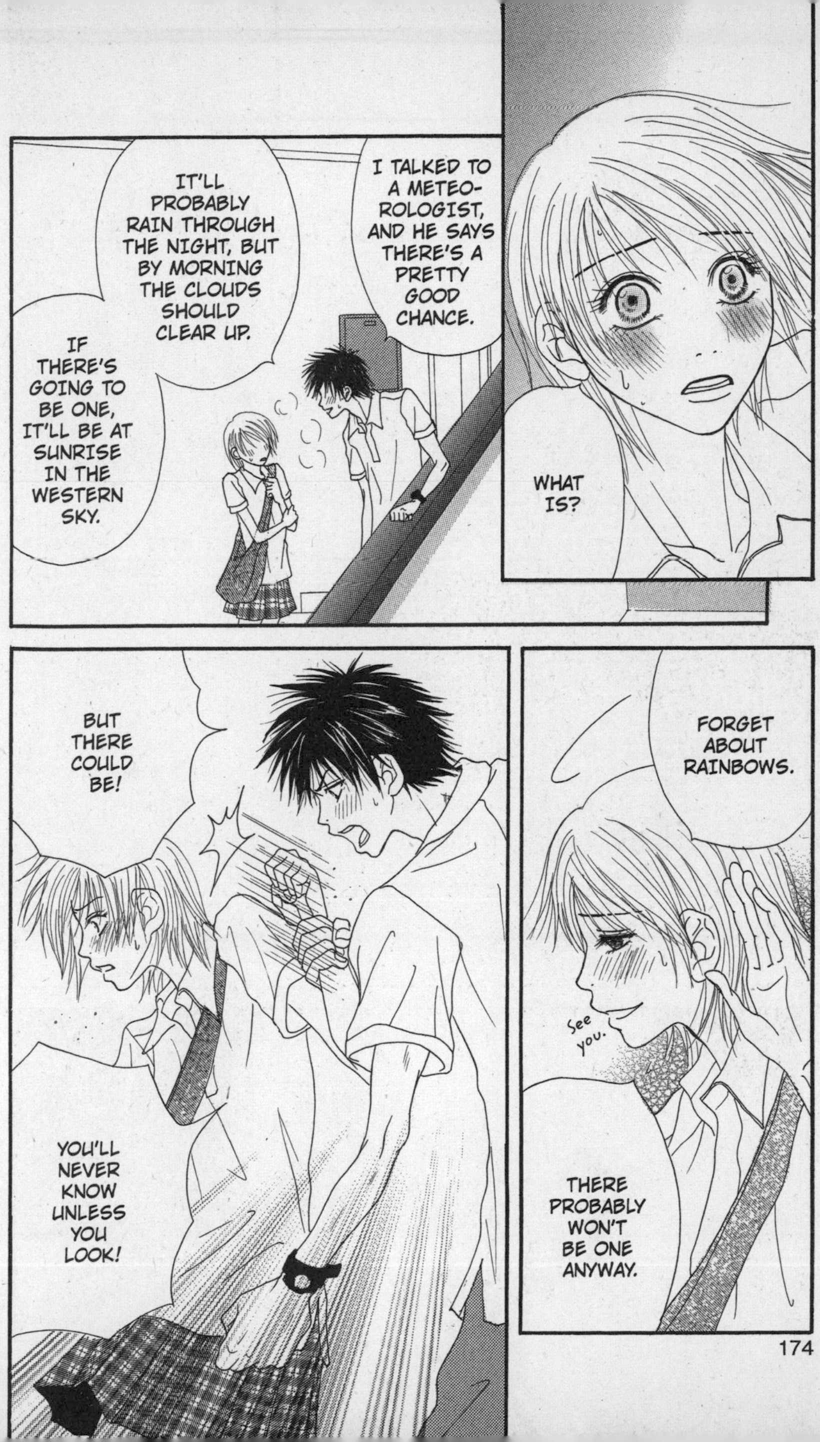
WHAT IS?
I TALKED TO A METEO-ROLOGIST, AND HE SAYS THERE'S A PRETTY GOOD CHANCE.
IT'LL PROBABLY RAIN THROUGH THE NIGHT, BUT BY MORNING THE CLOUDS SHOULD CLEAR UP.
IF THERE'S GOING TO BE ONE, IT'LL BE AT SUNRISE IN THE WESTERN SKY.
FORGET ABOUT RAINBOWS.
See you.
THERE PROBABLY WON'T BE ONE ANYWAY.
BUT THERE COULD BE!
YOU'LL NEVER KNOW UNLESS YOU LOOK!

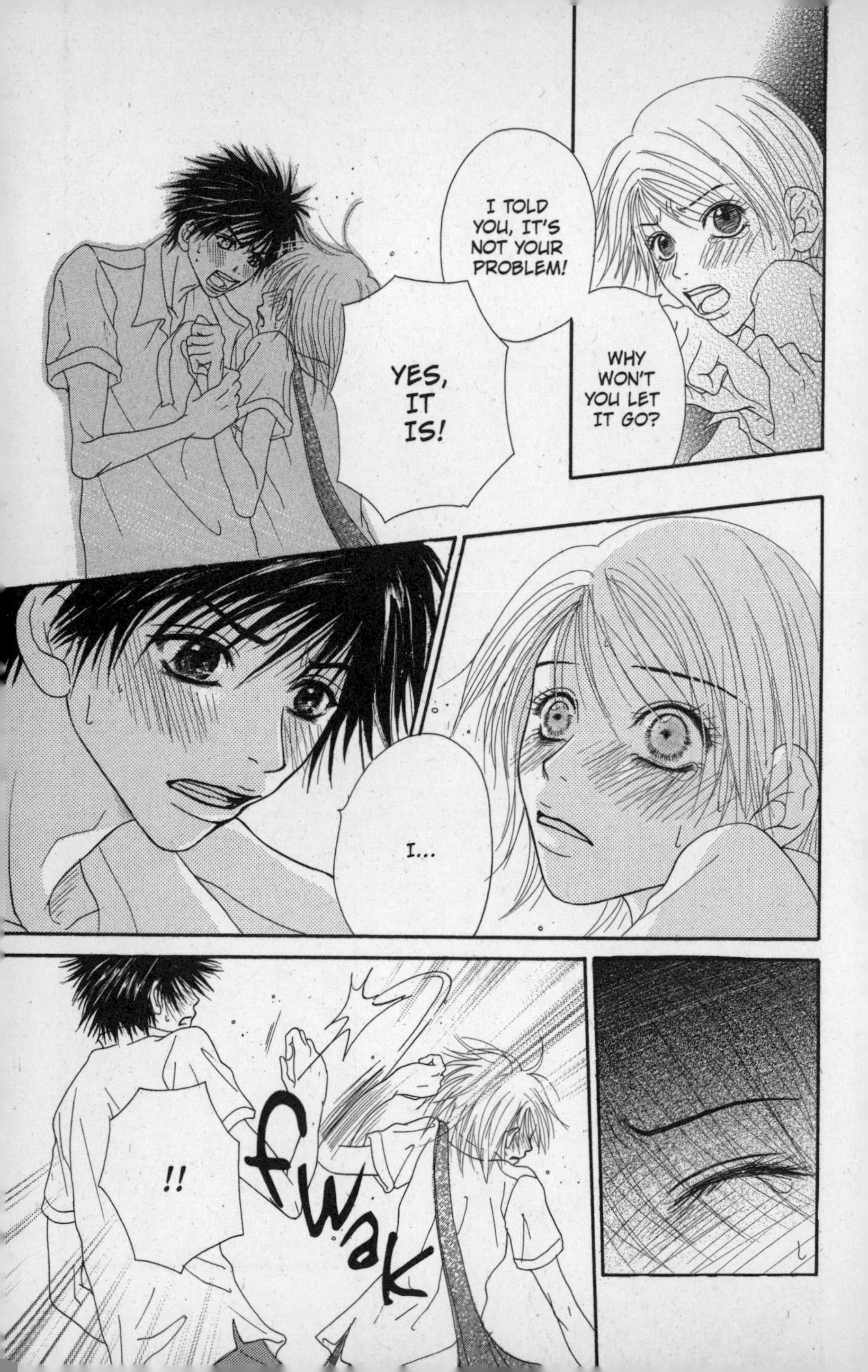
I TOLD YOU, IT'S NOT YOUR PROBLEM!
WHY WON'T YOU LET IT GO?
YES, IT IS!
I...
!!
fwak

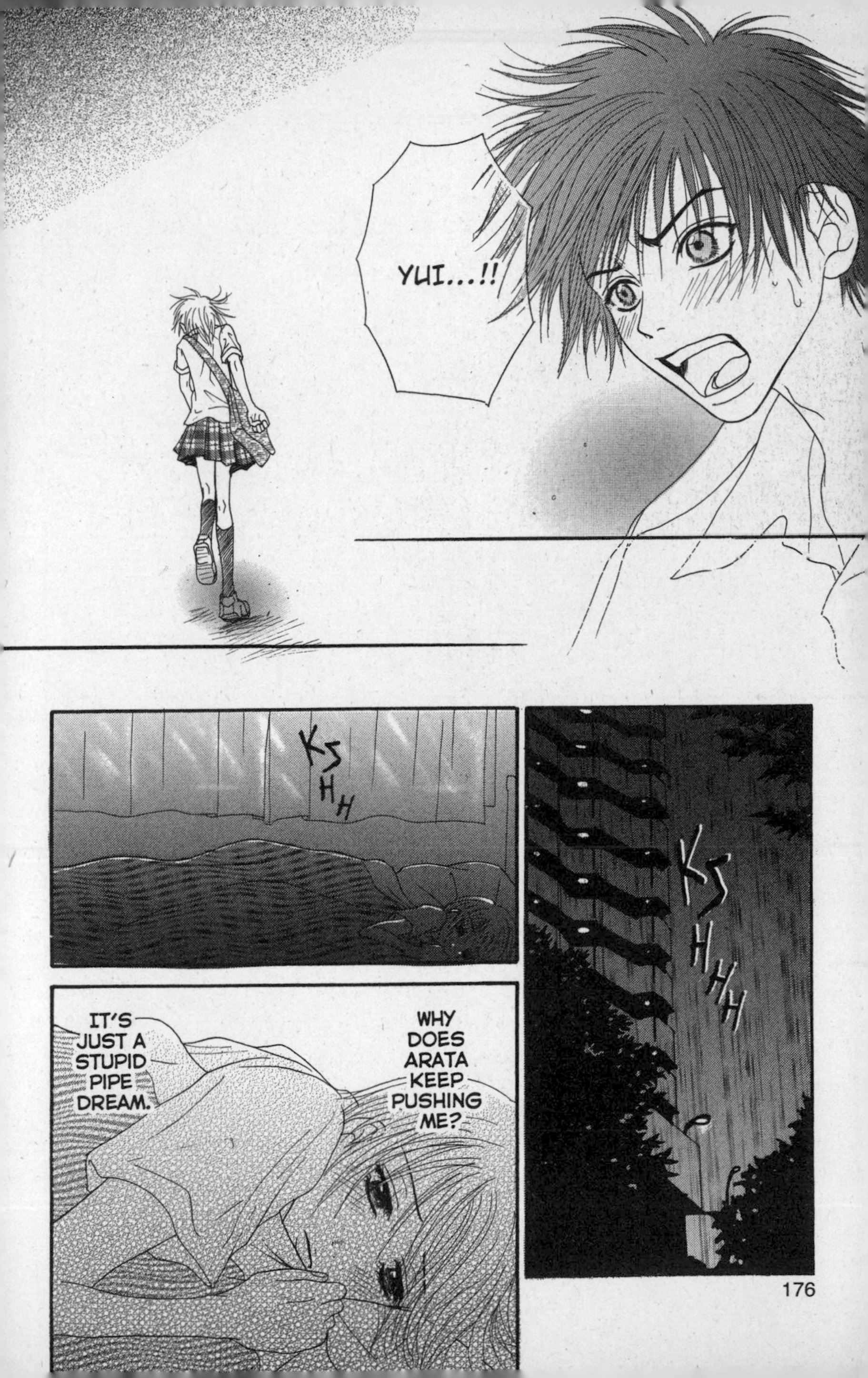
YUI...!!
KSHHH
KSHH
WHY DOES ARATA KEEP PUSHING ME?
IT'S JUST A STUPID PIPE DREAM.

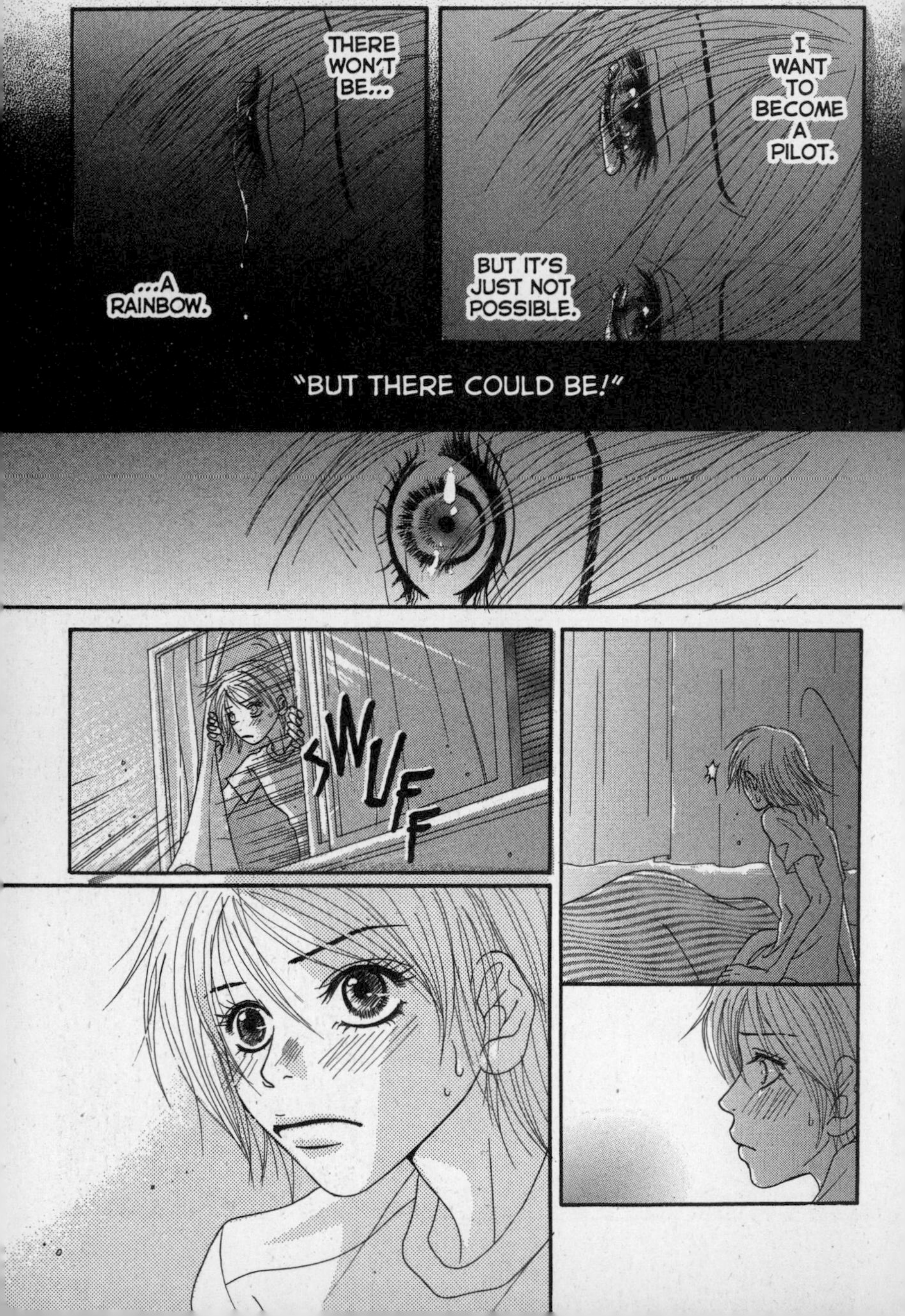
I WANT TO BECOME A PILOT.
BUT IT'S JUST NOT POSSIBLE.
THERE WON'T BE...
...A RAINBOW.
"BUT THERE COULD BE!"
SWUFF

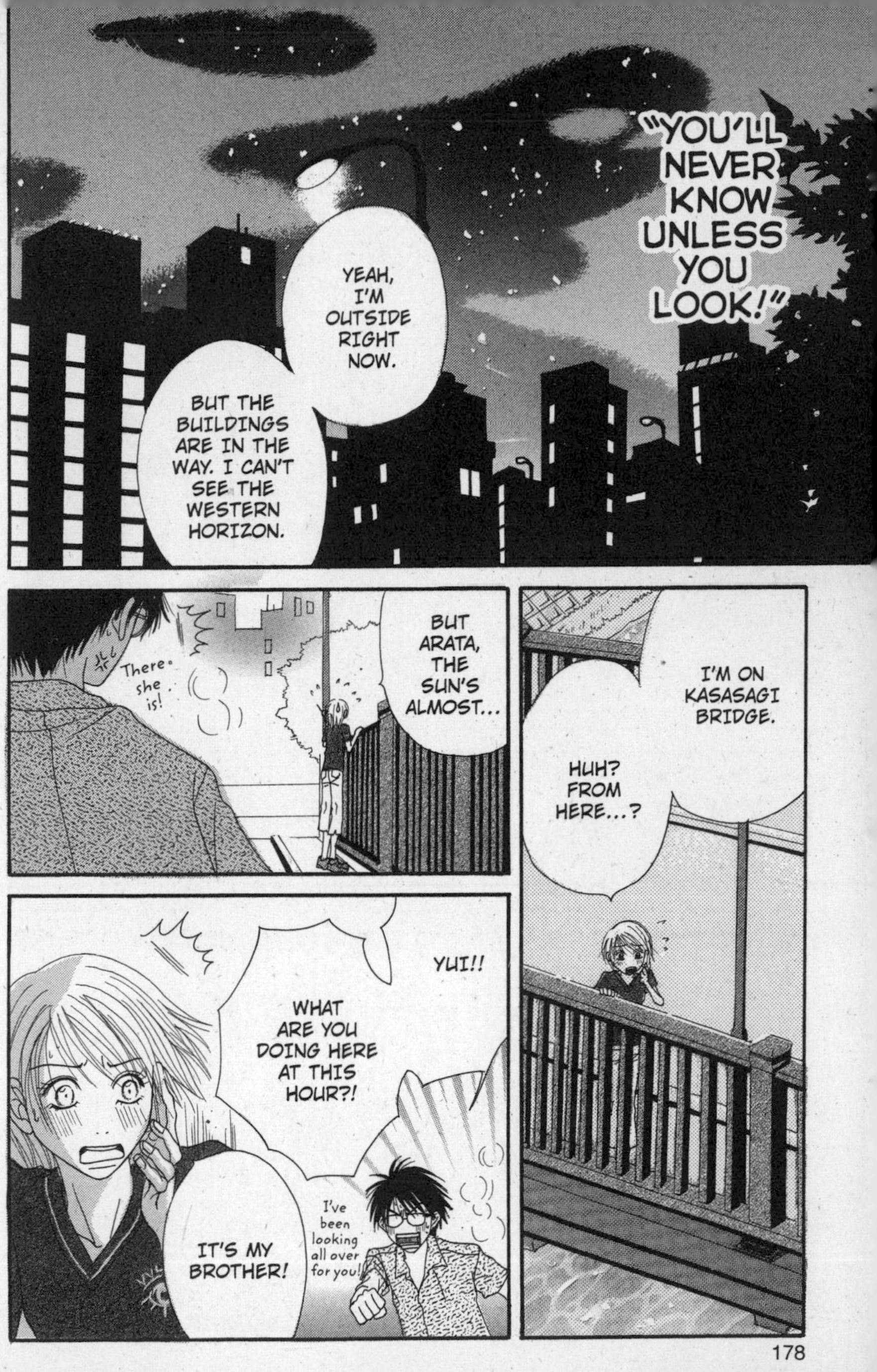
"YOU'LL NEVER KNOW UNLESS YOU LOOK!"
YEAH, I'M OUTSIDE RIGHT NOW.
BUT THE BUILDINGS ARE IN THE WAY. I CAN'T SEE THE WESTERN HORIZON.
I'M ON KASASAGI BRIDGE.
HUH? FROM HERE...?
BUT ARATA, THE SUN'S ALMOST...
There she is!
YUI!!
WHAT ARE YOU DOING HERE AT THIS HOUR?!
I've been looking all over for you!
IT'S MY BROTHER!

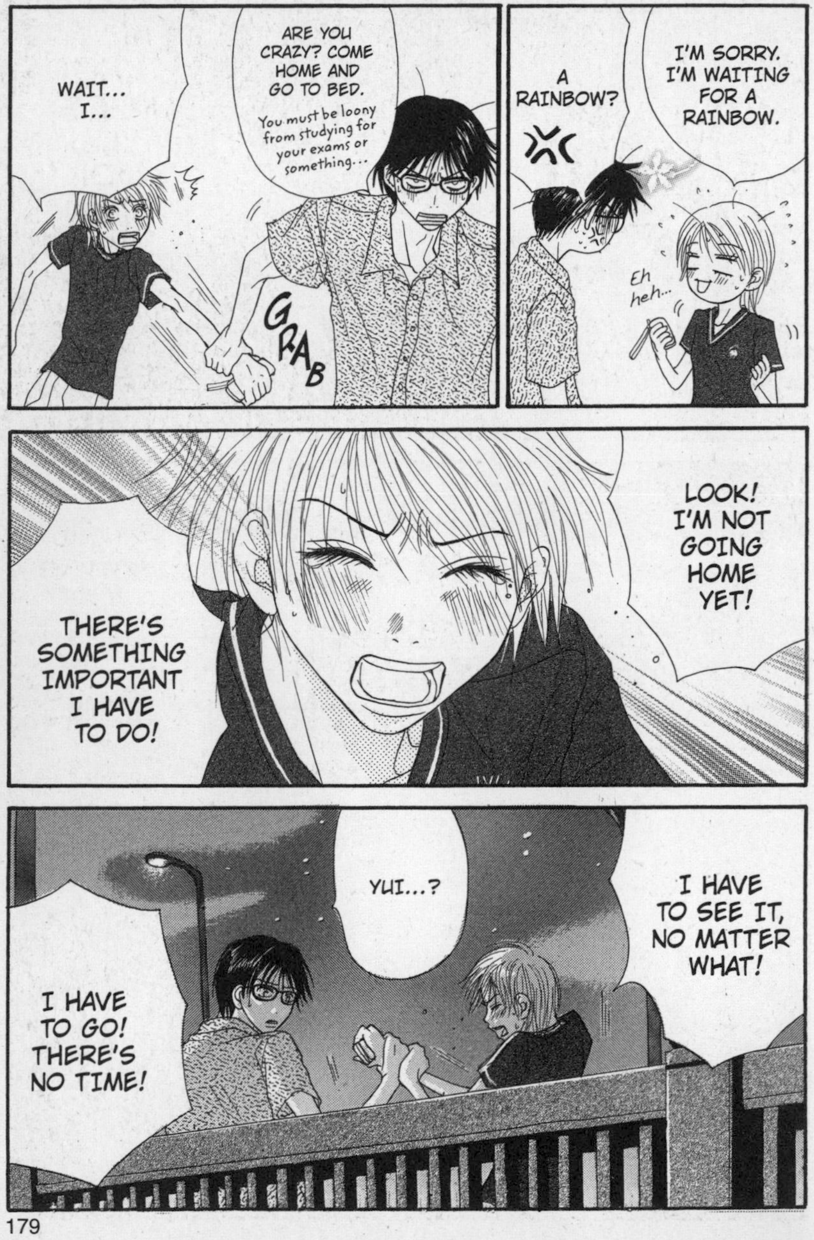
I'M SORRY. I'M WAITING FOR A RAINBOW.
A RAINBOW?
Eh heh...
ARE YOU CRAZY? COME HOME AND GO TO BED.
You must be loony from studying for your exams or something...
WAIT... I...
GRAB
LOOK! I'M NOT GOING HOME YET!
THERE'S SOMETHING IMPORTANT I HAVE TO DO!
I HAVE TO SEE IT, NO MATTER WHAT!
YUI...?
I HAVE TO GO! THERE'S NO TIME!

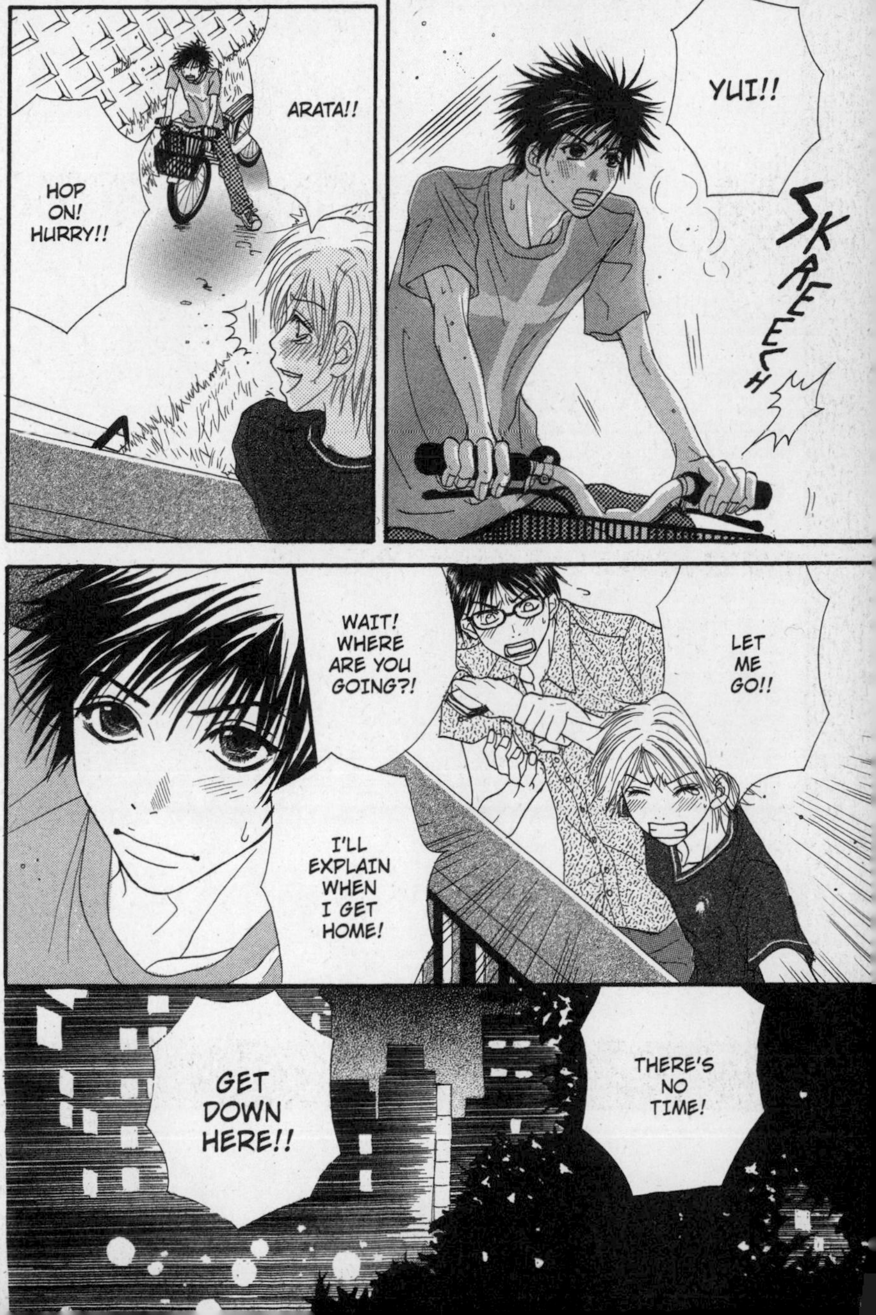
YUI!!
SKREEEH
ARATA!!
HOP ON! HURRY!!
LET ME GO!!
WAIT! WHERE ARE YOU GOING?!
I'LL EXPLAIN WHEN I GET HOME!
THERE'S NO TIME!
GET DOWN HERE!!

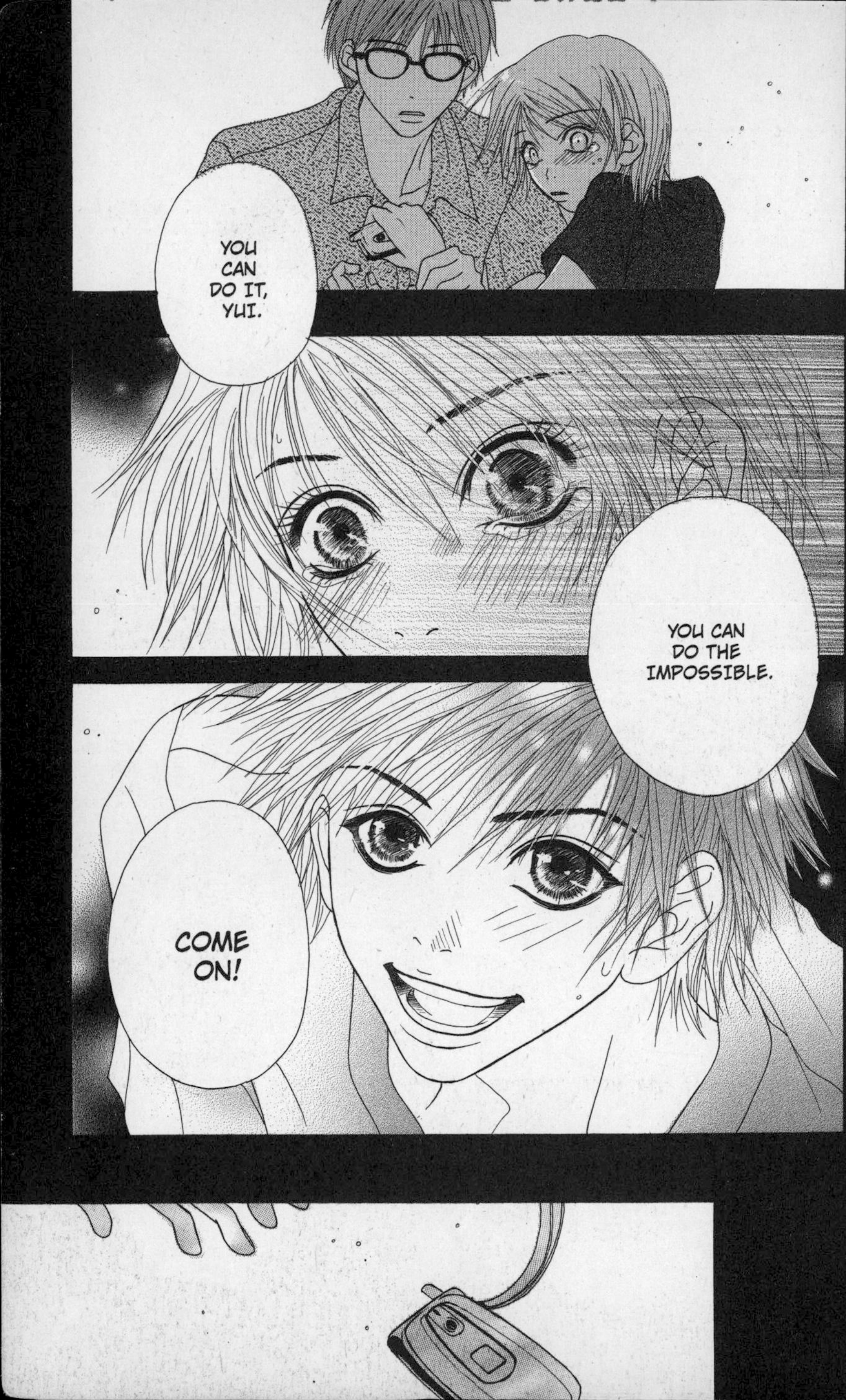
YOU CAN DO IT, YUI.
YOU CAN DO THE IMPOSSIBLE.
COME ON!

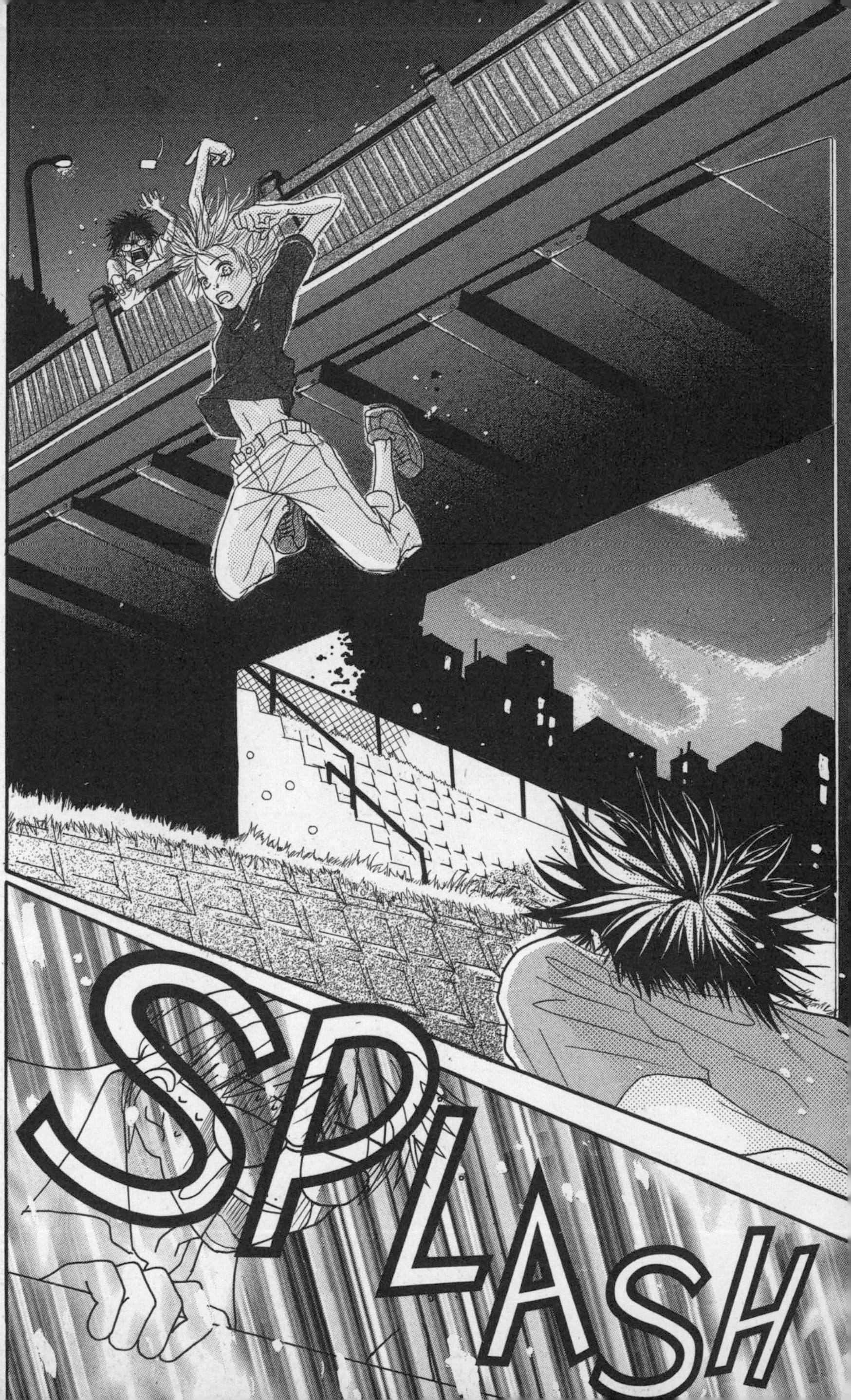
SPLASH

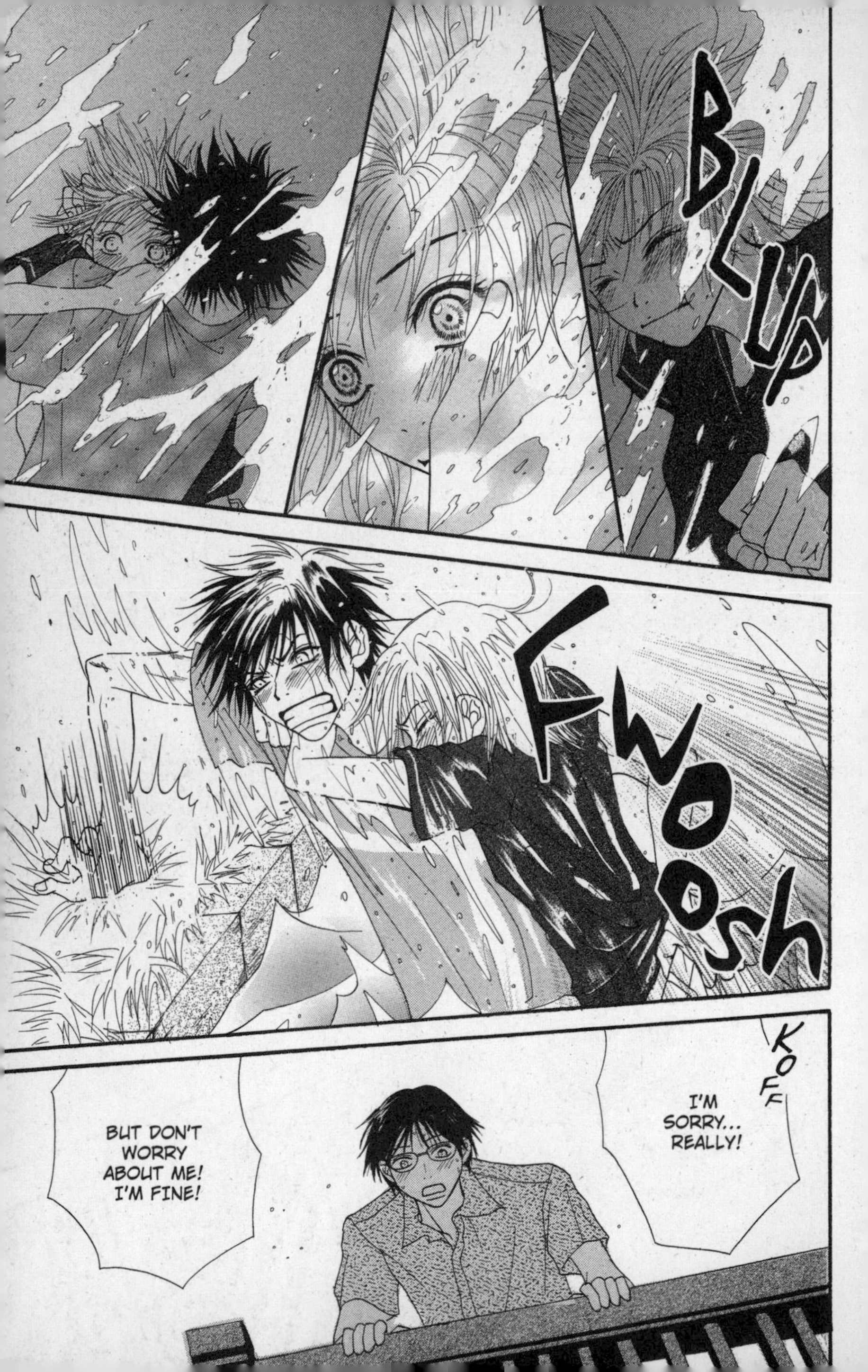
BLUP
FWOOSH
KOFF
I'M SORRY... REALLY!
BUT DON'T WORRY ABOUT ME! I'M FINE!

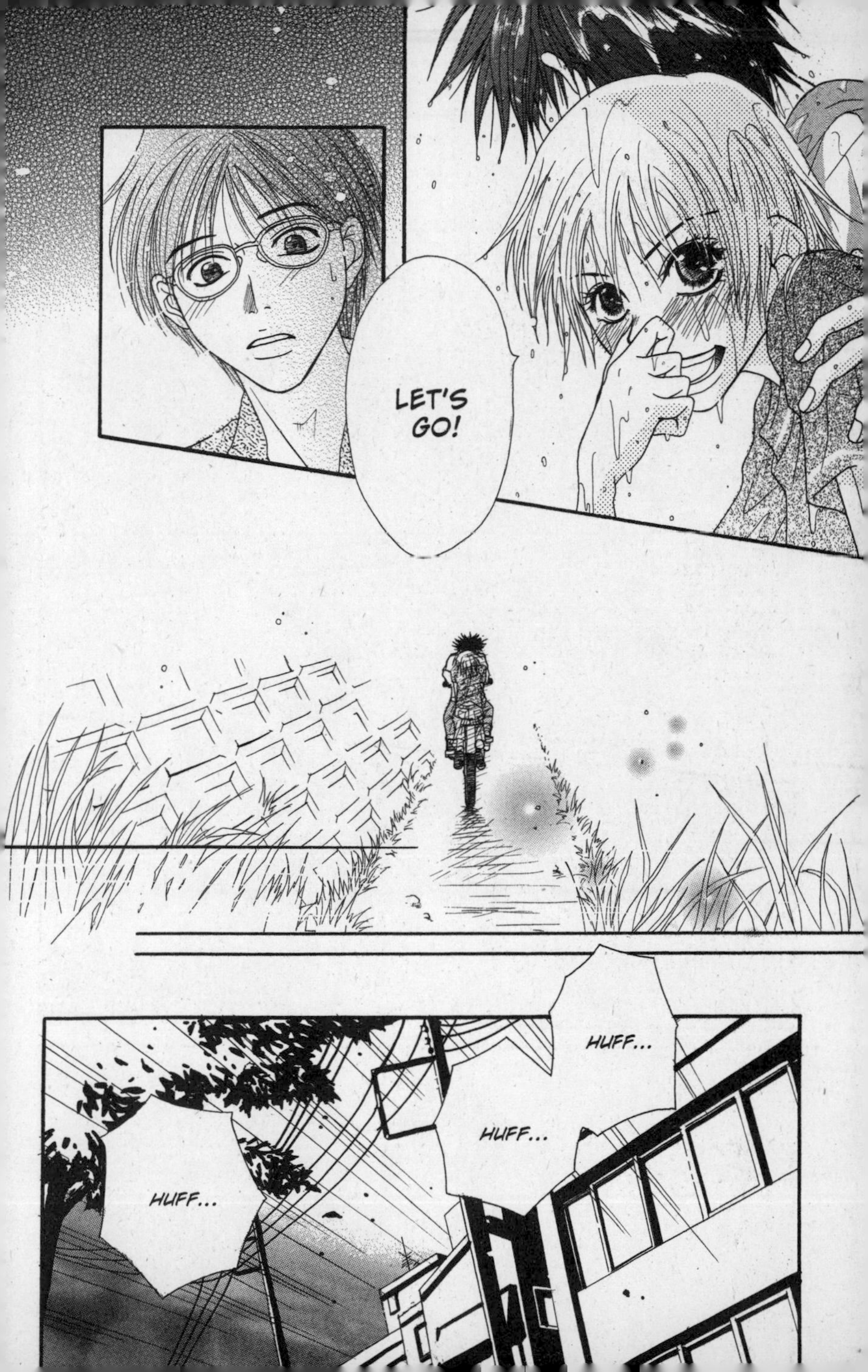
LET'S GO!
HUFF...
HUFF...
HUFF...

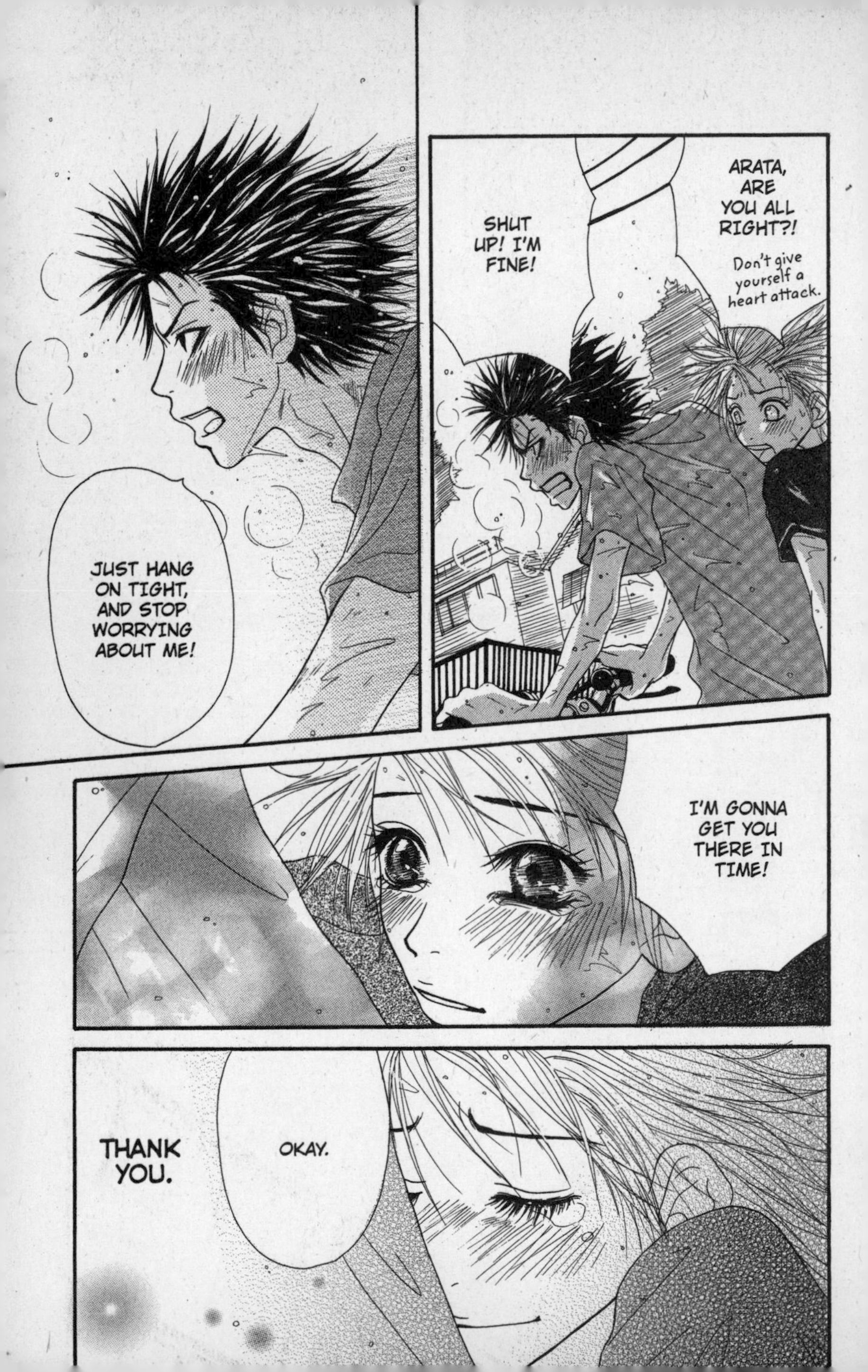
ARATA, ARE YOU ALL RIGHT?!
Don't give yourself a heart attack.
SHUT UP! I'M FINE!
JUST HANG ON TIGHT, AND STOP WORRYING ABOUT ME!
I'M GONNA GET YOU THERE IN TIME!
OKAY.
THANK YOU.

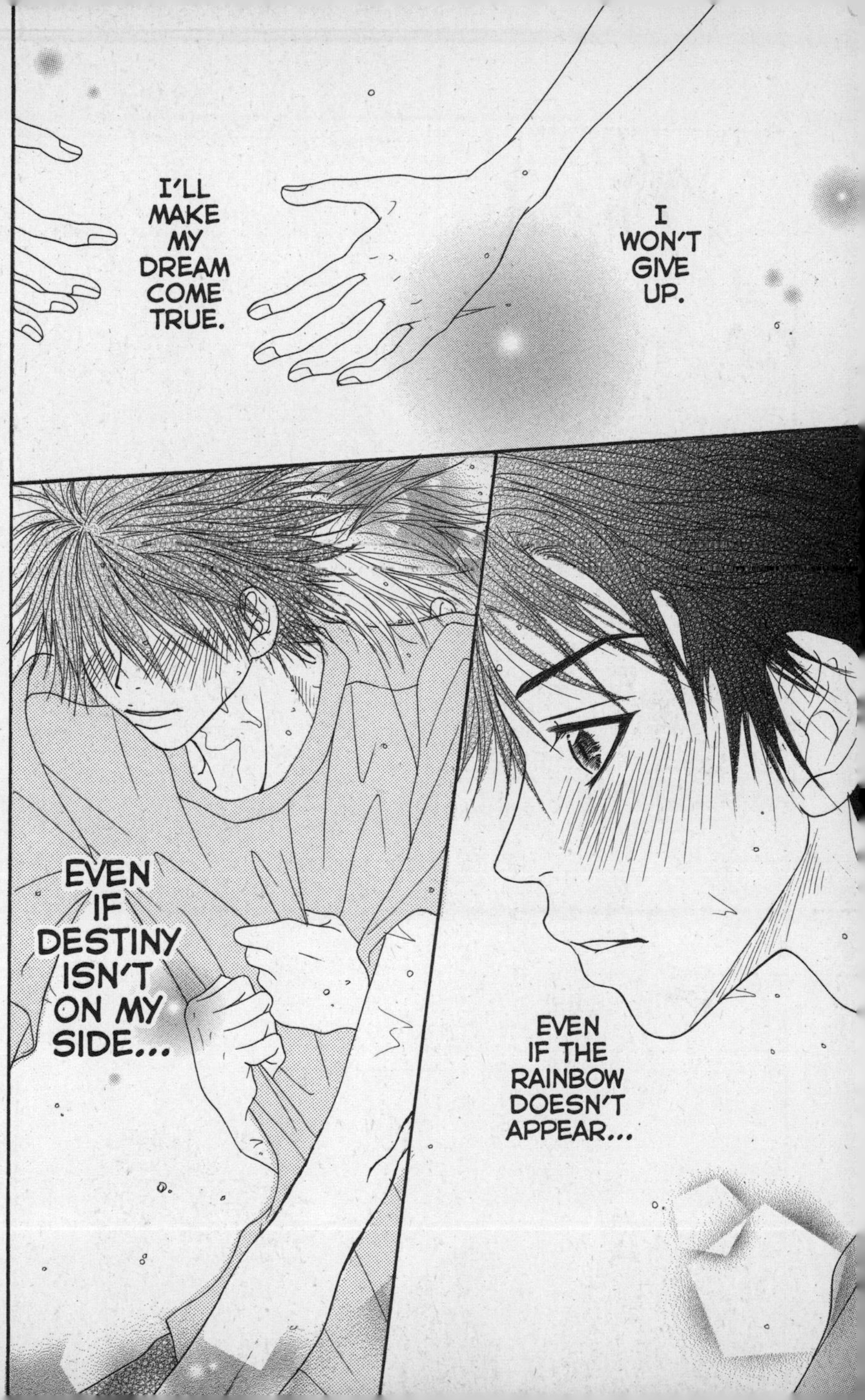
I WON'T GIVE UP.
I'LL MAKE MY DREAM COME TRUE.
EVEN IF THE RAINBOW DOESN'T APPEAR...
EVEN IF DESTINY ISN'T ON MY SIDE...

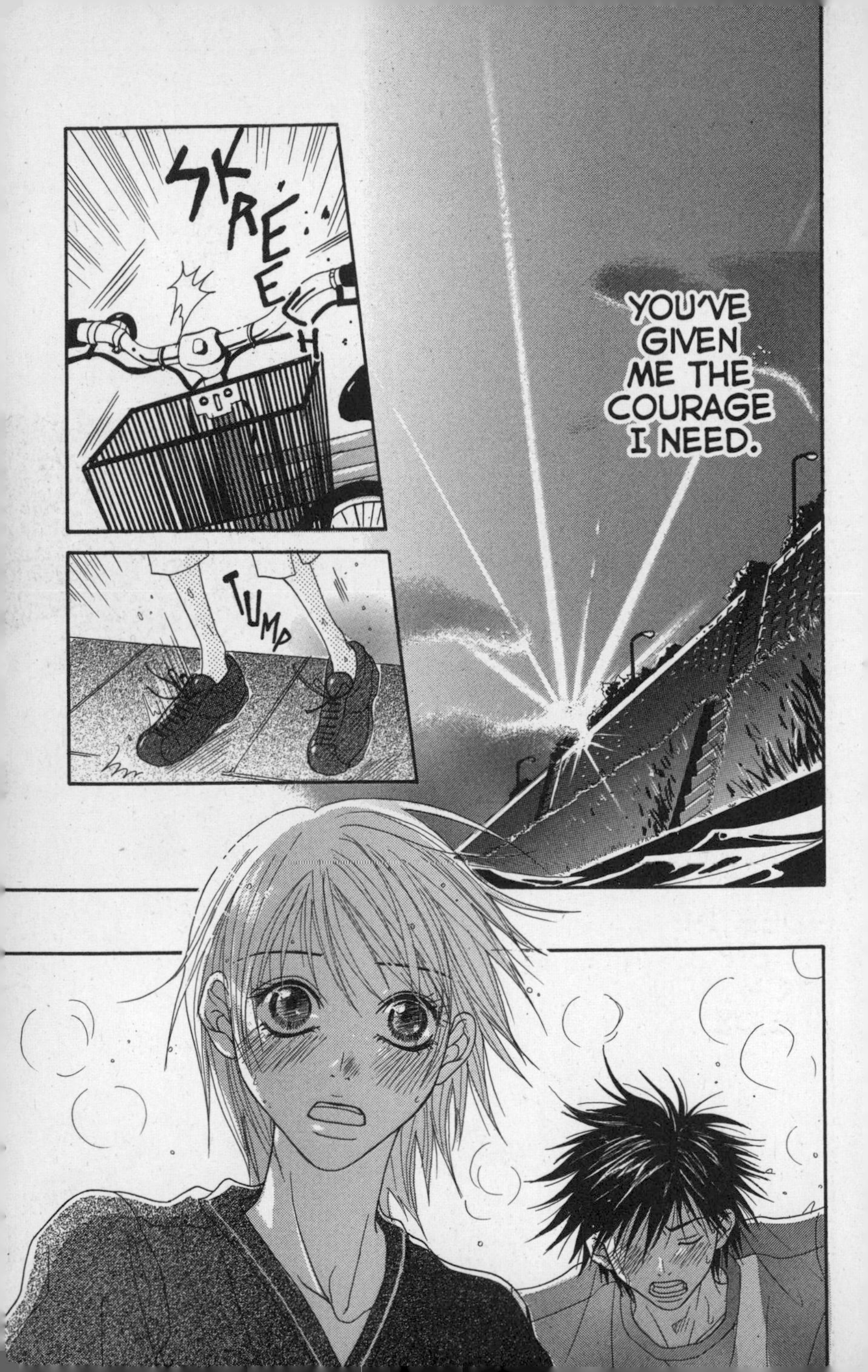
YOU'VE GIVEN ME THE COURAGE I NEED.
SKREECH
TUMP

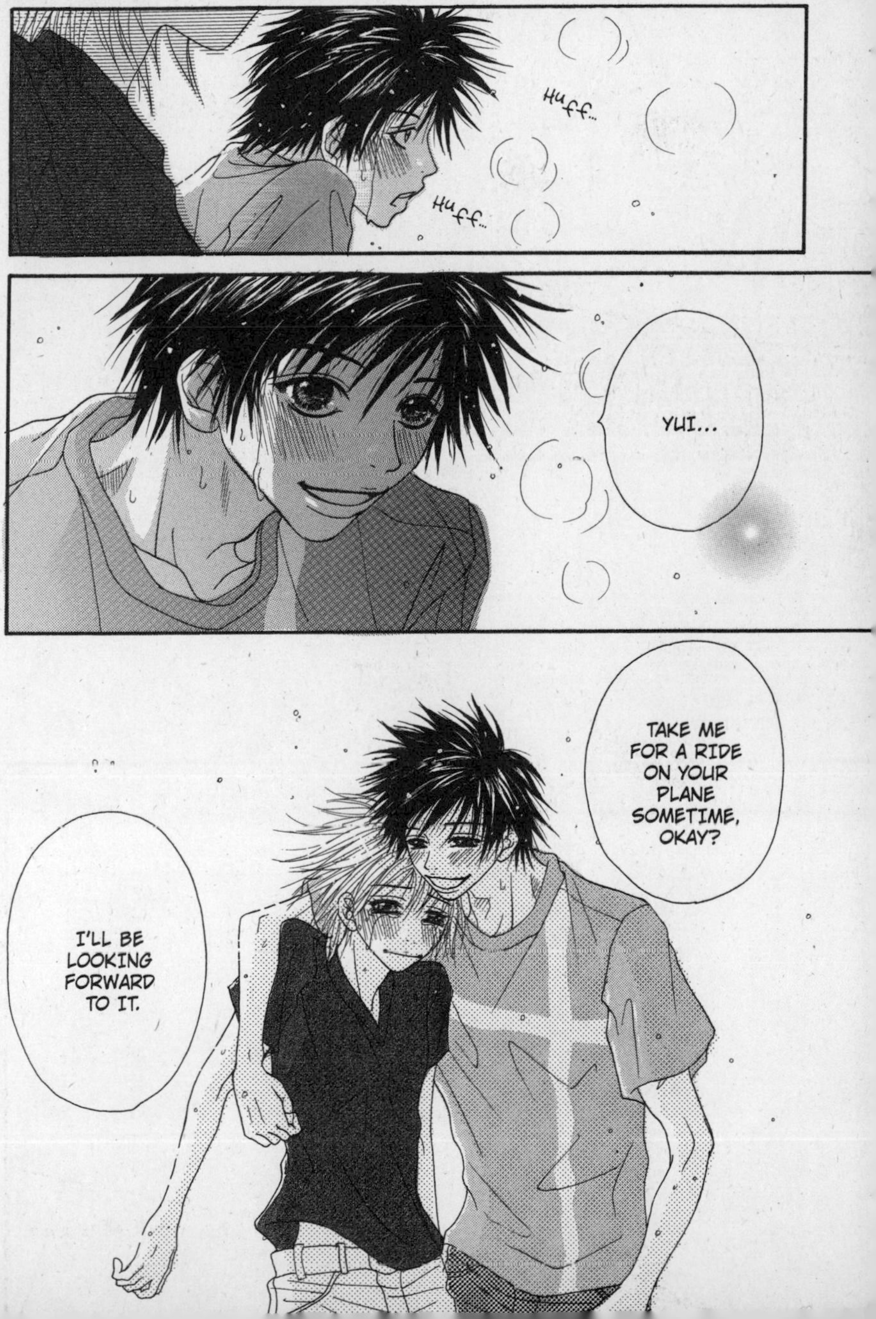
Huff...
Huff...
YUI...
TAKE ME FOR A RIDE ON YOUR PLANE SOMETIME, OKAY?
I'LL BE LOOKING FORWARD TO IT.

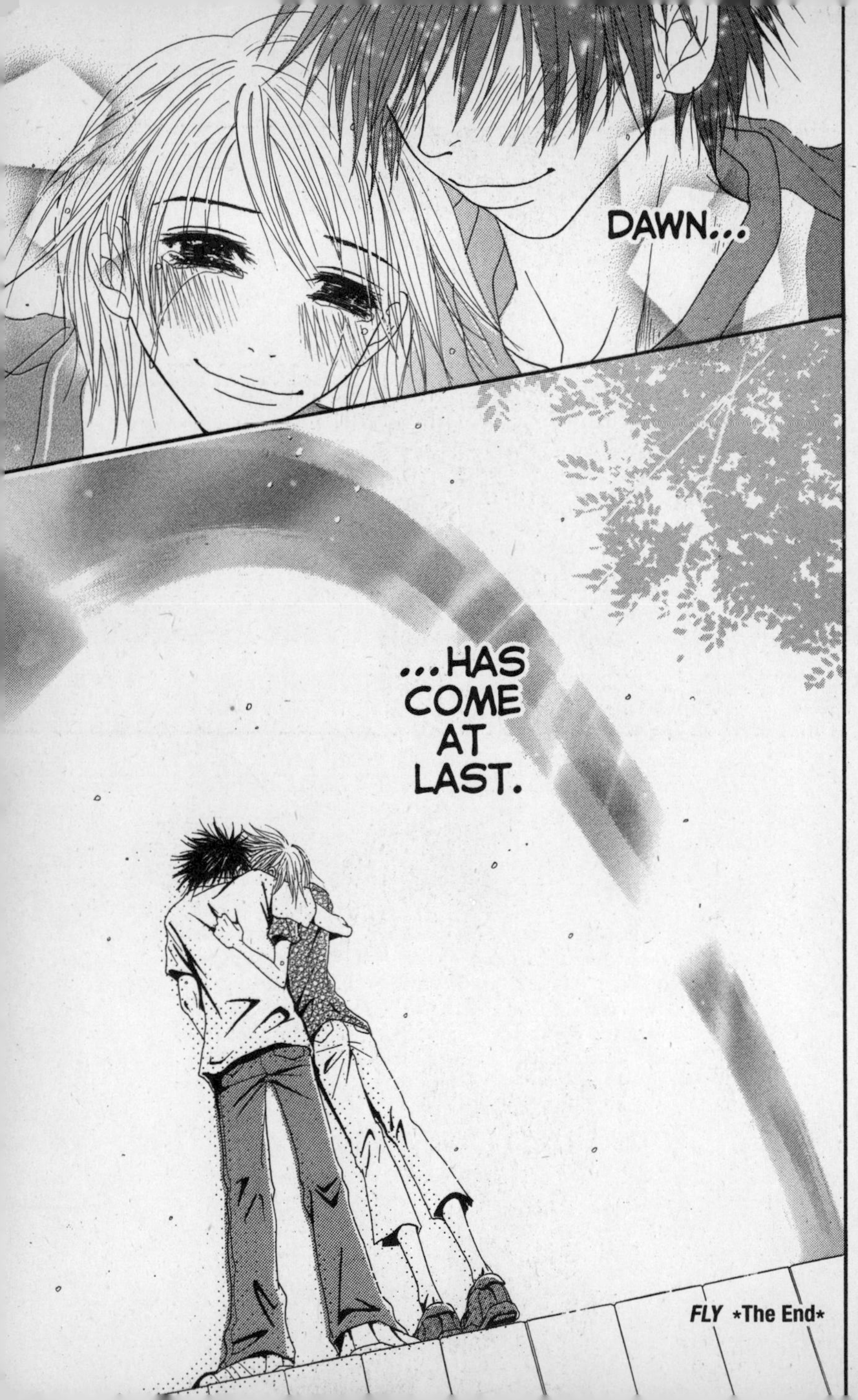
DAWN...
...HAS COME AT LAST.
FLY *The End*

It was expensive...

...so I have to use it all up.

I'm constantly working on my manga, so I don't have time to cook a lot. I decided I could at least make miso soup every day, so I splurged and bought some miso that cost about $7. It was expensive! If my mom back home found out I'd wasted that kind of money, she'd yell at me.

-Kyousuke Motomi

Born on August 1 (a Leo!), Kyousuke Motomi debuted in *Betsucomi* with *Hetakuso Kyupiddo* (No Good Cupid) in 2002. She is the creator of *Otokomae! Biizu Kurabu* (Handsome! Beads Club), and her latest work *Dengeki Deiji* (Electric Daisy) is currently being serialized in *Betsucomi*. Motomi enjoys sleeping, tea ceremonies, and reading Haruki Murakami.